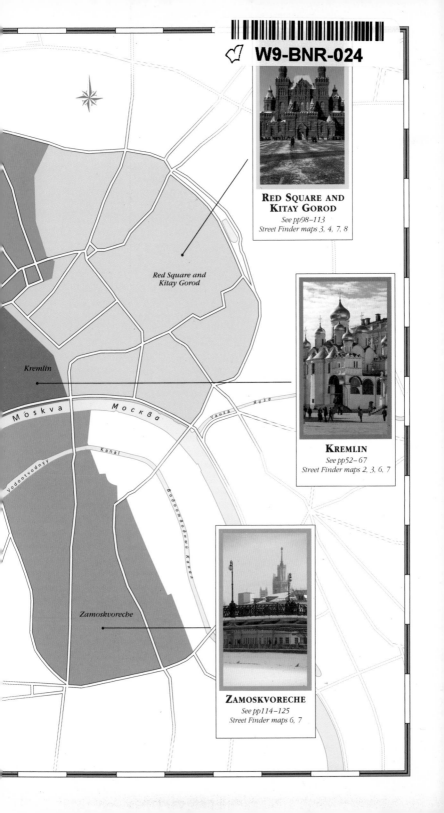

**W9-BNR-024**

**RED SQUARE AND KITAY GOROD**
*See pp98–113*
Street Finder maps 3, 4, 7, 8

**KREMLIN**
*See pp52–67*
Street Finder maps 2, 3, 6, 7

**ZAMOSKVORECHE**
*See pp114–125*
Street Finder maps 6, 7

Red Square and
Kitay Gorod

Kremlin

Móskva   Москва      Яуза  Яуза

Kanal

Vodootvodnyy

Bodorodni Kanal

Zamoskvoreche

EYEWITNESS *TRAVEL GUIDES*

# Moscow

# EYEWITNESS *TRAVEL GUIDES*

# MOSCOW

*Main contributors:*
CHRISTOPHER AND MELANIE RICE

DK PUBLISHING, INC.

# A DK PUBLISHING BOOK

PROJECT EDITOR Marcus Hardy
ART EDITOR Marisa Renzullo
EDITORS Catherine Day, Jane Oliver, Lynda Warrington
US EDITORS Michael Wise, Mary Sutherland
DESIGNERS Gillian Andrews, Carolyn Hewitson,
Paul Jackson, Elly King, Nicola Rodway
VISUALIZER Joy Fitzsimmons
MAP CO-ORDINATORS Emily Green, David Pugh

SENIOR EDITOR Anna Streiffert
MANAGING EDITORS Fay Franklin, Georgina Matthews
MANAGING ART EDITOR Annette Jacobs
SENIOR MANAGING EDITOR Vivien Crump
DEPUTY ART DIRECTOR Gillian Allan

PRODUCTION Jo Blackmore, David Proffit
PICTURE RESEARCH Brigitte Arora
DTP DESIGNER Pamela Shiels

MAIN CONTRIBUTORS
Christopher Rice, Melanie Rice

MAPS
Maria Donnelly (Colourmap Scanning Ltd)

PHOTOGRAPHER
Demetrio Carrasco

ILLUSTRATORS
Stephen Conlin, Richard Draper, Stephen Gyapay,
Claire Littlejohn, Chris Orr & Associates

Text film output by Graphical Innovations, London
Reproduced by Colourscan, Singapore
Printed and bound in China by L.Rex Printing Co., Ltd.

First American Edition, 1998
2 4 6 8 10 9 7 5 3 1

Published in the United States by
DK Publishing, Inc.,
95 Madison Avenue, New York, New York 10016
Copyright © 1998 Dorling Kindersley Limited, London
Visit us on the World Wide Web at htttp://www.dk.com

Library of Congress Cataloging-in-Publication Data
Moscow.
   p.   cm. -- (Eyewitness travel guides)
Includes index.
ISBN 0-7894-3529-2
1. Moscow (Russia) -- Guidebooks.  I. Series.
DK597.M557 1998           98-7232
914.7'31 -- dc21               CIP

Floors are referred to throughout in accordance with American
usage; i.e., the "first floor" is at ground level. Details such as
telephone numbers, opening hours, prices, and travel information
are correct at the time of going to press, but are liable to change.
The publishers cannot accept responsibility for any consequences
arising from the use of this book.

We would be delighted to receive any corrections and
suggestions for incorporation in the next edition. Please write to:
Senior Editor, Eyewitness Travel Guides,
DK Publishing, Inc., 95 Madison Ave., New York, NY 10016.

# CONTENTS

## HOW TO USE THIS GUIDE 6

Socialist-Realist sculpture of Soviet
farm workers at the All-Russian
Exhibition Center (see p145)

# INTRODUCING MOSCOW

## PUTTING MOSCOW ON THE MAP
10

## THE HISTORY OF MOSCOW 16

## MOSCOW THROUGH THE YEAR
32

## MOSCOW AT A GLANCE
36

The Tretyakov Gallery (see pp118–
21), housing Russian fine art

# MOSCOW AREA BY AREA

## THE KREMLIN
52

Magnificent iconostasis at the Danilovskiy Monastery *(see pp136–7)*

Blinis with black and red caviar
*(see p176)*, a Russian specialty

The Tsar Bell *(see p57)*, created
for Tsarina Anna, in the Kremlin

St. Basil's Cathedral
*(see pp108–9)*

# How to Use this Guide

THIS GUIDE WILL HELP you get the most from your visit to Moscow. It provides expert recommendations together with detailed practical information. *Introducing Moscow* maps the city and sets it in its geographical, historical, and cultural context, and the quick-reference timeline on the history pages gives the dates of Russia's rulers and significant events. *Moscow at a Glance* is an overview of the city's main attractions. *Moscow Area by Area*

**Neo-Classical statue, Kuskovo, *(see pp142–3)***

starts on page 50 and describes all the important sights, using maps, photographs, and illustrations. The sights are arranged in three groups: those in Moscow's central districts, those a little farther afield, and finally those beyond Moscow that require one- or two-day excursions. Hotel, restaurant, and entertainment recommendations can be found in *Travelers' Needs*, and the *Survival Guide* includes tips on everything from transportation to personal safety.

## FINDING YOUR WAY AROUND THE SIGHTSEEING SECTION

Each of the seven sightseeing areas is color-coded for easy reference. Every chapter opens with an introduction to the area it covers, describing its history and character. For central districts, this is followed by

a Street-by-Street map illustrating a particularly interesting part of the area; for sights farther away, by a regional map. A simple numbering system relates sights to the maps. Important sights are covered by several pages.

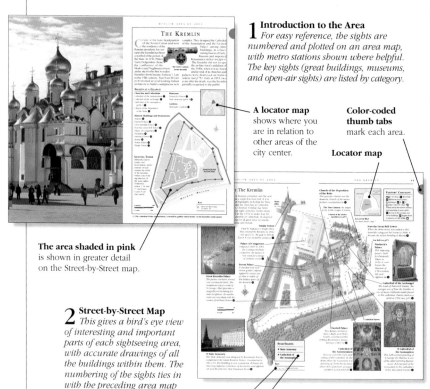

**1 Introduction to the Area**
*For easy reference, the sights are numbered and plotted on an area map, with metro stations shown where helpful. The key sights (great buildings, museums, and open-air sights) are listed by category.*

**A locator map** shows where you are in relation to other areas of the city center.

**Color-coded thumb tabs** mark each area.

**Locator map**

**The area shaded in pink** is shown in greater detail on the Street-by-Street map.

**2 Street-by-Street Map**
*This gives a bird's eye view of interesting and important parts of each sightseeing area, with accurate drawings of all the buildings within them. The numbering of the sights ties in with the preceding area map and with the fuller descriptions on the pages that follow.*

**Suggested walking route**

**A list of star sights** recommends the places that no visitor should miss.

## MOSCOW AREA MAP

The colored areas shown on this map *(see pp14–15)* are the five main sightseeing areas into which central Moscow has been divided for this guide. Each is covered in a full chapter in the *Moscow Area by Area* section *(pp50–125)*. The areas are also highlighted on other maps throughout the book. In *Moscow at a Glance (pp36–49)*, for example, they help you locate the most important sights that no visitor should miss. The maps' colored borders match the colored thumb tabs at the top corner of each page.

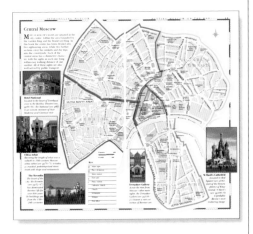

**Numbers** refer to each sight's position on the area map and its place in the chapter.

**Practical information** lists all the information you need to visit every sight, including a map reference to the *Street Finder* maps *(pp220–37)*.

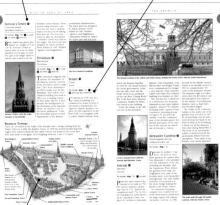

### 3 Detailed information on each sight

*All the important sights are described individually. They are listed to follow the numbering on the area map at the start of the section. The key to the symbols summarizing practical information is on the back flap.*

**A visitors' checklist** provides the practical information you will need to plan your visit.

**Illustrated maps** show in detail the layout of extensive sights.

### 4 Moscow's Major Sights

*These are given more extensive coverage, sometimes two or more full pages. Historic buildings are dissected to reveal their interiors; museums and galleries have color-coded floor plans to help you find important exhibits.*

**Stars** indicate the best features or works of art.

**Story boxes** provide details on famous people or historical events.

# INTRODUCING MOSCOW

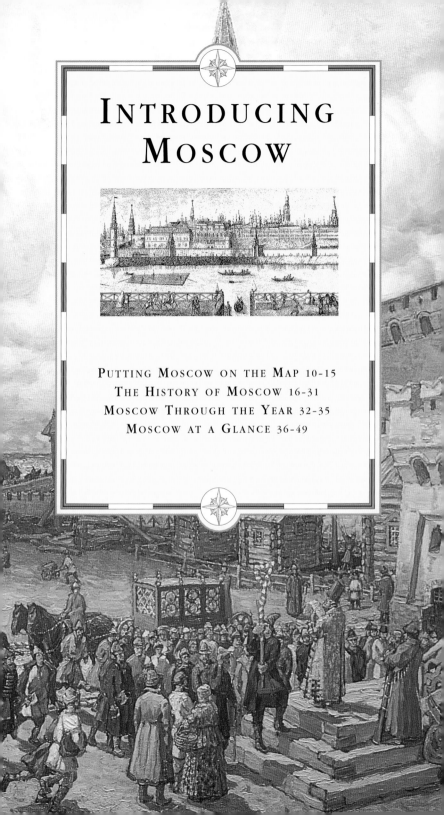

# Putting Moscow on the Map

THE RUSSIAN FEDERATION (usually simply known as Russia) stretches from the Baltic to the Pacific. With an area of 17 million sq km (6.6 million sq miles), it was the largest of the USSR's 15 republics and is now the world's largest country, almost twice the size of the US. Moscow, the capital with 9 million inhabitants, lies at the heart of European Russia. St. Petersburg is Russia's second largest city. Russia is a member of the CIS – a commonwealth of most of the former Soviet republics.

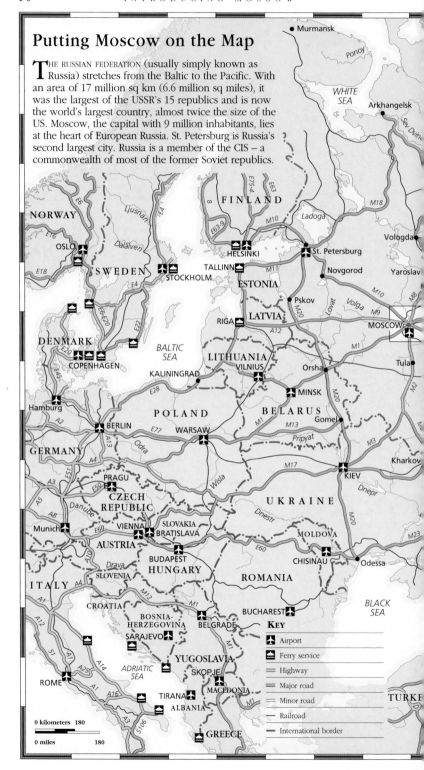

**KEY**

| | |
|---|---|
| ✈ | Airport |
| ⛴ | Ferry service |
| ═ | Highway |
| ▬ | Major road |
| ═ | Minor road |
| — | Railroad |
| ─ | International border |

0 kilometers 180

0 miles 180

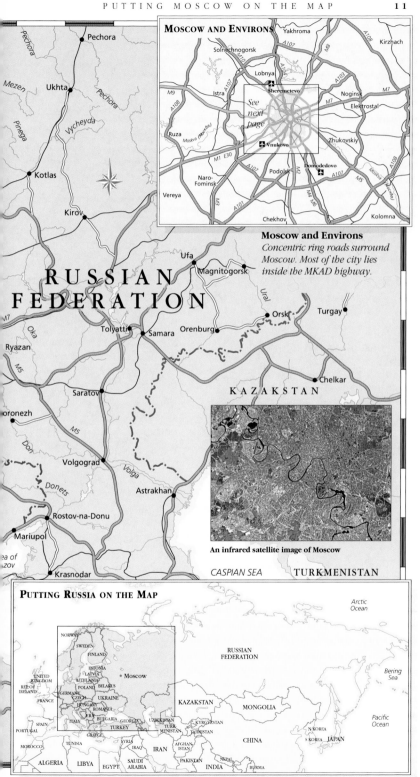

## MOSCOW AND ENVIRONS

Yakhroma
A107
A108
Kirzhach
M8

Solnechnogorsk
A107
Lobnya
A104

Istra
M9
A107
Sheremetevo
Noginsk
M7
Elektrostal

*See next page*

Ruza
Moskva (Moscow)

Vnukovo
Zhukovskiy

M1 E30
A107
Podolsk
M2
Domodedovo
A107
A108

Naro-Fominsk
M4 M6
Moskva

Vereya
A101

Chekhov
Kolomna

### Moscow and Environs
*Concentric ring roads surround Moscow. Most of the city lies inside the MKAD highway.*

## RUSSIAN FEDERATION

Pechora
Pechora

Mezen
Ukhta
Pechora

Pinega
Vycheyda

Kotlas

Kirov

Ufa
Magnitogorsk

Ural

Orsk
Turgay

M7
Oka
Tolyatti
Samara
Orenburg

Ryazan

KAZAKSTAN

Saratov

oronezh
M5

Don
Chelkar

Volgograd
Volga

Donets
Astrakhan

Mariupol
Rostov-na-Donu

ea of zov

Krasnodar

CASPIAN SEA
TURKMENISTAN

**An infrared satellite image of Moscow**

## PUTTING RUSSIA ON THE MAP

Arctic Ocean

NORWAY
SWEDEN
FINLAND

ESTONIA
LATVIA
LITHUANIA
POLAND
BELARUS

UNITED KINGDOM
REP. OF IRELAND
GERMANY
CZECH
UKRAINE
Moscow

RUSSIAN FEDERATION

Bering Sea

FRANCE
HUNGARY
ROMANIA

SPAIN
ITALY
BULGARIA
GEORGIA
UZBEKISTAN
TURK-MENISTAN
KYRGYZSTAN
TAJIKISTAN
MONGOLIA

KAZAKSTAN

Pacific Ocean

PORTUGAL
GREECE
TURKEY

N KOREA
JAPAN
S KOREA

MOROCCO
TUNISIA
SYRIA
IRAQ
IRAN
AFGHAN-ISTAN
CHINA

ALGERIA
LIBYA
EGYPT
SAUDI ARABIA
PAKISTAN
NEPAL
INDIA
BURMA

# Greater Moscow

A<small>N ENORMOUS, SPRAWLING CITY,</small> Moscow has grown rapidly over the past decades and, as a result, consists mostly of high-rise suburbs surrounding a relatively compact historic center. Most areas of the city are served by the famously efficient metro system as well as buses, trams, and trolleybuses *(see pp214–17)*. Much, but not all, of the city lies within the MKAD orbital motorway, which is one of six concentric ring roads.

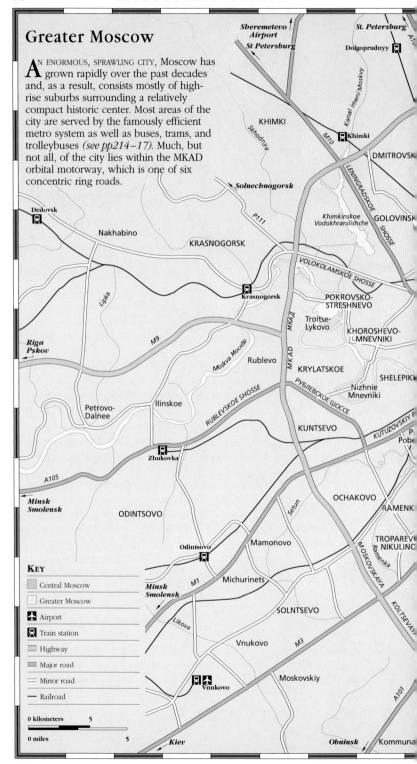

**KEY**

| | |
|---|---|
| | Central Moscow |
| | Greater Moscow |
| ✈ | Airport |
| 🚉 | Train station |
| | Highway |
| | Major road |
| | Minor road |
| | Railroad |

0 kilometers    5

0 miles          5

# Central Moscow

MOST OF MOSCOW'S SIGHTS are situated in the city center, within the area bounded by the Garden Ring and the Boulevard Ring. In this book the center has been divided into five sightseeing areas, while two other sections cover the outskirts and day trips into the countryside. Each of the central areas has a distinctive character, with the sights in each one lying within walking distance of one another. All of these sights well served by public transportation.

**Hotel National**
*Located in the heart of Tverskaya, close to the Bolshoy Theater (see pp90–91), the National (see p89) is an eclectic mixture of Style Moderne and Classical style.*

**Ulitsa Arbat**
*Running the length of what was a suburb in 15th-century Moscow, ulitsa Arbat (see pp70–71) is today a crowded pedestrian street, lined with shops and restaurants.*

**The Kremlin**
*The heart of the city, the Kremlin (see pp52–67) has dominated Russian life for over 800 years. Its buildings are from the 15th–20th centuries.*

## KEY

| | |
|---|---|
| ▦ | Major sight |
| ▦ | Place of interest |
| Ⓜ | Metro station |
| 🚢 | River boat pier |
| 🛡 | Police station |
| ✛ | Orthodox church |
| ✝ | Non-Orthodox church |
| ✡ | Synagogue |
| ☾ | Mosque |
| ⊠ | Post office |

0 meters 400
0 yards 400

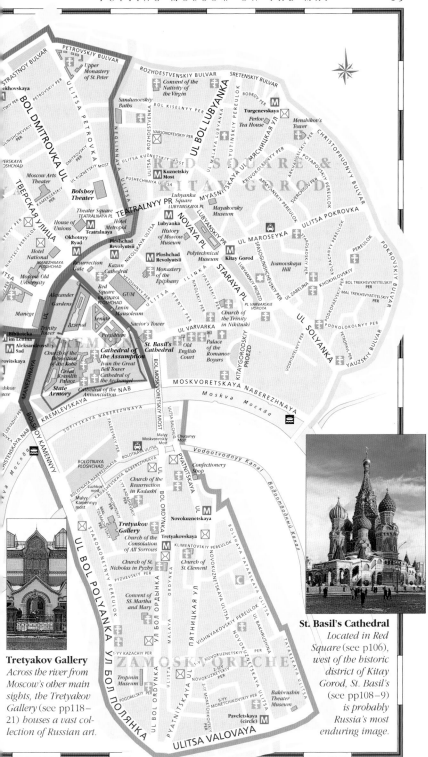

**Tretyakov Gallery**
*Across the river from Moscow's other main sights, the Tretyakov Gallery (see pp118–21) houses a vast collection of Russian art.*

**St. Basil's Cathedral**
*Located in Red Square (see p106), west of the historic district of Kitay Gorod, St. Basil's (see pp108–9) is probably Russia's most enduring image.*

# THE HISTORY OF MOSCOW

FROM HER 12TH-CENTURY ORIGINS *as an obscure defensive outpost, Moscow came to govern one-sixth of the land area on Earth and cast her shadow even farther. The story of her rise is laced with glory and setbacks, including the two centuries when St. Petersburg was the capital of Russia and Moscow lived the life of a dignified dowager.*

### THE FIRST SETTLERS

The forested area around Moscow was sparsely populated, but the fertile lands of southern Russia and the Ukraine had long supported trade routes between the Orient and Europe. It was here that the Slavs, the ancestors of the Russian people, first settled. They came from Eastern Europe in the 6th century and established isolated villages along the major rivers. In the 8th century they came into contact with the Varangians (Vikings), who navigated these waterways to trade amber, furs, and fair-skinned slaves.

**Mongol warriors going into battle on horseback, as depicted on a 15th-century lacquer box**

### KIEVAN RUS

Endemic infighting between the Slavic tribes was quelled when Rurik, a Varangian chief, assumed power in the region. Rurik settled in Novgorod, but his successor Oleg took Kiev and made it his capital. In 988 Grand Prince Vladimir I, a descendant of Rurik, was baptized into Orthodox Christianity *(see p137)* and married the sister of the

**Vladimir's conversion in the *Baptism of Russia* by Vasnetsov**

Byzantine emperor. Vladimir's conversion deeply affected the future of Russia, which remained an Orthodox country into the 20th century.

### THE MONGOL INVASION

By the 12th century, Kiev's supremacy had already been challenged by the powerful Russian principalities to the north, including Rostov-Suzdal *(see p155)*, of which the wooden kremlin at Moscow formed part. As a result, when the fierce horse-borne Mongols invaded in 1237, the disunited Russians fell easy victims to the well-organized troops of Batu Khan. For the next 240 years the Russian principalities paid an exorbitant yearly tribute to the khans, though they were left to govern themselves.

## TIMELINE

| | | | | |
|---|---|---|---|---|
| **C8** Varangians arrive in the region to trade and find local tribes in conflict | *Rurik, Varangian chief*<br><br>**988** Grand Prince Vladimir I converts to Christianity | | **1147** Moscow first documented, as the site of a hunting lodge | **1156** Prince Yuriy Dolgorukiy builds Moscow's first wooden kremlin | **1240** Mongols control most of Rus after the sack of Kiev |

| 800 | 900 | 1000 | 1100 | 1200 |
|---|---|---|---|---|

| | | | |
|---|---|---|---|
| **862** Rurik takes Novgorod and establishes a Varangian stronghold | **882** Rurik's successor Oleg takes Kiev and makes it capital<br><br>**863** Missionaries Cyril and Methodius invent the Cyrillic alphabet, based on the Greek one; literacy grows with the spread of Christianity | **1108** The town of Vladimir *(see p155)* is founded | **1223** First Mongol raid<br><br>**1236–42** Prince Aleksandr Nevskiy of Novgorod defeats first the invading Swedes and then the Teutonic Knights |

◁ **The symbol of Moscow, St. George and the Dragon, on a 15th-century icon housed in the Tretyakov Gallery**

### THE RISE OF MOSCOW

In the 14th century, the Mongols chose Moscow's power-hungry Grand Prince Ivan I, "Kalita" or "Moneybags" (1325–40), to collect tribute from all their conquered principalities, giving the city supremacy over its neighbors. Ivan had already shown his obsequiousness by crushing a revolt against the Mongols led by his neighbor, the Grand Prince of Tver. Yet the Mongols were sealing their own fate, for, as Moscow flourished under their benevolence, she ultimately became a real threat to their power.

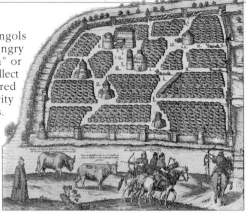

Map of 15th-century Moscow, showing neat rows of wooden houses and several churches behind the city's first stone walls

Within 50 years an army of soldiers from several Russian principalities, led by Moscow's Grand Prince Dmitriy Donskoy (1359–89), inflicted their first defeat on the Mongols, and the idea of a Russian nation was born.

It was not until the reign of Ivan III, "the Great" (1462–1505), when Moscow ruled a kingdom that stretched as far as the Arctic Ocean and the Urals, that the Mongols were finally vanquished. Ivan married the niece of the last emperor of Byzantium, who had fled Constantinople when it had fallen to the Ottomans in 1453. This increased Moscow's prestige further, and particularly her claim to being the last defender of true Orthodoxy. Ivan also sought to assert Moscow's status through a huge building program. He started the tradition of importing foreign architects, including the Italians (*see p44*) who built the present Kremlin walls.

Ivan the Terrible (1533–84)

### IVAN THE TERRIBLE

It was Ivan the Great's grandson, Ivan IV, "the Terrible" (1533–84), who transformed himself from Grand Prince of Moscow to "Tsar of All the Russias." During his reign Russia expanded beyond the Urals into Siberia and strong trading links were established with England. Moscow's walls were strengthened because the Crimean Mongols continued to venture sporadic attacks on the Russian capital as late as 1571.

Yet, powerful though he was, Ivan suffered dreadful paranoia. After the death of his beloved wife Anastasia, he became convinced that she had been poisoned by the boyars (*see p20*) and set up Russia's first police state. A sinister force of black-hooded agents called the *oprichniki* murdered whole villages to stamp out the tsar's supposed enemies. Ivan also imposed restrictions on the aristocracy and peasantry alike, establishing those

## TIMELINE

| | | | | |
|---|---|---|---|---|
| **1328** Ivan I becomes Grand Prince of Vladimir | **c.1345** St. Sergius founds the Trinity Monastery of St. Sergius (*see pp156–9*) | **1380** Dmitriy Donskoy defeats the Mongols at the pivotal Battle of Kulikovo (*see p155*) | **1453** Constantinople, previously Moscow's Orthodox ally, falls to the Ottomans | **1470s** The Cathedral of the Assumption is built |
| **1300** | **1350** | **1400** | | **1450** |
| **1300** Metropolitan See is transferred from Kiev to Vladimir | **1328** Metropolitan See is transferred from Vladimir to Moscow | **1367** Dmitriy Donskoy rebuilds Kremlin walls in limestone | | **1462–1505** Reign of Ivan III |
| | **1325–40** Ivan I rules Moscow and strengthens its position | *Rebuilding of the Kremlin walls* | | **1476** Ivan III stop paying tribute to Mongol |

autocratic traditions that were to prove the country's downfall. Ivan's more immediate legacy was his contribution to the end of the Varangian dynasty, the murder of his only competent son, also named Ivan, in a paranoid rage.

## THE TIME OF TROUBLES

This ushered in a period known as the Time of Troubles. For fourteen years, Ivan's disabled son Fyodor (1584–98) ruled under the guidance of Boris Godunov, a former and much-hated *oprichnik*. When Fyodor died childless, Godunov installed himself in the Kremlin, but he soon become target of a pretender to the throne. The pretender claimed to be Ivan the Terrible's dead youngest son Dimitry, sought support from Poland, and marched on Moscow with an army of 4,000 in 1604. With the death of Boris Godunov in 1605 he was installed on the throne.

**Boris Godunov (1598–1605)**

However, the pretender soon enraged the Moscow boyars; they killed him and installed an imposter of their own, Vasiliy Shuiskiy, in his place. Faced with a second "False Dmitry" marching on Moscow in 1607, Shuiskiy appealed to Sweden for help – only to provoke a new Polish intervention. The Poles reached Moscow in 1610, and Shuiskiy was then deposed by the boyars. In the north, the Swedes used the internal instability of Russia to capture Novgorod. Only in these desperate circumstances did the Russians finally unite to expel the occupying Poles under the leadership of Minin and Prince Pozharskiy *(see p108)*. The siege of the Kremlin thus ended in 1612.

## THE FIRST ROMANOVS

Determined to put an end to this period of anarchy, Moscow's leading citizens came together to nominate the 16-year old Mikhail Romanov, great-nephew of Ivan's first wife Anastasia, as hereditary tsar, thus initiating the 300-year rule of the Romanovs. Under Mikhail (1613–45), who ruled with his father, Filaret, the patriarch of Moscow, Russia recovered from her exhausting upheavals. His greatest legacy, however, was his heir Alexis (1645–76). An intelligent and pious man, Alexis tried to modernize the state. He oversaw the first codification of Russian law and encouraged an influx of foreign technicians, against the will of the Church. During the reign of Alexis the Church saw difficult times due to the schism between the reformers, led by Patriarch Nikon *(see p57)*, and the conservative Old Believers. Nikon, however, grew too important for his own good, which resulted in Alexis asserting the power of the State over the Church.

Ambassadors of the Council of the Realm entreating young Mikhail Romanov to accept the tsar's crown in 1613

| 1485 Ivan III commissions Italian architects to rebuild the Kremlin walls | 1533–84 Reign of Ivan IV | 1561 Building of St. Basil's Cathedral is completed | | 1589 Moscow attains status of Patriarchate | 1613 Mikhail is elected first tsar of the Romanov dynasty | 1653–67 Religious schism between Patriarch Nikon, and the Old Believers |
|---|---|---|---|---|---|---|
| **1500** | | **1550** | | **1600** | | **1650** |
| 1478 Ivan III revokes Novgorod's charter of independence | 1547 Ivan IV takes title "Tsar" 1552 Victory over Mongols as Ivan IV takes town of Kazan | 1570 Ivan IV orders massacre of Novgorod | 1571 Mongols raid Moscow 1598–1605 Reign of Boris Godunov | | 1610 Moscow falls to the Poles but they are driven out two years later | 1654–67 Second war with Poland *Patriarch Nikon* |

# Medieval Moscow

**M**OSCOW DEVELOPED in 400 years from an isolated wooden fortress (kremlin), built in 1156, into a thriving capital city, "shining like Jerusalem from without, but like Bethlehem inside." Its circle of outer walls enclosed a series of smaller districts centered on the Kremlin, whose wooden stockade was replaced with white limestone in 1367 to protect the city from Mongol raids, and by massive brick walls in 1485. It boasted a clutch of stone cathedrals, befitting its role as the "Third Rome" after the fall of Constantinople in 1453. Next to the Kremlin lay Red Square, where public spectacles ranged from executions to fairs. The rest of the city housed boyars, merchants, servants, hawkers, and artisans.

**EXTENT OF THE CITY**

◼ *13th century* ☐ *1590*

**The public sauna** *(banya)* was always placed near water, isolated where possible from the dense crush of wooden housing.

**Andrey Rublev (c.1370–1430)**
*Moscow's finest icon painter, Andrey Rublev, is seen here painting a fresco at the Monastery of the Savior and Andronicus (see p140). Icons (see p61) were used for the religious education of the people.*

**A Silver Kovsh**
*Originally made in wood, this ceremonial drinking vessel, known as a kovsh, began to be crafted in metal in the 14th century. Elaborately decorated kovshi were often given by the tsar to favored subjects. These treasured artifacts would be displayed as a symbol of wealth when not in use.*

**THE WALLED CITY**
Vasnetsov's *(see p144)* painting of the Kremlin in the 15th century shows the warren of wooden houses that surrounded the palaces and churches. Among them were the renowned Kremlin workshops.

**Boyars and Merchants**
*Though richly dressed, boyars (noblemen) in medieval Russia were largely illiterate and often crude in their habits. Their material needs were looked after by merchants who traded in furs from the north and silk from Turkey.*

### Foreigners in Moscow

*From the 16th century, foreign diplomats and traders began to visit the isolated and xenophobic Russia. The adventurer Richard Chancellor, who attempted to find the northwest passage to the Orient but ended up in Russia, managed to negotiate a trading treaty with Ivan the Terrible.*

**Wooden houses** could be bought prefabricated from a market outside the city walls. They quickly replaced houses that were lost in Moscow's frequent fires.

**Limestone walls, erected by Dmitriy Donskoy** *(see p155)*

## WHERE TO SEE MEDIEVAL MOSCOW

The Kremlin's medieval buildings include its Cathedrals of the Assumption *(see pp58–9)*, the Archangel *(p60)*, and the Annunciation *(p60)*. The State Armory *(pp64–5)*, also in the Kremlin, displays medieval artifacts and armor, while the daily life of the nobility is re-created in the Palace of the Romanov Boyars *(pp102–3)*. St. Basil's Cathedral *(pp108–9)* also dates from this time.

***The dining room** in the Palace of the Romanov Boyars*

### Building a Cathedral

*During the reign of Ivan I (1325–40), when the first stone Cathedral of the Assumption was built, Metropolitan Peter moved to Moscow to be head of the Orthodox Church. This manuscript illustration shows him blessing the new cathedral.*

**Cathedral of the Assumption**

**Small trading vessels** thronged the banks of the Moskva River, unloading goods for the growing city. Russia's rivers were her trading routes and were far more efficient than travel by land.

### Ivan the Terrible

*Though Ivan IV's reign (1533–84) did much to benefit Russia, he certainly deserved his epithet. Among the many souls on his conscience was his only worthy son and heir, Ivan, killed in a fit of rage, which the tsar regretted for the rest of his life.*

## PETER THE GREAT

The extraordinary reign of Alexis's son Peter I, "the Great," really put Russia back on her feet. Brought up in an atmosphere of reform, Peter was determined to make Russia a modern European state. In 1697, he became the first tsar ever to go abroad, with the particular aim of studying shipbuilding and other European technologies. On his return, he began immediately to build a

Vasiliy Surikov's portrayal of Peter the Great watching Streltsy Guards being led to their deaths in 1698, as punishment for their earlier rebellion

Russian navy, reformed the army, and insisted on Western-style clothing for his courtiers. At Poltava in 1709, Peter dramatically defeated the Swedes, who had been a threat to Russia for a century, and stunned Europe into taking note of an emerging power.

Peter's effect on Moscow was double-edged. At the age of ten he had seen relatives murdered in the Kremlin during the Streltsy Rebellion. This revolt had sprung from rivalry between his mother's family, the Naryshkins, and that of his father's first wife, the Miloslavskiys, over the succession. In the end Peter was made co-tsar with his half-brother Ivan, but developed a pathological distrust of Moscow. He took a long-awaited and grim revenge on the Streltsys 16 years

later, when he executed over a thousand of them. He also began to build a new city on the boggy banks of the Neva to the north and ordered the imperial family and government to move. In 1712 he declared the cold, damp St. Petersburg capital of Russia. For the next 200 years Moscow was Russia's second city.

Tsar Peter the Great (1682–1725)

Tsarina Elizabeth (1741–62)

## WOMEN'S RULE

After Peter the Great's death in 1725, Russia was ruled by women for most of the 18th century: Catherine I, Anna, Elizabeth, and Catherine II. Though they were all crowned in the Cathedral of the Assumption *(see pp58–9)*, most preferred to live in Europeanized St. Petersburg. However, Elizabeth, Peter's boisterous, fun-loving daughter, insisted on periodically living in Moscow. During Peter's reign constructions in stone outside St. Petersburg had been banned, but under Elizabeth a flurry of new buildings appeared in Moscow, especially since some of Russia's leading families preferred to live there.

## TIMELINE

| | | | | |
|---|---|---|---|---|
| **1696** Ivan dies. Peter I is sole ruler | **1698** The Streltsys are crushed | **1721** Peter I replaces patriarchiate with less-powerful church synod | | **1773–4** Pugachev Rebellion |
| | **1700–21** Great Northern War against Sweden | **1730–40** Reign of Anna | **1741–62** Reign of Elizabeth | **1768–74** First Russo-Turkish War |

| **1700** | | **1725** | | **1750** |
|---|---|---|---|---|

| | | | | | | |
|---|---|---|---|---|---|---|
| **1682** The Streltsy Rebellion; Peter I is co-tsar with half-brother Ivan V and his half-sister Sophia as regent | **1709** Great Russian victory at the Battle of Poltava | **1712** Capital is transferred to St. Petersburg | **1725–7** Reign of Catherine I | *Tsarina Anna* | **1762** Peter III is killed. His wife seizes the throne as Catherine II | |
| | | **1727–30** Reign of Peter II. Moscow is capital for two years | | | **1755** Mikhail Lomonosov founds Moscow University | |

Elizabeth founded Russia's first university in Moscow *(see p94),* under the guidance of Russia's 18th-century Renaissance man, the poet, scientist and academic Mikhail Lomonosov. But Moscow was still protected from the Westernization affecting the capital, and thus retained a more purely Russian soul and identity.

### CATHERINE THE GREAT

In 1762 Catherine II, "the Great," a German princess, usurped the throne of her feeble husband Peter III with the help of her lover Grigoriy Orlov, a guards officer. Under her energetic, intelligent leadership, the country saw another vast expansion in its prestige and made territorial gains

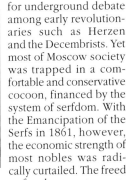
Catherine the Great (1762–96)

at the expense of Turkey and its old adversary Poland. Catherine purchased great collections of European art and books (including Voltaire's library) and in 1767 published her *Nakaz* (Imperial Instruction) upon which a reform of Russia's legal system was to be based. Not surprisingly, this modern European monarch regarded Moscow as inward-looking and backward and spent little time there.

### 19TH-CENTURY MOSCOW

Napoleon's invasion in 1812 and the heroic part played in his defeat by Moscow *(see pp24–5)* appeared to reinvigorate the city. Aleksandr Herzen *(see p71)* claimed that "Moscow was again made the 'capital' of the Russian people by Napoleon," and, indeed, the destruction of two-thirds of the city by fire resulted in a bold new archi-

tectural plan. The Napoleonic Wars also marked a turning point in Russian political history, as soldiers returned from Europe bringing with them the seeds of liberal ideas. Far from the court of Nicholas I, the Iron Tsar, Moscow became a fertile environment for underground debate among early revolutionaries such as Herzen and the Decembrists. Yet most of Moscow society was trapped in a comfortable and conservative cocoon, financed by the system of serfdom. With the Emancipation of the Serfs in 1861, however, the economic strength of most nobles was radically curtailed. The freed serfs, who were too poor to buy their own land, flocked to the factories of mercantile and industrial entrepreneurs. In Moscow, at the old heart of the empire, these entrepreneurs came to usurp the position of the aristocrats, making vast fortunes from trade, textiles, railroads, banking, and publishing, and financing a renaissance in the Russian arts on the proceeds.

The Bolshoy Theater, along with balls and lavish suppers, were all favored by Moscow's aristocracy.

| 1787–92 Second Russo-Turkish War | 1805–7 War with France; Russia is defeated at battles of Austerlitz, Friedland | *Tsar Nicholas I* | 1835 First modern law code comes into effect | 1851 The Nicholas Railroad between Moscow and St. Petersburg is opened | 1853–6 Crimean War |
|---|---|---|---|---|---|
| **1800** | | | **1825** | | **1850** |
| 1796 Death of Catherine II. Paul I accedes | 1807 Treaty of Tilsit | 1816–19 Emancipation of serfs in Baltic provinces | 1855 Nicholas I dies. Alexander II succeeds | | |
| 1801 Paul I is assassinated. Alexander I becomes tsar and begins a program of reforms | 1812 Napoleon invades Moscow but has to retreat | | 1825 Nicholas I becomes tsar. The Decembrist Rebellion is crushed in St. Petersburg | 1861 Emancipation of all serfs | 1865–9 Tolstoy publishes *War and Peace* |

# War and Peace

R USSIA'S GLORIOUS RISE to the ranks of a world power accelerated in the period between 1800 and 1830. After inflicting severe defeats on France, including the 1805 Battle of Austerlitz, Russia signed the Treaty of Tilsit in 1807. The uneasy peace ended in 1812, with the invasion of Napoleon's Grande Armée. But Russia turned disaster into victory, and in 1814–15 Tsar Alexander I sat down to decide Europe's future at the Congress of Vienna. The war marked an important cultural shift in Russia as liberal Western European political ideas first filtered into the country, although their time had not yet come.

**EXTENT OF THE CITY**

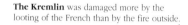
☐ *1812, before the fire*

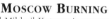
☐ *Areas razed by the fire*

**Alexander I (1801–25)**
*The handsome young tsar was initially infected by the ideals of enlightened government, but became increasingly influenced by his reactionary advisers.*

**The Kremlin** was damaged more by the looting of the French than by the fire outside.

**Napoleon** stayed in the tsar's apartments for a few days before retreating to safety outside the city.

## MOSCOW BURNING

After Field Marshal Mikhail Kutuzov's retreat at Borodino, the French army was able to enter Moscow. But Muscovites set fire to their city and fled. In just days, two-thirds of the city burned down, leaving the army without shelter or provisions. Combined with Alexander I's refusal to negotiate while Napoleon remained on Russian territory, this resulted in the French emperor's defeat.

**The French soldiers** soon fell to undisciplined drinking and looting.

**Battle of Borodino, September 1812**
*The Battle of Borodino (see p152) lasted 15 hours, causing the death of 70,000 men, half of them French. Yet Napoleon declared the battle a victory and advanced on Moscow.*

**Retreat of Napoleon's Grande Armée**
*Facing the winter without supplies, the army began its retreat in October. Only 30,000 out of 600,000 men made it back.*

**Empire Style**
*Many things, from chairs to plates, were designed in the pop-ular Empire style (see p45). This cup and saucer with a Classical motif were made at the Popov factory near Moscow in 1810.*

## WHERE TO SEE NEO-CLASSICAL MOSCOW

Early examples of Neo-Classicism can be seen at the palaces of Ostankino *(see p144)* and Kuskovo *(pp142–3)*, at Pashkov House

**Pediment, Kuskovo Palace**

*(p75)*, and at Moscow Old University *(p94)*. The fire of 1812 allowed vast areas to be developed to an Empire-style city plan. Bolshaya Nikitskaya ulitsa *(p93)*, ulitsa Prechistenka *(p74)*, and Theater Square *(p88)* are lined with fine buildings from this era.

**Moscow University**
*It was after the Napoleonic Wars that the University of Moscow, founded in 1755, gained a reputation as a hotbed of liberalism. However, political discussions still had to be conducted at secret salons.*

**Alexander Pushkin**
*The great Romantic poet Alexander Pushkin (see p73) captured the spirit of the time. Pushkin and his wife Natalya were often invited to court balls, such as the one shown here. This enabled Nicholas I to keep an eye on the liberal poet as well as on his enchanting wife.*

**New fires** were started deliber-ately throughout the city, on the orders of the tsarist governor.

**The river** proved no barrier to the fire, whipped up by a fierce wind.

**The Millstone of Serfdom**
*In the shadow of the nobility's easy life, and to a great extent enabling it, were millions of serfs toiling in slavery on large estates. This painting shows a serf owner settling his debts by selling a girl to a new master.*

## THE END OF AN EMPIRE

Although the 1890s saw rapid advances in industrialization, Russia experienced a disastrous slump at the turn of the 20th century. Nicholas II's diversionary war with Japan backfired, causing economic unrest, adding to the misery of the working classes, and finally culminating in the 1905 Revolution. On January 9, 1905, a demonstration in St. Petersburg carried a petition of grievances to the tsar and was met by bullets. News of this "Bloody Sunday" spread like wildfire, and strikes broke out all over the country. To avert further disaster Nicholas had to promise basic civil rights and an elected parliament, which he simply dissolved whenever it displeased him. This high-handed behavior, along with the imperial family's friendship with the "holy man" Rasputin, further damaged the Romanovs' reputation.

The outbreak of World War I brought a surge of patriotism, which the inexperienced Nicholas rode on by taking personal command of the troops. By

*The Bolshevik* by Boris Kustodiev, painted in 1920

late 1916, however, Russia had lost 3,500,000 men, morale at the front was very low, and supplies of food at home had become increasingly scarce.

## REVOLUTION AND CIVIL WAR

In early 1917 strikes broke out in St. Petersburg. People took to the streets, jails were stormed, and the February Revolution began. The tsar was forced to abdicate and his family was placed under house arrest. Exiled revolutionaries flooded back into the country to set up workers' and soldiers' soviets. Elected by the workers as an alternative to an unelected provisional government, they formed a powerful anti-war lobby. In October the leadership of the Bolsheviks, urged on by Lenin, decided on an armed uprising, under the rallying cries of "All power to the soviets!" and "Peace, bread, and land." In the early hours of October 26th, they arrested the provisional government in St. Petersburg's Winter Palace.

Within months the Bolsheviks had shown themselves as careless of democracy as the tsar, dismissing the constituent assembly and setting up their own secret police, the Cheka.

Tatiana
Olga
Maria
Anastasia

Tsar Nicholas II surrounded by his wife Alexandra, their four daughters, and Tsarevich Alexis in 1913

## TIMELINE

| | | | | |
|---|---|---|---|---|
| **1881** Alexander II is killed by the "People's Will" group. Accession of Alexander III | **1894** Alexander III dies after an oppressive and reactionary reign. Nicholas II accedes | **1905** The 1905 Revolution is followed by the inauguration of the Duma (1906) <br> **1902** Lenin's *What is to be Done?* is published | | **1912** First issue of *Pravda* is published |

**1880** **1900**

| | | | |
|---|---|---|---|
| **1881–2** Pogroms against Jews <br><br> **1887** Lenin's brother is hanged for attempt on the tsar's life | **1898** Foundation of Social-Democratic Workers' Party <br><br> **1903** Pro-violence Bolsheviks (under Lenin) secede from Social-Democratic Workers' Party | **1904–5** Russo-Japanese War | **1913** 300th anniversary of Romanov dynasty <br><br> **1914** World War I begins |

In March 1918, however, they stayed true to their promise and took Russia out of World War I, instead plunging the soldiers straight into a vicious civil war. The capital was moved back to Moscow, and from here Lenin and his government directed their "Red" army against the diverse coalition of anti-revolutionary groups known as the "Whites." When White soldiers got closer to the exiled Romanovs in Yekaterinburg in July 1918, the royal family was brutally butchered by its captors. But the Whites were a disparate force, and by November 1920 Soviet Russia was rid of them, only to face two years of appalling famine.

Cathedral of the Redeemer, torn down on the orders of Stalin as part of his new city plan *(see pp74–5)*

A 1933 propaganda poster showing Joseph Stalin

## THE STALIN YEARS

In the five years after Lenin's death in 1924, Joseph Stalin used his position as General Secretary of the Communist Party to remove such rivals as Leon Trotsky and establish his dictatorship.

The terror began in the countryside, with the collectivization of agriculture that forced the peasantry to give up their land, machinery, and livestock to collective farms in return for a salary. During this time, and in the ensuing famine of 1931–2, up to 10 million people are thought to have died.

The first major purge of intellectuals took place in urban areas in 1928–9. Then, in December 1934, Sergey Kirov, the local party leader in Leningrad, was assassinated on the secret orders of Stalin, although the murder was blamed on an underground anti-Stalinist cell. This was the catalyst for five years of purges, by the end of which over a million people had been executed and some 15 million arrested and sent to labor camps, where they often died.

In his purge of the Red Army in 1937–8, Stalin dismissed or executed three quarters of his officers. When the Germans invaded in 1941 they were able to advance rapidly, subjecting Leningrad to a horrendous siege of nearly 900 days. But Moscow was never taken because Hitler, like Napoleon before him, under-estimated both the harshness of the Russian winter and his enemies' willingness to fight.

After the German defeat, the Russian people, who had lost over 20 million souls in the war, were subjected to a renewed internal terror by Stalin, which lasted until his death in 1953.

"Let us defend our beloved Moscow," 1941 propaganda poster

*Sergey Kirov*

# The Russian Revolution

THE RUSSIAN REVOLUTION, which began in St. Petersburg and made Moscow once more a capital city, was pivotal to the history of the 20th century. By late 1916, with Russia facing defeat in World War I and starvation at home, even ministers and generals were doubting the tsar's ability to rule. In 1917 there were two uprisings: the February Revolution, which began with massive strikes and led to the abdication of Nicholas II; and the October Revolution which overturned the provisional government and swept the Communists to power. They emerged victoriously from the Civil War that followed, to attempt to build a new society.

**EXTENT OF THE CITY**

▨ *1917*      ☐ *Today*

**The Ex-Tsar**
*Nicholas II, seen here clearing snow during his house arrest outside St. Petersburg, was later taken with his family to Yekaterinburg in the Urals. There, in 1918, they were shot and their bodies thrown down a mine shaft.*

**Many soldiers** deserting from the front were happy to put on the new Red Army uniform instead.

**Middle-class people** as well as the poor took part in the Revolution.

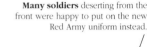

## REDS OUTSIDE THE KREMLIN

In October, the fight for control of the Kremlin was intense in comparison to the one in St. Petersburg. The Bolshevik seizure was reversed after three days, and it took the revolutionaries another six days to overcome loyalist troops in the fortress and elsewhere in the city.

**Women** took part in demonstrations and strikes.

**Comrade Lenin**
*A charismatic speaker, depicted here by Viktor Ivanov, the exiled Lenin returned in April to lead the Revolution. By late 1917 his Bolshevik party had gained power.*

**Revolutionary Plate**
*Ceramics with revolutionary themes, mixed with touches of Russian folklore, were produced to commemorate special events. This plate marks the founding of the Third International Communist group in 1919.*

**Leon Trotsky**
*The intellectual Trotsky played a leading military role in the Revolution. In 1928, during the power struggle after Lenin's death, he was exiled by Stalin. He was murdered in Mexico, in 1940, by a Stalinist agent.*

**Propaganda**
*One hallmark of the Soviet regime was its powerful propaganda. Many talented artists were employed to design posters, which spread the Socialist message through striking graphics. During the Civil War (1918–20), posters such as this one extolled the "pacifist army of workers" to support War Communism.*

Banner proclaiming freedom to the world

**Avant-Garde Art**
*Even before 1917, Russia's artists had been in a state of revolution, producing the world's first truly abstract paintings. A fine example of avant-garde art is* Supremus No. 56, *painted in 1916 by Kazimir Malevich.*

**Old and young** were swept away by the revolutionary fervor.

**New Values**
*Traditions were radically altered by the Revolution; instead of church weddings, couples exchanged vows under the red flag. Loudly trumpeted sexual equality meant that women had to work twice as hard – at home and in the factories.*

## TIMELINE

| **February** Revolution in St. Petersburg | **March** The tsar is persuaded to abdicate. Provisional government is led by Prince Lvov | **October** Bolsheviks storm Winter Palace in St. Petersburg, after signal from *Aurora*, and oust provisional government | **March** Bolsheviks sign Brest-Litovsk peace treaty with Germany, taking Russia out of World War I. Capital is moved to Moscow |
|---|---|---|---|
| **1917** | | **1918** | |
| **July** Kerenskiy becomes prime minister of provisional government | *Battleship* Aurora | **January** Trotsky becomes Commissar of War<br><br>**December** Lenin forms the Cheka (secret police) | **July** Start of Civil War. Tsar and family murdered in prison at Yekaterinburg |

The Washington Dove of Peace (1953), a Russian caricature from the days of the Cold War

## BEHIND THE IRON CURTAIN

Three years after Stalin's death his successor, Nikita Khrushchev, denounced his crimes at the 20th Party Congress, and the period known as "The Thaw" began. Thousands of political prisoners were released, and books critical of Stalin were published. In foreign affairs, things were not so liberal. Soviet tanks invaded Hungary in 1956 and in 1962 Khrushchev's decision to base nuclear missiles on Cuba brought the world to the brink of nuclear war.

## FIRST IN SPACE

Under Khrushchev the Soviet Union achieved her greatest coup against the West, when she sent *Sputnik 1* into space in 1957. That same year the dog Laika was the first living creature in space, on *Sputnik 2*. She never came back but, four years later, Yuriy Gagarin made history as the first man in space, returning as a hero. The Soviets lost the race to put a man on the moon, but the space program was a powerful propaganda tool, backing the claims of politicians that Russia would soon catch up with and overtake the West.

*Sputnik 2* and the space dog Laika, 1957

When Leonid Brezhnev took over in 1964, the intellectual climate froze once more. The first ten years of his office were a time of relative plenty, but beneath the surface there was a vast black market and growing corruption. The party apparatchiks, who benefited from the corruption, had no interest in rocking the boat. When Brezhnev died in 1982, the Politburo was determined to prevent the accession of a younger generation. He was succeeded by the 68-year-old Andropov, followed by the 72-year-old Chernenko.

## GLASNOST AND PERESTROIKA

It was only in 1985 when the new leader, 53-year-old Mikhail Gorbachev, announced his policies of perestroika (restructuring) and *glasnost* (openness), that the true bankruptcy of the old system became apparent. Yet he had no idea of the immense changes that they would bring in their wake. For the first time since 1917, the elections to the Congress of People's Deputies in 1989 contained an element of true choice, with rebels such as human-rights campaigner Andrey Sakharov and Boris Yeltsin winning seats. In the autumn and winter of that year the Warsaw Pact disintegrated as country after country in Eastern Europe declared its independence from the Soviet Union. Local elections within the Union in 1990 brought nationalist candidates to power in the republics and democrats in the most important Russian local councils.

Mikhail Gorbachev with George Bush

## TIMELINE

| 1950 | 1960 | 1970 |
|---|---|---|
| **1950–54** Korean War | **1962** Khrushchev bases missiles in Cuba after the US intervention, leading to near nuclear war | **1969** Strategic Arms Limitation Talks (SALT) with US |
| **1961** Stalin's body is removed from the Kremlin Mausoleum | | *Leonid Brezhnev* |
| **1953** Stalin dies | **1957** *Sputnik 1* is launched | |
| **1955** Warsaw Pact | **1961** Building of Berlin Wall. Yuriy Gagarin is first man in space | **1964** Brezhnev takes over the role of General Secretary after Khrushchev | **1968** Soviet troops enter Czechoslovakia to suppress "Prague Spring" |
| **1956** Stalin denounced at 20th Party Congress. Hungarian uprising crushed | *Nikita Khrushchev* | |

Communist hero fallen from grace after the 1991 coup

soak up their desire to party. Much of the city was renovated in 1997 in honor of Moscow's 850th anniversary. The Cathedral of Christ the Redeemer *(see p 74)*, de-molished by Stalin in 1931, was rebuilt as part of the restoration pro-gram. This was also a sign of the renewed im-portance of the Orthodox Church, which was forced underground during the Soviet era. Churches are now filled once again for weddings, baptisms, and religious holidays. The crime rate has fallen from its dizzying high in 1995, as the city's cri-minal groups, or *mafiya*, have resolved their territorial bat-tles. Moscow's mayor in the mid-1990s, Yuriy Luzhkov, has used the city's affluence to cosmetic aplomb and yet, for most citizens, in contrast to the New Russians, the riches are just a mirage. Moscow is now among the most expensive cities in the world, yet plenty of work-ers take home salaries that would seem more typical of the Third World.

In 1991 the Baltic Republics and Russia herself seceded from the Soviet Union. With his massive victory in the elec-tion for President of the Russian Republic, Yeltsin gained the man-date he needed to deal the death-blow to the Soviet Union. It came after the military coup against Gorbachev in August 1991, when Yeltsin's stand against the tanks in Moscow made him a hero. After Gorbachev's return from house arrest in the Crimea, Yeltsin forced him to outlaw the Com-munist Party. By year's end the Soviet Union was no more; all the republics had declared their independence.

Moscow 850-years poster

## MOSCOW TODAY

The 1990s have had a profound effect on the drab old Moscow of Soviet times. With Russia's vast natural resources attracting a rush of inward investment, Moscow saw the lion's share of that money passing through its hands. A wealthy elite, the "New Russians," sud-denly had a vastly improved standard of living. For instance, car ownership in the city quadrupled in 1991–7. No amount of nightclubs seemed able to

A church wedding, popular once more since religion has gained new importance among the young

| 1982 Brezhnev dies and is replaced by Andropov | 1984 Andropov is replaced by Chernenko. USSR boycotts Olympic Games in Los Angeles | 1989 USSR leaves Afghanistan. East European countries become independent | |
| | | 1993 Counter coup stopped by Yeltsin | 1994 Luzhkov, mayor of Moscow, initiates reconstruction program in city |
| **1980** | | **1990** | **2000** |
| 1980 Olympics in Moscow are boy-cotted by the West | 1986 Chernobyl nuclear disaster | 1991 Yeltsin is elected president of Russia. August coup fails; the USSR is dissolved in December | 1997 Moscow celebrates 850-years anniversary |
| 1979 USSR invades Afghanistan | 1985 Gorbachev is elected General Secretary of Communist Party | 1990 Gorbachev is awarded Nobel Peace Prize. Independence of Latvia, Lithuania, Estonia | *Boris Yeltsin with the Russian flag* |

# MOSCOW THROUGH THE YEAR

USCOVITES are ready to celebrate at any time and take their public holidays seriously. Flowers play a particularly important role, from mimosa for International Women's Day to lilac as a symbol that summer is on its way. All the official holidays, as well as some local festivals such as City Day, are marked with concerts and nighttime fireworks all over the city. Music,

**Lilac, a sign that summer is coming**

whether classical, folk, or contemporary, is the central theme of a large number of festivals, bringing in talent from all over the world. For really big celebrations, top Russian and international singers perform for crowds of thousands in Red Square. Even without an official holiday, people love to get out and about, whether skiing in winter, picnicking in spring or summer, or gathering mushrooms in autumn.

**Performers wearing papier-mâché costumes at The Rite of Spring**

## SPRING

WHEN FLOCKS of rooks appear in the city, usually in late March, and the violets and snowdrops bloom, spring has arrived.

To warm themselves up after the months of cold, locals celebrate *maslennitsa*, the feast of blini-making before Lent. Willow branches with catkins are gathered as a symbol of the approaching Palm Sunday, and on Forgiveness Sunday, just before Lent, people ask forgiveness of those they may have offended in the past year.

**Easter service, Trinity Monastery of St. Sergius (see pp156–9)**

Wealthy Muscovites usually make a first visit to their dachas at this time to put the yard in order and to plant their own fruits and vegetables.

## MARCH

**International Women's Day** *(Mezhdunarodnyy den zhenshchin)*, Mar 8. Men buy flowers for their womenfolk and congratulate them on the holiday with the words *"s prazdnikom."* Theaters hold special performances.
**The Rite of Spring** *(Vesenniy obryad)*, mid-Mar. Avant-garde festival of contemporary arts.
**St. Patrick's Day**, first Sunday after March 16. Arranged by Moscow's Irish community. Guinness is drunk at a few local marches and concerts.
**Easter Sunday** *(Paskha)*, March–early May, following the Orthodox calendar. Churches are filled with chanting, and candles. After the greeting *Khristos voskres* (Christ is risen) and the reply *Voistine voskres* (He is truly risen), people kiss one another three times.

## APRIL

**April Fool's Day** *(Den durakov)*, Apr 1. Russians play tricks with particular glee.
**Cosmonauts' Day** *(Den kosmonavtiki)*, Apr 12. Space exploration was one of the glories of the Soviet Union and is celebrated with fireworks.
**Alternative Festival**, end Apr–May. Annual modern music festival in Gorky Park.
**Moscow Forum**, end Apr–May. Annual festival of classical and modern music held at various city venues.

**War veterans on parade in Red Square on Victory Day**

## MAY

**Labor Day** *(Den truda)*, May 1. In the Soviet era, huge military parades filled Red Square. Now much more low-key, with impromptu concerts.
**Victory Day** *(Den pobedy)*, May 9. War veterans fill Red Square and Tverskaya ulitsa in memory of the 1945 Nazi surrender. A military parade is held in Red Square.
**Border Troopers' Day** *(Den pogranichnika)*, May 28. Retired Border Troopers gather at the Bolshoy Theater and in Gorky Park to drink, sing, and watch fireworks.

## AVERAGE DAILY HOURS OF SUNSHINE

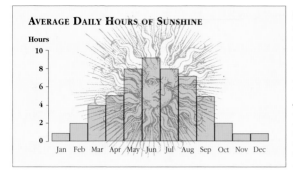

**Sunshine Chart**
*Moscow is often thought of as a cold and snowy city. However, it has more hours of sunshine in the summer months than many cities in northern Europe. May, June, and July are the sunniest months. The short, cold days of winter provide a stark contrast, with an average of only around one hour of sunshine a day.*

## SUMMER

LIFE IN MOSCOW is much less hectic in July and August as most enterprises close down for their summer breaks and many Muscovites move out of the city, either to their dacha or to spend vacations abroad. Although most of the theaters also close or go on tour for these two months, there is still plenty going on in and around the city for the visitor to enjoy. Some of the large estates and stately homes outside Moscow, such as Kuskovo *(see pp142–3)* and Ostankino Palace *(see pp144–5)*, hold outdoor concerts at this time of year. Gorky Park offers a number of options on a fine summer day – from bungee jumping or renting a row- or pedal-boat to enjoying a picnic. Outdoor cafés and bars

**Women in national costume for Peter the Great's birthday**

are a favorite with Muscovites remaining in the city, and there is even an outdoor casino at the Marilyn Entertainment Complex, at Krasina ulitsa 14.

## JUNE

**Trinity Sunday** *(Troitsa)*, late May–late June. Believers and atheists alike go to tidy the graves of their loved ones and drink a toast to their souls.
**Independence Day** *(Den neza-visimosti)*, Jun 12. The day Russia became independent of the Soviet Union is marked with firework displays.
**Peter the Great's Birthday** *(Den rozhdeniya Petra Pervovo)*, first Sunday after Jun 9. Costumed celebrations held at Kuskovo *(see pp142–3)*.
**International Music Assemblies Festival**, mid-June. Russian music through eight centuries performed at concert halls and art galleries.

## JULY

**Festival of Symphonies in Moscow Courtyards**, late Jun–early Jul. Impromptu concerts are staged in historic courtyards around the city.
**US Independence Day**, Jul 4. A big celebration by Moscow's huge American community and pro-Western Muscovites at the Kuskovo estate.
**Navy Day** *(Den voenno-morskovo flota)*, first Sunday after Jul 22. Fireworks and costumed celebrations across the city. Since Moscow is not a port city, celebrations are not as big as in St. Petersburg.
**Moscow International Film Festival**, held every two years (in odd-numbered years) in July or August *(see p193)*. An event attended by celebrities and featuring the latest releases from all over the world.

## AUGUST

**Tchaikovsky International Competition**, Aug (or sometimes end of Jul), held every four years (next in 2002). Musicians gather to compete for one of the most world's most prestigious musical awards *(see p192)*. Concerts are held throughout the city.
**Summer Music Festival**, throughout Aug. Evening recitals of classical music featuring distinguished graduates of the Moscow Conservatory.
**Moscow Annual Airshow**, toward the end of Aug. A chance to see Russian airplanes, including MiGs and SUKHOIs. Aerobatic displays.
**Russian Cinema Day**, Aug 27. Showings of favorite, mostly Russian, films on television and in theaters all over the city.

**Relaxing on a summer's day at an outdoor café in Arbatskaya**

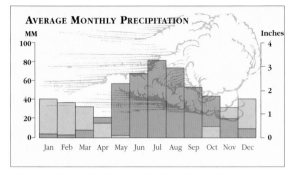

**AVERAGE MONTHLY PRECIPITATION**

MM / Inches

Jan Feb Mar Apr May Jun Jul Aug Sep Oct Nov Dec

**Precipitation Chart**
*In the winter months, precipitation falls mainly as snow, most of which settles until the spring, reaching a depth of 35 cm (14 in). In summer, even hot days are often interrupted by brief but heavy rain showers.*

Rainfall (from axis)

Snowfall (from axis)

## AUTUMN

CITY LIFE begins to pick up as people return from the country and prepare their children for school. In the last weeks of August, Moscow is filled with posters proclaiming the opening of school, and stores are packed with parents buying new school clothes and books. Theaters open again in September, with premieres of plays and operas.

The crisp autumn weather is perfect for mushroom gathering. Muscovites often head out early in the morning to the forests around the city to hunt for white and brown mushrooms, orange-cap boletes, chanterelles, and oyster mushrooms. However, dangerously poisonous as well as edible mushrooms abound, and gathering them is best left to the experts.

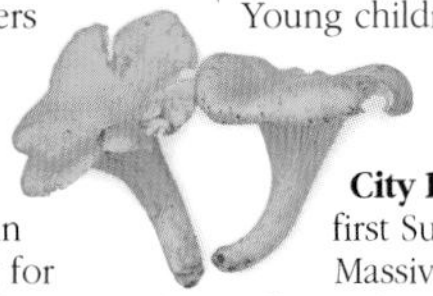

**Chanterelle mushrooms**

Other popular autumnal pastimes include horseback riding at the Hippodrome *(see p194)* and taking a boat trip along the Moskva river.

## SEPTEMBER

**New Academic Year** *(Novyy uchebnyy god),* Sep 1. Moscow is full of children heading for their first day back at school. Young children, especially those going for the first time, take flowers with them.
**City Day** *(Den goroda),* first Sunday in Sep. Massive costumed celebrations, concerts, and theater performances are held all over the city to celebrate the founding of Moscow in 1147 *(see p86).*

## OCTOBER

**Talents of Russia** *(Talanty Rossii),* Oct 1–10. Festival of classical music, with musicians from all over the country.

**Children with flowers for teachers at the start of the new school year**

**Punk Festival,** early Oct. Russian bands play in Gorky Park and at other venues.

## NOVEMBER

Students of the Moscow ballet schools give the first of their annual winter performances at various venues. This is the worst month to visit as Moscow is dirty and slushy.
**Day of Reconciliation** *(Den primireniya),* Nov 7. Previously called the Day of the Great October Socialist Revolution. Now celebrated mainly by the Communist Party.

### PUBLIC HOLIDAYS

**New Year's Day** (Jan 1)
**Russian Orthodox Christmas** (Jan 7)
**International Women's Day** (Mar 8)
**Easter Sunday** (Mar/Apr/May)
**Labor Day** (May 1)
**Victory Day** (May 9)
**Independence Day** (Jun 12)
**Day of Reconciliation** (Nov 7)
**Constitution Day** (Dec 12)

**Open-air folk dancing at Moscow's City Day celebrations**

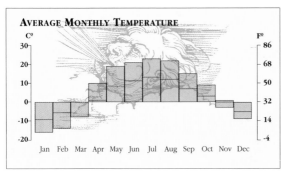

**AVERAGE MONTHLY TEMPERATURE**

**Temperature Chart**
*The chart shows the average minimum and maximum temperatures for each month. Winter temperatures well below freezing may seem daunting, and do limit the length of time it is possible to stay out, but the cold is dry and can be exhilarating and there is very little wind.*

## WINTER

As the ice thickens and the snow deepens, people head outdoors. Gorky (see p129), Sokolniki, and Luzhniki Parks become the venues for ice-skating and skiing. The hardened locals, the so-called "walruses," break the ice at Serebryaniy Bor on the western outskirts of Moscow to take a dip early every morning.

In the midst of winter sports come New Year and Christmas. New Year is the big holiday, while Christmas is celebrated on January 7, in accordance with the Orthodox calendar. Many people also still celebrate Old New Year, which falls a week later on January 14.

One great pleasure of this season is the Christmas ballet, *The Nutcracker*, performed at the Bolshoy Theater (see pp90–91) largely by children.

## DECEMBER

**Constitution Day** (*Den konstitutsii*), Dec 12. Fireworks are set off at 10pm to mark President Yeltsin's constitution.
**New Year's Eve** (*Novyy god*), Dec 31. Still the biggest holiday of the year, New Year's Eve is celebrated with the local *shampanskoe* (see p179). This

**An ice sculpture of an octopus, part of the festival in Gorky Park**

is a family celebration: at circuses and balls, actors dress up as the traditional bringers of presents, the Snow Maiden and Grandfather Frost.
**Svyatoslav Richter December Nights** (*Dekabrskie vechera imeni Svyatoslava Rikhtera*), throughout Dec. Classical music dedicated to the Russian conductor at the Pushkin Museum of Fine Arts (see pp78–81).
**Russian Winter** (*Russkaya zima*), end Dec–mid Jan. Classical music festival.

## JANUARY

**Russian Orthodox Christmas** (*Rozhdestvo*), Jan 7. Christmas is celebrated in a quieter fashion than Easter, with a traditional visit to an evening service on Christmas eve, when bells ring out through the frosty air from all over Moscow. Children's celebrations are held at various venues, including the Great Kremlin Palace (see p63). The parties are called *Yolka* (Christmas tree).
**Christmas Premier Festival**, end Dec–mid Jan. Annual classical music festival.
**Christmas in Moscow**, first two weeks in Jan. Festival of medieval and classical music.
**Ice Sculpture Festival in Gorky Park**. This festival lasts for several months, but it is never possible to tell exactly

**Fisherman fishing through a hole in the ice**

when it will start. It depends entirely on the weather, and some years it can start as early as December. During the festival Gorky Park is taken over by numerous ice sculptures, usually of fairy-tale characters, which remain in the park until the thaw.
**Tatyana's Day** (*Tatyanin den*), Jan 25. St. Tatyana's feast day is largely a holiday for students rather than a religious holiday, since the decree founding Moscow University (see p94) was signed on this day in 1755.

## FEBRUARY

**International Festival of the Orthodox Church**, throughout Feb. The music and cultural heritage of the Orthodox Church is celebrated in various city venues.
**Valentine's Day** (*Den svyatovo Valentina*), Feb 14. A recent addition to Moscow's calendar, although it is not as popular as it is in the West.
**Defenders of the Motherland Day** (*Den zashchitnikov rodiny*), Feb 23. Low-key male version of Women's Day. Elderly veterans, and men generally, receive presents.

**Street entertainer**

# MOSCOW AT A GLANCE

MORE THAN 100 places of interest are described in the *Area by Area* section of this book. These range from the historic treasures of State and Church, enclosed within the Kremlin walls, to galleries housing incomparable religious icons among spectacular collections of Russian and Western art. The city's liveliest streets and most beautiful parks, which offer different attractions in winter and summer, are also included. To help make the most of a visit, the next 12 pages offer a guide to the very best that Moscow has to offer. Museums and architecture each have their own section, and there is a special feature on Moscow's grandiose metro stations. The sights mentioned here are cross-referenced to their own full entries for ease of use. Below is a selection of the top sights that no visitor should miss.

## MOSCOW TOP TEN ATTRACTIONS

**Bolshoy Theater**
*See pp90–91.*

**St. Basil's Cathedral**
*See pp108–9.*

**Tretyakov Gallery**
*See pp118–21.*

**Red Square**
*See p106.*

### KREMLIN SIGHTS

**State Armory**
*See pp64–5.*

**Cathedral of the Assumption**
*See pp58–9.*

**Kolomenskoe**
*See pp138–9.*

**Lenin Mausoleum**
*See p107.*

**Pushkin Museum of Fine Arts**
*See pp78–81.*

**Kuskovo**
*See pp142–3.*

◁ **The Ivan the Great Bell Tower, with the huge Tsar Bell in front of it and the Assumption Belfry to the right**

# Moscow's Best: Metro Stations

Not many of the world's underground rail systems can claim to be tourist attractions and artistic monuments in their own right. The Moscow metro is an exception. Its station platforms and concourses resemble miniature palaces with chandeliers, sculptures, and lavish mosaics. Moreover, this is one of the busiest and most efficient metro networks in the world. Some of the finest stations are shown here and further information can be found on pp40–41. Practical details about using the metro are given on pp214–16.

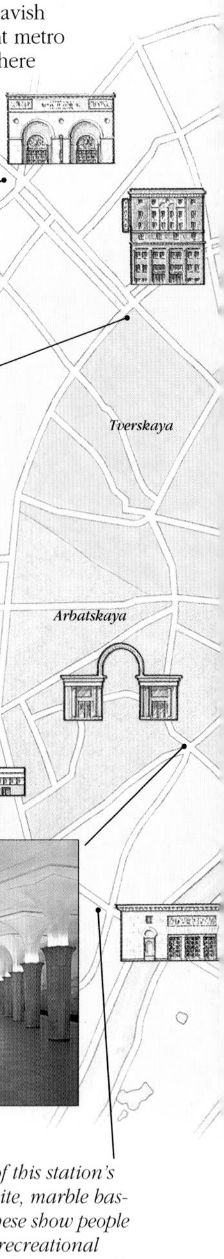

### Belorusskaya
*Named after the nearby Belorusskiy train station, Belorusskaya has a central hall with mosaics of rural scenes and a tiled floor based on a traditional pattern from a Belorussian rug.*

### Mayakovskaya
*A bust of poet Vladimir Mayakovsky stands in this station, which is named in his honor. Recesses in the ceiling contain a series of mosaics depicting planes and sports scenes.*

*Tverskaya*

*Arbatskaya*

### Kievskaya
*Large, ostentatious mosaics decorate the walls of this station. They include idealized scenes representing Russia's friendship with the Ukraine and pictures of Soviet agriculture.*

### Kropotkinskaya
*Clean lines and simple colors distinguish this elegant station, designed by Aleksey Dushkin in the 1930s. It is named after anarchist Prince Pyotr Kropotkin.*

### Park Kultury
*Niches in the walls of this station's central hall hold white, marble bas-relief medallions. These show people involved in various recreational activities such as ice skating, reading, playing chess, and dancing.*

**Teatralnaya**
*The differing cultures of the republics of the former Soviet Union provide the theme for this station. The ceiling panels depict some of their national costumes.*

**Komsomolskaya**
*This is the main entrance to Komsomolskaya station, named in honor of the Communist Youth League (Komsomol) that helped to construct the metro.*

Red Square and
Kitay Gorod

0 meters    600

0 yards     600

Kremlin

Zamoskvoreche

**Ploshchad Revolyutsii**
*The main hall of this station contains lifesize bronze statues of ordinary citizens, such as a farmer, who helped to build the Soviet State.*

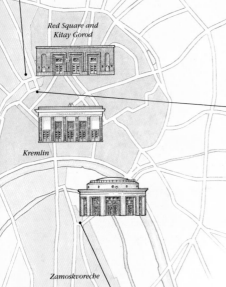

**Novokuznetskaya**
*A bas-relief frieze runs along the central hall of this station, which was constructed in 1943. The frieze shows a variety of Russian military heroes, such as World War II soldiers.*

# Exploring the Moscow Metro

**Bas-relief at Park Kultury**

W HEN THE IDEA of an underground railroad was first proposed for Moscow in 1902 the idea was rejected by one local newspaper as "a staggeringly impudent encroachment on everything Russian people hold dear in the city of Moscow." By the 1930s, however, the need for better transportation had become urgent as the population of the city more than doubled to meet the demands of rapid industrialization. Two prominent young Communists, Nikita Khrushchev and Lazar Kaganovich, were entrusted with building a metro that would serve as a showcase for socialism and the achievements of workers and peasants.

**Members of the Communist Youth League helping to build the metro**

## BUILDING THE METRO

C ONSTRUCTION WORK on the metro began in December 1931, during the period of Stalin's first Five Year Plan of 1928–33. The Communist Party decreed that "the whole country will build the metro," so workers – both men and women – were drafted in from all over the Soviet Union. They were assisted by soldiers of the Red Army and by over 13,000 members of the Communist Youth League (Komsomol).

The latter worked as volunteers in their free time, and their massive contribution was commemorated by naming **Komsomolskaya** after them. The materials, too, came from different parts of the country: rails from the steelworks of Kuznetsk, marble from the Urals and Caucasus, and granite from Karelia and the Ukraine.

Work was completed on the first 11.6-km (7.2-mile) section of track linking Sokolniki with **Park Kultury** in February 1935, and the first 13 stations were opened in May. Many of

those who had worked on the project were subsequently rewarded with medals, including the much-coveted Order of Lenin. Construction work continued rapidly, and by 1939 there were 22 stations serving over one million passengers.

## METRO DECORATION

S OME OF THE Soviet Union's finest artists were employed to decorate the metro. Working within the confines of Socialist Realism (see p135), many dealt with themes such as the Revolution, national defense, and the Soviet way of life.

The earliest metro stations are generally regarded as the most architecturally successful. **Mayakovskaya**, designed by Aleksey Dushkin in 1938, won the Grand Prix at the New York World's Fair. Its spacious halls are supported by columns of stainless steel and marble. **Kropotkinskaya** (1935) and **Ploshchad Revolyutsii** (1938) are also by Dushkin. The main hall of the latter has a series of

marble-lined arches. On either side of each stands a life-size bronze figure cast by sculptor Matvey Manizer. Red Guards, workers, sailors, sportsmen and women, a Young Pioneer, and a mother and child are among the "everyday heroes" who made the Revolution possible or helped to build the subsequent Soviet State.

Several stations, including **Komsomolskaya**, consist of two or more linked sections on different metro lines. One of Komsomolskaya's two sections, on the Kirovo-Frunzenskaya line, was built in 1935. Its decor is relatively restrained, with rose-colored marble pillars and majolica panels by Yevgeniy Lanseray showing heroic metro workers. The other station, on the circle line, was completed 17 years later and is much more ostentatious, with florid stucco moldings and glittering chandeliers. Designed by leading architect Aleksey Shchusev, it was also a prizewinner at the New York

**The simple, yet stylish, Mayakovskaya, designed by Aleksey Dushkin**

World's Fair. The gold mosaics showing military parades and figures from Russian history are the work of artist Pavel Korin.

Martial themes predominated during and after World War II. At **Novokuznetskaya** (1943), for example, architects Vladimir Gelfreikh and Igor Rozhin commissioned a bas-relief frieze from Nikolay Tomskiy showing Russian military heroes as diverse as Minin and Pozharskiy *(see p108)* and Field Marshal Kutuzov *(see p152)*.

The decor of the metro was intended to inspire people, and many of the stations built in the 1940s and 1950s extol the virtues of the Soviet regime. Ceramic panels at **Teatralnaya** (1940) celebrate the arts of the Soviet Republics, while mosaics at **Belorusskaya** (1952) and **Kievskaya** (1937 and 1954) show healthy, contented peasants celebrating agricultural abundance. These ignore the terrible famine resulting from Stalin's forced collectivization policy of the early 1930s.

In the Soviet mind, athletic prowess was the natural preparation for heroic achievement. Sports and recreation are the twin themes of the bas-reliefs by artist Sergey Rabinovich at **Park Kultury** (1935 and 1949).

Even the station exteriors above ground were designed to work as propaganda. Seen from above, the entrance to **Arbatskaya** (1935) is in the shape of the Soviet red star.

Although financial constraints now impose limits on artists and architects working on the metro, artistic leeway has still been possible in the design of some of the newer stations such as **Chekhovskaya**, built in 1987.

Part of Komsomolskaya, designed by architect Aleksey Shchusev

## THE METRO AND WAR

T HE EARLY METRO lines were laid deep underground so that they could be used as bomb shelters in times of war. By November 1941 German troops had reached the outskirts of Moscow and the Soviet Union was fighting for survival. **Mayakovskaya**, completed just three years earlier, became the headquarters of the Anti-Aircraft Defense Forces. It was in the station's spacious central hall that Stalin addressed generals and party activists the evening before the Red Army marched off to the front.

Kirovskaya (now known as **Chistye Prudy**) was the headquarters of the General Staff throughout World War II. It was here that Stalin and his advisors planned the first offensives against the Nazis. Consequently, the metro system became an important symbol of resistance to the Nazi invasion. In fact, its propaganda value was deemed so great that the designs for the mosaics at **Novokuznetskaya** were evacuated from St. Petersburg when their creator, Viktor Frolov, died there during the prolonged siege of 1941–4.

## METRO MUSEUM

T HE HISTORY and workings of the Moscow metro are fully explained in this interesting museum, located above the main hall of Sportivnaya in Sparrow Hills *(see p129)*. Some rather dated photomontages show the construction of the track and stations. There are displays of equipment, including signal points and ticket barriers, models of trains and escalators, a reconstruction of a driver's cabin, and the first ticket, sold in 1935.

🏛 **Moscow Metro Museum**
Sportivnaya metro. 📞 222 7309.
🕐 9am–4pm Tue–Fri, 11am–6pm Mon. 📷 (book in advance).

Revolutionary figures at Belorusskaya

The entrance to Arbatskaya, in the shape of the Soviet red star

# Moscow's Best: Architecture

V ISITORS TO MOSCOW ARE OFTEN pleasantly surprised by the wealth and variety of architecture the city has to offer. As well as magnificent palaces and cathedrals, such as those in the Kremlin, there are also smaller churches and chapels, homey boyars' residences, imposing Neo-Classical mansions, and some beautiful municipal buildings. A stark contrast to this older architecture is provided by early 20th-century Constructivist buildings and Communist landmarks such as Stalinist-Gothic skyscrapers. For further information about architecture see pp44–5.

**Moscow Old University**
*The colonnade of pillars along the front of this building and its ocher and white coloring are typical Neo-Classical features.*

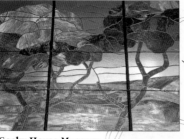

**Gorky House-Museum**
*Stunning stained-glass windows grace the Gorky House-Museum, a Style-Moderne masterpiece built by Fyodor Shekhtel in 1900.*

*Tverskaya*

*Krem*

*Arbatskaya*

**Cathedral of the Assumption**
*A miraculous fusion of Renaissance and Early-Russian styles, this superb cathedral was built in 1475–9 to a design by Italian architect Aristotele Fioravanti.*

**Foreign Ministry**
*This is one of seven skyscrapers designed in a hybrid style often referred to as Stalinist Gothic. The Foreign Ministry building was finished in 1952 shortly before Stalin's death.*

**Pashkov House**
*The colonnaded porch of the Neo-Classical Pashkov House has a low, wide pediment with relief sculptures.*

**Polytechnical Museum**
*The central part of the Polytechnical Museum, built in 1877, is the work of Ippolit Monighetti. It is an outstanding example of Russian Revival, a style that draws heavily on the architecture of Russia's past.*

**St. Basil's Cathedral**
*Pointed roofs over the entrance steps and tiers of arched gables typify the stunning architectural diversity of this Early-Russian cathedral, built in 1555–61 for Ivan the Terrible.*

Red Square and
Kitay Gorod

**Old English Court**
*Presented to an English trade delegation in 1556, this 16th-century whitewashed stone house has a wooden roof and few windows.*

0 meters    600

0 yards     600

Zamoskvoreche

**Church of the Resurrection in Kadashi**
*This Moscow-Baroque church has tiers of ornate limestone carvings in place of the kokoshniki gables normally seen on Early-Russian churches. The church's onion domes are a traditional feature, but they are an unusual jade green color.*

# Exploring Moscow Architecture

**Part of a floral fresco in St. Basil's Cathedral**

**R**USSIAN ARCHITECTURE has always been innovative. The medieval Novgorod, Yaroslavl, and Pskov schools of architecture developed several of the distinctive features found on Moscow's churches. These included the onion dome, rounded *zakomary* gables, and *kokoshniki* gables, which are semicircular or shaped like the cross-section of an onion. In later centuries Moscow's architects became increasingly influential, developing new styles, such as Constructivism, and giving a Russian flavor to others.

**The Baroque Gate Church of the Intercession at Novodevichiy**

**Study in the Palace of the Romanov Boyars**

In the 15th and 16th centuries the tsars employed a succession of Italian architects to construct prestigious buildings in the Kremlin. They combined the Early-Russian style with Italian Renaissance features to create magnificent buildings such as the **Cathedral of the Assumption** *(see pp58–9).*

Another 16th-century innovation was the spirelike tent roof, used, for example, on **St. Basil's Cathedral** *(see pp108–9).* In the mid-17th century Patriarch Nikon banned its use, insisting that plans for new churches must be based on ancient Byzantine designs.

The majority of Moscow's early secular buildings have not survived. The few exceptions include the ornate 16th-century **Palace of the Romanov Boyars** *(see pp102–3)* and the charming early 16th-century **Old English Court** *(see p102).*

## EARLY RUSSIAN

**M**OSCOW'S EARLIEST buildings were constructed entirely from wood. From around the 14th century, stone and brick began to be used for important buildings, but wood continued to be the main building material until the great fire of 1812 *(see p24),* when much of the city burned to the ground.

The majority of Moscow's oldest surviving buildings are churches. One of the earliest is the Cathedral of the Savior in the **Monastery of the Savior and Andronicus** *(see p140).*

## BAROQUE

**T**HE BRIDGE TOWER (1670s) at **Izmaylovo Park** *(see p141)* is an early example of Moscow Baroque. Its filigree limestone trimmings and pilaster decoration, set against a background of red brick, are typical of the style. The gate churches in the **Novodevichiy Convent** *(see pp130–31),* the buildings of the **Krutitskoe Mission** *(see p140),* and the spectacular **Church of the Resurrection in Kadashi** *(see p122),* with its limestone ornamentation carved to resemble lace, are also fine examples of this style of architecture.

A number of Baroque buildings, including the **Church of the Intercession in Fili** *(see p128),* were built with money from the wealthy and powerful Naryshkin family. This has led to Moscow Baroque also being known as Naryshkin Baroque.

## NEO-CLASSICAL

**T**HE ACCESSION of Catherine the Great in 1762 heralded a new direction for Russian architecture. She favored the Neo-Classical style, which drew on simple geometric shapes from the architecture of ancient Greece and Rome. This style has been used to great effect in the remarkable **Pashkov House** *(see p75),* thought to have been designed by Vasiliy Bazhenov in 1784.

Bazhenov's assistant, the prolific Matvey Kazakov, demonstrated the flexibility of Neo-Classicism in his designs for a wide range of buildings,

### THE NEW PATRIOTISM

The reconstruction of the city's pre-Revolutionary buildings, including the **Kazan Cathedral** *(see p105)* and the **Cathedral of Christ the Redeemer** *(see p74),* is evidence of a growing nostalgia for Russia's past, and a renewed interest in the nation's architectural heritage. The revival of the Orthodox Church, in particular, has led to the restoration of hundreds of churches across Moscow.

**The Cathedral of Christ the Redeemer, rebuilt in 1994–7**

including churches, hospitals, the **Moscow Old University** *(see p94)*, and the **House of Unions** *(see pp88–9)*. He is best known for the **Senate** *(see pp66–7)* in the Kremlin.

The huge fire that followed Napoleon's brief occupation of the city in 1812 led to a wholesale reconstruction. Moscow's nobility built new homes along **ulitsa Prechistenka** *(see p74)* in the newly fashionable Empire style. Leading architects of this more decorative style included Afanasiy Grigorev and Osip Bove, who designed **Theater Square** *(see p88)*.

The House of Friendship, a wonderful example of Eclecticism

A Neo-Classical bas-relief in the House of Unions, built in the 1780s

## HISTORICISM AND STYLE MODERNE

HISTORICISM replaced Neo-Classicism in the mid-19th century. It arose from a desire to create a national style by reviving architectural styles from the past. The **Great Kremlin Palace** *(see p63)* and **State Armory** *(see pp64–5)*, both designed by Konstantin Ton around 1840, are typical. They combine various styles including Renaissance, Classical, and Baroque. Ton also designed the extravagant Byzantine-style

The Style-Moderne Gorky House-Museum

**Cathedral of Christ the Redeemer** *(see p74)*, finished in 1883 and rebuilt in 1994–7.

Eclecticism combined past and present architectural styles to create fantastical buildings such as the **House of Friendship** *(see p95)*, which was designed by Vladimir Mazyrin in 1898.

Traditional wooden architecture and folk art were rich sources of inspiration for the architects who formulated the Russian-Revival style. The flamboyant **Historical Museum** *(see p106)* and **Polytechnical Museum** *(see p110)* are fine examples of the genre. However, the finest, and most functional, is **GUM** *(see p107)*, designed by Aleksandr Pomerantsev.

Style Moderne was a radical new

Mosaic of irises from the frieze around the Gorky House-Museum

architectural style akin to Art Nouveau. An early example is the **Hotel Metropol** *(see p88)*, designed in 1899 by Englishman William Walcot. The greatest advocate of Style Moderne was Fyodor Shekhtel. The mansion he built for Stepan Ryabushinskiy is now the **Gorky House-Museum** *(see p95)*. It is highly unconventional and uses mosaic friezes, glazed brick, and stained glass.

## ARCHITECTURE AFTER THE REVOLUTION

CONSTRUCTIVISM was a novel attempt to combine form and function and was the most popular style to emerge in the decade after the Revolution. The offices of the newspaper **Izvestiya**, on Pushkin Square *(see p97)*, were designed by Grigoriy Barkhin in 1927. His use of glass and reinforced concrete to create geometrical designs is typical of the Constructivist style. Another leading Constructivist was Konstantin Melnikov. The unique **Melnikov House** *(see p72)*, which consists of two interlocking cylinders, is the home he built for himself in 1927.

In the 1930s Stalin formulated a grand plan to rebuild large areas of the city. He favored a new monumental style, and Constructivism went out of vogue. The monumental style is exemplified by Aleksey Shchusev's grandiose "proletarian" apartments at the lower end of Tverskaya ulitsa and culminates in Stalinist Gothic. This term is used to describe the seven matching skyscrapers erected at key points in the city in the 1940s and 1950s. The **Foreign Ministry** building *(see p70)*, designed by architects Mikhail Minkus and Vladimir Gelfreikh, is typical of this style, which is often called "wedding-cake" architecture.

# Moscow's Best: Museums

Moscow has more than 80 museums
offering a fascinating insight into
the history and culture of the people
of Russia. Some, such as the Tretyakov
Gallery and State Armory, have collections including works by world-famous
artists and craftsmen, while others
house exhibits of local or special
interest. Among the most evocative are
those commemorating the lives of artists, writers, and musicians. The rooms
where they lived and worked have
been lovingly preserved. For further
information on museums see pp48–9.

### State Armory
*This elaborate 17th-
century enamel work
is exhibited in the
State Armory, along
with a dazzling array
of gold and silverware,
jewelry, and royal
regalia. The current
Armory building
was constructed in
1844 on the orders
of Tsar Nicholas I.*

### Shalyapin House-Museum
*Portraits of the opera star
Fyodor Shalyapin on dis-
play in his former home
include formal paint-
ings, images of him
on stage and draw-
ings by his children.*

Tverskaya

Arbatskaya

### Pushkin Museum
### of Fine Arts
*In addition to a magnificent
collection of European art,
this gallery houses artifacts
from ancient Egypt, Greece,
and Rome, including this
Egyptian funeral mask.*

0 meters    600

0 yards     600

### Tolstoy House-Museum
*For over 20 years this traditional
house was the winter home of Leo
Tolstoy, author of the epic novel* War
and Peace. *It is now an evocative
museum that recaptures the daily
lives of the writer and his family.*

**Lenin Mausoleum**
*The red and black pyramid of the Lenin Mausoleum was erected in 1930 to a design by architect Aleksey Shchusev. It contains the embalmed body of Vladimir Lenin, the first Soviet leader.*

**Mayakovsky Museum**
*This thought-provoking museum commemorates the revolutionary poet, playwright, and artist Vladimir Mayakovsky. The abstract exhibits in this room symbolize his childhood in Georgia.*

**Palace of the Romanov Boyars**
*The restored interiors and luxurious clothes and possessions in this house effectively evoke the daily lives of the Moscow aristocracy in the 16th and 17th centuries. The house was constructed for boyar Nikita Romanov.*

Red Square and Kitay Gorod

Kremlin

Zamoskvoreche

**Tretyakov Gallery**
*Valentin Serov's Girl with Peaches (1887) in the Tretyakov Gallery is part of the largest collection of Russian art in the world.*

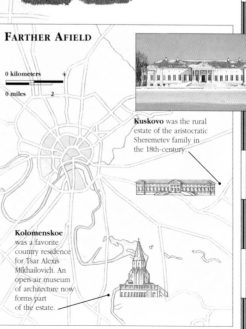

**FARTHER AFIELD**

0 kilometers 4

0 miles 2

**Kuskovo** was the rural estate of the aristocratic Sheremetev family in the 18th-century.

**Kolomenskoe** was a favorite country residence for Tsar Alexis Mikhailovich. An open-air museum of architecture now forms part of the estate.

# Exploring Moscow's Museums

**W**HEREVER VISITORS' INTERESTS LIE, whether in painting and the fine arts, science, the Revolution, the history of the Russian theater, or the lives of the nobility, there will be something in Moscow's museums to appeal to them. As well as the many museums in the city, there are a number of country estates in the area around Moscow. Several of these, including Kuskovo and Kolomenskoe, are easily accessible by metro and make good half-day or day excursions *(see p219)*. However, one should remember that a number of museums are currently undergoing much-needed renovation and, in some cases, ideological reassessment.

Nijinsky's ballet shoe, Bakhrushin Theater Museum

The elegant drawing room of the Lermontov House-Museum

*Young Acrobat on a Ball* by Picasso, in the Pushkin Museum of Fine Arts

## PAINTING AND DECORATIVE ARTS

**T**HE WORLD'S most important collection of Russian art is on display in the recently renovated **Tretyakov Gallery** *(see pp118–21)*. The gallery owns over 100,000 works, but only a fraction of them are on show at any one time. They include paintings by most of the group of artists called the Wanderers *(peredvizhniki)*. The gallery's collection of post-Revolution art is now housed in the **New Tretyakov Gallery** *(see p135)*. A further selection of the Tretyakov's 20th-century paintings may be moved there soon.

The **Tropinin Museum** *(see pp124–5)* has a fine collection of works by the 19th-century portrait artist Vasiliy Tropinin and his contemporaries.

The **Museum of Private Collections** *(see p75)* is a new gallery, housed in a 19th-century building. It exhibits previously unseen drawings, watercolors, sketches, and paintings, mainly by Russian artists of the 19th and 20th centuries.

Next door is the **Pushkin Museum of Fine Arts** *(see pp78–81)*, which is particularly known for its collection of works by Impressionist, Post-Impressionist, and 20th-century artists. Visitors can also see earlier paintings by artists such as Botticelli, Rembrandt, and Rubens, and archaeological artifacts such as the treasures excavated by Heinrich Schliemann at the site of the ancient city of Troy.

A superb collection of decorative and applied art spanning the last seven centuries or so is housed in the **State Armory** *(see pp64–5)* in the Kremlin. There are rooms devoted to arms and armor, jewelry, gold, and silverware, religious vestments, and imperial regalia.

A 16th-century Persian shield on display in the State Armory

## HOUSE-MUSEUMS

**T**HE HOUSES and apartments where many important Russian cultural figures lived have been preserved as museums. The timber-framed **Tolstoy House-Museum** *(see p134)* contains many personal possessions that belonged to Leo Tolstoy. The novelist and his family spent many winters here. Among their regular visitors was the playwright Anton Chekhov. The house where this writer began his career in the 1880s is also open to the public as the **Chekhov House-Museum** *(see p96)*. Across the road from Chekhov's house is the **Shalyapin House-Museum** *(see p83)*, where the great opera singer Fyodor Shalyapin lived. Visitors can enjoy the beautifully furnished rooms while listening to old recordings of his singing.

The **Stanislavsky House-Museum** *(see p93)* is the former home of Konstantin Stanislavsky, theatrical director and the cofounder of the Moscow Arts Theater *(see p92)*. It contains costumes, props, and other memorabilia.

Along with a few items once owned by Alexander Pushkin, the **Pushkin House-Museum** *(see p73)* contains an interesting display of pictures that show what Moscow was like in 1831, when the poet lived here. The **Bely House-Museum** *(see p73)*, in the building next door, was once the home of the Symbolist poet, Andrei Bely. Nearby is the **Skryabin House-Museum** *(see p72)*, the last home of composer Aleksandr Skryabin.

The high-rises of Novyy Arbat dwarf the **Lermontov House-Museum** *(see pp82–3)*, the simple timber house where Pushkin's contemporary, the poet Mikhail Lermontov, was brought up by his grandmother in the early 1830s.

The extraordinary life of Vladimir Mayakovsky is brilliantly realized in the displays in the **Mayakovsky Museum** *(see p111)*. This apartment, near the former KGB building *(see p112)*, is where the Futurist poet lived from 1919–30.

The artist Viktor Vasnetsov designed his own home. In his studio, now the **Vasnetsov House-Museum** *(see p144)*, visitors can see his enormous canvases based on folk tales.

The **Tchaikovsky House-Museum** *(see p153)* at Klin still contains furnishings used by composer Pyotr Tchaikovsky, including the desk where he finished his *Sixth Symphony*.

## COUNTRY ESTATES

SEVERAL PALACES and estates on the outskirts of Moscow are open to the public. **Ostankino Palace** *(see pp144–5)*, built in the 18th century for the fabulously wealthy Sheremetev family, is famous for its exquisite theater, where serf actors and musicians once took the stage. **Kuskovo** *(see pp142–3)* was also built for the Sheremetevs. In the palace's beautiful gardens is a ceramics museum.

A number of superb 16th- and 17th-century buildings still stand at the former royal estate of **Kolomenskoe** *(see pp138–9)*. Also on the estate is a fascinating museum of wooden architecture.

Picturesque, Gothic-style ruins are all that remain of the palace at **Tsaritsyno** *(see p137)*. This ambitious project, commissioned by Catherine the Great, was never finished.

Works of art by 19th- and 20th-century Russian artists are on display at the **Abramtsevo Estate-Museum** *(see p154)*, formerly an artists' colony.

Candy wrappers, boxes, and scales in the Museum of the Revolution

## HISTORY MUSEUMS

A NUMBER OF MUSEUMS and other sites in and around the city provide fascinating glimpses into Moscow's past.

The **History of Moscow Museum** *(see p111)* traces the city's history, with earliest exhibits including archaeological finds from around the Kremlin. There is speculation that the museum may be moved.

The life of the boyars *(see p20)* in Moscow in the early 17th century is recreated in the **Palace of the Romanov Boyars** *(see pp102–3)*.

Clay sledge in the History of Moscow Museum

Visitors interested in Napoleon's winter invasion of Russia in 1812 *(see pp23–4)* will want to make the day trip to **Borodino** *(see p152)*. This was the scene of one of the bloodiest encounters of the campaign. There are over 30 monuments around the battlefield, and a nearby museum tells the story of the battle. They may also like to visit the **Borodino Panorama Museum** *(see p129)* on Kutuzovskiy prospekt. This circular pavilion contains an enormous painting of the famous battle.

The monumental scale of the **Lenin Mausoleum** *(see p107)*, containing Lenin's embalmed body, gives an insight into the importance of the role played by Lenin *(see pp27–8)* in 20th-century Russian history.

Displays at the **Museum of the Revolution** *(see p97)* cover Russian history from 1900 until the collapse of the Soviet Union in 1991. Candy wrappers depicting Marx and Lenin and homemade grenades are among the exhibits.

The **Museum of the Great Patriotic War** *(see p129)* has dioramas of major battles from World War II, shown largely from a Soviet viewpoint.

## SPECIAL MUSEUMS

A MONG THE CITY's handful of special interest museums is the **Polytechnical Museum** *(see p110)*, which charts developments in science and technology in Russia.

The **Bakhrushin Theater Museum** *(see p125)* has a collection of theater memorabilia, including ballet shoes worn by Nijinsky, while the **Shchusev Museum of Architecture** *(see p82)* gives a history of Russian architecture.

A model of a reactor from a nuclear power station, one of the displays at the Polytechnical Museum

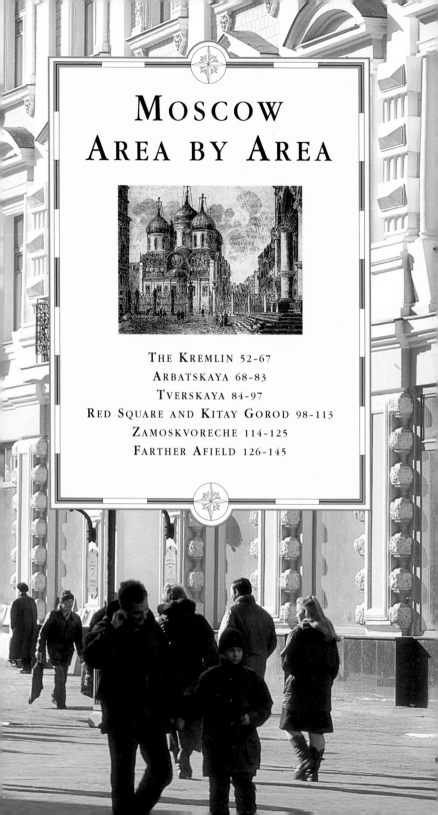

# MOSCOW
# AREA BY AREA

# THE KREMLIN

CITADEL OF THE TSARS, headquarters of the Soviet Union, and now the residence of the Russian president, for centuries the Kremlin has been a symbol of the power of the State. In 1156, Prince Yuriy Dolgorukiy chose the confluence of the Moskva and Neglinnaya Rivers as the site for the first wooden Kremlin (*kreml* means "fortress"). Late in the 15th century, Tsar Ivan III *(see p18)* invited several leading Italian architects to build a sumptuous new complex. They designed the Cathedral of the Assumption and the Faceted Palace, among other buildings, in a fascinating fusion of Early-Russian and imported Renaissance styles *(see pp44)*.

The Kremlin did not escape the architectural vandalism of the 1930s, when it was closed and several of its churches and palaces were destroyed on Stalin's orders *(see p75)*. Only in 1955, two years after his death, was the Kremlin partially reopened to the public.

**The Tsar's Cannon in the Kremlin**

## SIGHTS AT A GLANCE

### Churches and Cathedrals
Cathedral of the Annunciation ❼
Cathedral of the Archangel ❻
*Cathedral of the Assumption pp58–9* ❺
Church of the Deposition of the Robe ❾

### Historic Buildings and Monuments
Arsenal ❶❻
Faceted Palace ❽
Great Kremlin Palace ⓫
Ivan the Great Bell Tower ❹
Palace of Congresses ❷
Presidium ⓮
Savior's Tower ⓭
Senate ⓯
Terem Palace ❿
Trinity Tower ❶

### Museums
Patriarch's Palace ❸
*State Armory pp64–5* ⓬

### Gardens
Alexander Gardens ⓱

### GETTING THERE
Biblioteka imeni Lenina and Borovitskaya metro stations are just outside the walls of the Kremlin, within easy walking distance of the main sights. Trolleybus routes 2, 16, 33, and 37 and buses 6 and 25 are also useful.

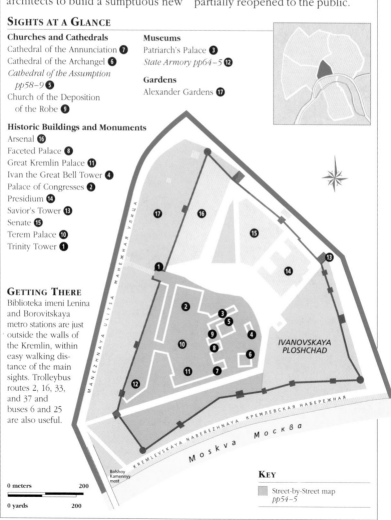

IVANOVSKAYA PLOSHCHAD

МАНЕЖНАЯ УЛИЦА

МАНЕЖНАЯ УЛИЦА

КРЕМЛЕВСКАЯ НАБЕРЕЖНАЯ

КРЕМЛЕВСКАЯ НАБЕРЕЖНАЯ

Moskva  Москва

Bolshoy Kamennyy most

0 meters        200
0 yards         200

### KEY
Street-by-Street map pp54–5

◁ **The Cathedral of the Annunciation, crowned by golden onion domes, on the Kremlin's main square**

# Street by Street: The Kremlin

THE KREMLIN IS HOME to the Russian president and the seat of his administration. As a result, less than half of it is accessible to the public, but highlights, including the State Armory, the Patriarch's Palace and the churches in Cathedral Square are open to visitors. Christians have worshiped on this site for more than eight centuries, but their early stone churches were demolished in the 1470s to make way for the present magnificent ensemble of cathedrals. In imperial times, these were the setting for great state occasions such as coronations, baptisms, and burials.

**Ticket office**

**Trinity Tower**
*Napoleon marched in triumph through this gate when he entered the Kremlin in 1812* (see pp23–5). *He left defeated a month later* ❶

**Palace of Congresses**
*Originally built in 1961 for Communist Party congresses, the palace is now used for a range of cultural events* ❷

**Terem Palace**
*A checkered roof and 11 golden cupolas topped by crosses are all that is visible of this hidden jewel of the Kremlin* ❿

**Great Kremlin Palace**
*The palace contains several vast ceremonial halls. The sumptuous stucco work of St. George's Hall provides a magnificent backdrop for state receptions. Its marble walls are inscribed with the names of military heroes* ⓫

0 meters          50

0 yards          50

**★ State Armory**
*The State Armory was designed by Konstantin Ton to complement the Great Kremlin Palace. Constructed in 1844–51, this building is now a museum. It houses the stunning imperial collections of decorative and applied art and the priceless State Diamond Fund* ⓬

**STAR SIGHTS**

★ State Armory

★ Cathedral of the Assumption

**KEY**

– – –  Suggested route

## Church of the Deposition of the Robe
*This graceful church was the domestic church of the metropolitans and patriarchs* ❾

**The Tsar Cannon**, cast in 1586, weighs a massive 40 tons.

**Church of the Twelve Apostles** *(see p56)*

**LOCATOR MAP**
*See Street Finder, maps 6 & 7*

## Ivan the Great Bell Tower
*When the third story was added to this beautiful octagonal bell tower in 1600, it became the tallest building in Russia* ❹

**Tsar Bell** *(see p57)*

## Patriarch's Palace
*This imposing palace, rebuilt for Patriarch Nikon in 1652–6, now houses the Museum of 17th-Century Life and Applied Art* ❸

## Cathedral of the Archangel
*The tomb of Tsarevich Dmitry, the younger son of Ivan the Terrible, is one of many elaborate tombs found in this cathedral. Dmitry died as a child in 1591 (see p19)* ❻

**Cathedral Square**

## Faceted Palace
*Two Italian architects, Marco Ruffo and Pietro Solario, constructed this striking Renaissance palace between 1485 and 1491* ❽

## Cathedral of the Annunciation
*Frescoes cover the walls and ceiling of this cathedral. In the dome above the iconostasis is a painting of Christ Pantocrator, above tiers of pictures of angels, prophets, and patriarchs* ❼

## ★ Cathedral of the Assumption
*This 12th-century painting of St. George the Warrior is one of the oldest surviving Russian icons. It forms part of the iconostasis in the cathedral's richly decorated interior* ❺

**Trinity Tower, with the modern Palace of Congresses on the right**

# Trinity Tower ❶
Троицкая башня
*Troitskaya bashnya*

The Kremlin. **Map** 7 A1.

THIS TOWER takes its name from the Trinity Monastery of St. Sergius *(see pp156–9)*, which once had a mission nearby. The tower's Trinity Gate used to be the entrance for patriarchs and the tsars' wives and daughters. Today it is one of only two that admit visitors. The other is in the Borovitskaya Tower *(see p66)* to the southwest.

At 76 m (249 ft) high, the seven-story Trinity Tower is the Kremlin's tallest. It was built in 1495–9 and in 1516 was linked by a bridge over the Neglinnaya River to the Kutafya Tower. The river now runs underground, and the Kutafya Tower is the sole survivor of the circle of towers that were originally built to defend the Kremlin walls.

In September 1812 Napoleon triumphantly marched his army into the Kremlin through the Trinity Gate – they left only a month later when the Russians set fire to the city *(see pp24–5)*.

# Palace of Congresses ❷
Дворец Съездов
*Dvorets Sezdov*

The Kremlin. **Map** 7 A1. ◯ for *performances only.*

COMMISSIONED BY Russian premier Nikita Khrushchev in 1959 to host Communist Party conferences, the Palace of Congresses is the Kremlin's only modern building. It was completed in 1961 by a team of architects led by Mikhail Posokhin. Roughly 120 m (395 ft) long and constructed largely from concrete and glass, the palace was sunk 15 m (49 ft) into the ground so that the surrounding buildings would not be dwarfed.

Until 1991 the 6,000-seat auditorium was the venue for political meetings. Now it is used by the Kremlin Ballet Company *(see p192)* and for staging operas and rock concerts.

# Patriarch's Palace ❸
Патриарший дворец
*Patriarshiy dvorets*

The Kremlin. **Map** 7 A1.
◯ 10am–5pm Fri–Wed.

THE METROPOLITANS of the Russian Orthodox Church lived on the site of the current Patriarch's Palace for many years. The patriarchate was created in the 16th century, and the patriarch took over from the metropolitans as the most senior figure in the Russian Church. As a result the metropolitans moved to Krutitskoe Mission *(see p140)* while the patriarch lived in the Kremlin.

When Nikon became the patriarch in 1652, he felt that the existing residence and the small Church of the Deposition of the Robe *(see pp62–3)* were not grand enough for him. He had the residence extended and renovated to create the Patriarch's Palace, with its integral Church of the Twelve Apostles. Completed in 1656, the work was carried out by a team of master builders led by Ivan Semenov and Aleksey Korolkov.

**Tsarevich Alexis's school book**

The palace is now the Museum of 17th-Century Life and Applied Art, which comprises more than 1,000 exhibits drawn from the State Armory collection *(see pp64–5)* and from churches and monasteries that were destroyed by Stalin in the 1930s *(see p75)*.

Entry to the museum is up a short flight of stairs. The first room houses an exhibition on the history of the palace. In the Gala Antechamber is a dazzling array of 17th-century patriarchs' robes. Some of Nikon's own vestments are on display, including a chasuble *(sakkos)*, a set of beautifully carved staffs, and a cowl made from damask and satin, and embroidered with thread of gold, gemstones, and pearls.

Two rooms in the museum have been refurbished in the style of a 17th-century boyar's apartment. In one of them is a display of old, handwritten

**Refurbished residence of a boyar in the Patriarch's Palace**

books, including Tsarevich Alexis's primer. Each page features one letter of the alphabet and a selection of objects beginning with that letter.

The impressive Chamber of the Cross, to the left of the stairs, has an area of 280 sq m (3,013 sq ft). When this ceremonial hall was built, it was the largest room in Russia without columns supporting its roof. Its ceiling is painted with a delicate tracery of flowers. The room was later used for producing consecrated oil called *miro* for all the churches in Russia, and the silver vats and ornate stove used still stand in the room.

Nikon's rejection of new architectural forms, such as tent roofs, dictated a traditional design for the Church of the Twelve Apostles. Located to the right of the stairs, it houses some brilliant icons, including works by master iconographers such as Semen Ushakov. The iconostasis dates from around 1700. It was brought to the church from the Kremlin Convent of the Ascension prior to its demolition in 1929.

Ivan the Great Bell Tower, with the Assumption Belfry and annex

## PATRIARCH NIKON

A zealous reformer of the Russian Orthodox Church, Patriarch Nikon was so intent on returning it to its Byzantine roots that he caused his adversaries, the Old Believers, to split from the rest of the Church. Nikon also advocated the supremacy of Church over State, angering Tsar Alexis (*see p19*). His autocratic style made him unpopular, and he retreated to a monastery outside the city. He was deposed in 1667.

# Ivan the Great Bell Tower ❹

Колокольня Ивана Великого
*Kolokolnya Ivana Velikovo*

The Kremlin. **Map** 7 A1.

THIS ELEGANT OCTAGONAL bell tower was built in 1505–8 to a design by Marco Bon Friazin. It takes its name from the Church of St. Ivan Climacus, which stood on the site in the 14th century. The bell tower is called "the Great" because of its height. In 1600 it became the tallest building in Moscow when Tsar Boris Godunov had a third story added to extend it to 81 m (266 ft).

The four-story Assumption Belfry, with its single gilded dome, was built beside the bell tower by Petrok Maliy in 1532–43. It holds 21 bells, the largest of which, the 64-ton Assumption Bell, traditionally tolled three times when the tsar died. A small museum on the first floor houses changing displays about the Kremlin.

The tent-roofed annex next to the belfry was commissioned by Patriarch Filaret in 1642.

Outside the bell tower is the enormous Tsar Bell. The largest in the world, it weighs over 200 tons. Tsar Alexis commissioned the original, which fell from the bell tower and shattered in a fire in 1701. The fragments were used in a second bell ordered by Tsarina Anna. This still lay in its casting pit when the Kremlin caught fire again in 1737. Cold water was poured over the hot bell and a large piece (displayed beside the bell) broke off.

**The Tsar Bell, the largest in the world, with the 11-ton section that broke off**

# Cathedral of the Assumption ➎

Успенский собор
*Uspenskiy sobor*

**F**ROM THE EARLY 14TH CENTURY, the Cathedral of the Assumption was the most important church in Moscow. It was here that princes were crowned and the metropolitans and patriarchs of the Orthodox Church were buried. In the 1470s Ivan the Great *(see p18)* decided to build a more imposing cathedral, to reflect the growing might of the nation during his reign. When the first version collapsed in an earthquake, Ivan summoned the Italian architect Aristotele Fioravantito to Moscow. He designed a light and spacious masterpiece in the spirit of the Renaissance.

**The golden domes** stand on towers inset with windows which allow light to flood into the interior of the cathedral.

**Scenes from the Life of Metropolitan Peter**
*Attributed to the great artist Dionysius* (see p61), *this 15th-century icon is located on the cathedral's south wall. It depicts different events in the life of this religious and political leader.*

**Orthodox cross**

**★ Frescoes**
*A team of artists headed by Sidor Pos-eeyev and Ivan and Boris Paisein painted these frescoes in 1642–4. The walls of the cathedral were first gilded to give the look of an illuminated manuscript.*

**Metropolitans' and patriarchs' tombs** line the walls of the nave and the crypt. Almost all of the leaders of the Russian Orthodox Church are buried in the cathedral.

**The Tsarina's Throne** (17th–19th centuries) is gilded and has a double-headed eagle crest.

**STAR FEATURES**

★ **Frescoes**

★ **Iconostasis**

**Western door and main entrance**

**The Tabernacle** contains holy relics including the remains of Patriarch Hermogen, who starved to death in 1612 during the Polish invasion *(see p19).*

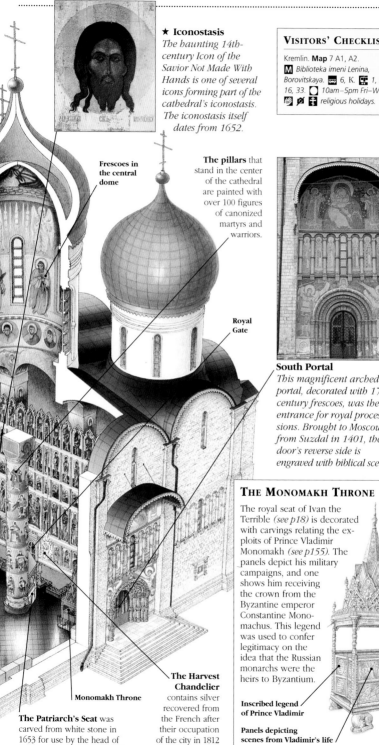

★ **Iconostasis**
*The haunting 14th-century Icon of the Savior Not Made With Hands is one of several icons forming part of the cathedral's iconostasis. The iconostasis itself dates from 1652.*

**Frescoes in the central dome**

**The pillars** that stand in the center of the cathedral are painted with over 100 figures of canonized martyrs and warriors.

**Royal Gate**

**South Portal**
*This magnificent arched portal, decorated with 17th-century frescoes, was the entrance for royal processions. Brought to Moscow from Suzdal in 1401, the door's reverse side is engraved with biblical scenes.*

**THE MONOMAKH THRONE**

The royal seat of Ivan the Terrible *(see p18)* is decorated with carvings relating the exploits of Prince Vladimir Monomakh *(see p155)*. The panels depict his military campaigns, and one shows him receiving the crown from the Byzantine emperor Constantine Monomachus. This legend was used to confer legitimacy on the idea that the Russian monarchs were the heirs to Byzantium.

**Inscribed legend of Prince Vladimir**

**Panels depicting scenes from Vladimir's life**

**The Harvest Chandelier** contains silver recovered from the French after their occupation of the city in 1812 *(see pp23–5).*

**Monomakh Throne**

**The Patriarch's Seat** was carved from white stone in 1653 for use by the head of the Russian Orthodox Church.

## Cathedral of the Archangel ❻

Архангельский собор
*Arkhangelskiy sobor*

The Kremlin. **Map** 7 A2. 📷 🚫

THIS WAS the last of the great cathedrals in the Kremlin to be built. It was commissioned by Ivan III in 1505, shortly before his death. Designed by a Venetian architect, Aleviz Novyy, it is a skillful combination of Early-Russian and Italian Renaissance architecture. The most striking of the Italian features is the scallop shell motif underneath the *zakomary* gables *(see p44)*.

This site was the burial place for Moscow's princes and tsars from 1340, first in an earlier cathedral and then in the current building. The tombs of the tsars, white stone sarcophagi with bronze covers inscribed in Old Slavonic, are in the nave. The tomb of Tsarevich Dmitry, the youngest son of Ivan the Terrible *(see p18)*, has a carved, painted canopy above it. The tsars were no longer buried here after the capital city was moved to St. Petersburg in 1712. Peter II, who died of smallpox in Moscow in 1730, was the only later ruler to be buried here.

The walls, pillars, and domes of the cathedral are covered with superb frescoes painted in 1652–66 by a team of artists led by Semen Ushakov, the head of the icon workshop in the State Armory *(see pp64–5)*. There are over 60 full-length idealized portraits of Russian rulers, as well as some striking images of the Archangel Michael, traditionally the protector of the rulers of early Moscow.

The fresco in the cathedral's central cupola depicts the threefold nature of God. The Father holds the Son on his lap and the Holy Spirit, in the form of a white dove, hovers between them.

The four-tiered iconostasis was constructed in 1680–81. However, the Icon of the Archangel Michael on the lowest tier dates from the 14th century.

## Cathedral of the Annunciation ❼

Благовещенский собор
*Blagoveshchenskiy sobor*

The Kremlin. **Map** 7 A2. 📷 🚫

UNLIKE THE OTHER Kremlin cathedrals, which were created by Italians, the ornate Cathedral of the Annunciation is a wholly Russian affair. Commissioned by Ivan III in 1484 as a royal chapel, it stands beside the Faceted Palace *(see p62)*, which is all that remains of a large palace built for Ivan III around the same time. The cathedral, built by architects from Pskov *(see p44)*, originally had three domes and open galleries on all sides but, after a

The glorious Cathedral of the Annunciation

fire in 1547, the corner chapels were added and the galleries were enclosed. On the south facade is the Groznenskiy Porch, added by Ivan the Terrible when he contravened church law by marrying for the fourth time in 1572. Barred from attending religious services, he could only watch through a grille in the porch.

The whole of the interior of the cathedral, including the galleries, is painted with frescoes. The artwork around the iconostasis was painted in 1508 by the monk Feodosius, the son of the icon painter Dionysius who worked on the Cathedral of the Assumption *(see pp58–9)*. The warm colors of the frescoes create an atmosphere of intimacy (this was the tsars' family church). At the same time the vertical thrust of the pillars draws the eye upward to the cupola and its awe-inspiring painting of Christ Pantocrator (Christ as ruler of the universe).

Three of the greatest masters of icon painting in Russia contributed to the iconostasis, widely considered the finest in Russia. Theophanes the Greek painted the images of Christ, the Virgin, and the Archangel Gabriel in the Deesis Tier, while the Icon of the Archangel Michael on this tier is attributed to Andrey Rublev. Several of the icons in the Festival Tier, including *The Annunciation* and *The Nativity*, were also painted by Rublev. Most of the other icons in this tier, including the *The Last Supper* and *The Crucifixion*, are the work of Prokhor Gorodetskiy.

The fresco in the central cupola of the Cathedral of the Archangel

# The Art of Icon Painting in Russia

THE RUSSIAN ORTHODOX church uses icons for both worship and teaching, and there are strict rules for creating each image. Icons were thought to be imbued with power from the saint they depicted and were invoked for protection during wars. Because content was more important than style, old revered icons were often repainted. The first icons were brought to Russia from Byzantium. Kiev was Russia's main icon painting center until the Mongols conquered it in 1240. Influential schools then sprang up in Novgorod and the Vladimir-Suzdal area. The Moscow school was born in the late 15th century when Ivan the Terrible decreed that artists must live in the Kremlin. Dionysius, Theophanes, the Greek and Andrey Rublev were all members of this renowned school.

**Festival Tier Icon**

*The Virgin of Vladimir, from 12th-century Byzantium, is highly venerated and has had a profound influence on Russian iconography.*

*Theophanes the Greek (c.1340–1405) is thought to have painted this icon of the Assumption (ascent into heaven) of the Virgin Mary. Originally from Byzantium, Theophanes became famous first in Novgorod and then in Moscow. The figures in his icons are famous for their delicate features and individual expressions.*

## ICONOSTASIS

Separating the sanctuary from the main part of the church, the iconostasis also symbolizes the boundary between the spiritual and temporal worlds. The icons are arranged in tiers (usually four, five, or six), each with its own subject matter and significance.

**The Festival Tier** depicts important feast days and holidays in the Russian Orthodox calendar.

**The top tier** of the iconostasis depicts patriarchs and prophets of the Old Testament.

**Christ Enthroned** is always shown at the center of the Deesis Tier, and is normally flanked by the Virgin Mary and John the Baptist.

**The Deesis Tier** is the most important in the iconostasis and depicts saints, apostles, and archangels.

**An additional tier** between the Local and Deesis Tiers often depicts the months of the year.

**The Royal Gate,** at the center of the Local Tier, is usually decorated with panels showing the four apostles and the Annunciation – when Mary learns she is to bear the Son of God. The gate represents the entrance from the temporal to the spiritual world.

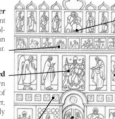

*Andrey Rublev became a monk at the Trinity Monastery of St. Sergius (see pp156–9). Later he moved to a monastery in Moscow. Rublev painted this icon of the Archangel Michael in about 1410. The benevolent appearance of the archangel is typical of Rublev's figures.*

**The Local Tier** contains icons of saints with a strong link to the church, such as the church's namesake or saints after whom patrons of the church were named.

The enormous vaulted main hall of the Faceted Palace, which was lavishly repainted in the 1880s

## Faceted Palace ❽

Грановитая палата
*Granovitaya palata*

The Kremlin. **Map** 7 A2. ● *to public.*

IN THE 19TH CENTURY, the Faceted Palace, along with the Terem Palace, was incorporated into the Great Kremlin Palace. Named after its distinctive stonework facade, the Faceted Palace is all that is left of a larger 15th-century royal palace. It was commissioned by Ivan III *(see p18)* in 1485 and finished six years later. The Faceted Palace is the work of two Italian architects, Marco Ruffo and Pietro Solario.

The first floor of the Faceted Palace consists of the main hall and adjoining Sacred Vestibule. Both are decorated with rich frescoes and gilded carvings. The splendid vaulted main hall has an area of about 500 sq m (5,380 sq ft). It was the throne room and banquet hall of the tsars and was used for state banquets until the days of perestroika *(see pp30–31)*.

On the palace's southern facade is the Red Staircase. The tsars passed down this staircase on their way to the Cathedral of the Assumption for their coronations. The last such procession was at the coronation of Nicholas II in 1896.

In the Streltsy Rebellion of 1682 *(see p22)* several of Peter the Great's relatives were hurled down the Red Staircase onto the pikes of the Streltsy guard.

Demolished by Stalin in the 1930s, the staircase was rebuilt in 1994 at great expense.

## Church of the Deposition of the Robe ❾

Церковь Ризположения
*Tserkov Rizpolozheniya*

The Kremlin. **Map** 7 A1. ▨ ∅

CROWNED BY a single golden dome, this beautiful, but simply designed, church was built as the domestic church of the metropolitans in 1484–6. It was designed by architects from Pskov *(see p44)*.

The church is named after a Byzantine feast day, which celebrates the arrival, in the city of Constantinople, of a robe supposed to have belonged to the Virgin Mary. The robe is believed to have saved the city from invasion several times.

The exterior of the church has distinctive *ogee* arches, which are shaped like the cross-section of an onion and feature on many Russian churches from this

The southern facade of the Faceted Palace, with the Red Staircase

period. They are a favorite device of the Pskov school of architecture. Inside the church, the walls and slender columns are covered with 17th-century frescoes by artists including Ivan Borisov, Sidor Pospeev, and Semen Abramov. Many depict scenes from the life of the Virgin. Others depict Christ, the prophets, royalty, and the Moscow metropolitans.

The impressive iconostasis was created by Nazariy Istomin in 1627. To the left of the royal gate is a splendid image of the Trinity, and to its right is the patronal Icon of the Deposition of the Virgin's Robe.

**The ornately decorated anteroom in the Terem Palace**

Beyond this are the throne room, the tsar's bedchamber, and a small prayer room.

Most of the splendid Terem Palace is not visible from the areas of the Kremlin to which the public do have access. The eleven richly decorated onion domes of the private chapel, at one end of the palace, are all that can be seen.

## Great Kremlin Palace ⓫

Большой Кремлёвский дворец

*Bolshoy Kremlevskiy dvorets*

The Kremlin. **Map** 7 A2. ● *to public.*

THE IMPRESSIVE 125 m (410 ft) facade of this yellow and white palace is best admired from the Kremlin embankment, outside the Kremlin walls. The Great Kremlin Palace was built to replace the 18th-century

Kremlin Palace that previously stood on the site but had become dilapidated. In 1837 Tsar Nicholas I commissioned the Great Kremlin Palace as the Moscow residence of the royal family, where they stayed when visiting from St. Petersburg, then the capital. Designed by a team of architects led by Konstantin Ton *(see p45)*, it took 12 years to build. Ton's design integrated the Terem and Faceted Palaces with the new palace, creating a single complex. He also rebuilt the State Armory *(see pp64–5)*.

On the palace's ground floor are the luxurious private rooms of the royal family. The state chambers, on the first floor, include several vast ceremonial halls. The imposing St. George's Hall has white walls engraved in gold with the names of those awarded the Order of St. George, one of Russia's highest military decorations.

Despite spending massive amounts on the interior, the tsar rarely used the palace. In the 1930s two of the halls were joined to form a huge meeting room for the Supreme Soviet. Now the palace's halls are used to receive foreign dignitaries.

**The small, single-domed Church of the Deposition of the Robe**

## Terem Palace ⓾

Теремной дворец

*Teremnoy dvorets*

The Kremlin. **Map** 7 A2. ● *to public.*

COMMISSIONED BY Tsar Mikhail Romanov *(see p19)*, the Terem Palace was built next to the Faceted Palace in 1635–7. It was constructed by a team of stonemasons led by Bazhen Ogurtsov. The palace takes its name from the *terem*, a pavilion-like structure with a red and white checkered roof on top of the main building. The interior has small, low-vaulted, simply furnished rooms.

The tsar had five sumptuous rooms situated on the third floor of the palace. The anteroom, where boyars *(see p20)* and foreign dignitaries waited to be received, leads into the council chamber, where the tsar held meetings with boyars.

**The Great Kremlin Palace viewed from the Kremlin embankment**

# State Armory ⓬
Оружейная палата
*Oruzheynaya palata*

THE COLLECTION OF THE STATE ARMORY represents the wealth accumulated by Russian princes and tsars over many centuries. The first written mention of a state armory occurs in 1508, but there were forges in the Kremlin making helmets, shields, and other accoutrements of war as early as the 13th century. Later, gold- and silversmiths, workshops producing icons and embroidery, and the Office of the Royal Stables all moved into the Kremlin. The original armory was demolished in 1960 to make way for the Palace of Congresses *(see p56)*. The current State Armory was constructed as a museum on the orders of Nicholas I. It was designed by Konstantin Ton *(see p45)* in 1844.

**★ Fabergé Eggs**
*This egg, also a music box, was made in 1904 in the St. Petersburg workshops of the famous House of Fabergé. The egg forms part of a stylized model of the Kremlin.*

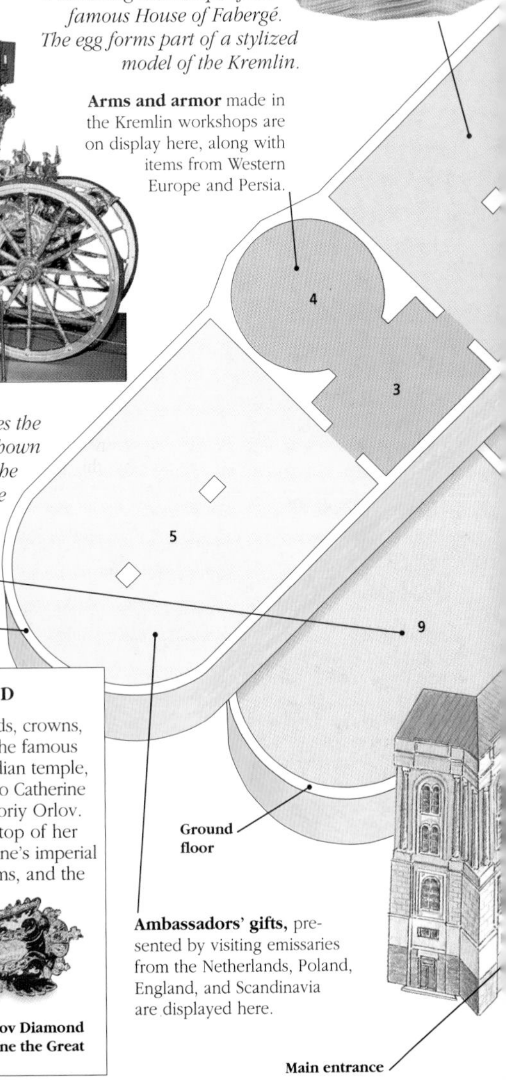

**Arms and armor** made in the Kremlin workshops are on display here, along with items from Western Europe and Persia.

4

3

**Carriages and Sleds**
*This magnificent collection includes the beautiful gilded summer carriage shown here. It was presented to Catherine the Great (see p23) by Count Orlov. The oldest carriage displayed was a gift from King James I of England to Boris Godunov.*

5

**First Floor**

9

## THE STATE DIAMOND FUND

This dazzling exhibition of diamonds, crowns, jewelry, and state regalia includes the famous Orlov Diamond. Taken from an Indian temple, it was one of many presents given to Catherine the Great by her lover Count Grigoriy Orlov. The tsarina had it mounted at the top of her scepter. Also on display are Catherine's imperial crown, inset with almost 5,000 gems, and the Shah Diamond, which was given to Tsar Nicholas I by Shah Mirza.

**The Orlov Diamond on the scepter of Catherine the Great**

**Ground floor**

**Ambassadors' gifts,** presented by visiting emissaries from the Netherlands, Poland, England, and Scandinavia are displayed here.

**Main entrance**

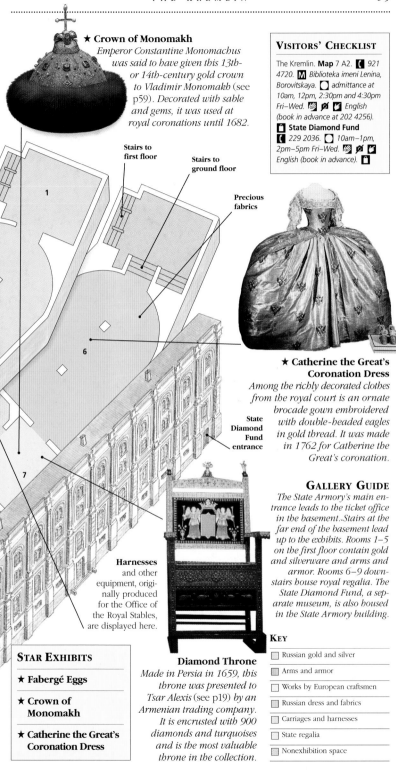

★ **Crown of Monomakh**
*Emperor Constantine Monomachus was said to have given this 13th- or 14th-century gold crown to Vladimir Monomakh (see p59). Decorated with sable and gems, it was used at royal coronations until 1682.*

## VISITORS' CHECKLIST

The Kremlin. **Map** 7 A2. 921 4720. Biblioteka imeni Lenina, Borovitskaya. admittance at 10am, 12pm, 2:30pm and 4:30pm Fri–Wed. English (book in advance at 202 4256).
**State Diamond Fund** 229 2036. 10am–1pm, 2pm–5pm Fri–Wed. English (book in advance).

Stairs to first floor

Stairs to ground floor

Precious fabrics

1

6

State Diamond Fund entrance

7

★ **Catherine the Great's Coronation Dress**
*Among the richly decorated clothes from the royal court is an ornate brocade gown embroidered with double-headed eagles in gold thread. It was made in 1762 for Catherine the Great's coronation.*

## GALLERY GUIDE
*The State Armory's main entrance leads to the ticket office in the basement. Stairs at the far end of the basement lead up to the exhibits. Rooms 1–5 on the first floor contain gold and silverware and arms and armor. Rooms 6–9 downstairs house royal regalia. The State Diamond Fund, a separate museum, is also housed in the State Armory building.*

**Harnesses** and other equipment, originally produced for the Office of the Royal Stables, are displayed here.

## KEY

| | |
|---|---|
| ☐ | Russian gold and silver |
| ☐ | Arms and armor |
| ☐ | Works by European craftsmen |
| ☐ | Russian dress and fabrics |
| ☐ | Carriages and harnesses |
| ☐ | State regalia |
| ☐ | Nonexhibition space |

## STAR EXHIBITS

- ★ **Fabergé Eggs**
- ★ **Crown of Monomakh**
- ★ **Catherine the Great's Coronation Dress**

**Diamond Throne**
*Made in Persia in 1659, this throne was presented to Tsar Alexis (see p19) by an Armenian trading company. It is encrusted with 900 diamonds and turquoises and is the most valuable throne in the collection.*

## Savior's Tower ⓭
Спасская башня
*Spasskaya bashnya*

The Kremlin. **Map** 7 B1.

R ISING MAJESTICALLY above Red Square to a height of 70 m (230 ft), Savior's Tower is named after an icon of Christ installed over its gate in 1648. The gate is no longer open to the public, but it used to be the Kremlin's main entrance.

**Savior's Tower, once the main entrance to the Kremlin**

Every person using Savior's Gate, even the tsar, had to indicate respect for the icon by taking his hat off. The icon was removed after the Revolution.

Savior's Tower was built in two stages. The lower part was designed by Italian architect Pietro Solario in 1491. Bazhen Ogurtsov and Englishman Christopher Holloway added the upper part and tent roof in 1625. Originally the chimes of the clock played the Tsarist National Anthem. In 1917 they were changed to play a revolutionary anthem. Now they play the Russian National Anthem.

## Presidium ⓮
Президиум
*Prezidium*

The Kremlin. **Map** 7 A1. ◓ *to public.*

T WO IMPORTANT religious institutions, the Monastery of the Miracles and the Convent of the Ascension, used to stand here. They were demolished in 1929 to make way for the Presidium. This Classical-style, yellow building was erected in 1932–4 as a training school for Red Army officers. It later

became the headquarters of the Presidium of the Supreme Soviet, an executive arm of the Soviet parliament. Today the Presidium houses several departments of the Russian presidential administration.

**The Classical-style Presidium**

## Senate ⓯
Сенат
*Senat*

The Kremlin. **Map** 7 A1. ◓ *to public.*

C OMPLETED IN 1790, this Neo-Classical building was constructed to house several of the Senate's departments. Designed by Matvey Kazakov (*see pp44–5*), who regarded it as his best work, it is triangular, with a central, domed rotunda, from which the Russian flag flies.

### KREMLIN TOWERS
There are 19 towers in the walls of the Kremlin, with a bridge leading from the Trinity Tower to a 20th, the Kutafya Tower. In 1935 the double-headed imperial eagles were removed from the five tallest towers and replaced two years later with stars made of red glass, each weighing between 1 and 1.5 tons.

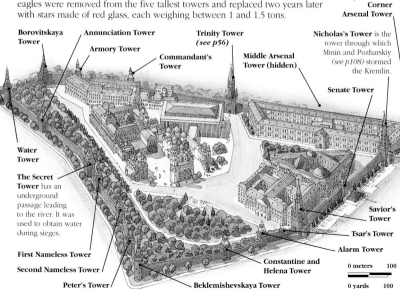

**Corner Arsenal Tower**

**Borovitskaya Tower**

**Annunciation Tower**

**Armory Tower**

**Trinity Tower** (*see p56*)

**Commandant's Tower**

**Middle Arsenal Tower (hidden)**

**Nicholas's Tower** is the tower through which Minin and Pozharskiy (*see p108*) stormed the Kremlin.

**Senate Tower**

**Water Tower**

**The Secret Tower** has an underground passage leading to the river. It was used to obtain water during sieges.

**Savior's Tower**

**Tsar's Tower**

**Alarm Tower**

**First Nameless Tower**

**Second Nameless Tower**

**Peter's Tower**

**Constantine and Helena Tower**

**Beklemishevskaya Tower**

0 meters 100

0 yards 100

**The domed rotunda of the yellow and white Senate, behind the Senate Tower and the Lenin Mausoleum**

From 1918 to 1991, the Senate housed the Soviet government. Lenin had his office here, and his family lived in a apartment on the top floor. During World War II the Red Army Supreme Command, headed by Stalin, was based in the building.

Today the Senate is the official seat of the president of the Russian Federation.

**Corner Arsenal Tower with the Arsenal and Nicholas's Tower**

## Arsenal ⓰

Арсенал

*Arsenal*

The Kremlin. **Map** 7 A1. ⬤ *to public.*

PETER THE GREAT ordered the Arsenal built in 1701, but various setbacks, including a fire in 1711, delayed its completion until 1736. In 1812 the building was partly blown up by Napoleon's army *(see pp23–5)*. Architects Aleksandr

Bakarev, Ivan Tamanskiy, Ivan Mironovskiy, and Evgraf Tyurin were commissioned to design a new Arsenal. Their attractive yellow and white Neo-Classical building was finished in 1828.

The Arsenal was constructed as a storehouse for weapons, ammunition, and other military supplies. Around 750 cannons, including some that were captured from Napoleon's retreating troops, are lined up outside. Now the command post of the Kremlin guard, the interior and much of the exterior of the Arsenal are strictly out of bounds to visitors.

## Alexander Gardens ⓱

Александровский сад

*Aleksandrovskiy sad*

The Kremlin. **Map** 7 A1.

DESIGNED BY architect Osip Bove *(see p45)* in 1821, these gardens are named after Tsar Alexander I, who presided over the restoration of the city, including the Kremlin, after the Napoleonic Wars. Before the gardens were built, the Neglinnaya River, part of the Kremlin moat, was channeled underground. The only visible reminder of its presence is the stone bridge linking the Kutafya and Trinity Towers.

In front of the Middle Arsenal Tower in the northern half of the gardens is an obelisk erected in 1913 to mark 300 years of the Romanov dynasty. The

imperial eagle was taken down after the Revolution and the inscription was replaced by the names of revolutionary thinkers such as Karl Marx and Friedrich Engels.

The Tomb of the Unknown Soldier, a short distance away, was unveiled in 1967. Its eternal flame was lit with a torch lit from the flame at the Field of Mars in St. Petersburg. It burns for all the Russians who died in World War II. The body of a soldier is buried beneath the monument, which bears an inscription, "Your name is unknown, your deeds immortal."

In 1996, an huge shopping complex was constructed beneath Manezhnaya ploshchad, the large square to the north of Alexander Gardens.

**Path through Alexander Gardens, with the Trinity Tower behind**

# ARBATSKAYA

THE NAME "ARBAT" is thought to derive from a Mongol word meaning suburb, and was first applied in the 15th century to the entire area west of the Kremlin, then inhabited by the tsar's artisans and equerries. Though still commemorated in street names, the artisans generally moved elsewhere in the late 18th century. The aristocracy moved in followed by Moscow's professionals,

**Fayoum portrait, Pushkin Museum**

the intellectual elite, and artists, attracted by the area's rambling backstreets, cottages, and overgrown courtyards. In the Old Arbat, with its pedestrian main street, there are historic churches, timber houses, and early 19th-century mansions around pereulok Sivtsev Vrazhek. Not far away are the kiosks, cafés, and huge Soviet-era apartments and shops of the New Arbat.

## SIGHTS AT A GLANCE

**Museums and Galleries**

Bely House-Museum **5**
Lermontov House-Museum **13**
Museum of Private Collections **8**
Pushkin House-Museum **4**
*Pushkin Museum of Fine Arts pp78–81* **9**
Shalyapin House-Museum **14**
Shchusev Museum of Architecture **11**
Skryabin House-Museum **1**

**Cathedrals**

Cathedral of Christ the Redeemer **7**

**Historic Buildings**

Melnikov House **3**
Pashkov House **10**

**Streets and Squares**

Arbat Square **12**
Spasopeskovskiy Pereulok **2**
Ulitsa Prechistenka **6**

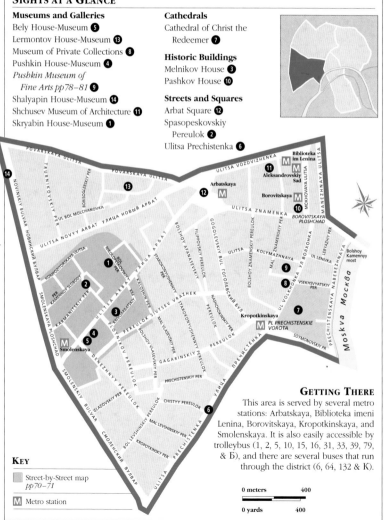

## GETTING THERE

This area is served by several metro stations: Arbatskaya, Biblioteka imeni Lenina, Borovitskaya, Kropotkinskaya, and Smolenskaya. It is also easily accessible by trolleybus (1, 2, 5, 10, 15, 16, 31, 33, 39, 79, & Б), and there are several buses that run through the district (6, 64, 132 & K).

**KEY**

Street-by-Street map pp70–71

M Metro station

0 meters        400
0 yards         400

◁ **Busy ulitsa Arbat, the heart of the Old Arbat, overlooked by the monumental Stalinist Foreign Affairs Ministry**

# Street-by-Street: Old Arbat

AT THE HEART OF THE OLD ARBAT is the pedestrian ulitsa Arbat.
It is lined with antique shops, boutiques, souvenir stalls,
sidewalk cafés, and a variety of restaurants, from pizzerias and
burger joints to lively examples of the traditional Russian pub
(*traktir*). In the 19th century, the Old Arbat was the haunt of artists,
musicians, poets, writers, and intellectuals. Some of their homes
have been preserved and opened as museums, and are among the
district's many houses of that era that have been lovingly restored
and painted in pastel shades. Today, sidewalk artists
and musicians and street poets give it a renewed
bohemian atmosphere.

**Spaso House**
is a grand Neo-
Classical mansion.
It has been the
residence of the
US ambassador
since 1933.

**This small garden**
contains a statue of the
poet Alexander Pushkin.

Novyy
Arbat ↑

★ **Pushkin House-Museum**
*The poet Alexander Pushkin for a while
lived here just after his marriage. The
interior of the house has been completely restored to look as it did then* ❹

**Ulitsa Arbat**
During the Soviet era ulitsa Arbat retained
a discreet bohemian character and was a
magnet for dissenting musicians, artists,
and students. It was pedestrianized in
1985, and its shops, restaurants, and cafés
are now popular with Muscovites
and visitors to the city alike.

Smolenskaya

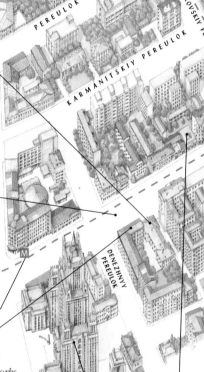

**Bely House-
Museum**
*Andrei Bely, best
known for two works,
a novel,* Petersburg,
*and his memoirs, lived
in this apartment for
his first 26 years. It is
now a museum, and the exhibits on
display include this photo of Bely
with his wife and the fascinating
illustration,* Line of Life *(see p73)* ❺

**Georgian
Center**

**The Foreign Ministry**
is one of Moscow's
seven Stalinist-Gothic
skyscrapers *(see p45)*.

**Spasopeskovskiy Pereulok**
*On one side of this peaceful lane is the 18th-century Church of the Savior on the Sands, with its white bell tower. It overlooks a secluded square and garden, a reminder that the Arbat was at that time a genteel suburb* **2**

**LOCATOR MAP**
*See Street Finder, map 6*

TVERSKAYA

ARBATSKAYA

**The Vakhtangova Theater** was established here in 1921 by Yevgeniy Vakhtangov, one of Moscow's leading theater directors. The current theater building dates from 1947.

BOLSHOY NIKOLOPESKOVSKIY PEREULOK

**Arbat Square**

ULITSA ARBAT

KALOSHIN PEREULOK

**★ Skryabin House-Museum**
*This comfortable apartment has been preserved as it was in 1913–15 when experimental composer Aleksandr Skryabin lived here. The furniture in the rooms is Style Moderne and the lighting is dim, since Skryabin disliked direct light* **1**

**Pushkin Museum of Fine Arts**

**The Herzen House-Museum** was the home of the radical writer Aleksandr Herzen for three years from 1843.

| 0 meters | 100 |
| 0 yards | 100 |

**STAR SIGHTS**

★ **Pushkin House-Museum**

★ **Skryabin House-Museum**

**These pre-Revolution apartments**, designed for wealthy Muscovites, are decorated with fanciful turrets and sculptures of knights.

**Melnikov House**
*This unusual cylindrical house is now dwarfed by the apartments on ulitsa Arbat. It was built in the 1920s by Constructivist architect Konstantin Melnikov, who lived here until his death in 1974* **3**

**KEY**

– – – Suggested route

## Skryabin House-Museum ❶

Дом-музей АН Скрябина

*Dom-muzey AN Skryabina*

Bolshoy Nikolopeskovskiy pereulok 11.
**Map** 6 D1. **C** *241 1901.* **M** *Smolenskaya, Arbatskaya.* ◯ *Noon–6pm Wed, Fri, 10am–4:30pm Thu, Sat–Sun.* 🎟️ 🎫 *English (book in advance).*

T HE APARTMENT WHERE the pianist and composer Aleksandr Skryabin (1872–1915) died, at the age of 43, has been preserved as it was when he lived there. Skryabin studied at the Moscow Conservatory *(see p94),* where he established an international reputation as a concert pianist. He was also a highly original composer and musical theorist, best known for orchestral works such as *Prometheus* and *A Poem of Ecstasy.* Skryabin's music influenced Igor Stravinsky (1882–1971), and Sergei Rachmaninov (1873–1943) was a regular visitor to his apartment.

Although Skryabin spent much of his time abroad giving concerts, he was an aesthete and paid great attention to furnishing and decorating his fashionable apartment. The rooms house his pianos, autographed manuscripts, and Style-Moderne furniture. However, the most original item on show is a device for pro-

**A room in Aleksandr Skryabin's apartment, with one of his pianos**

**The Classical-style Spaso House on Spasopeskovskaya ploshchad**

jecting flickering light, which Skryabin used to "illuminate" his music. Regular concerts are held in the rooms on the ground floor.

## Spasopeskovskiy Pereulok ❷

Спасопесковский переулок

*Spasopeskovskiy pereulok*

**Map** 6 D1. **M** *Smolenskaya.*

T HE CHARMS of the Old Arbat have been preserved in this secluded lane and the peaceful adjoining square, Spasopeskovskaya ploshchad. In 1878, Vasiliy Polenov painted *A Moscow Courtyard,* depicting Spasopeskovskaya ploshchad as a bucolic haven in the midst of the city. Today the square still provides a respite from the hustle and bustle prevailing elsewhere.

At the center of Polenov's picture, now in the Tretyakov Gallery *(see pp118–21),* is the white bell tower of the Church of the Savior on the Sands (Tserkov Spas na Peskakh) from which the lane gets its name. This 18th-century church still dominates the square. In front of it is a small garden dedicated to the poet Alexander Pushkin.

The handsome Classical-style mansion standing on the far side of the square was built in 1913 as a private residence. Known as Spaso House, it has been the home of the US ambassador since 1933.

## Melnikov House ❸

Дом Мельникова

*Dom Melnikova*

Krivoarbatskiy pereulok 10.
**Map** 6 D1. **M** *Smolenskaya.*
◯ *to public.*

T HIS UNIQUE HOUSE, almost hidden by office building, was designed by Konstantin Melnikov (1890–1974), one of Russia's greatest Constructivist architects *(see p45),* in 1927.

Made from brick overlaid with white stucco, the house consists of two interlocking cylinders. These are studded

**Viktor Melnikov's studio in the Melnikov House**

with rows of hexagonal windows, creating a curious honeycomb effect. A spiral staircase rises through the space where the cylinders overlap, linking the light, airy living spaces. Melnikov's house was built for his family, but it was also to have been a prototype for future housing developments. However, his career was blighted when Stalin encouraged architects to adopt a new monumental style *(see p45).* Although he had won the Gold Medal at the Paris World's Fair in 1925, Melnikov's work was ridiculed or ignored. However, he did remain in his house for the rest of his life, one of the very few residents of central Moscow allowed to live in a privately built dwelling.

Melnikov's son, artist Viktor Melnikov, now has a studio on the top floor of the house.

## ALEXANDER PUSHKIN

Born in 1799 into Russia's aristocracy, Pushkin is Russia's most famous poet. He had established a reputation as both a poet and a rebel by the time he was 20. In 1820, he was sent into exile because the Tsarist government did not approve of his liberal verse, but he later returned to Russia.

Pushkin's early work consisted of narrative poems such as *The Robber Brothers* (1821), and his most famous work is *Eugene Onegin* (1823–30), a novel in verse. From 1830 on he wrote mostly prose. He developed a unique style in pieces such as *The Queen of Spades* (1834) and is credited with giving Russian literature its own identity.

# Pushkin House-Museum ❹

Музей-квартира АС Пушкина
*Muzey-kvartira AS Pushkina*

Ulitsa Arbat 55. **Map** 6 D2.
🇨 241 4212. Ⓜ *Smolenskaya.*
🕐 11am–6pm Wed–Sun. 📷 🚫
📖 *English (book in advance).*

ALEXANDER PUSHKIN rented this elegant, blue and white Empire-style flat for the first three months of his marriage to society beauty Natalya Goncharova. They were married in the Church of the Great Ascension on Bolshaya Nikitskaya ulitsa *(see p93)* in February 1831, when she was 18 years old. Pushkin wrote to his friend Pyotr Pletnev: "I am married – and happy. My only wish is that nothing in my life should change; I couldn't possibly expect anything better."

However, by May 1831 Pushkin had tired of life in Moscow, and the couple moved to St. Petersburg, where sadly a tragic fate awaited him. Gossip began to circulate there that Pushkin's brother-in-law, a French officer called d'Anthès, was making advances to Natalya. Upon receiving letters informing him that he was now the "Grand Master to the Order of Cuckolds,"

Pushkin challenged d'Anthès to a duel. Mortally wounded in the contest, Pushkin died two days later.

The exhibition located in the museum's ground-floor rooms gives an idea of what the city was like in the period when Pushkin was growing up, before the great fire of 1812. Among the prints, lithographs, and watercolors are some unusual wax figures of a serf orchestra that belonged to the Goncharova family.

A portrait of Pushkin's wife, Natalya Goncharova

Pushkin and Natalya lived on the first floor. There are few personal possessions here, although the poet's writing desk and some family portraits are displayed. The atmosphere resembles a

shrine more than a museum. Pushkin holds a special place in Russians' hearts and they treat his work, and memory with reverence.

# Bely House-Museum ❺

Музей-квартира Андрея Белого
*Muzey-kvartira Andreya Belovo*

Ulitsa Arbat 55. **Map** 6 D2.
🇨 241 7702. Ⓜ *Smolenskaya.*
🕐 11am–6pm Wed–Sun. 📷 🚫 📖

IN THE ADJOINING building to the Pushkin House-Museum is the childhood home of the symbolist writer Andrei Bely. Bely was born Boris Bugaev in 1880, but later adopted the name by which he is known as a writer. He grew up here before becoming a student at Moscow University *(see p94)*, where he began to write verse. He is best known, however, for *Petersburg*, a novel completed in 1916, and for his memoirs.

Only two rooms of the Bugaev family apartment have been preserved. A photographic exhibition on the writer's life and work is housed in one room. The most interesting item in the museum is the *Line of Life*, an illustration by Bely to show how his mood swings combined with cultural influences to direct his work.

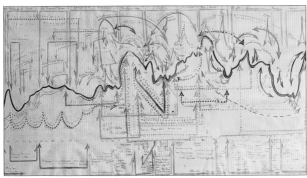
The *Line of Life* illustration drawn by the symbolist writer Andrei Bely

Stone eagles among the ornate decoration on No. 20 ulitsa Prechistenka

## Ulitsa Prechistenka **6**

Улица Пречистенка
*Ulitsa Prechistenka*

**Map** 6 D3–E2. **M** *Kropotkinskaya.*

Moscow's ARISTOCRACY first settled on this street in the late 18th century, and their elegant mansions still line it today. In Soviet times it was known as Kropotkinskaya ulitsa, after Prince Pyotr Kropotkin, a famous anarchist *(see p23)*.

The Empire-style house at No. 12 ulitsa Prechistenka is now the Pushkin Literary Museum (not to be confused with the Pushkin House-Museum, *see p73).* The house was originally designed for the Krushchev family by Afanasiy Grigorev *(see p45),* one of the leading exponents of this style in Moscow. The building has a wooden frame, skillfully hidden by Classical columns and ornate stucco decoration.

**Lion at No. 16 ulitsa Prechistenka**

Across the street another great writer is honored at No. 11 in the Tolstoy Literary Museum. In contrast to the Tolstoy House-Museum *(see p134),* it concentrates on the man's work rather than his life. The building has no connection with Tolstoy; it was built in 1822, also to a design by Afanasiy Grigorev, for the noble Lopukhin family. On display are letters, manuscripts, and family portraits.

At No. 20 is an elegant two-story mansion decorated with eagles, urns, heraldic symbols, and scallop shells. Until 1861 it was home to General Aleksey Yermolov, a commander-in-chief in the Russian army. After the Revolution, the American dancer Isadora Duncan and the poet Sergey Yesenin lived here during their brief, tempestuous marriage. The two spoke no common language, and Yesenin stated his feelings by writing the Russian for "I love you" in lipstick on the bedroom mirror.

The most distinguished house on ulitsa Prechistenka is at No. 19. Rebuilt after the 1812 fire *(see p24)* for the Dolgorukov family, it has an ocher and white facade with a central, columned portico framed by loggias. Adjoining it, at No. 21, is another early 19th-century mansion, now the Academy of Arts, where exhibitions are sometimes held.

## Cathedral of Christ the Redeemer **7**

Храм Христа Спасителя
*Khram Khrista Spasitelya*

Ulitsa Volkhonka 15. **Map** 6 F2.
**M** *Kropotkinskaya.*

REBUILDING this cathedral, blown up on Stalin's orders in 1931, was the most ambitious of the construction projects undertaken by the enterprising mayor of Moscow, Yuriy Luzhkov. The basic structure of the new cathedral was built between 1994–97,

although work is still being carried out on the interior. For much of the intervening time, the site was occupied by an outdoor swimming pool, but this was eventually filled in.

The project brought controversy from the start, both on grounds of taste and cost. In 1995 a presidential decree declared that not a kopek of public money should be spent on it – funds were to be raised through donations from the public, the Russian Church, and foreign donors among the big multinational companies operating in Russia. However, in practice, the better part of the total bill of over $200 million came from the state budget, which raised objections at a time when Muscovites were suffering extreme poverty.

The original cathedral was built to commemorate the miraculous deliverance of Moscow from Napoleon's Grande Armée *(see pp23–4).* Begun in 1839, but not completed until 1883, it was designed by Konstantin Ton *(see p45).* The cathedral was the tallest building in Moscow at that time, the gilded dome rising to a height of 103 m (338 ft) and dominating the skyline for miles around. With a floor area of 9,000 sq m (97,000 sq ft), it could accommodate more than 10,000 worshipers.

In 1998, a small museum and a church on the ground floor opened to the public. There will be spectacular views of the city when elevators to the dome go into service.

**Cathedral of Christ the Redeemer, rebuilt in the 1990s at huge cost**

## STALIN'S PLAN FOR A PALACE OF SOVIETS

The original Cathedral of Christ the Redeemer was to have been replaced by a Palace of Soviets – a soaring tower, 315 m (1,034 ft) high, topped by a 100-m (328-ft) statue of Lenin. It was designed as the highlight of Stalin's reconstruction of Moscow, much of the rest of which was realized: broad boulevards, skyscrapers, and the metro system *(see pp38–41)* are now familiar features of the city. The result was also, however, the destruction of many supposedly unnecessary buildings, especially churches and monasteries, even inside the Kremlin. The plan for the Palace of Soviets eventually abandoned and the cathedral was rebuilt in the 1990s.

**Artist's impression of Stalin's proposed awe-inspiring Palace of Soviets**

**The Museum of Private Collections, housed in a former hotel**

## Museum of Private Collections ❽

Музей личных коллекции
*Muzey lichnykh kollektsiy*

Ulitsa Volkhonka 14. **Map** 6 F2.
📞 *203 1546.* 🕐 *10am–5pm Wed–Sun.* Ⓜ *Kropotkinskaya.* 📷 🚫

**B**EFORE THE REVOLUTION the Knyazhiy Dvor hotel, whose guests included Maxim Gorky and artist Ilya Repin, occupied this building.

The museum opened in 1994 and is based on private collections. The largest is that of Ilya Zilberstein, which includes a vast range of work by prominent Russian artists such as Ivan Shishkin, Ilya Repin, and Konstantin Somov. There are also works by Aleksandr Rodchenko, and rooms devoted to periodic special exhibitions.

## Pushkin Museum of Fine Arts ❾

See pp78–81.

## Pashkov House ❿

Дом Пашкова
*Dom Pashkova*

Ulitsa Znamenka 6. **Map** 6 F1.
⬤ *to public.* Ⓜ *Borovitskaya, Biblioteka imeni Lenina.*

**T**HIS MAGNIFICENT mansion was once the finest private house in Moscow and enjoys a wonderful hilltop location overlooking the Kremlin. It was built in the Neo-Classical style in 1784–8 for the fabulously wealthy Captain Pyotr Pashkov. Pashkov encouraged his architect, who is thought probably to have been Vasiliy Bazhenov *(see p44),* to surpass himself – and every other residence in Moscow – with the grandeur of the design. The mansion's height was achieved by placing it on an enormous stone base, and the building is surmounted by a beautifully proportioned rotunda. Surprisingly, the most impressive facade is at the rear of the building, which originally led to a riverside garden. The original main entrance is through an ornate stone gateway located on Starovagankovskiy pereulok.

In 1839, a relative of Captain Pashkov sold the house to the Moscow Institute for Nobles, which occupied the premises until 1861. It was then taken over by the Rumyantsev Museum, which moved to the capital from St. Petersburg at that time. The museum brought with it an art collection and a library of more than one million volumes.

After the Revolution, the library was nationalized and renamed the Lenin Library. A new, and infinitely less attractive, extension for the rapidly expanding book collection was begun next door in 1928 and completed during the 1950s. Now known as the Russian State Library, it contains some 40 million items including books, periodicals, manuscripts, recordings, microfilms, and pictures.

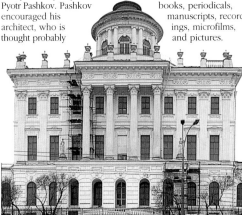

**The imposing Pashkov House overlooking the Kremlin**

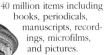

# Pushkin Museum of Fine Arts ❾
Музей изобразительных искусств имени АС Пушкина
*Muzey izobrazitelnykh iskusstv imeni AS Pushkina*

FOUNDED IN 1898, the Pushkin Museum houses an excellent collection of French Impressionist and Post-Impressionist paintings. It also has an enviable collection of old masters. Following the collapse of the Soviet Union *(see pp30–31)*, the curators admitted that they had countless works of art hidden away for ideological reasons. Some of these are now on show, including paintings by Russian-born artists Vasily Kandinsky and Marc Chagall. The museum building was designed by Roman Klein. It was originally built to house plaster casts of classical sculptures for Moscow University art students to use for research.

**Room 23** houses mostly 19th-century French paintings.

★ **Nude** *(1876)*
*The natural beauty of the female body is captured in this picture by Impressionist painter Pierre Auguste Renoir. The gallery owns a number of other paintings by Renoir including* Bathing in the Seine.

**Stairs to ground floor**

**First floor**

**Room 5** houses Italian, German, and Dutch paintings from the 15th and 16th centuries.

## GALLERY GUIDE
*The ticket office is in the entrance hall. The displays are spread over two floors, but although the museum halls are numbered, the layout is not strictly chronological. Paintings from the 17th and 18th centuries are on the ground floor, while works from the 19th and 20th centuries are upstairs. Collections of art that date from before the 17th century can be found on both floors. The cloakroom and toilets are in the basement.*

★ **Annunciation**
*Painted around 1490 by Italian artist Sandro Botticelli, this work was originally part of a large altarpiece. It shows the angel Gabriel telling the Virgin Mary she is to bear the Son of God.*

## STAR EXHIBITS

★ **Annunciation by Botticelli**

★ **Nude by Renoir**

★ **Montagne Ste-Victoire by Cézanne**

**Altar Triptych**
*The panels of this altarpiece were painted by Pietro di Giovanni Lianori in the 14th century. Above the central image of the Virgin and Child is a picture of the crucifixion. Figures of the saints are painted on the triptych's wings.*

★ **Montagne Ste-Victoire** *(1905)*
*This work by Paul Cézanne is one of the many views he painted of this mountain, east of Aix-en-Provence, after he settled in the region in 1886.*

**VISITORS' CHECKLIST**

Ulitsa Volkhonka 12. **Map** 6 F2.
[📞] 203 9578. [M] Kropotkinskaya.
[🚌] 1, 2, 16, 33. [🕐] 10am–7pm
Tue–Sun. [💰] English (book
in advance). [📷] [🎧] English.

**Room 17** houses a collection of early works by Picasso.

**Goldfish (1911–12)**
*Henri Matisse painted this remarkable still life of goldfish, with its bright, clear colors, in his workshop at Issy-les-Moulineaux, near Paris. His friend, the Russian collector Sergey Shchukin, purchased it on sight the following year.*

**The Treasure of Troy** is an exhibition of artifacts excavated from the ancient city by Heinrich Schliemann. It includes many valuable items such as beautiful golden goblets and jewelry.

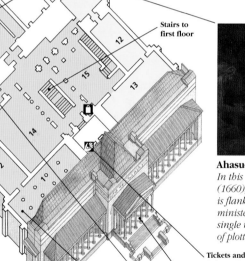

**Stairs to first floor**

**Ground floor**

**Tickets and information**

**Entrance**

**Ahasuerus, Haman, and Esther**
*In this biblical scene by Rembrandt (1660), the Persian king, Ahasuerus, is flanked by his Jewish wife and his minister, Haman. Esther, lit by a single ray of light, accuses Haman of plotting to destroy the Jews.*

**KEY**

| | |
|---|---|
| ☐ | Art of ancient civilizations |
| ☐ | European art 13th–16th centuries |
| ☐ | European art 17th–18th centuries |
| ☐ | European art 19th century |
| ☐ | Post-Impressionist and 20th-century European art |
| ☐ | Temporary exhibition space |

**Fayoum Portrait**
*Painted in the 1st century AD, this is one of a collection of portraits discovered at a burial ground at the Fayoum oasis in Egypt in the 1870s. They were painted while the subjects were still alive to be used as death masks on their mummies when they died.*

# Exploring the Pushkin Museum of Fine Arts

**Religious icon (c.14th–15th century)**

THE ACCUMULATED TREASURES of the Pushkin Museum of Fine Arts reflect the tastes of many private collectors, whose holdings were nationalized by the Soviet government after the Revolution. The most important of these belonged to two outstanding connoisseurs, Sergey Shchukin and Ivan Morozov. By 1914, Shchukin had acquired more than 220 paintings by French artists, including many by Cézanne. Even more importantly, Shchukin championed Matisse and Picasso when they were still relatively unknown. Morozov also collected canvases by these two painters along with pictures by Renoir, Van Gogh, and Gauguin.

**Greek marble sarcophagus, dating from around AD 210**

## ART OF ANCIENT CIVILIZATIONS

THE MUSEUM's archaeological exhibits come from as far afield as ancient Mesopotamia and the Mayan Empire. Among them is a fascinating collection donated by the Egyptologist Vladimir Golenishchev in 1913. The display includes tomb portraits from Fayoum and two exquisite ebony figurines of the high priest Amen-Hotep and his wife, the priestess Re-nai.

There is also an assortment of items from ancient Greece and Rome. Some are originals, others are plaster-cast replicas. The most interesting display in this part of the museum is the Treasure of Troy. These fabulous gold artifacts, excavated from the ancient city in the 1870s, were brought secretly to Moscow as war booty in 1945.

## EUROPEAN ART 13TH–16TH CENTURIES

THE PUSHKIN MUSEUM contains a small, but memorable, collection of Medieval and Renaissance art. It includes a series of altar panels painted

in the Byzantine tradition by Italian artists. Siena was a major artistic center in the 14th century, and Simone Martini was a leading master of the Sienese school. His naturalistic images of St. Augustine and Mary Magdalene, painted in the 1320s, are among the exhibits.

There are also a number of later religious pieces on display, including a triptych by Pietro di Giovanni Lianori. Two outstanding old masters painted in the 1490s are also displayed here: the superb *Annunciation*, painted by Sandro Botticelli, and the *Madonna and Child* by Pietro Perugino.

The museum is not so well endowed with German and Flemish art of the period. However, two notable exceptions are Pieter Breughel the Younger's *Winter Landscape with Bird Trap* and Lucas Cranach the Elder's *Virgin and Child*. Painted on wood, the latter places the Virgin and Child in the context of a typical German landscape.

## EUROPEAN ART 17TH–18TH CENTURIES

THE PUSHKIN MUSEUM has an enviable collection of 17th-century Dutch and Flemish masters. It includes Anthony Van Dyck's accomplished portraits of the wealthy burgher Adriaen Stevens and his wife, Maria Boschaert, both painted in 1629, and some evocative landscapes by Jan Van Goyen and Jacob van Ruysdael. Also on display are still lifes by Frans Snyders, some delightful genre scenes by Jan Steen, Pieter de Hooch, and Gabriel Metsu, and several works by Peter Paul Rubens, including the characteristically flamboyant and sensual *Bacchanalia* (c.1615).

Six of Rembrandt's masterly canvases, along with some of his drawings and etchings, are displayed in the gallery. The paintings include the biblical *Ahasuerus, Haman and Esther* (1660), *Christ Driving the Money-Changers from the Temple* (1626) and *An Old Woman*, a sensitive portrait of the artist's mother (1654).

The gallery has a modest collection of Spanish and Italian paintings from the 17th and 18th centuries. Of the Spanish artists, Bartholomé Esteban Murillo, known for his religious scenes and portraits, is probably the best known. The works on display by Italian artists include *Betrothal of the Doge and the Sea* (1729–30) by

**A section of the *Virgin and Child*, painted by Lucas Cranach the Elder in about 1525**

Canaletto, widely considered the master of the style of urban landscape known as *veduta*.

The Pushkin Museum is justly famous for its collection of French art, which includes paintings of classical and epic subjects by a variety of artists. Among the paintings on display are Nicolas Poussin's dramatic work, *The Battle of the Israelites with the Amorri* (c.1625) and François Boucher's painting *Hercules and Omphale* (1730s). The latter depicts the myth of Hercules, who was sold as a slave to Queen Omphale.

**Hercules and Omphale, painted in the 1730s by François Boucher**

## EUROPEAN ART 19TH CENTURY

IN THE EARLY 19th century Classicism in art gradually yielded to Romanticism. Works such as *After the Shipwreck* (1847) by Eugène Delacroix, which portrays the sea as a force of nature, unpredictable and hostile to man, were the result of this shift. Works by other artists of the period, such as the landscape painters John Constable and Caspar David Friedrich, are also on show.

The Pushkin Museum has a fine collection of paintings by artists of the French Barbizon school, who were the predecessors of the Impressionists. These include landscapes by Camille Corot, François Millet, and Gustave Courbet.

Paintings from the enormous collection of works by the Impressionists themselves are displayed in rotation. Visitors can look forward to a selection of canvases by artists such as Edouard Manet, Edgar Degas,

Pierre Auguste Renoir, and Claude Monet. The museum owns eleven paintings by Monet, including *Lilac in the Sun* (1873) and two from a series of 20 paintings of the cathedral at Rouen. There are also some excellent paintings by Renoir including *Nude* and the radiant *Portrait of the Actress Jeanne Samary* (1877). Alongside landscapes and street scenes by Alfred Sisley and Camille Pisarro are *Blue Dancers* (c.1899) and *Dancers at a Rehearsal* (1875–77), two of Degas' many ballet scenes.

Sculptures by Auguste Rodin are also part of the collection. They include a bust of Victor Hugo and preparatory studies for the famous *Kiss* (1886) and *Burghers of Calais* (1884–6).

**Claude Monet's *Rouen Cathedral at Sunset*, painted in 1894**

## POST-IMPRESSIONIST AND 20TH-CENTURY EUROPEAN ART

POST-IMPRESSIONISM is the term generally used to describe the various styles of painting developed by the generation of artists that came after the

***Improvisation No 20* by the Futurist Vasily Kandinsky**

Impressionists. This school includes Vincent Van Gogh, Paul Cézanne, and Paul Gauguin.

A marvelous array of paintings by Paul Cézanne is on display in the gallery, including his *Self-portrait* (early 1880s), *Pierrot and Harlequin* (1888), and a late version of *Montagne Ste-Victoire* (1905).

In 1888, Paul Gauguin stayed with Van Gogh for two months in Arles. Gauguin's *Café in Arles* and Van Gogh's intense *Red Vineyards in Arles*, both painted during the visit, hang in the Pushkin Museum.

The gallery also has several later works by Van Gogh, including *The Prison Courtyard* (1890) and *Wheatfields in Auvers, After the Rain* (1890).

In 1891 Gauguin moved to Tahiti and a number of works from this period, including *Are You Jealous?* (1892) and *The Great Buddha* (1899), are also displayed here.

Some of Henri Matisse's greatest masterpieces are in the Pushkin Museum, including *The Painter's Studio* (1911) and *Goldfish* (1911). There are also over 50 paintings by Matisse's friend, Pablo Picasso, including *Young Acrobat on a Ball*, painted in 1905, *(see p48)* and *Harlequin and His Companion*, dating from 1901.

A number of other 20th-century artists are also represented in the collection. Highlights include *The Artist and His Bride* (1980) by Marc Chagall and the abstract *Improvisation No. 20* by Vasily Kandinsky.

The wide expanse of Arbat Square, located between the Old and New Arbat

## Shchusev Museum of Architecture ⓫

Музей архитектуры имени АВ Щусева
*Muzey arkhitektury imeni AV Shchuseva*

Ulitsa Vozdvizhenka 5. **Map** 6 F1.
**【** *290 4855.* **M** *Biblioteka imeni Lenina, Borovitskaya, Arbatskaya.*
**Main building** ⭘ *11am–6pm Tue–Sun.* **Apothecary's Office** ⭘ *10am–6pm Tue–Sun.* 🌀 ∅ 📷 *English.*

A<small>N ENORMOUS</small> 18th-century mansion houses this museum dedicated to Russian architecture through the ages. It is named after the Soviet architect Aleksey Shchusev *(see p45),* who carried out parts of Stalin's reconstruction of Moscow during the 1930s and also designed the Lenin Mausoleum *(see p107).*

The museum's exhibits cover architectural development from medieval times to the present day. They include scale models, building plans and elevations, drawings,

A model of the Lenin Mausoleum in Red Square, in the Shchusev Museum of Architecture

lithographs, and watercolors, many of them considered works of art in their own right. They also shed light on the countless forgotten palaces, churches, monasteries, and monuments that were destroyed in the Soviet era on Stalin's orders *(see p75).*

Exhibitions are also mounted in the 17th-century former Apothecary's Office to the rear of the main museum.

## Arbat Square ⓬

Арбатская площадь
*Arbatskaya ploshchad*

**Map** 6 E1. **M** *Arbatskaya.*

A<small>CHAOTIC MASS</small> of kiosks, traffic, and underpasses, Arbat Square is the link between the vividly contrasting areas of Old and New Arbat. Beneath the square, the underpasses contain a society of their own. Expect to come across an impromptu rock concert, kittens and puppies for sale, and, in late summer, children selling bulbous, hand-picked mushrooms (though buying these may not be advisable).

On the corner of ulitsa Arbat is the yellow wedge-shaped Praga restaurant *(see p181),* dating from before the Revolution, but reconstructed in 1954. Despite still retaining the elegance of its dining halls, it became a fairly uninspiring snack bar during the later Soviet era. However, it has now been entirely

refurbished to reemerge as a very elegant establishment serving high-quality cuisine in a variety of national styles.

The small white building at the other end of the underpass dates from 1909, but it was redesigned three years later by Fyodor Shekhtel *(see p45)* for the pioneering Russian movie studio boss Aleksandr Khanzhonkov. Now known as the Arts Cinema *(see p193),* it was one of the first movie houses to open in Moscow.

## Lermontov House-Museum ⓭

Дом-музей МЮ Лермонтова
*Dom-muzey MYu Lermontova*

Ulitsa Malaya Molchanovka 2. **Map** 6 D1. **【** *291 5298.* **M** *Arbatskaya.* ⭘ *2pm–4pm Wed, Fri, 11am–4pm Thu, Sat–Sun.* 🌀

A portrait of the poet and novelist Lermontov (1814–41) as a child

T<small>UCKED AWAY</small> behind the high-rises of the New Arbat is the modest timber house that was once home to Mikhail Lermontov. The great Romantic poet and novelist lived here with his grand-mother, Yelizaveta Arseneva, from 1829–32 while he was a student at Moscow University. While here, he wrote an early draft of his narrative poem *The Demon* (1839).

Lermontov was more interested in writing poetry than in his studies and left school without graduating. He then became a guardsman. However, he was exiled to the Caucasus for a year because of the bitter criticisms of the authorities expressed in his

**Lermontov's tranquil study in the Lermontov House-Museum**

poem *Death of a Poet* (1837). This poem about the death of Pushkin *(see p73)* marked a turning point in Lermontov's writing and is generally agreed to be the first of his mature works. His most famous composition, the novel *A Hero of our Time*, was written in 1840. Lermontov died the next year, at just 26. Like Pushkin, he was killed in a duel.

There are only five rooms in the museum, but each bears testament both to Lermontov's dazzling intellectual gifts and also to his zest for life. The study on the mezzanine was his favorite room. Here he would play the guitar, piano, and violin, and even compose music.

The drawing room, which still contains many of its original furnishings, was often the site of lively dancing, singing, and masquerades.

Many of Lermontov's manuscripts are on display downstairs, together with drawings and watercolors, some by Lermontov himself.

## Shalyapin House-Museum ⑭
Дом-музей ФИ Шаляпина
*Dom-muzey FI Shalyapina*

Novinskiy bulvar 25. **Map** 1 C5.
205 6236. Ⓜ Smolenskaya, Barrikadnaya. ☐ 11:30am–7pm Wed, Thu, 10am–6pm Tue, Sat, 10am–4pm Sun.

A STONE BUST and inscription outside a yellow Empire-style mansion record that one of the greatest opera singers of the 20th century once lived here. The renowned Russian bass, Fyodor Shalyapin, occupied this large house from 1910 until he emigrated from Soviet Russia in 1922.

Born in Kazan in 1873, Shalyapin began his career in great poverty, working as a stevedore on the Volga before his unique vocal talent was discovered. He made his international debut at La Scala, Milan, in 1901, and went on to sing a variety of the great operatic bass roles, including *Don Quixote*, *Ivan the Terrible*, and *Boris Godunov*.

Shalyapin died in Paris in 1938, but his remains have since been returned to Russia and were

**Stone bust of opera singer Shalyapin**

reburied in the Novodevichiy Cemetery *(see p131)* alongside other famous Russians.

This is one of Moscow's newer house-museums and one of the best. Amusing drawings of Shalyapin by his children and a china doll bought in France decorate the green-upholstered sitting room. The mementos in the blue study, meanwhile, include portraits of the singer in his various operatic roles.

The carved chair in front of the dining room stove was a gift from writer Maxim Gorky *(see p95)*, and the paintings on the walls are by the artist Konstantin Korovin.

The heavily labeled trunks stored in the box room are a reminder that Shalyapin was also in great demand at opera houses abroad. Other items on display in the house include the singer's makeup table and one of his wigs. In the concert room visitors can listen to recordings of Shalyapin at work.

After singing for his guests, Shalyapin would often take them next door for a game of billiards. Shalyapin was not a very good loser, and, depending on his mood, his wife would invite only friends with grace enough to let him win.

**Pictures drawn by Shalyapin's children, on display in the sitting room**

# TVERSKAYA

A T HEART A COMMERCIAL district, Tverskaya centers on the road of the same name, which originally led to St. Petersburg and was the processional route used by the tsars. Now Moscow's premier shopping street, Tverskaya ulitsa underwent a major redevelopment in the 1930s during the huge reconstruction of Moscow ordered by Stalin (see p75). At that time many buildings were torn down

**Shell detail on the House of Friendship**

so that the street could be widened and massive new apartment buildings were erected for workers. These looming gray buildings make the street a showcase of the monumental style of architecture (see p45) favored by Stalin. The area's surprisingly tranquil backstreets have been home to many famous artists, writers, and actors, and, despite Stalin's best efforts, still have some interesting pre-Revolutionary houses.

## SIGHTS AT A GLANCE

**Museums**
Chekhov House-Museum ⑯
Gorky House-Museum ⑮
Museum of the Revolution ⑲
Stanislavskiy House-Museum ⑨

**Historic Buildings**
Hotel Metropol ①
Hotel National ⑤
House of Friendship ⑭
House of Unions ④
Manège ⑬
Morozov Mansion ⑰
Moscow Conservatory ⑪
Moscow Old University ⑫

**Monasteries**
Upper Monastery of St. Peter ㉑

**Streets and Squares**
Bolshaya Nikitskaya Ulitsa ⑩
Bryusov Pereulok ⑧
Patriarch's Pond ⑱
Pushkin Square ⑳
Theater Square ②
Tverskaya Ulitsa ⑥

**Theatres**
Bolshoy Theater pp90–91 ③
Moscow Arts Theater ⑦

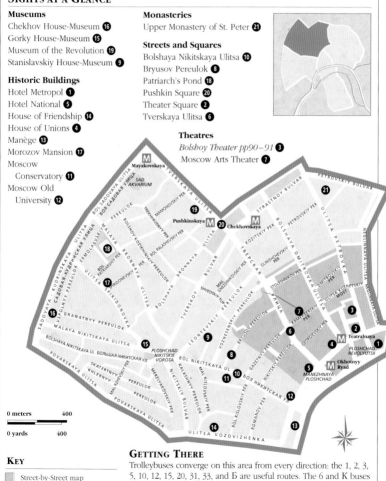

**KEY**

Street-by-Street map pp86–7

Ⓜ Metro station

0 meters 400
0 yards 400

## GETTING THERE

Trolleybuses converge on this area from every direction: the 1, 2, 3, 5, 10, 12, 15, 20, 31, 33, and Б are useful routes. The 6 and K buses run to a number of sights in the district. Metro stations in the area include Okhotnyy Ryad, Teatralnaya, Chekhovskaya, Tverskaya, Pushkinskaya, Mayakovskaya, and Biblioteka imeni Lenina.

◁ **The exquisitely ornate interior of the 19th-century Yeliseev's Food Hall (see p89) on Tverskaya ulitsa**

# Street-by-Street: Around Theater Square

Moscow's THEATERLAND is centered, appropriately, around Theater Square. Dominating the square is one of the most famous opera and ballet stages in the world, the Bolshoy Theater. The Malyy (Small) Theater is on the east side of the square, while the Russian Academic Youth Theater is on the west. Farther to the west is the city's main shopping street, Tverskaya ulitsa, and two more theaters, the Yermolova Theater and the Moscow Arts Theater. There are several restaurants and bars in this lively neighborhood, including the MKhAT Club in the Moscow Arts Theater.

**Yuriy Dolgorukiy,**
Moscow's founder *(see p17),* is depicted in this statue. It was unveiled in 1954, seven years after the city's 800th anniversary.

**Pushkin Square**

**Bryusov Pereulok**
*A granite archway leads from Tverskaya ulitsa to this quiet lane, once home to director Vsevolod Meyerhold. The 17th-century Church of the Resurrection is visible farther down the lane* **8**

**Tverskaya Ulitsa**
*Most of the imposing Stalinist buildings on Moscow's main shopping street date from the 1930s, but a few older buildings survive* **6**

**Bolshaya Nikitskaya ulitsa**

**Central Telegraph Office**

**Yermolova Theater**

**Lower Chamber of the Russian Parliament**

**Moscow Arts Theater**
*This famous theater will always be associated with the dramatist Anton Chekhov (see p93). Several of his plays, including* The Cherry Orchard, *were premiered here* **7**

| STAR SIGHTS |
| --- |
| ★ **Bolshoy Theater** |
| ★ **House of Unions** |

**Okhotnyy Ryad**

**Hotel National**
*Designed by Aleksandr Ivanov, the National (see p169) is a mix of Style Moderne and Classical style. Now fully restored, its decor is as impressive as it was before the Revolution, when it was Moscow's finest hotel* **5**

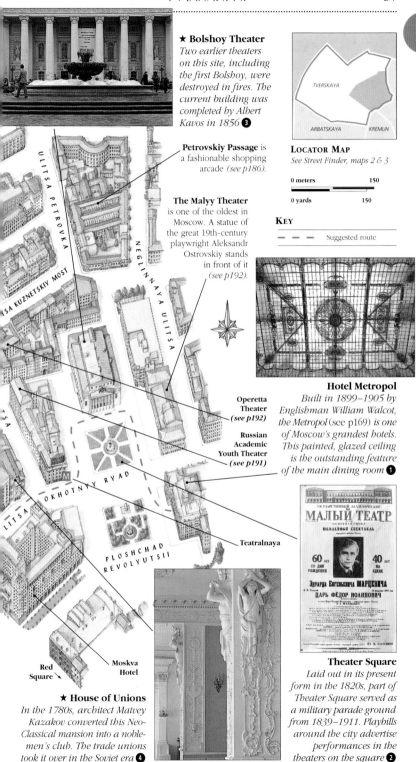

★ **Bolshoy Theater**
*Two earlier theaters on this site, including the first Bolshoy, were destroyed in fires. The current building was completed by Albert Kavos in 1856* ❸

**Petrovskiy Passage** is a fashionable shopping arcade *(see p186).*

**The Malyy Theater** is one of the oldest in Moscow. A statue of the great 19th-century playwright Aleksandr Ostrovskiy stands in front of it *(see p192).*

**LOCATOR MAP**
*See Street Finder, maps 2 & 3*

0 meters          150
0 yards           150

**KEY**

– – –          Suggested route

Operetta
Theater
*(see p192)*

Russian
Academic
Youth Theater
*(see p191)*

**Hotel Metropol**
*Built in 1899–1905 by Englishman William Walcot, the Metropol (see p169) is one of Moscow's grandest hotels. This painted, glazed ceiling is the outstanding feature of the main dining room* ❶

Teatralnaya

Red
Square

Moskva
Hotel

★ **House of Unions**
*In the 1780s, architect Matvey Kazakov converted this Neo-Classical mansion into a noble-men's club. The trade unions took it over in the Soviet era* ❹

**Theater Square**
*Laid out in its present form in the 1820s, part of Theater Square served as a military parade ground from 1839–1911. Playbills around the city advertise performances in the theaters on the square* ❷

**The statue of Aleksandr Ostrovskiy in front of the Malyy Theater**

# Hotel Metropol ❶

Гостиница Метрополь

*Gostinitsa Metropol*

Teatralnyy prospekt 1/4. **Map** 3 A5.
927 6000. Ⓜ *Teatralnaya. See*
***Where to Stay*** *p169.*

THE HOTEL METROPOL, built
by William Walcot and Lev
Kekushev in 1899–1905, is a
fine example of Style-Moderne
architecture *(see p45)*. The exterior walls display a number
of ceramic panels, including
Mikhail Vrubel's large work at
the top of the facade. Called
*The Daydreaming Princess*, it is
based on scenes from the play
*La Princesse Lointaine*, written
in 1895 by Edmond Rostand,
author of *Cyrano de Bergerac*.
The building also has ornate
wrought-iron balconies and a
superb painted glass roof in
its Metropol Zal restaurant.
   Over the years the Metropol
has welcomed guests as varied
and famous as Irish dramatist
George Bernard Shaw and
American pop star
Michael Jackson.

**The facade of the Hotel Metropol, designed by William Walcot**

# Theater Square ❷

Театральная площадь

*Teatralnaya ploshchad*

**Map** 3 A5. Ⓜ *Teatralnaya, Ploshchad
Revolyutsii, Okhotnyy Ryad.*

THIS ELEGANT SQUARE is named
after the theaters on three
of its sides. Originally this area
was marshy ground, regularly
flooded by the Neglinnaya
River. In the 1820s it was paved
over, and the square was laid
out to a design by Osip Bove
*(see p45)*. In 1839–1911 a
military parade ground occupied part of the square. Today,
Theater Square is dominated
by the Bolshoy Theater.
   On the square's east
side is a converted private
mansion that houses the
Malyy (Small) Theater
*(see p192)*. The Malyy is
particularly associated
with playwright Aleksandr
Ostrovskiy (1823–86),
whose satirical plays were
performed here. A somber
statue of him by Nikolay
Andreev was erected in
the courtyard in 1929.
   The Russian Academic
Youth Theater *(see p191)*,
with its elaborate Neo-
Classical porch, stands on
the square's west side. Originally designed by Osip Bove
*(see p45)*, it was almost entirely
rebuilt by Boris Friedenberg in
1882. The theater has occupied
this building since 1936.
   To the northwest of Theater
Square is the Operetta Theater
*(see p192)*. In the 1890s the
private opera company
of the wealthy
industrialist and arts patron
Savva Mamontov (1842–1914)
performed here. The careers of
opera singer Fyodor Shalyapin
*(see p83)*, composer Sergei
Rachmoninoff, and artist Vasiliy
Polenov, who designed sets
and costumes, all began here
with Mamontov's company.
   In the center of the square is
a granite statue of Karl Marx.
Sculpted in 1961 by Leonid
Kerbel, it bears the words
"Workers of the world unite!"

# Bolshoy Theater ❸

*See pp90–91.*

**The well-proportioned Hall of Columns in
the elegant, 18th-century House of Unions**

# House of Unions ❹

Дом Союзов

*Dom Soyuzov*

Bolshaya Dmitrovka ulitsa 1.
**Map** 3 A5. ⬤ *to public.*
Ⓜ *Teatralnaya, Okhotnyy Ryad.*

THIS GREEN AND WHITE Neo-
Classical mansion was
originally built in the first half
of the 18th century. In the
early 1780s it was bought by
a group of Moscow nobles
who commissioned architect
Matvey Kazakov *(see pp44–5)*
to turn it into a noblemen's
club. Kazakov added a number
of rooms to the existing building, including the magnificent
ballroom, known as the Hall
of Columns. It was here, in
1856, that Tsar Alexander II
addressed an audience of the
Russian nobility on the need
to emancipate the serfs.
   After the Revolution, unions
took over the building, hence
its current name. In 1924 the
hall was opened to the public
for more than a million

people to file past Lenin's open coffin. Many of his closest colleagues, members of the guard of honor on that occasion, were later tried here during the show trials of 1936–8 *(see p27)*. Stalin, who was behind these mockeries of justice, also lay in state here in 1953.

Nowadays the House of Unions is used for concerts and public meetings.

## Hotel National ❺

Гостиница Националь
*Gostinitsa Natsional*

Mokhovaya ulitsa 15/1. **Map** 2 F5.
📞 *258 7000.* Ⓜ *Okhotnyy Ryad.*
♿ ✉ *See* **Where to Stay** *p169.*

Designed in 1903 by architect Aleksandr Ivanov, the Hotel National is an eclectic mixture of Style-Moderne and Classical-style architecture *(see pp44–5)*. The facade is decorated with sculpted nymphs and ornate stone tracery, but is topped by a mosaic from the Soviet era. This features factory chimneys belching smoke, oil derricks, electricity towers, train engines, and tractors.

The National's most famous guest was Lenin, who stayed in room 107 at the hotel for a week, in March 1918, before he moved to the Kremlin.

**Lobby of the Hotel National, with Style-Moderne windows and Classical statues**

**Tverskaya ulitsa, one of Moscow's most popular shopping streets**

The National was completely refurbished in the early 1990s, and its Style-Moderne interiors have been faithfully restored to their original splendor.

## Tverskaya Ulitsa ❻

Тверская улица
*Tverskaya ulitsa*

**Map** 2 F5, F4, E3. Ⓜ *Okhotnyy Ryad, Tverskaya, Pushkinskaya.*

Tverskaya ulitsa was the grandest thoroughfare in Moscow in the 19th century, when it was famous for its restaurants, theaters, hotels, and purveyors of French fashions. Stalin's reconstruction of the city in the 1930s resulted in Tverskaya ulitsa being widened by 42 m (138 ft) and its name being changed to ulitsa Gorkovo to commemorate the writer Maxim Gorky. Many buildings were torn down to make way for huge apartment buildings for Soviet workers, such as those at Nos. 9–11. Other buildings were rebuilt farther back to stand on the new, wider road. Now called Tverskaya ulitsa again, the street carries a huge volume of traffic. However, it is still one of the city's most popular places to eat out and shop.

At No. 7 is the Central Telegraph Office, a building with an illuminated globe outside. It was designed by Ilya Rerberg in 1927. Through the arch on the other side of the road is a green-tiled building with floral friezes and tent-roofed turrets. Built in 1905, this was the Moscow mission of the Savvinskiy Monastery. It is now luxury apartments and offices.

Farther up the street is the soulless Tverskaya square, dominated by an equestrian statue of Moscow's founder, Prince Yuriy Dolgorukiy *(see p86)*. On the west side of the square looms the red and white city hall. Designed in 1782 by Matvey Kazakov *(see pp44–5)*, it was the residence of the governor-general before the Revolution and later became the Moscow City Soviet or town hall. In 1944–6 extra stories were added, more than doubling its height.

Beyond Tverskaya square, at No. 14, is Moscow's most famous delicatessen. It is now known by its pre-Revolutionary name, Yeliseev's Food Hall *(see p186)*, but in Soviet times it was called Gastronom No. 1. In the 1820s this mansion was the home of Princess Zinaida Volkonskaya, whose soirées were attended by great literary figures of the day, including Alexander Pushkin *(see p73)*. In around 1898 Grigoriy Yeliseev bought the building and had it lavishly redecorated with stained-glass windows, crystal chandeliers, elaborately carved pillars, polished wood counters, and large mirrors. It now stocks a wide range of imported and Russian delicacies.

# Bolshoy Theater ❸

Большой театр
*Bolshoy teatr*

H OME TO ONE OF THE OLDEST, and probably the most famous, ballet companies in the world, the Bolshoy Theatre is also one of Moscow's major landmarks. The first Bolshoy Theatre opened in 1780 and presented masquerades, comedies and comic operas. It burnt down in 1805, but its successor was completed in 1825 to a design by Osip Bove *(see p45)* and Andrey Mikhaylov. This building too was destroyed by fire, in 1853, but the essentials of its highly praised design were retained in Albert Kavos' reconstruction of 1856. Today the theatre still provides a magnificent setting for performances of ballet and opera by the Bolshoy Theatre company.

★ **Royal Box**

*Situated at the center of the gallery, the royal box, hung with crimson velvet, is one of over 120 boxes. The imperial crown on its pediment was removed in the Soviet era but has now been restored.*

**Neo-Classical Pediment**

*The relief on the Neo-Classical pediment was an addition by Albert Kavos during his reconstruction of the theater. It depicts a pair of angels bearing aloft the lyre of Apollo, the Greek god of music and light.*

★ **Apollo in the Chariot of the Sun**

*This eye-catching sculpture by Pyotr Klodt, part of the original 1825 building, was retained by Albert Kavos. It depicts Apollo driving the chariot on which he carried the sun across the sky.*

**Entrance**

**Vestibule**

*Patrons entering the theater find themselves in this grand, black and white tiled vestibule. Magnificent staircases, lined with white marble, lead up from either side of the vestibule to the spacious main lobby.*

**Eight-columned portico**

**Beethoven Hall**
*This ornately decorated room was formerly known as the Imperial Foyer. It is now used for occasional chamber concerts and lectures. The stuccoed decoration on the ceiling includes approximately 3,000 rosettes, and the walls are adorned with delicately embroidered panels of crimson silk.*

Main stage

**VISITORS' CHECKLIST**

Teatralnaya ploshchad 1.
**Map** 3 A4. [ 927 6982. M
Teatralnaya. 3. Tue – Sun,
for performances. July – August.
in auditorium.
interval buffet available.

**The backstage area** provides jobs for over 700 workers, including craftsmen and women making ballet shoes, costumes, and stage props.

**Apollo and the Muses**
*The ten painted panels decorating the auditorium's ceiling are by Pyotr Titov. They depict Apollo dancing with the nine muses of Greek myth, each of which is connected with a different branch of the arts or sciences.*

**STAR FEATURES**

★ **Apollo in the Chariot of the Sun**

★ **Royal Box**

Artists' dressing room

**The auditorium** has six tiers and a seating capacity of 2,500. When Kavos rebuilt it he modified its shape to improve the accoustics.

**The main lobby** extends around the whole of the front of the building on the first floor. Its vaulted ceiling is decorated with paintings and elaborate stuccowork.

## THE BOLSHOY BALLET IN THE SOVIET ERA

In the 1920s and 1930s new ballets conforming to Revolutionary ideals were created for the Bolshoy, but the company's heyday was in the 1950s and 1960s. Ballets such as *Spartacus* were produced and the dancers toured abroad for the first time to widespread acclaim. Yet a number of dancers also defected to the West in this period, in protest at the company's harsh management and a lack of artistic freedom.

**A production of *Spartacus* (1954), by Aram Khachaturian, at the Bolshoy**

Arch at the entrance to Bryusov pereulok, a street where artists and musicians lived in the 1920s

## Moscow Arts Theater ❼

МХАТ имени АП Чехова
*MKhAT imeni AP Chekhova*

Kamergerskiy pereulok 3. **Map** 2 F5.
**C** 229 8760. **M** *Teatralnaya, Okhotnyy Ryad.* ◻ *performances only. See* **Entertainment** *p192.*

THE VERY FIRST performance at the Moscow Arts Theater (MKhAT) took place in 1898. The theater was founded by a group of young enthusiasts, led by the directors Konstantin Stanislavskiy and Vladimir Nemirovich-Danchenko. The MKhAT company had an early success with their production of Anton Chekhov's

**The Moscow Arts Theater entrance with** *The Wave* **bas-relief above**

play *The Seagull* in the theater's first year. When the play had been performed three years earlier in St. Petersburg, it had been a disastrous flop but, performed using Stanislavskiy's new Method acting, it was extremely well received.

In 1902 architect Fyodor Shekhtel (*see p45)* completely reconstructed the interior of the theater, adding innovations such as a central lighting board and a revolving stage. The auditorium had very little decoration, so that audiences were forced to concentrate on the performance.

The theater continued to flourish after the Revolution, but its repertoire was restricted by state censorship. Most of the

**Stylized seagull on the exterior of the Moscow Arts Theater**

plays produced were written by Maxim Gorky, whose work was in favor with the government. The frustrations and compromises of the period were brilliantly satirized in the 1930s by Mikhail Bulgakov (who also worked as an assistant director in the theater) in his novel *Teatralnyy Roman*. These problems continued and in the 1980s part of the company moved to the Gorky Arts Theater on Tverskoy bulvar.

Today a variety of productions are staged at the Moscow Arts Theater, including many of Anton Chekhov's plays.

## Bryusov Pereulok ❽

Брюсов переулок
*Bryusov pereulok*

**Map** 2 F5. **M** *Okhotnyy Ryad, Arbatskaya.*

A GRANITE ARCH on Tverskaya ulitsa marks the entrance to this quiet side street. It is named after the Bruces, a Scottish family who were involved with the Russian court.

In the 1920s new apartments here were assigned to the staff of the Moscow state theaters. No. 17 was the home of two actors from the Moscow Arts Theater, Vasiliy Kachalov and Ivan Moskvin. No. 12 was home to the avant-garde director Vsevolod Meyerhold, who directed premieres of Vladimir Mayakovskiy's satires. He lived here from 1928 until his arrest in 1939 at the height of Stalin's Great Purge (*see p27).*

The Composers' Union was at Nos. 8–10. It was here that composers Sergey Prokofiev and Dmitriy Shostakovich were forced to read an apology for works that deviated from Socialist Realism (*see p135).*

About halfway along Bryusov pereulok is the 17th-century single-domed Church of the Resurrection. This was one of the few churches to remain open during the Soviet era.

## Stanislavskiy House-Museum ❾

Дом-музей КС Станиславского
*Dom-muzey KS Stanislavskovo*

Leontevskiy pereulok 6. **Map** 2 E5. *229 2855.* *Arbatskaya, Tverskaya.* *11am–6pm Thu, Sat–Sun, 2pm–8pm Wed, Fri.* *public holidays.*

This 18th-century mansion was the home of the great director and actor Konstantin Stanislavskiy. He lived on the first floor from 1920 until he died in 1938, at the age of 75.

Stanislavskiy had enrolled in the Moscow Theater School, but soon left, disillusioned with its conservative ethos. He created an outlet for his innovative ideas by founding the Moscow Arts Theater (MKhAT) in 1898. After moving into this flat, he converted his ballroom into a makeshift theater where he rehearsed his experimental Opera Dramatic Group. Later, when he was too ill to go out, he also rehearsed the MKhAT company here.

Stanislavskiy's living room and study, the dining room, and the bedroom of his wife, Maria Lilina, are all open. Also on display are an early Edison phonograph and a vase that was a gift from the dancer Isadora Duncan. Downstairs are props and costumes from Stanislavskiy's productions.

### Stanislavskiy and Chekhov

Konstantin Stanislavskiy in the play *Uncle Vanya* by Chekhov

Konstantin Stanislavskiy's successful production of Anton Chekhov's *The Seagull* took the theater world by storm. Stanislavskiy's secret was his new school of Method acting, in which performers explored their characters' inner motives. Stanislavskiy and Chekhov collaborated on the premieres of other Chekhov plays and the success of the productions was such that their names have been linked ever since.

## Bolshaya Nikitskaya Ulitsa ❿

Большая Никитская улица
*Bolshaya Nikitskaya ulitsa*

**Map** 2 F5, E5. *Arbatskaya, Okhotnyy Ryad, Biblioteka imeni Lenina.*

This historic street, once the main road to Novgorod, is named after the Nikitskiy Convent which was founded in the 16th century, but torn down by Stalin in the 1930s.

Prominent aristocratic families such as the Menshikovs and Orlovs built their palaces here in the 18th century. The finest is the former residence of Prince Sergey Menshikov, which can be reached via Gazetniy pereulok. The pale blue facade was reconstructed following the great fire of 1812 *(see pp24–5)*. The Neo-Classical rear facade, which survived the fire, dates from around 1775.

Just opposite the Moscow Conservatory *(see p94)* is the attractive white Church of the Little Ascension. Built around the end of the 16th century, it was restored in 1739 following a fire. Behind it is the Gothic tower of St. Andrew's Anglican Church. It was built for Moscow's English community in 1882 by British architect Richard Freeman.

Stone relief on Church of the Great Ascension

The heavily ornamented redbrick building at Nos. 19–20 was once called the Paradise Theater. It was renamed the Mayakovsky Theater after the poet Vladimir Mayakovsky *(see p111)*. His plays *Bath House* and *The Bed Bug* were premiered here in 1928 and 1929, directed by avant-garde director Vsevolod Meyerhold. One of the greatest innovators of his era, Meyerhold was executed by the State in 1940, largely because his work did not agree with the canons of Socialist Realism *(see p135)*.

About halfway along the road is Nikitskie Vorota ploshchad, named after the medieval St. Nicholas's Gate, which used to stand here. On the square is a modern white building with a sign in the shape of a large globe hanging beneath its porch. This is the ITAR-TASS news agency, the mouthpiece of the Communist Party in the Soviet era and now Russia's main news agency.

Opposite is the Church of the Great Ascension. Begun in 1798, it was rebuilt after the 1812 fire. Alexander Pushkin *(see p73)* married Natalya Goncharova here in 1831.

Sign in the shape of a globe hanging outside the ITAR-TASS news agency

The Bolshoy Zal (Great Hall) in the Moscow Conservatory

# Moscow Conservatory ⓫

Московская Консерватория

*Moskovskaya Konservatoriya*

Bolshaya Nikitskaya ulitsa 13. **Map** 2 F5. **C** 229 7412. **M** *Arbatskaya, Pushkinskaya.* ⃝ *performances only.*

THE LARGEST MUSIC SCHOOL in Russia, the Moscow Conservatory was founded in 1866 by Nikolay Rubinstein, the brother of composer and pianist Anton Rubinstein.

One of the Conservatory's teachers was the young Pyotr Tchaikovsky, who taught here until 1878. In the courtyard is his statue, wielding a baton despite the fact that Tchaikovsky detested conducting. The work of Vera Mukhina, it dates from 1954. The pattern on the courtyard railings is made up of the opening notes from some of Tchaikovsky's works.

Portraits of famous composers adorn the walls of the light, airy Bolshoy Zal (Great Hall). Used for concerts since 1898, it is also the setting for the prestigious Tchaikovsky International Competition *(see p192)*. The Conservatory has a small museum that is open during performances.

The Conservatory has always been an important training ground for young Russian composers and performers. Among its best-known alumni are pianist-composers Sergei Rachmaninov and Aleksandr Skryabin *(see p72)*. Dmitriy Shostakovich, the great Soviet composer, lived nearby, at the Composers' Union on Bryusov pereulok *(see p92)* . He taught at the Conservatory from 1942 until he fell from favor and was fired six years later for "professional incompetence" during Stalin's Purges *(see p27)*.

# Moscow Old University ⓬

Московский Университет

*Moskovskiy Universitet*

Mokhovaya ulitsa 9. **Map** 2 F5. **M** *Okhotnyy Ryad, Biblioteka imeni Lenina.*

MOSCOW UNIVERSITY was founded by the scholar Mikhail Lomonosov in 1755, and is the oldest university in Russia. It moved into this imposing building (now called the Old University) in 1793. Designed by Matvey Kazakov *(see pp44–5)*, it was extensively rebuilt by Domenico Gilardi after the 1812 fire *(see pp24–5)* and is a fine example of Neo-Classical architecture *(see pp44–5)*. Outside are statues of radical writers Nikolay Ogarev and Aleksandr Herzen.

In 1836 the university acquired a building on the far side of Bolshaya Nikitskaya ulitsa. In front of the New University is a statue of Mikhail Lomonosov. Nearby is the chapel of St. Tatyana, whose feast day is celebrated by the students.

# Manège ⓭

Манеж

*Manezh*

Manezhnaya ploshchad 1. **Map** 6 F1. **C** 202 8976. **M** *Biblioteka imeni Lenina, Okhotnyy Ryad.* ⃝ *exhibitions only.*

THE MANEGE was originally built in 1817 as a military parade ground to a design by General Augustin de Béthencourt. The 45-m- (148-ft-) wide roof had no supporting columns, leaving an uninterrupted floor space large enough for an infantry regiment to practise in. However, in the 1930s the roof started to sag and had to be reinforced with interior pillars.

In 1823–5 Osip Bove *(see p45)* added a colonnade and decorative frieze to the exterior.

The Manège became the Central Exhibition Hall in 1957, and it was at an exhibition here in 1962 that Nikita Khrushchev *(see p30)* famously condemned abstract art. The brunt of the attack was borne by the sculptor Ernst Neizvestniy but, strangely, in his will Khrushchev chose Neizvestniy to design his tombstone *(see p131)*. Today the Manège is still mostly used to house exhibitions.

**Statue of Mikhail Lomonosov**

The Manège, designed by Augustin de Béthencourt in 1817

**The extravagant interior of the 19th-century House of Friendship**

# House of Friendship 🄬

Дом Дружбы

*Dom Druzhby*

Vozdvizhenka ulitsa 16. **Map** 6 E1. 📞 290 2069. Ⓜ *Arbatskaya, Biblioteka imeni Lenina.* ⬭ *performances only.*

THIS INCREDIBLE MANSION has towers encrusted with stone shells and topped by lacelike stonework. Vladimir Mazyrin designed it at the end of the 19th century for the playboy Arseny Morozov, a member of the wealthy Morozov family *(see p96)*. The interior is as showy as the facade. Its rooms include a Greek atrium and a hunting hall filled with carved animal heads. The only way to see inside is to attend a concert or lecture held here. In Soviet times the mansion was used by the Union of Friendship Societies, hence its name.

# Gorky House-Museum 🄯

Дом-музей АМ Горького

*Dom-muzey AM Gorkovo*

Malaya Nikitskaya ulitsa 6/2. **Map** 2 E5. 📞 290 0535. Ⓜ *Pushkinskaya.* ⬭ *10am–5pm Thu, Sat–Sun, 12pm–7pm Wed, Fri.* ♿ 🚫 📷 *English.*

A FRIEZE OF IRISES against a background of blue and purple clouds runs round the top of the yellow glazed-brick walls of this extraordinary mansion. Fyodor Shekhtel designed this masterpiece of Style-Moderne architecture *(see p45)* in 1900. The house belonged to arts patron and millionaire banker Stepan Ryabushinskiy until he left Russia with his family after the Revolution. In 1931 Stalin presented the mansion to the writer Maxim Gorky, who died here five years later.

The interior of the house is spectacular, featuring ceilings with elaborate moldings, stained-glass windows, and carved door frames. However, the *pièce de résistance* is the flowing staircase of polished Estonian limestone, which ends in a twisted post with a bronze lamp resembling a jellyfish.

By the time Gorky moved to this house, his career as a novelist and playwright was in decline. While living here, he wrote only one play, *Yegor Bulichev and Others* (1932), and part of a novel, *The Life of Klim Samgin* (unfinished at his death). However his fame and his earlier support for the Bolshevik Party made him a useful propaganda tool for the Soviet government. He served this function by being president of the Union of Writers, which explains why the rooms are full of photos of the author in the company of aspiring dramatists, Young Pioneers, and ambitious Communist officials.

On display are Gorky's hat, overcoat, and walking stick, his remarkable collection of oriental carvings, and many of his letters and books, including some first editions.

Shortly after Gorky died in 1936, Genrikh Yagoda, the former head of the NKVD (secret police), was accused of murdering him. Although the charge was probably fabricated, Yagoda was found guilty in one of the last of the notorious show trials *(see p27)*. Rumors persist that Gorky was killed on Stalin's orders.

**The spectacular Style-Moderne staircase in the Gorky House-Museum**

## Chekhov House-Museum 🔟

Дом-музей АП Чехова
*Dom-muzey AP Chekhova*

Sadovaya-Kudrinskaya ulitsa 6.
**Map** 2 D5. 📞 291 6154.
Ⓜ *Barrikadnaya.* ⏲ *11am–2pm Tue, Thu, Sat, 2pm–5pm Wed, Fri.* 📷 🚫 📷 *(book in advance).*

A NTON CHEKHOV (1860–1904) lived in this two-story house in 1886–90. It was later refurbished in consultation with the author's widow, actress Olga Knipper-Chekhova, and opened as a museum in 1954. However, it is only partially successful in recreating a period feeling and contains few of Chekhov's possessions.

Chekhov was a qualified doctor and was practicing medicine when he lived here, as the brass plate by the front door testifies. He shared the house with his parents, his brother, Mikhail, and his sister, Mariya. As the family's main breadwinner, Chekhov could only write in his spare time, but it was here that he created his first major play, *Ivanov.* He also wrote many short stories and several one-act plays here.

Exhibits in the study, which doubled as an examination room, include Chekhov's doctor's bag, manuscripts, and pictures, including some of him with Leo Tolstoy *(see p134).*

Upstairs are a richly decorated living room and Mariya's room, which, in some ways, is the most attractive in the house. Its furnishings include a sewing machine, ornaments, and embroidered tablecloths.

There is also an exhibition about Chekhov's later career as a playwright *(see p93),* which includes promos for his plays and first editions of his works.

**Picture of Chekhov (on the left) talking with Leo Tolstoy, in the Chekhov House-Museum**

**The Gothic-style Morozov Mansion, designed by Fyodor Shekhtel**

## Morozov Mansion 🔟

Дом ЗГ Морозовой
*Dom ZG Morozovoy*

Ulitsa Spiridonovka 17. **Map** 2 D4.
Ⓜ *Mayakovskaya.* ⏲ *to public.*

F YODOR SHEKHTEL *(see p45)* built this house for his patron, Savva Morozov, in 1893–8. He was a wealthy textiles manufacturer and arts patron, a member of one of the city's richest families.

The mansion was built in the Gothic style to resemble a baronial castle, with turrets, gargoyles, and arched windows. Some of the stained-glass windows were designed by the Symbolist artist Mikhail Vrubel.

The Foreign Ministry now owns the building and uses the Grand Hall for entertaining.

## Patriarch's Pond 🔟

Патриаршие пруды
*Patriarshie prudy*

**Map** 2 D4. Ⓜ *Mayakovskaya.*

J UST A FEW MINUTES' WALK from the busy Garden Ring is a secluded, tree-lined square with the large Patriarch's Pond at its heart. The pond is named after the patriarch, the head of the Russian Orthodox Church *(see p137),* who formerly owned the land.

Near the children's playground is a bronze statue of the 19th-century playwright and writer of popular fables Ivan Krylov. Sculptures of the creatures from his stories are dotted among the trees.

Patriarch's Pond is probably best known as the setting for the opening scene in Mikhail Bulgakov's novel *The Master and Margarita,* in which the Devil causes havoc in Moscow. In 1921–4 Bulgakov lived near Patriarch's Pond, on Bolshaya Sadovaya ulitsa. He began the novel in 1928, but only finished it just before his death in 1940. It was not published until 1966 for political reasons.

**Graffiti at Bulgakov's flat by enthusiasts of his work**

## MIKHAIL BULGAKOV

Many of the satirical, anti-Bolshevik plays of Mikhail Bulgakov (1891–1940) were banned by the authorities. In 1930 Bulgakov became so frustrated that he wrote to Stalin asking to be exiled. Instead he was given a job at the Moscow Arts Theater *(see p92),* and, in 1932, Stalin lifted the ban on *The Days of the Turbins.* Most of Bulgakov's work, including *The Master and Margarita,* was published only after his death.

**Maxim gun used in the Civil War, in the Museum of the Revolution**

# Museum of the Revolution ⓳

Музей Революции

*Muzey Revolyutsii*

Tverskaya ulitsa 21. **Map** 2 E4.
📞 299 6724. Ⓜ *Pushkinskaya, Tverskaya.* ⭕ *10am–6pm Tue–Sat, 10am–5pm Sun.* 📷 🚫 🎦 *English.*

A PAIR OF STONE LIONS guards this elegant red mansion, built in the late 18th century. The wings and Empire-style facade *(see p45)* were added some decades later. In 1831 the mansion became a gentlemen's club, known as the English Club, and until the Revolution, the Muscovite aristocracy drank and gambled here and made use of the club's superb library.

It is not without irony that the Communists chose this building, with all its aristocratic associations, for a Museum of the Revolution. Since the Soviet Union broke up in 1991, the displays have been reorganized to give a more objective view of 20th-century Russian history.

Laid out chronologically, the exhibits cover 1900–91. They include home-made grenades, a Maxim gun on a converted carriage (used in the Civil War), candy wrappers depicting Marx and Lenin, and former premier Nikita Khrushchev's hat and camera from his 1959 trip to the United States. The collection of so-called propaganda porcelain and a display of gifts presented to Soviet rulers are also interesting.

# Pushkin Square ⓴

Пушкинская площадь

*Pushkinskaya ploshchad*

**Map** 2 F4. Ⓜ *Pushkinskaya, Tverskaya, Chekhovskaya.*

THE BRONZE STATUE of poet Alexander Pushkin was unveiled in the presence of two other Russian literary giants, Fyodor Dostoevsky and Ivan Turgenev, in 1880. The statue, located on the north side of Pushkin Square, was sculpted by Alexander Opekushin.

Pushkin has long epitomized the spirit of freedom in Russia, and the statue became a rallying point for dissident human rights demonstrations in the 1960s and 1970s. These often ended in violent clashes between the KGB and demonstrators.

Before the Revolution Pushkin Square was called Strastnaya ploshchad (Passion Square) after the 17th-century Convent of the Passion that used to stand here. The convent was demolished in 1935 to make way for the monstrous Rossiya theater *(see p193)*.

**The statue of poet Alexander Pushkin, on Pushkin Square**

Just beyond the theater, on Malaya Dmitrovka ulitsa, is the Church of the Nativity of the Virgin in Putniki. Built in 1649–52, this attractive church has clustered tent roofs, tiered *kokoshniki* gables *(see p44)*, and blue onion domes.

On the northeast corner of the square stand the offices of the newspaper *Izvestiya*. Once an official mouthpiece of the Soviet government, *Izvestiya* is now one of Russia's independent daily newspapers.

# Upper Monastery of St. Peter ㉑

Высоко-Петровский монастырь

*Vysoko-Petrovskiy monastyr*

Ulitsa Petrovka 28. **Map** 3 A3. 📞 923 7580. Ⓜ *Pushkinskaya, Chekhovskaya.* ⭕ *10am–5pm daily.* 🎦

THIS MONASTERY was founded in the reign of Ivan I *(see p18)*. It was rebuilt in the late 17th century with sponsorship from the Naryshkin family, relatives of Peter the Great. Its six churches include the Church of the Metropolitan Peter, after which the monastery is named. This single-domed church was built in 1514–17 to a design by Aleviz Novyy. The Church of the Icon of the Virgin of Bogolyubovo commemorates three of Peter the Great's uncles killed in the 1682 Streltsy Rebellion *(see p22)*. The Refectory Church of St. Sergius has five cupolas and scallop-shell decoration. The monastery complex also includes a green-domed bell tower and the monks' cells.

**Iconostasis in the Baroque bell tower of the Upper Monastery of St. Peter**

# RED SQUARE AND KITAY GOROD

**M**OSCOW'S FIRST suburb, Kitay Gorod, was settled as early as the 12th century by tradesmen and artisans employed by the tsar. The word *kitay* is thought to refer to the wattle used to build the ramparts around the suburb. Red Square was created as a market square beside the Kremlin *(see pp52–67)* in the late 15th century. Behind it, trading rows were set up, each line of wooden cabins

**Icon of St George, Resurrection Gate**

specializing in a particular item, such as icons, pots, or hats. In the 16th century, a number of boyars *(see p20)*, including Russia's future rulers, the Romanovs, built their estates nearby, while the presence of merchants from Novgorod and as far away as England was actively encouraged. Later, in the 19th century, Kitay Gorod became Moscow's financial district, home to the Stock Exchange and major banks.

## SIGHTS AT A GLANCE

**Cathedrals, Churches, Convents, and Monasteries**

Church of the Trinity in Nikitniki ④
Convent of the Nativity of the Virgin ㉒
Kazan Cathedral ⑧
Monastery of the Epiphany ⑥
*St. Basil's Cathedral pp108–9* ⑬

**Streets and Squares**

Chistoprudnyy Bulvar ⑲
Ivanovskaya Hill ⑭
Lubyanka Square ⑱
Nikolskaya Ulitsa ⑦
Red Square ⑩
Ulitsa Ilinka ⑤
Ulitsa Varvarka ①

**Historic Buildings**

GUM ⑫
Menshikov's Tower ⑳
Old English Court ②
Perlov Tea House ㉑
Resurrection Gate ⑨
Sandunovskiy Baths ㉓

**Museums and Galleries**

History of Moscow Museum ⑯
Lenin Mausoleum ⑪
Mayakovsky Museum ⑰
Palace of the Romanov Boyars ③
Polytechnical Museum ⑮

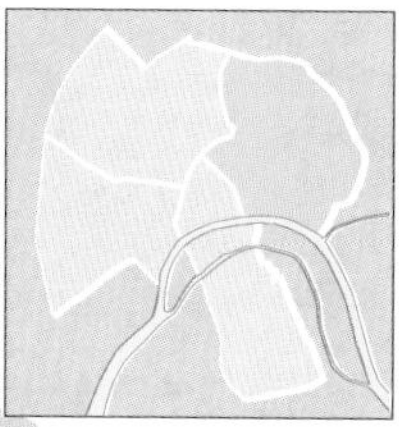

0 meters    400
0 yards    400

## KEY

▢ Street-by-Street map *pp100–101*
Ⓜ Metro station
▰ River boat pier

**GETTING THERE**
This area is well served by trolleybuses (2, 9, 16, 25, 33, 45, 48, 63 & 83), buses (25 & 158), and trams (3, 39 & A). The metro runs to Ploshchad Revolyutsii, Kitay Gorod, Lubyanka, Kuznetskiy Most, or Turgenevskaya.

◁ **The Russian-Revival façade of the Historical Museum at the northern end of Red Square**

# Street-by-Street: Kitay Gorod

COMMERCE AND RELIGION go hand-in-hand
in this ancient part of the city. The heart
of Moscow's financial district is Birzhevaya
ploshchad, and the surrounding area has
been home to traders for centuries. Among
the banks and offices are an increasing
number of upscale stores, especially lining
Nikolskaya ulitsa, and the area now rivals
Russia's best-known shopping arcade,
GUM (*see p107*). At one time there
were more than 40 churches and
monasteries dotted about these
narrow streets. Only around a
dozen have survived, and
most of these are now
undergoing
painstaking
restoration.

**Monastery of
the Epiphany**
*Founded in 1296,
this is the second
oldest monastery
in Moscow. Its
cathedral, built
between 1693–6,
is a fine example
of florid Moscow
Baroque* ⑥

**Russian Supreme Court**

**Ploshchad
Revolyutsii**

**Red
Square**

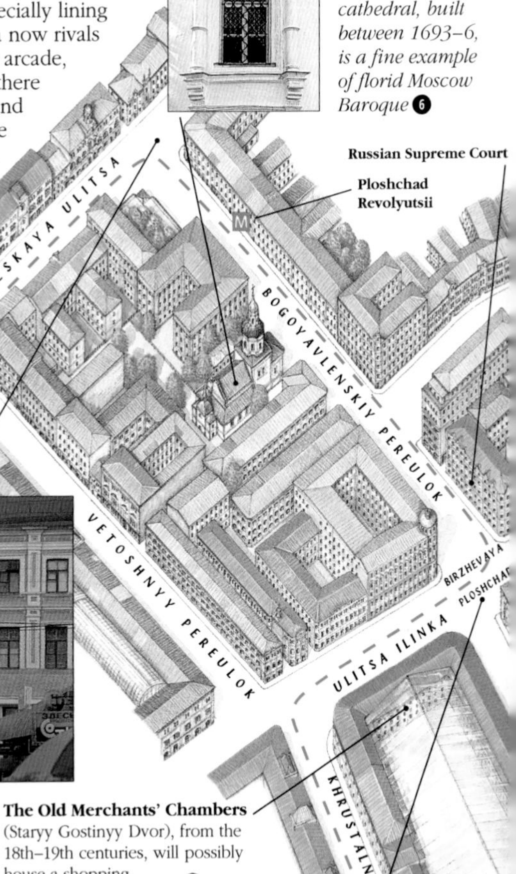

**Nikolskaya Ulitsa**
*Well-to-do shoppers now
head to this street's boutiques
and jewelry stores. Among
its more colorful sights is
the Gothic-style Synodal
Printing House, which dates
from the 19th century* ⑦

**The Old Merchants' Chambers**
(Staryy Gostinyy Dvor), from the
18th–19th centuries, will possibly
house a shopping
arcade.

**Ulitsa Ilinka**
*Halfway along ulitsa Ilinka is Birzhevaya
ploshchad, where the former Stock Exchange
is located. Constructed in 1873–5 by Aleksandr
Kaminskiy, this attractive, pink, Classical-
style building is now the home of the Russian
Chamber of Industry and Commerce* ⑤

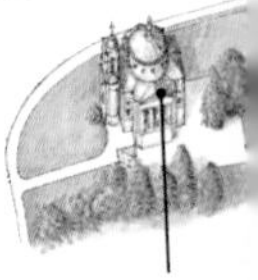

**Church of
St. Barbara**

---

**STAR SIGHTS**

★ **Church of the
Trinity in Nikitniki**

★ **Palace of the
Romanov Boyars**

**KEY**

– – – Suggested route

**Ulitsa Varvarka**
*Several historic churches line this ancient route out of Moscow. Among them is the Church of St. Maxim the Blessed, which was paid for by Novgorod merchants trading in Kitay Gorod and consecrated in 1698* **1**

**LOCATOR MAP**
*See Street Finder, maps 3 & 7*

★ **Church of the Trinity in Nikitniki**
*Commissioned by the wealthy merchant Grigoriy Nikitnikov and completed in 1635, the Church of the Trinity in Nikitniki is famous for both its exuberant architecture and the vivid frescoes that decorate its interior* **4**

**This house** belonged to Simon Ushakov, a leading 17th-century icon and fresco painter. He worked on the nearby Church of the Trinity in Nikitniki.

★ **Palace of the Romanov Boyars**
*This palace was originally lived in by powerful Muscovite boyar* (see p20) *Nikita Romanov. It is now a fascinating museum that evokes the life of noble families in the 16th and 17th centuries* **3**

LITSA ILINKA

NIKOLSKIY PEREULOK

IPATEVSKIY PEREULOK

Y PEREULOK

ULITSA VARVARKA

**Kitay Gorod metro**

**Church of St. George**

**Monastery of the Sign**

**Old English Court**
*Recently restored to its 17th-century appearance, this merchants' residence was given to visiting English traders by Ivan the Terrible in the hope of securing arms and other goods from them* **2**

| 0 meters | 100 |
| 0 yards | 100 |

# Ulitsa Varvarka ❶

Улица Варварка

*Ulitsa Varvarka*

**Map** 7 B1–C1. **M** *Kitay Gorod.*

THE HEART OF the former merchants' quarter of Zaryade, ulitsa Varvarka is one of Moscow's oldest streets. It is named after the original Church of St. Barbara (Varvara) the Martyr. This earlier building was demolished in 1796 to make way for a new pink and white Neo-Classical church of the same name, designed by Rodion Kazakov.

A little further along is the single-domed Church of St. Maxim the Blessed. Built by traders from Novgorod to house the bones of St. Maxim, it was consecrated in 1698. Between the two churches stands the Old English Court.

Across the road are the Old Merchants' Chambers (Staryy gostinyy dvor), which are fronted by a row of Corinthian columns. Italian architect Giacomo Quarenghi drew up plans for this market in 1790, and the work was supervised by Moscow architects Semen Karin and Ivan Selekhov. The Old Merchants' Chambers are currently being restored. Beyond the Church of St. Maxim are the 17th-century Monastery of the Sign and the Palace of the Romanov Boyars.

At the end of ulitsa Varvarka is the Church of St. George, built in 1657–8 by merchants from Pskov, a town known for its architects *(see p44).*

**The five domes of the Church of St. George on ulitsa Varvarka**

To the right, on Kitaygorodskiy proezd, is one of the few sections of the old city walls to survive. At the end of this street, beside the Moskva river, is the charming mid-16th-century Church of the Conception of St. Anna.

# Old English Court ❷

Старый английский двор

*Staryy angliyskiy dvor*

Ulitsa Varvarka 4a. **Map** 7 B1. **(** 298 3952. **◯** *10am–6pm Tue, Thu, Sat–Sun, 11am–7pm Wed, Fri.* **M** *Ploshchad Revolyutsii.* 🈯 🚫 ✅ *English.*

IN 1553, while searching the northern coast of Russia for a passage to the east, the English merchant adventurer Richard Chancellor *(see p21)* was shipwrecked. He was taken to Moscow and received by Ivan the Terrible, whose desire to trade with England later led him to propose

marriage to Queen Elizabeth I. On returning to Russia in 1556, Chancellor and his trading mission were given this large property in Zaryade. It was to serve as a storage and trading house and as accommodations for English merchants.

In the mid-17th century, the estate passed into Russian hands, and by the 1900s it had been extensively altered. After the Revolution *(see pp26–9),* the house was restored. It later reopened as a museum during the official visit of Queen Elizabeth II to Russia in 1994.

Inside, an exhibition sheds light on the history of the Old English Court and its role in the development of Anglo-Russian relations. Winding stone staircases lead down to the cellars and the official chamber used for negotiations and functions. The English merchants fitted the traditional Russian stove in this chamber with an open hearth to remind themselves of home.

**Spartan interior of the official chamber in the Old English Court**

# Palace of the Romanov Boyars ❸

Музей-палаты в Зарядье

*Muzey-palaty v Zaryade*

Ulitsa Varvarka 10. **Map** 7 B1. **(** 298 3706. **◯** *10am–5pm Sun. Pre-booked groups only: 10am–5pm Thu–Sat, Mon, 11am–6pm Wed.* **M** *Kitay Gorod.* 🈯 🚫 ✅ *English.*

ONLY THE UPPER stories of this palace can be seen from ulitsa Varvarka. This is largely because the palace is built on a steep slope leading away from the street down toward the Moskva River.

The palace was originally built by the boyar *(see p20)* Nikita Romanov in the 16th century. It was home to the Romanovs until 1613 when

**A view along ulitsa Varkarva, with the Old English Court straight ahead**

Mikhail Romanov *(see p19)* became tsar and the family moved to the Kremlin. The palace has been protected as a museum since 1859.

The main entrance is reached via a courtyard; a double-headed eagle, the Romanov family crest, adorns the archway leading to the courtyard.

The ground and first floors of the palace probably date from the 17th century. In the painted hall, personal effects of the early Romanovs are displayed, including gold dishes, ancient title deeds, ledgers inlaid with precious gems, and the robes of Nikita's eldest son, Patriarch Fyodor Filaret. The rooms have been refurbished in the lavish style of the period, with walls covered in gilt-embossed leather or painted in rich reds, greens, and golds.

In the 16th and 17th centuries even the richest families had to tolerate rather cramped and dim conditions. The portals in the palace are so low that a man of average height has to stoop, and little light is let in by the windows as they are made of mica, a translucent mineral, rather than glass.

In the mid-19th century the light and airy, wooden upper story was added to the building. The main hall on this level has a beautifully carved wooden ceiling. An anteroom has a display of embroidery.

The vaulted cellars are the least interesting rooms of the museum and contain an odd mix of baskets, trunks, and kitchen equipment.

Gilded iconostasis in the Church of the Trinity in Nikitniki

Ornate dining room in the Palace of the Romanov Boyars

## Church of the Trinity in Nikitniki ❹

Церковь Троицы в Никитниках

*Tserkov Troitsy v Nikitnikakh*

Nikitnikov pereulok 3. **Map** 7 C1.
Ⓜ *Kitay Gorod.* ⬤ *to public.*

LIKE THE CHURCHES on ulitsa Varvarka, this marvelous church is dwarfed by monstrous post-war buildings that were formerly Communist Party offices. When it was founded in 1635 by the wealthy merchant, Grigoriy Nikitnikov, the church dominated the local skyline. It is at present closed while it is being restored.

Carvings on the porch of the Church of the Trinity in Nikitniki

The church has five green domes, a profusion of decoration and painted tiles, and tiers of *kokoshniki* gables *(see p44)*. The equally elaborate tent-roofed bell tower, which is linked to the main building by an enclosed gallery, was added shortly after the church was finished.

The Church of the Trinity is famous for its frescoes, which were finished in 1656, shortly after Nikitnikov died from the plague. They portray scenes from the Gospels, such as *The Parable of the Rich Man*, in direct, emotional terms.

Among the artists who made an important contribution to the church's decoration was the great fresco and icon painter Semen Ushakov. He painted a number of the frescoes and several of the panels in the splendid gilded iconostasis. Among his works is the *Annunciation of the Virgin*, which can be seen to the left of the Royal Gate *(see p61)* on the iconostasis. Members of the Nikitnikov family are commemorated in the frescoes in the corner Chapel of St. Nikita the Martyr.

Semen Ushakov was a parishioner, and his house is around the corner from the church on Ipatevskiy pereulok. It is an unremarkable 17th-century, red-brick building.

**Striking 19th-century commercial buildings lining ulitsa Ilinka**

## Ulitsa Ilinka ❺
Улица Ильинка
*Ulitsa Ilinka*

**Map** 7 B1. Ⓜ *Kitay Gorod.*

IN THE 19TH CENTURY this narrow but majestic street was the commercial heart of Kitay Gorod and home to numerous banks and trading offices. Their richly decorated façades were intended to impress and are still the chief pleasure of a stroll along the street. Today, ulitsa Ilinka is once more the location of a number of commercial and financial institutions, including the Ministry of Finance.

The name Ilinka refers to the former Ilinskiy Monastery, of which no traces now remain. The monastery once stood where part of the 17th-century Church of St. Elijah can now be seen, at No. 3. Farther along, at No. 6, on the corner of Birzhevaya ploshchad, is a peach-colored building with a Neo-Classical portico, which at present houses the Russian Chamber of Industry and Commerce. Originally these were the premises of Moscow's Stock Exchange, which was re-built by Aleksandr Kamenskiy in 1873–5, having first opened in 1836. At that time many of Moscow's merchants still wore long patriarchal beards and the traditional kaftan, and were used to dealing with one another in the street. They at first refused to enter the new Stock Exchange and, in the end, were coralled into the building by the police.

Across the street from this building is the former Trinity Sergius Hostel, which was the city mission of the Trinity Monastery of St. Sergius *(see pp156–9)*. Now part of the Russian Supreme Court, it was built by Pavel Skomoroshenko in 1876 and is a restrained example of the Russian-Revival style *(see p45)*.

A building that formerly served as offices for the Soviet government stands at the corner of ulitsa Ilinka and Bolshoy Cherkasskiy pereulok. Uncompromisingly plain, with glazed tiles and rows of narrowly spaced windows, it was designed by Vladimir Mayat in the 1920s.

## Monastery of the Epiphany ❻
Богоявленский монастырь
*Bogoyavlenskiy monastyr*

Bogoyavlenskiy pereulok 2, stroenie 4.
**Map** 3 A5. Ⓒ *298 3771.*
Ⓜ *Ploshchad Revolyutsii.*
Ⓞ *8am–8pm daily.* ⦰

FOUNDED BY Prince Daniil, father of Grand Prince Ivan I *(see p18)* in 1296, the Monastery of the Epiphany is Moscow's second oldest monastery, after the Danilovskiy Monastery *(see pp136–7)*. It was built at what was at that time the edge of the city, be-yond the merchants' quarters.

The oldest building to sur-vive is the cathedral. This is an addition to the original medi-eval complex and dates from 1693–6. The building is distin-guished by its massive but

refined tower, a masterpiece of Moscow Baroque *(see p44)*. Among the other surviving features are a bishop's palace, a few 18th-century monastic cells, and some trading rows.

## Nikolskaya Ulitsa ❼
Никольская улица
*Nikolskaya ulitsa*

**Map** 3 A5.
Ⓜ *Lubyanka, Ploshchad Revolyutsii.*

BY THE END of the 12th century, this street, which is named after the Kremlin's Nicholas's Tower *(see p66)*, had been settled by merchants and traders. Trading stalls and shops remained a feature of the street until the Revolution. Following a dowdy period under communism, Nikolskaya ulitsa has recently moved up-scale with the arrival of several expensive clothing stores and jewelers.

Through the courtyard at No. 7 is a gateway leading into the Zaikonospasskiy Monas-tery, which was founded in the 15th century or earlier. The name means Savior Beyond the Icons and recalls the time when there was a brisk trade in icons here. The monastery church, with its dilapidated red brick tower and spire, dates from the 17th century. It is now open again for worship. From 1687–1814 the monastery also housed Moscow's first institute of higher education, referred

**Gothic-style facade of the Synodal Printing House, Nikolskaya ulitsa**

**Kazan Cathedral, a faithful 1990s reconstruction of the original cathedral**

## Kazan Cathedral 🔢

Казанский собор
*Kazanskiy sobor*

Nikolskaya ulitsa 3. **Map** 3 A5.
Ⓜ *Okhotnyy Ryad.* ♿

THIS DIMINUTIVE CATHEDRAL is a replica of an original demolished in 1936. Its predecessor was consecrated in 1637 and housed the Icon of the Kazan Virgin. The icon was revered as it had accompanied Prince Dmitriy Pozharskiy during his victorious campaign against the invading Poles 25 years earlier (*see p108*).

Detailed plans and photographs, preserved by architect Pyotr Baranovskiy, assisted reconstruction of the cathedral in 1990–93 (*see p44*). It was reconsecrated by Patriarch Aleksey II in the presence of President Boris Yeltsin and the mayor of Moscow, Yuriy Luzhkov. The Icon of the Kazan Virgin in the cathedral is a copy, the original having been removed to St. Petersburg in the early 19th century.

## Resurrection Gate 🔢

Воскресенские ворота
*Voskresenskie vorota*

Krasnaya ploshchad.
**Map** 3 A5. Ⓜ *Okhotnyy Ryad, Ploshchad Revolyutsii.*

REBUILT IN 1995 (*see p44*), this gateway, with its twin red towers topped by green tent spires, is an exact copy of the original completed on this site in 1680. The first gateway was demolished in 1931. Note the mosaic icons on the gate, one of which depicts Moscow's patron saint, St. George, slaying the dragon.

Within the gateway is the equally colorful Chapel of the Iverian Virgin, originally built in the late 18th century to house an icon. Whenever the tsar came to Moscow, he would visit this shrine before entering the Kremlin (*see pp52–67*). Visitors should try to see the gate at night, when it is impressively lit up.

to laboriously as the Slavic Greek Latin Academy. Among its pupils was the famous polymath and future founder of Moscow University, Mikhail Lomonosov (*see p94*).

At No. 15 are the fanciful Gothic-style spires of the Synodal Printing House. The pale blue building, with a lion and unicorn sculpted over its central window, contrasting with an incongruous hammer and sickle above, dates from 1810–14. The courtyard is enhanced by a colorful chequered roof and walls of blue and white tiles. In the chambers previously on this site Ivan Fyodorov produced Russia's first printed book, *The Acts of the Apostles*, in 1564.

Next door, in the courtyard of No. 17, is the Slavyanskiy Bazaar restaurant, which opened in 1870. Among its former patrons is Anton Chekhov (*see p96*). This restaurant is also where the theater directors Konstantin Stanislavskiy and Vladimir Nemirovich-Danchenko began a meeting which concluded with the founding of the Moscow Arts Theatre (*see p92*). Following a fire in 1994, the restaurant was closed for repair, but there are plans to reopen it when this has been completed.

On the opposite side of the road is a building that used to house the Chizhevskoe Inn, a combined inn and warehouse for traders passing through Kitay Gorod. In the courtyard behind it is the 17th-century Church of the Assumption.

**Floodlit Resurrection Gate, inside which is the Chapel of the Iverian Virgin**

The vast expanse of Red Square, with the Historical Museum at the far end

**RED SQUARE**

RESURRECTION GATE

HISTORICAL MUSEUM

KAZAN CATHEDRAL

GUM

RED SQUARE

KREMLIN WALL

LENIN MAUSOLEUM

LOBNOE MESTO

SAVIOUR'S GATE

ST BASIL'S CATHEDRAL

# Red Square ⑩

Красная площадь

*Krasnaya ploshchad*

**Map** 7 B1. **M** *Ploshchad Revolyutsii, Okhotnyy Ryad.* **Historical Museum** 📞 292 4012. 🕐 11am–7pm Wed–Mon 🏛 🚻 📷

Toward the end of the 15th century, Ivan III *(see p18)* gave orders for houses in front of the Kremlin to be cleared to make way for this square. It originally served as a market called the *torg*, but the wooden stalls burned down so often that the area later became popularly known as Fire Square. The current name dates from the 17th century and is derived from the Russian word *krasnyy*, which originally meant "beautiful" but later came to denote "red". The association between the color red and Communism is purely coincidental.

Red Square, which is approximately 500 m (1,600 ft) in length, was also the setting for public announcements and executions. At its southern end, in front of St. Basil's Cathedral *(see pp108–9)*, there is a small circular dais. Called Lobnoe Mesto, this is the platform from which the tsars and patriarchs would address the people. In 1606 the first "False Dmitry" *(see p19)*, an usurper of the throne, was mutilated and killed by a hostile crowd in Red Square. His body was finally left at Lobnoe Mesto.

Six years later, a second pretender to the throne, who like the first "False Dmitry" was backed by Poland, took

power. He was expelled from the Kremlin by an army led by the Russian heroes Dmitriy Pozharskiy and Kuzma Minin, who proclaimed Russia's deliverance from Lobnoe Mesto. In 1818, a statue was erected in their honor *(see p108)*. This now stands in front of St. Basil's.

Red Square has also long been a stage for pageants and processions. Before the Revolution *(see pp26–9)*, the patriarch would ride an ass through Savior's Gate *(see p66)* to St. Basil's each Palm Sunday to commemorate Christ's entry into Jerusalem.

Lobnoe Mesto, the platform from which the tsar spoke

Religious processions were abolished in the Communist era. Military parades took their place and were staged each year on May Day and on the anniversary of the Revolution. Rows of grim-faced Soviet leaders observed them from

outside the Lenin Mausoleum. They, in turn, would be closely studied by professional kremlinologists trying to work out the current pecking order.

Today the square is used for a variety of cultural events, concerts, fireworks displays, and other public occasions.

The red-brick building facing St. Basil's Cathedral was erected by Vladimir Sherwood in 1883 in the Russian-Revival style *(see p45)*. It houses the Historical Museum, only part of which is currently open. The museum boasts over four million exhibits covering the rise and expansion of the Russian state.

In front of the museum's façade on Manezhnaya ploshchad is a statue by Vyacheslav Klykov of one of the heroes of World War II *(see p27)*, Marshal Georgiy Zhukov. This statue of him was unveiled in 1995 to mark the 50th anniversary of the end of World War II.

Aleksey Shchusev's Lenin Mausoleum, with the Kremlin Wall behind

# Lenin Mausoleum ⓫
Мавзолей ВИ Ленина
*Mavzoley VI Lenina*

Krasnaya ploshchad. **Map** 7 A1.
**[** 923 5527. **M** *Ploshchad
Revolyutsii, Okhotnyy Ryad.* ☐ *10am–
1pm Tue–Thu, Sat–Sun.* **∅**

FOLLOWING LENIN'S DEATH in 1924, and against his wishes, it was decided to preserve the former Soviet leader's body for posterity. The body was embalmed and placed in a temporary wooden mausoleum in Red Square. Once it became clear that the embalming process had worked, Aleksey Shchusev *(see p45)* designed the current mausoleum of a pyramid of cubes cut from red granite and black labradorite.

Paying one's respects to Lenin's wan and whiskered mummy was once akin to a religious experience, and lines used to trail all over Red Square. In 1993, however, the goose-stepping guard of honor was replaced by a lone militiaman, and now the mausoleum attracts mostly tourists. There are rumors that Lenin will soon be moved elsewhere or buried.

Behind the mausoleum at the foot of the Kremlin Wall are the graves of other famous communists. They include Lenin's successors, Joseph Stalin (at one time laid alongside Lenin in the Mausoleum), Leonid Brezhnev, and Yuriy Andropov. Lenin's wife and sister are also buried here, as are the first man in space, Yuriy Gagarin, writer Maxim Gorky, and American John Reed. The latter was honored as the author of *Ten Days that Shook the World*, an account of the October Revolution.

The glass-roofed interior of Russia's largest department store, GUM

# GUM ⓬
ГУМ
*GUM*

Krasnaya ploshchad 3. **Map** 7 B1. **[**
921 5763. **M** *Ploshchad Revolyutsii,
Okhotnyy Ryad.* ☐ *8am–
8pm Mon–Sat, 11am–7pm Sun.* **[**

BEFORE THE REVOLUTION, this building was known as the Upper Trading Rows after the covered market that used to stand on the site. In fact, lines of stalls used to run all the way from here to the Moskva river. GUM has three separate arcades that are still called "lines." The store's name, Gosudarstvennyy universalnyy magazin, dates from its nationalization in 1921.

The building was designed by Aleksandr Pomerantsev in 1889–93 in the then fashionable Russian-Revival style. Its archways, wrought-iron railings, and stuccoed galleries inside are especially impressive when sunlight streams through the glass roof.

There were once more than 1,000 shops here, selling goods ranging from furs and silks to humble candles. For a period, however, during the rule of Stalin *(see p27)*, GUM's shops were requisitioned as offices. Nowadays, Western firms like Benetton, Estée Lauder, and Christian Dior dominate the prestigious ground floor along with a variety of Western-style cafés and restaurants.

## EMBALMING LENIN

"Do not raise monuments to him, or palaces to his name, do not organize pompous ceremonies in his memory." Such were the words of Lenin's widow, Krupskaya. Despite this, Lenin's body was embalmed by two professors and, after a delay to see if the process had worked, put on display. A laboratory is dedicated to preserving the body, which needs regular applications of special fluids. Rumors that parts or all of the body have been replaced with wax substitutes are vigorously denied.

# St. Basil's Cathedral ⑬
Собор Василия Блаженного
*Sobor Vasiliya Blazhennovo*

**Detail, Chapel of the Entry of Christ into Jerusalem**

COMMISSIONED BY Ivan the Terrible *(see p18)* to celebrate the capture of the Mongol stronghold of Kazan in 1552, St. Basil's Cathedral was completed in 1561. It is reputed to have been designed by the architect Postnik Yakovlev. According to legend, Ivan was so amazed at the beauty of his work that he had him blinded so that he would never be able to design anything as exquisite again. The church was officially called the Cathedral of the Intercession because the final siege of Kazan began on the Feast of the Intercession of the Virgin. However, it is usually known as St. Basil's after the "holy fool" Basil the Blessed, whose remains are interred within. The cathedral's design, which was inspired by traditional Russian timber architecture, is a riot of gables, tent roofs, and twisting onion domes.

**Bell tower**

**Chapel of the Trinity**

**★ Domes**

*Following a fire in 1583, the original helmet-shaped cupolas were replaced by ribbed or faceted onion domes. It is only since 1670 that the domes have been painted many colors; at one time St. Basil's was white with golden domes.*

**Chapel of St. Cyprian**

*This is one of eight main chapels commemorating the campaigns of Ivan the Terrible against the town of Kazan, to the east of Moscow. It is dedicated to St. Cyprian, whose feast is on October 2, the day after the last attack.*

## MININ AND POZHARSKIY

A bronze statue by Ivan Martos depicts two heroes from the Time of Troubles *(see p19)*, the butcher Kuzma Minin and Prince Dmitriy Pozharskiy. They raised a volunteer force to fight the invading Poles and in 1612 led their army to victory when they drove the Poles out of the Kremlin. The statue was erected in 1818, in the triumphal afterglow of the Napoleonic Wars.

Originally placed in the center of Red Square facing the Kremlin, it was moved to its present site in front of St. Basil's during the Soviet era.

**Monument to Minin and Prince Pozharskiy**

**The Chapel of St. Basil**, the ninth chapel to be added to the cathedral, was built in 1588 to house the remains of the "holy fool," Basil the Blessed.

**Chapel of the Three Patriarchs**

**The entrance** to the cathedral contains an exhibition on its history, and armor and weapons dating from the time of Ivan the Terrible.

**Tent roof on the Central Chapel**

**Chapel of St. Nicholas**

**Central Chapel of the Intercession**
*Light floods in through the windows of the tent-roofed central church, which soars to a height of 61 m (200 ft).*

★ **Main Iconostasis**
*The Baroque-style iconostasis in the Central Chapel of the Intercession dates from the 19th century. However, some of the icons contained in it were painted much earlier.*

**Chapel of St. Varlaam of Khutynskiy**

**Tiered gables**

**VISITORS' CHECKLIST**

Krasnaya ploshchad 2. **Map** 7
B1. ☎ 298 3304. ◯ *May–Nov:*
*10am–5pm Wed–Mon (Dec–Apr:*
*10am–4pm).* Ⓜ *Okhotnyy Ryad,*
*Ploschad Revolyutsii.* 🚌 *25.*
🚎 *37.* 📷 🚫 ☑ *English.*
✝ *religious holidays.*

**STAR FEATURES**

★ **Domes**

★ **Gallery**

★ **Main Iconostasis**

**The Chapel of the Entry of Christ into Jerusalem** was used as a ceremonial entrance during the annual Palm Sunday procession. On this day the patriarch rode from the Kremlin to St. Basil's Cathedral on a horse dressed up to look like a donkey.

★ **Gallery**
*Running around the outside of the Central Chapel, the gallery connects it to the other eight chapels. It was roofed over at the end of the 17th century, and the walls and ceilings were decorated with floral tiles in the late 18th century.*

**Chapel of Bishop Gregory**

# Ivanovskaya Hill ⓮

Ивановская горка
*Ivanovskaya gorka*

**Map** 3 C5. Ⓜ *Kitay Gorod.*

THIS HILLY AREA takes its name from the Ivanovskiy Convent on the corner of ulitsa Zabelina and Malyy Ivanovskiy pereulok. The convent's rather neglected remains can be seen behind a twin-towered gateway and high encircling walls.

Yelena Glinska, mother of Ivan the Terrible *(see p18)*, founded the convent in 1533 as a gesture of thanks for the birth of her son. Later, however, it doubled as a prison for many years – its most famous inmate was Avgusta Tarakanova, the illegitimate daughter of Tsarina Elizabeth *(see p22)* and Count Aleksey Razumovskiy. She was educated abroad before being brought to Russia in 1785 and put into the convent under an assumed name. She spent the rest of her life here as a solitary nun, forbidden to receive any visitors except for the mother superior. She died in 1810.

Across the road is the Church of St. Vladimir in the Old Gardens. It was built in 1514 by Italian architect Aleviz Novyy and altered at the end of the 17th century. Its name refers to the tsar's orchards, which used to occupy the slopes of the hill.

One of the pleasures of this area is exploring its quiet backstreets. At the end of Malyy Ivanovskiy pereulok, which runs down from the Ivanovskiy Convent, is Podkolokolnyy pereulok (Lane Beneath the Bells). This street is dominated by the Church of St. Nicholas the Wonder-worker, which dates from the mid-17th century and is recognizable by its red bell tower. Perhaps the most impressive church in the area is SS. Peter and Paul on Petropavlovskiy pereulok. It was built in 1700 and contains an icon of the Bogolyubovskaya Virgin, which used to hang in a chapel near the gate to the city at the end of ulitsa Varvarka *(see p102)*.

To the north, at No. 10 Kolpachiy pereulok, is the 17th-century mansion that reputedly belonged to the Ukrainian chief Ivan Mazepa. He fled to Turkish-controlled Moldova in 1709, after betraying Peter the Great *(see p22)* to the Swedes and then being defeated by him. Tchaikovsky set the story to music in his opera *Mazepa*. Kokhlovskiy pereulok may also have a Ukrainian link; Ukrainians used to be known as *khokhly* because of the tufts of hair they grew at the back of their shaved heads (*khokhly* means tufted in Russian). The

most notable building standing on ulitsa Maroseyka is the blue and white mansion at No. 17. This is now the Belarussian embassy.

**Russian space program exhibit at the Polytechnical Museum**

# Polytechnical Museum ⓯

Политехнический музей
*Politekhnicheskiy muzey*

Novaya ploshchad 3/4. **Map** 3 B5.
█ 923 4287. ☐ 10am–6pm
Tue–Sun. Ⓜ *Kitay Gorod.* ▓ 🗗
🗗 *English (book in advance).*

DESIGNED BY architect Ippolit Monighetti, the central section of this museum was built in 1877 and is a superb example of Russian-Revival architecture *(see p45)*, which was very popular in the late 19th century. The north and south wings were added in 1896 and 1907 respectively.

The items on display were originally assembled for an exhibition staged in the Alexander Gardens *(see p67)* in 1872. This marked the 200th anniversary of the birth of Peter the Great, himself an enthusiastic amateur scientist.

The museum is today a popular field trip for groups of Russian schoolchildren. Its original collection has been expanded to trace the development of Russian science and technology during the 19th and 20th centuries. Exhibits range from early clocks and cameras to cars and space capsules. Every two hours there are demonstrations of devices such as robots, working models, and sound equipment.

**A typically quiet, gently sloping backstreet on Ivanovskaya Hill**

## History of Moscow Museum 🔟

Музей истории города Москвы

*Muzey istorii goroda Moskvy*

Novaya ploshchad 12. **Map** 3 B5.
📞 *924 8490.* ⭕ *10am–6pm Tue, Thu, Sat–Sun; 11am–7pm Wed, Fri.*
Ⓜ *Lubyanka.* 🖼 💯 ☑

THIS MUSEUM was founded in 1896 and is housed in the 19th-century church of St. John the Divine Under the Elm. There has been some speculation about finding larger premises, but this has yet to be decided upon.

Only a fraction of the one million items in the collection can be displayed at any time. These include Iron and Bronze Age artifacts, colossal timbers from a medieval log cabin, unearthed during the building of the Palace of Congresses *(see p56)* in the Kremlin, and a growing treasure trove of jewelry, toys, and pottery. There are also priceless early maps, rare illuminated books, paintings, glass, ceramics, and scale models of the Kremlin and other historic buildings.

**Wooden model of the Kremlin in the History of Moscow Museum**

## Mayakovsky Museum 🔟

Музей-квартира ВВ Маяковского

*Muzey-kvartira VV Mayakovskovo*

Lubyanskiy proezd 3/6. **Map** 3 B5.
📞 *921 9387.* ⭕ *10am–6pm Fri–Tue, 1–9pm Thu.* Ⓜ *Lubyanka.*
🖼 💯 ☑

VLADIMIR MAYAKOVSKY, poet, iconoclast, exhibitionist, and consummate self-promoter, was above all a revolutionary. In his short but eventful life his poetry, plays, screenplays,

**The striking Constructivist entrance to the Mayakovsky Museum**

and poster art gave a strident voice to the Revolution and its vision of modernity. The propaganda posters he designed with Aleksandr Rodchenko are a prominent feature of the museum.

By nature, Mayakovsky was both provocative and extraordinary,

**Room designed to symbolize Mayakovsky's poetic origins**

and this is reflected in this apparently anarchic museum. Huge frameworks of metal bars, designed in the Constructivist style influential in the 1920s, lean at angles and provide a backdrop for the other exhibits. Mayakovsky's artworks and belongings are intermingled: chairs, old boots, typewriters, painted cannonballs, large posters, and photomontages, cracked mirrors, sewing machines, and manuscripts.

Mayakovsky actually lived in this building from 1919 until his death in 1930: a single room on the fourth floor has been furnished to look as it would have when he moved in. While living in this house, Mayakovsky continued his long-running love affair with Lilya Brik, the wife of his friend Osip Brik. This was also the period in which he wrote his best-known plays, the caustic satires *The Bed Bug* and *Bath House*.

The last part of the exhibition deals with Mayakovsky's suicide at the age of 37. On display are two death masks, one black and one white. After his death, Stalin *(see p27)* praised Mayakovsky as the most talented of Soviet poets and continued to use his work for propaganda purposes.

### VLADIMIR MAYAKOVSKY

Born in Georgia in 1893, Mayakovsky was brought up in Moscow, where he became involved in the revolutionary movement at the tender age of 14. Earning his revolutionary honors by being arrested three times in the space of two years, he was also drawn to the avant-garde and in 1912 became a founder of the Futurist movement by contributing to its manifesto, *A Slap in the Face for Public Taste*. Mayakovsky wholeheartedly endorsed the Revolution *(see p26–9)*, becoming one of its most effective propagandists, but became increasingly disillusioned with the rigid attitudes of Soviet society in the 1920s; this may have contributed to his suicide in 1930.

## Lubyanka Square ⓲
Лубянская площадь
*Lubyanskaya ploshchad*

**Map** 3 B5. Ⓜ *Lubyanka.*

SYNONYMOUS WITH terror and the secret police, the name Lubyanka struck fear into the hearts of generations of Soviet citizens. In 1918, the Cheka (the forerunners of the KGB), led by the hated "Iron" Feliks Dzerzhinskiy, took over what had been the Rossiya Insurance Offices at the northern end of the square.

In the 1930s the building was extended and the enormous, underground Lubyanka Prison added, where the KGB interrogated, tortured, imprisoned, and killed hundreds of thousands of people. By 1947 the incredible numbers of those accused in the course of Stalin's rule *(see p27)* led to the building of an additional wing, designed by Aleksey Shchusev *(see p45)*. Despite numerous changes of name (and claims of a change of ethics), the Russian intelligence services still occupy the building.

**Feliks Dzerzhinskiy
(1877–1926)**

A statue of Dzerzhinskiy used to stand in the center of Lubyanka square. It was unceremoniously toppled in front of a cheering crowd, following the unsuccessful coup against President Gorbachev in 1991 *(see p31)*. The statue can now be seen in the Graveyard of Fallen Monuments *(see p135)*.

With their customary lack of irony, the Soviet authorities built Russia's largest toy store, Detskiy Mir (Children's World) *(see p185)*, directly opposite the KGB headquarters in 1957.

## Chistoprudnyy Bulvar ⓳
Чистопрудный бульвар
*Chistoprudnyy bulvar*

**Map** 3 C4. Ⓜ *Chistye Prudy.*

THIS ROAD is part of the historic Boulevard Ring, which was laid out along the line of the old Belyy Gorod (White City) wall after the great fire of 1812 *(see p24)*. There are several fine houses located along Chistoprudnyy bulvar. At No. 19a is the elegant, Classical-style portico of the Sovremennik Theater, which was built as a movie house by Roman Klein in 1914. Just beyond is the mansion where Sergey Eisenstein, director of *October* and *Battleship Potemkin*, lived from 1920–34.

Chistoprudnyy bulvar is part of the area that used to be known as Myasnitskaya after the butchers *(myasniki)* who worked here in the 17th century. The *myasniki* are still commemorated in the name of Myasnitskaya ulitsa, which runs from Lubyanka Square to Chistoprudnyy bulvar.

Between the lanes of Chistoprudnyy bulvar is a large pond. It was created as

**Detail of the fine stone carvings on Menshikov's Tower**

a place for the butchers to dump innards and waste products but, by 1703, the stench and risk of disease were so bad that the pond was cleaned and renamed Chistye prudy (Clean Pond).

The beautiful, pale blue mansion standing around the corner, at No. 22 ulitsa Pokrovka, was built in 1766. In the 1920s it housed an industrial school. The school's alumni include Stalin's wife, Nadezhda, and Soviet leader Nikita Khrushchev *(see p30)*.

## Menshikov's Tower ⓴
Меньшикова башня
*Menshikova bashnya*

Arkhangelskiy pereulok 15.
**Map** 3 C4. Ⓜ *Turgenevskaya, Chistye Prudy.* ♿ 📷

THIS CHURCH was constructed on the orders of Prince Alexandr Menshikov, Peter the Great's advisor and favorite. With Peter the Great's backing, Menshikov rose from the position of lowly pie-seller to be one of most powerful and wealthy men in Russia. It was typical of the flamboyant Menshikov that, when he commissioned the church from Ivan Zarudnyy in 1701, he instructed the architect to make it just a little taller than the Ivan the Great Bell Tower *(see p57)*, until then the tallest structure in all of Russia.

Specialist stonemasons from Yaroslavl and Kostroma and a variety of Italian sculptors worked on the church, accounting for the beauty of the stone carvings and stuccoed festoons. The wooden spire was capped by a gilded angel and contained an expensive English clock, which chimed on the quarter-hour.

**The infamous former headquarters of the KGB on Lubyanka Square**

However, pious Muscovites remained unimpressed by the display of wealth, and when the tower was destroyed by lightning in 1723, many saw in it the hand of God. The tower was rebuilt without the spire in 1773–80. The church was one of the few to remain open during the Soviet era, and much of its interior decoration has survived.

Next to the tower is the small Church of St. Fyodor Stratilit, which was heated in winter for the benefit of the parishioners. It was built in 1806, probably by Ivan Yegotov.

The waiting area inside the luxurious Sandunovskiy Baths

## Perlov Tea House ㉑

Чай-кофе магазин
*Chay-kofe magazin*

Myasnitskaya ulitsa 19. **Map** 3 B4.
925 4656. 8am–1pm,
2pm–8pm Mon–Sat. Chistye
Prudy, Turgenevskaya.

THIS BUILDING WAS originally designed by Roman Klein in 1890 for the tea merchant Sergey Perlov. Five years later Perlov heard that the official representative of the Chinese emperor would be visiting Moscow. He hastily commissioned Karl Gippius to redesign the shop in the hope of receiving him. The façade is a fanciful vision of the Orient, including serpents, dragons, and pagoda-style details. Inside there are lacquered columns and counters painted with golden dragons. As it

Shelves of tea behind the counter of the elegant Perlov Tea House

turned out, the Chinese official mistakenly visited Perlov's nephew, who was also a tea merchant.

## Convent of the Nativity of the Virgin ㉒

Рождественский монастырь
*Rozhdestvenskiy monastyr*

Ulitsa Rozhdestvenka 20. **Map** 3 A4.
921 3986. 8am–3pm, 5pm–8pm daily. Kuznetskiy Most.

CONVERTED to provide housing in Soviet times, this small cluster of buildings was neglected until 1991, when it was returned to the Russian Orthodox Church.

Founded in 1386 by Princess Maria Serpukhovskiy, daughter-in-law of Ivan I *(see p18)*, the convent was one of a ring of fortified monasteries constructed around Moscow.

The beautifully proportioned cathedral, commissioned between 1501–5 by Tsar Ivan III *(see p18)*, has tiers of *kokoshniki* gables *(see p44)* surmounted by a single cupola.

The small Church of St. John of Zlatoust with five domes, has also survived, along with a short section of the original brick ramparts. The yellow, tiered bell tower was designed by Nikolay Kozlovskiy in 1835.

The bell tower of the
**Convent of the Nativity
of the Virgin**

## Sandunovskiy Baths ㉓

Сандуновские бани
*Sandunovskie bani*

Neglinnaya ulitsa 14, stroenie 4–7.
**Map** 3 A4. 925 4631. 8am–10pm Wed–Mon (last adm 8pm).
Kuznetskiy Most.

THE ORIGINAL Sandunovskiy Baths were built for actor Sila Sandunov in 1808. In 1895 they were replaced by this building designed by Boris Freidenberg and with a decorative Beaux Arts facade.

The main entrance is through an ornate archway, decorated with sculptures of nymphs on horseback, emerging from the sea and using triton shells as trumpets.

However, it is the sumptuous interiors, decorated in a flamboyant mix of Baroque, Gothic, and Moorish styles, that make the baths famous. The Alhambra Palace in Spain was one of the sources of inspiration for the ornate decoration. The baths can accommodate up to 2,000 customers a day. The best, most expensive, rooms are located off a series of narrow alleys on the first floor. Here patrons can still buy birch twigs to beat themselves with, an essential part of a Russian steam bath.

# ZAMOSKVORECHE

FIRST SETTLED in the 13th century, Zamoskvoreche (literally "beyond the Moscow River") acted as an outpost against the Mongols. Its main road, Bolshaya Ordynka, was the route to the *Orda*, or Golden Horde, the Mongols' headquarters on the Volga River. Later, under Ivan the Terrible, the Streltsy (royal guard) was stationed here. Artisans serving the court moved in, living in areas according to their trades, each of which sponsored a church. These historic churches, now in varying states of repair, and the fact that the area was almost untouched by the replanning of the 1930s, give it a more old-fashioned atmosphere than the center, which is dominated by massive Soviet architecture. In the 19th century wealthy merchants settled here, many of whom, such as Aleksey Bakhrushin and Pavel Tretyakov, were patrons of the arts. The Tretyakov Gallery is the nation's most important collection of Russian art.

**Icon at the Convent of SS Martha and Mary**

## SIGHTS AT A GLANCE

**Churches and Convents**
Church of the Consolation
of All Sorrows **4**
Church of the Resurrection
in Kadashi **2**
Church of St. Clement **5**
Church of St. Nicholas
in Pyzhy **6**
Convent of SS. Martha
and Mary **7**

**Museums and Galleries**
Bakhrushin Theater
Museum **9**
*Tretyakov Gallery*
*pp118–21* **1**
Tropinin Museum **8**

**Historic Buildings**
Confectionery Shop **3**

**Streets**
Sophia Embankment **10**

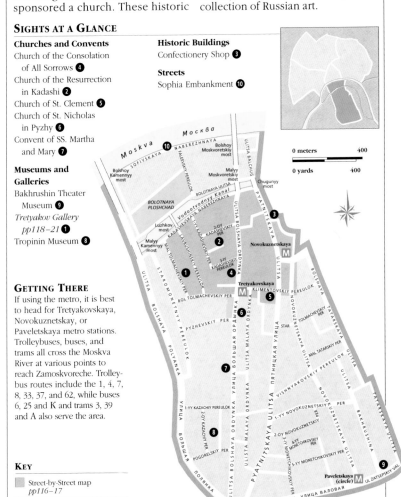

0 meters 400
0 yards 400

## GETTING THERE
If using the metro, it is best to head for Tretyakovskaya, Novokuznetskay, or Paveletskaya metro stations. Trolleybuses, buses, and trams all cross the Moskva River at various points to reach Zamoskvoreche. Trolleybus routes include the 1, 4, 7, 8, 33, 37, and 62, while buses 6, 25 and K and trams 3, 39 and A also serve the area.

## KEY

Street-by-Street map
*pp116–17*

**M** Metro station

◁ **The Vodootvodnyy canal in Zamoskvoreche, blanketed by snow in Moscow's freezing winter**

# Street-by-Street: Around Pyatnitskaya Ulitsa

A<small>N OLD-FASHIONED ATMOSPHERE</small> still prevails in the area around Pyatnitskaya ulitsa. The well-established streets are lined with attractive 19th-century churches and imposing Neo-Classical mansions. The busiest part of the district is the area around Tretyakovskaya metro. The market stalls in front of the station spill over onto Klimentovskiy pereulok, and nearby Pyatnitskaya ulitsa is the main shopping street. A short walk to the west is the stunning Tretyakov Gallery. To the north, the area is bordered by the Vodootvodnyy Canal, which was built in 1783–6 to prevent the regular spring flooding of the Moskva River.

**Vodootvodnyy Canal**

**★ Church of the Resurrection in Kadashi**
*With its tapering bell tower and lavish limestone ornamentation, this magnificent church is a fine example of the style known as Moscow Baroque (see p44)* ❷

**★ Tretyakov Gallery**
*The world's largest collection of Russian art is housed here. Taken down in the Soviet era, the statue of Pavel Tretyakov (see p120) has now been restored to its rightful place in front of the gallery* ❶

**The Demidov House** was built in 1789–91 by a family of well-known industrialists.

**Church of the Consolation of All Sorrows**
*Two of Moscow's best-known architects contributed to this much-loved church. Vasiliy Bazhenov designed the bell tower, and Osip Bove (see p45) the rotunda* ❹

..................................................................

**A Museum of Modern Glass** is housed in the former church of the Monastery of St. John.

**Kremlin**

**The Church of SS. Michael and Fyodor**, dating from the late 17th century, is named after two martyrs killed by Mongols when they refused to renounce Christianity.

**Church of St. John the Baptist**

**Cultural Center of Pan Slavism**

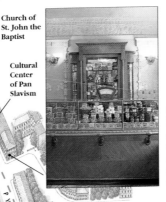

**LOCATOR MAP**
*See Street Finder, map 7*

**Confectionery shop**
*This enticing shop at No. 9 has birchwood counters, brass fittings, and stucco decoration. It looks much as it did when it first opened in the early 1900s* ❸

**PYATNITSKAYA ULITSA**

**Novokuznetskaya**

**Church of St. Clement**
*Building began on this splendid Baroque church in 1720 and continued in phases over the next few decades: in 1756–8 a rectory and belfry were added. The church has four black, star-spangled domes and a central golden dome* ❺

**KLIMENTOVSKIY PEREULOK**

**Tretyakovskaya**

**The market** on Klimentovskiy pereulok does a brisk trade in fruit, vegetables, and other basics.

```
0 meters        100
0 yards         100
```

**STAR SIGHTS**

★ **Tretyakov Gallery**

★ **Church of the Resurrection in Kadashi**

**The Dolgov House** has an elaborately decorated Neo-Classical exterior. This fine town house was built in the 1770s for a wealthy merchant named Dolgov, possibly by his son-in-law, Vasiliy Bazhenov *(see p44).*

**KEY**

– – – – Suggested route

# Tretyakov Gallery ❶

Третьяковская галерея
*Tretyakovskaya galereya*

IN 1892 THE MILLIONAIRE MERCHANT and textiles manufacturer Pavel Tretyakov presented his private museum of Russian art to the city of Moscow. His brother Sergey also donated a number of works, and the gallery's collection has been expanding ever since. Today the Tretyakov has the largest and finest collection of Russian art in the world. The building has a striking facade, designed by artist Viktor Vasnetsov, with a bas-relief of St. George and the dragon at its center. A new wing was added to the gallery in 1930. There are currently plans to rehouse some of the early 20th-century works in the New Tretyakov Gallery *(see p135)*.

**Stairs down to ground floor**

**Portraits by Ivan Kramskoy** *(see p120)*

**First floor**

**The Appearance of Christ to the People** is by the 19th-century Romantic artist Aleksandr Ivanov *(see p120)*.

**The Rooks Have Come** *(1871)*
*This bleak winter scene by Aleksey Savrasov contains a message of hope: rooks are taken by Russians as a sign of the coming spring.*

**Portrait of Arseny Tropinin, the Artist's Son** *(c.1818)*
*This portrait was painted by the renowned artist Vasiliy Tropinin. He was a serf for 47 years before gaining his freedom and finding commercial success.*

**Stairs from basement**

**Portraits by Ilya Repin** *(see p120)*

## GALLERY GUIDE

*The gallery has 62 rooms on two main floors. On entering the museum, visitors first descend to the basement ticket office, then head straight up to the first floor. Paintings are hung in chronological order in rooms 1–54; visitors take the stairs back down to the ground floor after viewing room 34. Russian jewelry is housed on the ground floor in room 55, and rooms 56–62 contain icons and jewelery.*

★ **Demon Seated** *(1890)* *This is one of several paintings by Mikhail Vrubel, who adopted a new, strikingly modern style. They are inspired by Mikhail Lermontov's Symbolist poem* The Demon *(see p82), with which Vrubel became obsessed.*

**Over the City** *(1924)*
*This picture, by Marc Chagall, shows the artist and his wife, Bella Rosenfeld, on a flight of freedom. Chagall believed love and freedom to be closely linked.*

**The Morning of the Execution of the Streltsy** is by Vasiliy Surikov, who specialized in using historical subjects to illustrate contemporary social issues.

**Ground floor**

**VISITORS' CHECKLIST**

Lavrushinskiy pereulok 10.
**Map** 7 A3. 951 1362.
Tretyakovskaya. 25. 1, 4, 7, 8, 33, 62. 10am–7:30pm Tue–Sun. English. English.

**★ The Trinity** *(1420s)*
*This beautiful icon was painted by Andrey Rublev (see p61) for the Trinity Monastery of St. Sergius (see pp156–9), where he had been a novice monk. He dedicated it to the monastery's founder, St. Sergius of Radonezh (see p159).*

Stairs from first floor

Stairs down to basement

Exit

Main entrance leading to basement for tickets, information, toilets, and cloakrooms

**Russian jewelry**

**Main Facade**
*The gallery's facade was designed in 1902 by Viktor Vasnetsov. An example of the Russian-Revival style (see p45), it has a frieze inspired by medieval manuscripts.*

**STAR EXHIBITS**

★ **The Trinity** by Rublev

★ **Demon Seated** by Vrubel

**KEY**

- 18th and early 19th centuries
- Second half of the 19th century
- Late 19th and early 20th centuries
- Drawings and watercolors of the 18th–20th centuries
- Icons and jewelry
- Nonexhibition space

# Exploring the Tretyakov Gallery

ALTHOUGH THE GALLERY'S COLLECTION began with the paintings donated by Pavel Tretyakov, it continued to expand after the Revolution as numerous private collections were nationalized by the Soviet regime. There are currently more than 100,000 Russian works in the collection. Paintings from after the Revolution – mainly Socialist-Realist works – are now exhibited in the New Tretyakov Gallery *(see p135)*, while the main gallery displays Russian art ranging from the icons of the medieval period to early 20th-century avant-garde paintings.

**Portrait of Ursula Mnichek by Dmitriy Levitskiy**

## 18TH AND EARLY 19TH CENTURIES

PAINTING IN RUSSIA was exclusively religious in character for over 600 years. However, a profound transformation occurred in the 18th century as secular art from Europe began to influence Russian artists. Portrait painting came into its own with technically accomplished canvases by artists such as Vladimir Borovikovskiy (1757–1825), Fyodor Rokotov (c.1736–1808), and Dmitriy Levitskiy (c.1735–1822), whose charming *Portrait of Ursula Mnichek* is among those in the gallery. The Romantic movement is represented in the collection by such pictures as Vasiliy Tropinin's refined but sentimental portrait of his son and Orest Kiprenskiy's famous *Portrait of the Poet Alexander Pushkin* (1827). Several of Aleksandr Ivanov's (1806–58) historical canvases are also displayed here, including his outstanding painting, *The Appearance of Christ to the People*. Begun in 1837, it took 20 years to finish.

## SECOND HALF OF THE 19TH CENTURY

THE ART OF THIS PERIOD was dominated by Realism. In 1870 a group of artists founded the Association of Traveling Art Exhibitions. Its members, who became known as the Wanderers *(peredvizhniki)*, began to produce "socially useful art" highlighting injustices and inequalities. One of the leaders of the movement was Vasiliy Perov (1834–82) whose satirical *Tea-drinking in Mytishchi* exposes hypocrisy among the clergy. Another Wanderer was Vasiliy Surikov, whose picture of *The Morning of the Execution of the Streltsy* (1881) instils new realism into a dramatic episode of Russian history. Ivan Kramskoy, the head of the group, aimed to portray the moral character of his subjects in paintings such as *Portrait of an Unknown Lady* and *Portrait of Pavel Tretyakov*.

Landscapes were popular subjects for the Wanderers, and the gallery's many examples

include Vasiliy Polenov's *A Moscow Courtyard* (1878) and *The Rooks Have Come* (1871) by Aleksey Savrasov.

A number of works by Ilya Repin (1844–1930), the most versatile of the Wanderers, is on display. They include the enormous canvases *Religious Procession in Kursk Province*, *They Did Not Expect Him*, and *Ivan the Terrible and his Son Ivan on November 16, 1581*, and striking portraits of Repin's friends and contemporaries.

**Portrait of an Unknown Lady**, painted by Ivan Kramskoy in 1883

*Bathing the Red Horse*, painted in 1912 by Kuzma Petrov-Vodkin

## LATE 19TH AND EARLY 20TH CENTURIES

DURING THE 1890s, the social ideals that inspired the Wanderers no longer appealed to a new generation of artists. Instead they rallied behind a call for "art for art's sake."

The innovative artist Mikhail Vrubel (1856–1910) was influenced by the poetry of the Russian Symbolists. Many of his dark, brooding works, such as *Demon Seated*, also reflect his troubled mental state.

French painting had a huge impact on this and subsequent generations of artists. This influence can be seen in the Impressionist work *Paris, Boulevard des Capucines*, painted in 1911 by Konstantin Korovin. The style of Valentin Serov's (1865–1911) early paintings was also close to Impressionism. His *Girl with Peaches (see p47)* is a charming portrait of the daughter of art patron Savva Mamontov.

In the decade leading up to World War I, Moscow was the center of Russia's avant-garde movement, receptive to developments from abroad, such as Cubism and Futurism, as well as taking ideas from indigenous folk art, which inspired Primitivism. Primitivist works feature bold shapes and bright colors. *Staro Basmannaya – Board No. 1* by Vladimir Tatlin (1885–1953) and *Bathing Horses* by Natalya Goncharova

(1881–1962) are among the gallery's works in this style. Kuzma Petrov-Vodkin's (1878–1939) main concern, in paintings such as *Bathing the Red Horse*, was technique.

Freedom of expression was not always possible for artists in Russia, and some, such as Marc Chagall (1887–1985) and Vasily Kandinsky (1866–1944), spent most of their lives abroad. However, a number of their paintings are displayed here, including *Over the City* (1924) by Chagall.

Some early 20th-century works may soon be moved to join the Socialist-Realist art in the New Tretyakov Gallery.

*The Transfiguration* (c.1403), painted by a follower of Theophanes the Greek

## DRAWINGS AND WATERCOLORS

THE GALLERY owns a substantial collection of sketches, lithographs, and watercolors by artists from the 18th–20th centuries, but to avoid the damaging effect of light, only a small proportion are on display at any time.

Among the watercolors are a delightful equestrian portrait by Karl Bryullov (1799–1852) and some preliminary biblical sketches by Aleksandr Ivanov. Landscapes by Isaak Levitan (1861–1900) and Konstantin Korovin contrast with delicate pencil portraits by artists as diverse as Ilya Repin, Valentin Serov, and Natalya Goncharova.

## ICONS AND JEWELRY

A FINE COLLECTION of religious icons dating from the 12th–17th centuries is housed in the Tretyakov. Russian icon painting inherited the dark colors and immobile, otherworldly images of the saints from Byzantine art. One of the most revered icons, the 12th-century Virgin of Vladimir *(see p61)*, originated in Byzantium but was brought to Moscow via Kiev and Vladimir.

However, Russian icon painters lightened their palettes, introducing shades such as yellow ocher, vermilion, and white. A typical example is *The Transfiguration* (c.1403), painted by a follower of Theophanes the Greek *(see p61)*. It shows Christ standing over cowering sinners.

Andrey Rublev's stunning icon *The Trinity* dates from around 1420.

Alongside it are icons by other masters of the Moscow school *(see p61)*, including Dionysius (c.1440 – c.1508).

Also on the ground floor is a room devoted to Russian jewelry from the 13th–20th centuries.

**The bell tower and domes of the Church of the Resurrection in Kadashi**

# Church of the Resurrection in Kadashi ❷

Церковь Воскресения в Кадашах

*Tserkov Voskreseniya v Kadashakh*

2-oy Kadashevskiy pereulok 7. **Map** 7 B3. **M** *Tretyakovskaya.* ● *to public.*

THIS FIVE-DOMED CHURCH is among the most striking examples of Moscow Baroque (*see p44*) and is thought to have been designed by Sergey Turchaninov, favorite architect of Patriarch Nikon (*see pp56–7*). The small group of buildings around it also includes a refectory, and tiered bell tower. It was paid for by a wealthy guild of weavers who had moved into the street by the 17th century. Before that an earlier church stood here, in what was at that time the district of Kadeshevo; hence the name that survives today.

The church was built around 1687, and the slender, tapering bell tower added in the 1690s.

Apart from the five green onion domes, visible from all over the neighborhood, the most notable features are the tiers of lacelike limestone balustrades just below the drums supporting the domes. The church is now an art restoration workshop.

# Confectionery Shop ❸

Кондитерский магазин

*Konditerskiy magazin*

Pyatnitskaya ulitsa 9/28. **Map** 7 B3. **M** *Tretyakovskaya.* ◯ *9am–1pm, 2–7pm Mon–Fri, 9am–1pm, 2–6pm Sat.*

DATING FROM THE early 1900s, the interior of the Confectionery Shop has been almost perfectly preserved. The original owner of this smart shop, the merchant Mikhail Babanin, was determined to impress his customers and left no detail of decoration to chance. The lavender-painted walls and ceiling, supported by round pillars, are decorated with a delicately molded frieze. Gleaming brass handrails and bronze light fittings add to the sense of luxury. The counters and glass-fronted display cases are made of the finest, gleaming birchwood. Those with a sweet tooth will be tempted by the array of chocolates and candy piled high on the counter and shelves.

# Church of the Consolation of All Sorrows ❹

Церковь Богоматери Всех Скорбящих Радость

*Tserkov Bogomateri Vsekh Skorbyashchikh Radost*

Ulitsa Bolshaya Ordynka 20. **Map** 7 B3. **M** *Tretyakovskaya.* ♿

BOTH the Church of the Consolation of All Sorrows and the Neo-Classical yellow mansion opposite belonged to the Dolgovs, a wealthy merchant family. After completion of their house in the 1770s, they commissioned the church from Vasiliy Bazhenov (*see p44*), a relative by marriage. He first built a new belfry and refectory, which are among the few surviving buildings in Moscow by this talented architect, and then replaced the existing medieval church in 1783–91. It was finished by the Kumanins, another merchant family.

That church, however, was destroyed in the great fire of 1812 (*see p24*). Another new one was designed by Osip

**Bowls of colorful candy ranged along the counter of the Confectionery Shop**

Bove *(see p45)*, who was the architect in charge of Moscow's reconstruction after the fire. His Empire-style rotunda and dome, which still survive today, were finished in 1833.

The interior is unusual in an Orthodox church due to its lavish Empire-style colonnade, theatrical iconostasis, and exuberant sculpted angels. On display in the church's left aisle, originally dedicated to the Transfiguration, is the Icon of Our Lady of Consolation of All Sorrows. It is said to have miraculously cured the ailing sister of Patriarch Joachim in the 17th century.

**The Empire-style Church of the Consolation of All Sorrows**

# Church of St. Clement ❺
Церковь Святого Клементия
*Tserkov Svyatovo Klementiya*

Klimentovskiy pereulok 7. **Map** 7 B3. Ⓜ *Tretyakovskaya*. ⬤ *to public*.

T̲HIS IMPOSING, red-painted 18th-century church is now in a sadly decayed state. In 1756–8 the present refectory and belfry were built onto a church dating from the 1720s. This, however, was torn down in the 1760s when a new church was commissioned by the merchant Kuzma Matveev, a wealthy parishoner. The resulting building is an outstanding example of late Moscow Baroque. The design is thought to have been conceived by the Italian architect Pietro Antonio Trezzini, who must have sent his plans from St. Petersburg, since he is not thought ever to have visited

**Baroque domes of the Church of St. Clement, completed in 1774**

Moscow. The building of the church was completed by 1774. It is named after Pope Clement III (1187–91).

The red and white facade is crowned by four black domes with golden stars surrounding a fifth, golden, cupola.

The church has been unsafe to enter for many years and it is unlikely that it will reopen in the near future.

# Church of St. Nicholas in Pyzhy ❻
Церковь Николая в Пыжах
*Tserkov Nikolaya v Pyzhakh*

Ulitsa Bolshaya Ordynka 27a/8. **Map** 7 B3. Ⓜ *Tretyakovskaya*.

S̲MALL CROWNS, as well as the traditional crosses, decorate the silver domes of this splendid church. It was constructed between 1670–72 in the area of the city once inhabited by the Streltsy, the royal guard, who provided the funds for it. Some of these men were later executed by Peter the Great for their role in the 1682 Streltsy Rebellion *(see p22)*. Funds were, in particular, generously lavished on the exterior decoration, which includes remarkable fretted cornices and finely chiseled window frames. The church's slender, tiered bell tower is one of the finest in the city.

The iconostasis contains some original icons as well as copies of more famous ones.

**The remarkably decorated, 17th-century Church of St. Nicholas in Pyzhy**

The Convent of SS. Martha and Mary, founded in 1908 and designed by Aleksey Shchusev

## Convent of SS. Martha and Mary ❼

Марфо-Мариинская обитель

*Marfo-Mariinskaya obitel*

Ulitsa Bolshaya Ordynka 34. **Map** 7 B4.
📞 951 8446. Ⓜ *Tretyakovskaya, Polyanka.* ⏰ *daily.* ♿ 📷

A LOW ARCHWAY leads from the street to this secluded compound, containing what appear at first glance to be medieval buildings. In fact they date from 1908–12 and were designed by Aleksey Shchusev *(see p45)*.

The convent was conceived to house a dispensary, a clinic, a small women's hospital, and a school. It was run by the Order of the Sisters of Charity, which was founded by the Grand Duchess Yelizaveta Fyodorovna, sister-in-law of Tsar Nicholas II. She had turned to charitable work after her husband was assassinated by a terrorist bomb in the troubled year of 1905 *(see p26)*. Yelizaveta also met a violent death: the day after the shooting of Tsar Nicholas II and his family in 1918, the Bolsheviks pushed her down a mine shaft with further members of the royal family.

When designing the Church of the Intercession, the convent's main building, Shchusev carried out considerable research into Russian religious architecture, particularly that of the Pskov and Novgorod schools *(see p44)*. However, it was the Church of the Savior in the Forest in the Kremlin (torn down by Stalin in the 1930s) that he is thought to have taken as the final model for his own church. Shchusev's ingenious design juxtaposed a highly traditional style with Style-Moderne features such as boldly pointed gables, limestone carvings of mythical creatures and Slavonic script on the outer walls.

The artist Mikhail Nesterov was commissioned to design and paint the frescoes in the interior of the church. He also designed the pale gray and white habits of the nuns.

After the Revolution the Order of the Sisters of Charity was suppressed and the church was used as a workshop for restoring icons for a number of years. The nuns have now returned to staff the clinic.

## Tropinin Museum ❽

Музей ВА Тропинина

*Muzey VA Tropinina*

Shchetininskiy pereulok 10. **Map** 7 B4.
📞 953 9750. Ⓜ *Dobryninskaya, Polyanka.* ⏰ *noon–6:30pm Mon, Thu–Fri; 10am–4:30pm Sat–Sun.* 📷 🚫 📷

A HIGHLY TALENTED portrait artist, Vasiliy Tropinin executed a staggering 3,000 paintings in his life. As well as painting figures in high society, he is noted as one of the first Russian artists to depict working people. Works spanning his career are displayed in this attractive museum set in a blue and white Neo-Classical house. The furnishings and ornaments are from Tropinin's time and are mostly in Empire style.

The museum's collection is based on works gathered by Feliks Vishnevskiy (1902–78). Having been a supporter of the Revolution, he was able to collect in the Soviet period when paintings were relatively cheap. In addition to Tropinin's oil portraits, there are works

*Girl in Ukrainian Dress* painted by Vasiliy Tropinin

## VASILIY TROPININ (1776–1857)

Though born a serf in Karpovo near Novgorod, Vasiliy Tropinin's prodigious talent was recognized at an early age. He was sent to the St. Petersburg Academy of Arts in 1798, but was withdrawn by his master and brought back to work as an interior decorator, pastrycook, and footman on his estates. Tropinin and his wife gained their freedom in 1823 and moved to Moscow, where Tropinin became a professional portrait artist. Unlike many other painters of the time, he did not limit himself to painting members of the aristocracy. Instead, his portraits depicted a cross-section of society, from peasants to nobles.

**Some of the Empire-style furnishings in the Tropinin Museum**

by some of his contemporaries, including Orest Kiprenskiy and Dmitriy Levitskiy. Like Tropinin, they were students at the St. Petersburg Academy of Arts. There are also some fine landscapes of 19th-century Moscow. The Tretyakov Gallery *(see pp118–21)* contains more works by these artists.

## Bakhrushin Theater Museum ❾
Театральный музей имени АА Бахрушина
*Teatralnyy muzey imeni AA Bakhrushina*

Ulitsa Bakhrushina 31/12. **Map** 7 C5.
**C** 953 4470. **M** *Paveletskaya.* **O** *noon–7pm Wed–Mon.* 🎦 📷 🎫 *English (book in advance).*

FOUNDED IN 1894 by Aleksey Bakhrushin, a merchant and patron of the arts, this museum contains probably the most important collection of theater memorabilia in Russia. Spread over two floors, the exhibits range from sets and costumes to theater tickets, programs, advertisements, and signed photographs.

The basement is filled with items relating to the career of the great opera singer Fyodor Shalyapin *(see p83).* One of the highlights is a richly brocaded costume he wore for the title role in Modest Mussorgsky's opera *Boris Godunov.*

A display on early Russian theater includes puppets, models of theaters and sets, and paintings and engravings of theatrical entertainments.

Exhibits on 19th-century theater include costumes and sets from the Ballets Russes. This famous company, formed by Sergey Diaghilev in 1909, revolutionized ballet. The sets include some designed by Michel Fokine, the company's inspired choreographer. A pair of ballet

shoes belonging to Vaslaw Nijinsky, one of the principal dancers, is also on display.

The room on 20th-century avant-garde theater includes stage models created for outstanding directors Konstantin Stanislavskiy *(see p93)* and Vsevolod Meyerhold *(see p92).*

**View of the Kremlin from the Sophia Embankment**

## Sophia Embankment ❿
Софийская набережная
*Sofiyskaya naberezhnaya*

**Map** 7 A2. **M** *Kropotkinskaya, Borovitskaya, Novokuznetskaya.*

SITUATED OPPOSITE the Kremlin, on the southern bank of the Moskva River, the Sophia Embankment stretches from the Bolshoy Kamennyy most (Great Stone Bridge) to the Bolshoy Moskvoretskiy most (Great Moscow River Bridge).

The embankment was built up to its current height at the end of the 18th century and was greatly improved in 1836. It offers spectacular views of the Kremlin and the city.

Novgorodians settled on the river bank in the 14th century and built the original Church of St. Sophia. The present church dates from the mid-17th century. Aleksandr Kaminskiy added the bell tower in 1862.

The mansion at No. 14 was designed by Vasiliy Zalesskiy in 1893 for a wealthy sugar baron and is now the British embassy. The interiors are by Fyodor Shekhtel *(see p45).*

**Set design by Michel Fokine, on show in the Bakhrushin Theater Museum**

# FARTHER AFIELD

Moscow's suburbs are generally rather bleak, but they conceal a surprising number of attractions, all accessible by metro. To the south of the center lie a number of fortified monasteries, built to defend the city against the Mongols and the Poles. The most spectacular of them is Novodevichiy Convent, a serene 16th-century sanctuary with a glorious cathedral, but the Donskoy Monastery is also well worth a visit. The Danilovskiy Monastery, with its handsome cathedral, is the oldest in the city.

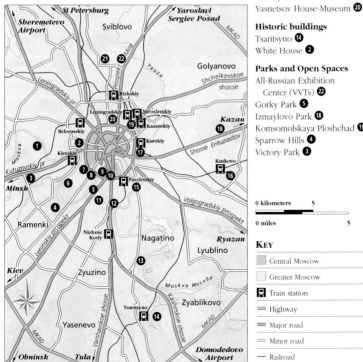

Cathedral fresco, Novodevichiy Convent

Visitors to Moscow are often surprised at the beauty and variety of its green spaces. Gorky, Izmaylovo, and Victory parks are all perfect places in which to relax, while Sparrow Hills offers fantastic views. The city's best-kept secrets, however, are the grand estates away from the center in what was formerly countryside. There the Sheremetev family built two elegant Neo-Classical summer residences, Kuskovo and Ostankino. Both have beautifully preserved gardens and palaces full of fine paintings and period furnishings.

## SIGHTS AT A GLANCE

**Churches, Convents, and Monasteries**
Church of the Intercession in Fili ❶
Church of St. John the Warrior ❿
Church of St. Nicholas of the Weavers ❽
Danilovskiy Monastery ⓬
Donskoy Monastery ⓫
Krutitskoe Mission ⓯
Monastery of the Savior and Andronicus ⓱
*Novodevichiy Convent pp130–31* ❻

**Palaces**
*Kuskovo pp142–3* ⓰
Ostankino Palace ㉑

**Museums and Galleries**
*Kolomenskoe pp138–9* ⓭
New Tretyakov Gallery ❾
Tolstoy House-Museum ❼
Vasnetsov House-Museum ⓴

**Historic buildings**
Tsaritsyno ⓮
White House ❷

**Parks and Open Spaces**
All-Russian Exhibition Center (VVTs) ㉒
Gorky Park ❺
Izmaylovo Park ⓲
Komsomolskaya Ploshchad ⓳
Sparrow Hills ❹
Victory Park ❸

0 kilometers  5

0 miles  5

### KEY

| | |
|---|---|
| | Central Moscow |
| | Greater Moscow |
| 🚉 | Train station |
| ═══ | Highway |
| ▬▬▬ | Major road |
| ═══ | Minor road |
| — | Railroad |

◁ **Ostankino's magnificent Italian Pavilion, designed by Moscow-based Italian architect Vincenzo Brenna**

# Church of the Intercession in Fili ❶

Церковь Покрова в Филях

*Tserkov Pokrova v Filyakh*

Ulitsa Novozavodskaya 6. **M** *Fili.*
◯ *11am–6pm Thu–Mon (May–Oct: upper church only).* 🅿 🗙

THIS STUNNING CHURCH was commissioned by an uncle of Peter the Great, Prince Lev Naryshkin, in the style known as Moscow, or Naryshkin, Baroque *(see p44)*. Built over a period of years from 1690–93 by an unknown architect, it is an extraordinary tiered structure of red brick, with lacelike ornamentation and pilasters of white stone.

Russian churches often comprise two churches: a grand, unheated one for summer, and a smaller, less elevated one with few or no windows that can be heated easily in winter.

Here, the winter church at ground level has changing displays of religious art. In front of it a double staircase rises to a terrace surrounding the upper summer church. This staircase would once have provided the setting for processions. Inside, there is an iconostasis, mainly the work of the 17th-century painter Karp Zolotarev, and a carved gilt pew used by Peter the Great.

**Gilded crest on the clock tower of the White House**

# White House ❷

Белый дом

*Belyy dom*

Krasnopresnenskaya naberezhnaya 2. **Map** 1 B5. **M** *Krasnopresnenskaya.* ⬤ *to public.*

A MARBLE-CLAD building with a gilded clock tower, the White House is still a "must-see" for tourists interested in recent political history.

Once the seat of the Russian Federation's parliament, it first claimed the world's attention in August 1991 when it was the focus of resistance to the Communist hardliners' coup against Mikhail Gorbachev, the president of the Soviet Union. The rebels detained Gorbachev at his Black Sea villa, where he was vacationing at the time, so it was Boris Yeltsin, the president of the smaller Russian Federation, who led the opposition to the coup. The world watched as he passed through the lines of tanks surrounding the White House without anyone daring to arrest him. Then he climbed onto a tank to proclaim: "You can build a throne of bayonets, but you cannot sit on it for long."

The coup failed, and the victory of Yeltsin and his supporters was soon followed by the breakup of the Soviet Union and the end of Communist rule.

However, in September 1993, a reversal of roles occurred at the White House when Yeltsin became the besieger. Hundreds of deputies locked themselves into it in protest when Yeltsin summarily suspended parliament over its increasing opposition to his new draft constitution. The siege ended after two weeks when army tanks bombarded the deputies into submission.

The charred building was quickly repaired, but never regained its former significance; today the Russian parliament occupies a building on ulitsa Okhotnyy ryad *(see p86)*, and the presidential offices are in the Kremlin *(see pp52–67)*.

**The Triumphal Arch, celebrating Napoleon's defeat in the 1812 war**

# Victory Park ❸

Парк победы

*Park pobedy*

Kutuzovskiy prospekt. **M** *Kutuzovskaya.* **Museum of the Great Patriotic War** 𝄃 *148 5550.* ◯ *10am–5pm Tue–Sun.* ♿ 🗙 **Borodino Panorama Museum** 𝄃 *148 1967.* ◯ *10am–6pm Sat–Thu.* 🅿 🗙

COMMEMORATING victory in the Great Patriotic War, the Russian name for World War II *(see p27)*, Victory Park was originally intended to have a vast monument to Mother Russia at its center. After the end of Communist rule, plans were scaled down, and the park was finally completed in 1995, in time for the 50th anniversary of the end of the war.

The park is formally laid out, with straight alleys dividing the sparsely treed grass. The main, fountain-lined avenue leads

**The elegant Church of the Intercession in Fili, the city's best example of Moscow Baroque**

**The Stalinist-Gothic skyscraper of the Moscow State University**

from Kutuzovskiy prospekt to the central Nike Monument, a towering, 142-m (466-ft) obelisk designed by Zurab Tsereteli to honor the Greek goddess of victory.

Behind the monument is the domed, semicircular Museum of the Great Patriotic War. The dioramas, models, maps, and weapons on display give an informative picture of the war as experienced by the Russians.

Just to the side of the central avenue is the simple Church of St. George the Victorious, built in 1995, probably the first to be built in Russia after the Revolution. Next to it is a monument to war victims.

East along Kutuzovskiy prospekt are two large-scale memorials to the war of 1812 (*see pp23–5*). Moscow's final deliverance from the French is celebrated by the grand Triumphal Arch. It was designed by Osip Bove (*see p45*), with sculptures of Russian and Classical warriors by Ivan Vitali and Ivan Timofeev. Originally built on Tverskaya ulitsa in 1834, the arch was dismantled in the 1930s during street-widening. The sculptures were preserved, and in 1968 the arch was rebuilt at its present site.

Farther along the street, at No. 38, is the circular Borodino Panorama Museum, which contains a vast painting, 115-m (377-ft) long and 14-m (46-ft) high. It was created by Franz Roubaud in 1912 to mark the centenary of the battle waged between Russian forces and Napoleon's army at Borodino (*see p152*) outside Moscow.

## Sparrow Hills ❹
Воробьёвы горы
*Vorobevy gory*

**Plaque at the entrance to Gorky Park**

Ⓜ *Universitet.*

THE SUMMIT of this wooded ridge offers unsurpassed views across the city. There is an observation point on ulitsa Kosygina and newlywed couples traditionally come here to have their photograph taken against the panorama. It is also a favorite spot for a large number of souvenir sellers.

The hills are dominated by the Moscow State University (MGU) building commissioned by Stalin, designed by Lev Rudnev and completed in 1953. At 36 floors high it is the tallest of the seven Stalinist-Gothic "wedding-cakes" (*see p45*).

The small, green-domed Church of the Trinity (1811) can also be seen close by, to the left of the observation platform. There are also a couple of long, but somewhat rickety, ski jumps on the hills.

On prospekt Vernadskovo, on the southeast edge of the hills, is the Palace of Youth and Creative Work, a studio complex built for the Communist youth organization. Also on this street are the silver-roofed New Moscow Circus (*see p190*) built in 1971, and the Nataliya Sats Children's Musical Theater (*see p191*).

## Gorky Park ❺
Парк культуры и отдыха имени М. Горького
*Park Kultury i otdykha imeni M. Gorkovo*

Krymskiy val 9. **Map** 6 E4. Ⓜ *Park Kultury, Oktyabrskaya.* ☎ *237 0707.* ⏰ *10am–10pm daily.* 🅿 ♿

MOSCOW'S MOST FAMOUS park is named in honor of the writer Maxim Gorky and extends for more than 297 acres along the banks of the Moskva River. Opened in 1928 as the Park of Culture and Rest, it incorporates the Golitsyn Gardens, laid out by Matvey Kazakov (*see p44*) in the late 18th century, and a 19th-century pleasure park. Later, during the Soviet era, loudspeakers were set up and used to broadcast speeches by Communist leaders across the park. Today the attractions include fairground rides, woodland walks, boating lakes, a 10,000-seat outdoor theater, and, in the winter months, an ice-skating rink.

The park was immortalized in the opening scenes of Michael Apted's film *Gorky Park*. However, because of the tense political climate of 1983, the film was actually shot in Finland.

**Outdoor ice-skating in Gorky Park, a popular activity in the winter months**

# Novodevichiy Convent ❻

Новодевичий монастырь
*Novodevichiy monastyr*

**P**ROBABLY THE MOST BEAUTIFUL of the semicircle of fortified religious institutions to the south of Moscow is Novodevichiy Convent, founded by Basil III in 1524 to commemorate the capture of Smolensk from the Lithuanians. Only the Cathedral of the Virgin of Smolensk was built at this time. Most of the other buildings were added in the late 17th century by Peter the Great's half-sister, the Regent Sophia. After Peter deposed her and reclaimed his throne in 1689 *(see p22)*, he confined her here for the rest of her life. In 1812 Napoleon's troops tried to blow up the convent but, according to a popular story, it was saved by the nuns, who snuffed out the fuses.

**The Church of the Assumption** and adjoining refectory were built in the 1680s on the orders of the Regent Sophia.

**Savior's Tower**

**Faceted Tower**

**Nuns' cells**

**Refectory**

**Setunskaya Tower**

**Gate Church of the Intercession**
*It is not known who designed this church, but it is believed to have been built in the second half of the 17th century.*

**The Palace of Irina Gudunova** was home to the widow of Tsar Fyodor I.

**Novodevichiy Cemetery**

**Church of St. Ambrose**

**Maria's Chambers** were used by the daughter of Tsar Alexis Mikhailovich, Maria.

**STAR FEATURES**

★ Cathedral of the Virgin of Smolensk

★ Bell Tower

★ Gate Church of the Transfiguration

**Vorobeva Tower**

**Shoemaker's tower**

★ **Cathedral of the Virgin of Smolensk**
*The oldest building in the convent is the cathedral, built in 1524. The five-tier iconostasis, the rich frescoes, and the onion domes all date from the 17th century.*

| 0 meters | 25 |
|---|---|
| 0 yards | 25 |

## Novodevichiy Cemetery

Many famous Russians are buried in this cemetery. Among the cultural figures are playwright Anton Chekhov, writer Nikolai Gogol, composers Sergey Prokofiev, Aleksandr Skryabin *(see p72)*, and Dmitriy Shostakovich, and opera singer Fyodor Shalyapin *(see p83)*. Numerous military and political dignitaries from the Soviet era, including the former Russian premier Nikita Khrushchev *(see p30)* are buried here.

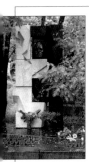

**The tombstone of Nikita Khrushchev**

## Visitors' Checklist

Novodevichiy proezd 1. 246 8526. Sportivnaya. 69, 132 (see p219). 10am–5pm Wed–Mon. Oct–Apr & some public hols. grounds only. English (book in advance). 8am, 5pm Mon–Sat, 7am & 10am Sun. **Cemetery** 10am–6pm daily.

Naprudnaya Tower
This guard house is where the Regent Sophia was imprisoned.
Entrance
Sportivnaya metro
Tsaritsa's Tower
St. Nicholas's Tower
Tailor's Tower
Hospital

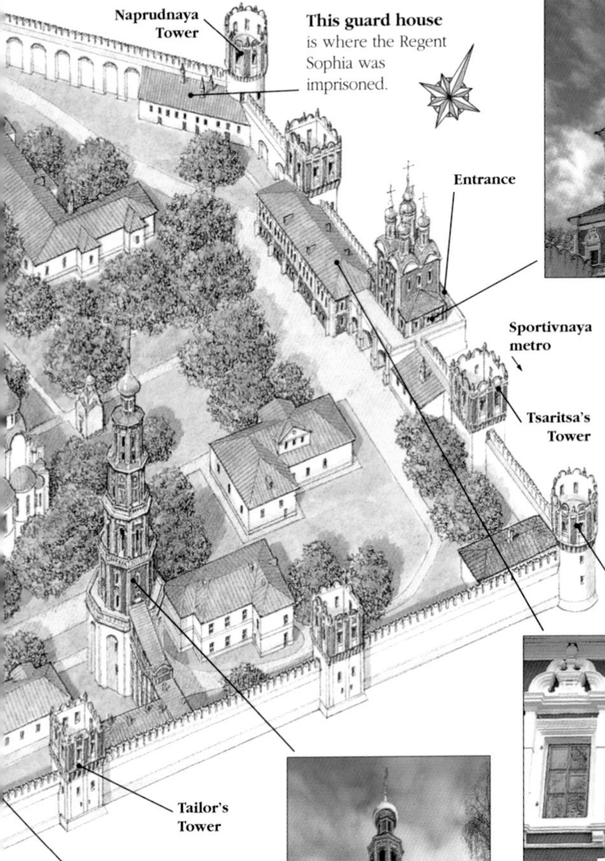

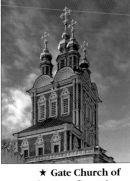

**★ Gate Church of the Transfiguration**
*A cornice of scallop-shell gables, topped by five gilded domes and crosses, crowns this grand Baroque church. It stands over the main gate to the convent and was completed in 1688.*

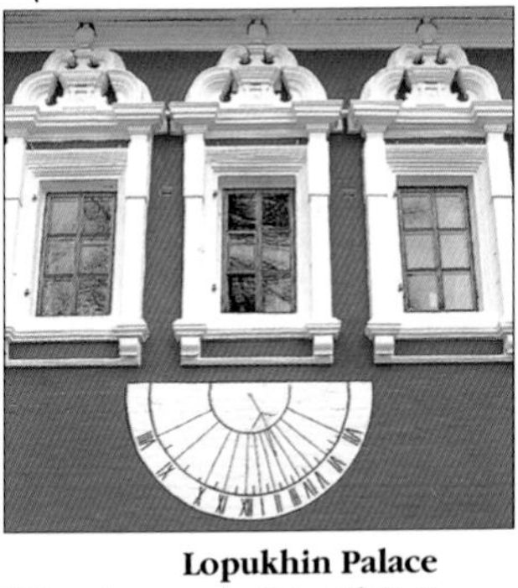

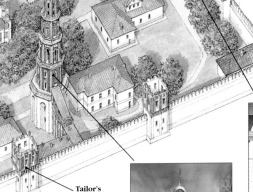

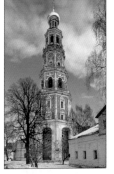

**Lopukhin Palace**
*This palace was built in 1687–9. After Peter the Great's death in 1725, his first wife, Yevdokiya Lopukhina, moved here from the Suzdal convent where she had been sent after Peter tired of her.*

**★ Bell Tower**
*Completed in 1690, this tower is one of the most exuberant examples of Baroque architecture in Moscow. The Church of St. John the Divine occupies the second story of the six-tiered, octagonal tower, which stands 72 m (236 ft) high.*

**Magnificent towers and domed churches of Novodevichiy, viewed from the north** ▷

## Tolstoy House-Museum ❼

Музей-усадьба ЛН Толстого
*Muzey-usadba LN Tolstovo*

Ulitsa Lva Tolstovo 21. **Map** 6 D4.
📞 246 9444. Ⓜ Park Kultury.
🕐 Apr–Sep: 10am–5pm Tue–Sun;
Oct–Mar: 10am–3:30pm Tue–Sun.
🎫 🚫 ✅ English (book in advance).

THE PRESENCE of one of Russia's greatest novelists can be felt in every corner of this evocative, wooden house. It was here that Leo Tolstoy (1828–1910) spent the winters between 1882 and 1901 with his long-suffering wife, Sofya Andreevna, and the nine surviving of their 13 children. The summers were spent on the Tolstoy ancestral estate at Yasnaya Polyana *(see p161)*, 200 km (124 miles) away.

The Moscow house was turned into a museum in 1921 on Lenin's orders and has been preserved much as it was when Tolstoy and his family lived here.

On the ground floor, the large table in the dining room is still set with china. The evening meal in the Tolstoy household always began promptly at 6pm to the summons of the cuckoo clock on the wall. Next door is the "corner room," where at one time, the elder sons, Sergey, Ilya, and Lev, would retire to play Chinese billiards.

**The simple desk in Tolstoy's study, where he wrote his final novel, *Resurrection***

### LEO TOLSTOY

By the time Tolstoy was in his 50s, he was an author of international renown and had written his two great masterpieces *War and Peace* (1865–9) and *Anna Karenina* (1875–7). He continued to write fiction, but later renounced his earlier books and the world they depicted. Instead Tolstoy concentrated on his highly individual brand of Christian Humanism, a doctrine that included nonviolence, vegetarianism, and total sexual abstinence. It was in this period that he wrote the stories *The Death of Ivan Ilych* and the *Kreutzer Sonata* and his last great novel, *Resurrection*, which strayed so far from Orthodoxy that the Holy Synod excommunicated him in 1901. Tolstoy left Moscow the same year for Yasnaya Polyana, where he devoted himself totally to mysticism and the education of the peasants on the estate.

**The dining room with a painting of Tolstoy's favorite daughter, Mariya**

The house exudes a sense of ordered, comfortable family life, but Tolstoy and his wife frequently quarreled violently, largely on account of his wish to renounce society and live as simply as possible. The couple were reconciled for a short time when Vanya, their much-loved youngest child, died of scarlet fever at the age of seven. His memory is preserved in his small bedroom near the scullery, where his high chair, rocking horse, and books can be seen.

The bedroom of Tolstoy's second daughter, Tatyana, is crammed with ornaments and keepsakes. She was a talented artist, and her own paintings and sketches are hung on the walls.

The stairs to the first floor open into the salon, a large hall where frequent guests were treated to supper. They included the young Sergei Rachmaninov who accompanied the bass, Fyodor Shalyapin *(see p83)*, on the piano here, the artist Ilya Repin, whose portrait of Tatyana now hangs in the "corner room," the music critic Vladimir Stasov, and the writer Maxim Gorky *(see p95)*, with whom Tolstoy would play chess. The drawing room next door was decorated by Sofya Andreevna herself.

The bedroom of Tolstoy's favorite child, Mariya, is rather spartan, testifying to her sympathy with her father's ideals and way of life.

At the far end of the upstairs hall is Tolstoy's study, a spacious room overlooking the garden. Reflecting his passion for austerity, the room is simply furnished in black leather. The plain, solid desk where he wrote his novel *Resurrection* is lit by candles. Rather than admit to being shortsighted, Tolstoy sawed off the ends of his chair legs to bring himself closer to his papers. In the adjoining washroom are dumbbells and a bicycle – evidence of his interest in keeping fit. Also on display are the tools he used for his hobby of shoemaking, with some of the pairs he made. The nearby back stairs lead to the garden, which is accessible only to those taking a guided tour.

The luxurious interior of the Church of St. Nicholas of the Weavers

## Church of St. Nicholas of the Weavers ❽
Церковь Николая в Хамовниках
*Tserkov Nikolaya v Khamovnikakh*

Ulitsa Lva Tolstovo 2. **Map** 6 D4.
Ⓜ Park Kultury. ◯ 11am–5.30pm Thu–Tue. ♿ 🚫

D EDICATED TO the patron saint of weavers, sailors, and farmers, this spectacular church was founded in 1679 by local weavers (*khamovniki*). Their aim was to surpass the Church of the Resurrection in Kadashi *(see p122)*, which was built a few years before by rival weavers across the river.

While staying at their winter home nearby, Tolstoy and his family used to attend services here until his rift with church authorities. The church continued to function throughout the Communist era.

The exterior is decorated with vivid orange and green gables and topped with five golden domes, and the walls are decorated with patterned tiles imitating woven motifs.

Inside the church there is an iconostasis featuring a 17th-century icon of St. Nicholas. A separate Icon of the Virgin, Helper of Sinners, is reputed to perform miracles.

## New Tretyakov Gallery ❾
Третьяковская галерея
*Tretyakovskaya galereya*

Krymskiy val 10. **Map** 6 F3.
Ⓒ 238 1378. Ⓜ Park Kultury, Oktyabrskaya. ◯ 10am–8pm Tue–Sun. 📷 ♿ 📷 English.

T HIS HUGE WHITE BOX of a building is an annexe of the Tretyakov Gallery *(see pp118–21)* in the center of town. It is devoted to Russian art from the Revolution to the present. Most of the canvases here belong to the official movement known as Socialist Realism and reflect the cultural straitjacket imposed by Stalin *(see p27)* in the 1930s. It had its roots in the Wanderers movement of the 1860s, which was based on the principle that art has, first and foremost, a

social role to play, though lyricism and beauty in paintings were also important *(see p120)*. In contrast, the hard-hitting art of the Communist era served the state's interests, reflecting socialist goals and achievements. A few examples of the titles given to the paintings say it all: *Life is Getting Better; Building New Factories; Unforgettable Meeting* (between Stalin and a spellbound young woman). Technological achievements were also immortalized in pictures such as *The First Russian Airship*.

Many people will find the Modernist paintings at the beginning of the exhibition more aesthetically pleasing. These include pictures by previously outlawed artists, such as the *Black Square* by Kazimir Malevich and works by Constructivists such as Aleksandr Rodchenko and the brothers Georgiy and Vladimir Stenberg.

Outside, on the Moskva river embankment, is the Graveyard of Fallen Monuments, a collection of some of the sculptures removed from around Moscow at the end of the Soviet era. Star position belongs to the huge statue of the secret police chief, Feliks Dzerzhinskiy, which was taken down from outside the KGB headquarters in Lubyanka Square *(see p112)* in 1991. A striking addition to the view from the Tretyakov's gardens is a huge statue of Peter the Great by Zurab Tsereteli, completed in 1997.

The vast statue of Peter the Great, erected in 1997, viewed from the Graveyard of Fallen Monuments

The Church of St. Nicholas of the Weavers, topped by golden domes

The distinctive, colorful Church of St. John the Warrior

# Church of St. John the Warrior ⑩

Церковь Иоанна Воина
*Tserkov Ioanna Voina*

Ulitsa Bolshaya Yakimanka 46.
**Map** 6 F4. 📞 238 2056.
Ⓜ *Oktyabrskaya.* ✎

THE PLANS FOR this famous church, attributed to the architect Ivan Zarudniy, are said to have been personally approved by Peter the Great *(see p22)*. Building took place from 1709–13, and the result is a notable example of Petrine Baroque, a style that had begun to flourish in St. Petersburg, the tsar's new capital. The church's most eye-catching feature is a tiered octagonal tower, with an elegant balustrade and colored roof tiles forming bold, geometric designs.

St. John the Warrior is one of the few churches to have stayed open after the Revolution, and a number of historic works of religious art were transferred here for safekeeping. These can still be seen in the church and include the 17th-century Icon of the Savior, which hung above the Savior's Gate *(see p66)* when it served as the main entrance leading into the Kremlin.

Across the road is the striking Igumnov House, built in 1893 for a rich merchant by Nikolay Pozdeev. A typically flamboyant example of Russian-Revival architecture *(see p45)*, it now houses the French Embassy.

# Donskoy Monastery ⑪

Донской монастырь
*Donskoy monastyr*

Donskaya ploshchad 1. 📞 952 1646.
Ⓜ *Shabolovskaya.* 🕐 *7am–7pm daily.* ♿ *grounds only.* ✎ 📷

The Old Cathedral, Donskoy Monastery

THE DONSKOY MONASTERY was founded in 1593 by Boris Godunov to honor the Icon of the Donskoy Virgin, credited with having twice saved Moscow from the Mongols. The first time was in 1380 when Prince Dmitriy Donskoy carried the icon into battle at Kulikovo *(see p155)*. Boris Godunov also used it to rally his troops in 1591 against the army of Khan Kazy Girei, which retreated after minor skirmishes. The crescent moons, placed many of the golden crosses on top of the monastery buildings, symbolize the defeat of Islam.

The modest scale of the original monastery is reflected in the beautifully understated Old Cathedral with its bright blue dome and *kokoshniki* gables *(see p44)*. Two orthodox prelates are buried within the Old Cathedral: Archbishop Amvrosiy, killed by a mob during a plague riot in 1771, and Patriarch Tikhon, who was imprisoned by the Bolsheviks after the Revolution.

In the late 17th century the monastery acquired greater prestige under the patronage of the Regent Sophia and her lover Golitsyn. The fortified outer walls and New Cathedral are additions from this period.

Built in 1684–98 in the Moscow-Baroque style *(see p44)*, the New Cathedral is a towering brick building with five domes. Inside are a stunning seven-tiered iconostasis and some exuberant frescoes, painted in 1782–5 by Italian artist Antonio Claudio. The Icon of the Donskoy Virgin is now in the Tretyakov Gallery *(see pp118–21)*, but a copy is on display in the Old Cathedral.

The Donskoy Monastery's imposing 17th-century New Cathedral

# Danilovskiy Monastery ⑫

Даниловский монастырь
*Danilovskiy monastyr*

Danilovskiy val 22. 📞 958 0502.
Ⓜ *Tulskaya.* 🕐 *7am–8pm daily.*
♿ 📷

FOUNDED BY Prince Daniil in 1298–1300, the Danilovskiy Monastery is the city's oldest. It was used as a factory and youth detention center after the Revolution, but since 1988 it has been the headquarters of

## THE RUSSIAN ORTHODOX CHURCH

Christianity was adopted as Russia's official religion in AD 988, when Vladimir I *(see p17)* married the sister of the Byzantine Emperor and had himself baptized in the Orthodox faith. In the 13th century monasteries became a focus for resistance against the invading Mongols. Thereafter the Church played a vital role in Russian life until the Revolution, when it was forced underground. As the Soviet Union broke up, the church revived, and, in 1992, Boris Yeltsin became the first Russian leader to attend church services since 1917.

**Delicate stone tracery on the Figured Gate at Tsaritsyno**

the Russian Orthodox Church, which has offices in its more modern, plainer buildings.

The green-domed Church of the Holy Fathers of the Seven Ecumenical Councils is the oldest of the three churches within the fortified walls. It was founded by Ivan the Terrible *(see p18)* in the 16th century. The main church, on the first floor, has a 17th-century iconostasis with contemporary icons.

At the heart of the monastery is the elegant yellow Cathedral of the Trinity, designed by Osip Bove *(see p45)* in 1833 and completed five years later.

The lovely pink bell tower in the northern wall contains the Gate Church of St. Simeon the Stylite. It was built in 1730–32, but torn down in the 1920s. The bells were sold to Harvard University, but have now been restored to the rebuilt gate and bell tower.

## Kolomenskoe ⓭

See pp138–9.

## Tsaritsyno ⓮

Царицыно
*Tsaritsyno*

Ulitsa Dolskaya 1. 321 0743. Orekhevo, Tsaritsyno. 11am–6pm Wed–Fri, 10am–6pm Sat–Sun (Oct–Mar: 10am–4pm).

CATHERINE THE GREAT *(see p23)* bought this tract of land in 1775 and changed its name from Chyornaya Gryaz (Black Mud) to Tsaritsyno (the Tsarina's Village). In doing so, she commissioned one of her most imaginative architects, Vasiliy Bazhenov *(see p44)*, to design and construct an imperial palace which would rival those in St. Petersburg.

Bazhenov conceived an innovative palace complex combining Gothic, Baroque, and even Moorish styles and Catherine approved the plans. She visited the site in 1785 and, although construction was well under way, proclaimed herself dissatisfied. Bazhenov's young colleague Matvey Kazakov *(see pp44–5)* was told to rebuild the palace but, after another decade of construction, lack of funds left it still incomplete.

Today the grounds boast charming lakes and woodland walks. Some of the ruins have been restored, but the forlorn remainder have a beauty that the completed palace might never have matched. Although the shell of Kazakov's Grand Palace is the most imposing building on the estate, some of Bazhenov's smaller structures are equally impressive. Visitors can see the Figured Gate with its elegant Gothic-style towers and lancet windows, the Figured Bridge and the ornate two-story Opera House, one of the few buildings Catherine approved. The extraordinary Bread Gate, with its arch of sharply pointed stone "teeth," leads to the kitchens, while the Octahedron was built as the servants' quarters. The attractive, white-domed Church of St. Nicholas, now restored, was added in the 19th-century.

A small museum on the estate displays icons, china, glass, and some Fabergé eggs as well as landscapes and architectural exhibits. However, only a fraction of the items in the cellars below the palace are on display at any one time.

**The iconostasis in the Church of the Holy Fathers, Danilovskiy Monastery**

# Kolomenskoe ⓭

Коломенское
*Kolomenskoe*

**The Falcon Tower** was constructed in 1627. It was used as a water tower.

**Refectory**

THE EARLIEST KNOWN REFERENCE to Kolomenskoe village is in the will of Ivan I (*see p18*), dated 1339. By the 16th century Kolomenskoe was a favorite country estate of the tsars. The oldest surviving building is the Church of the Ascension, constructed in 1532. A superb wooden palace was built for Tsar Alexis Mikhailovich (*see p19*) in 1667–71, but it was demolished in the 18th century. After the Revolution the park was designated a museum of architecture, and wooden buildings, such as Peter the Great's cabin from Archangel, were moved here from all over Russia. Also located on the estate is the Front Gate Museum. Its exhibits include a model of Tsar Alexis's palace and Russian craft objects, such as tile paintings and woodcarvings.

**★ Church of the Ascension**
*This magnificent church was erected by Basil III in 1532 to celebrate the birth of his son Ivan (later the Terrible). Its most striking feature is its tent-roofed tower, one of the first in Russia to be built from stone.*

**The Pavilion** is all that remains of Alexander I's palace, built in 1825.

**Church of St. George**
*The 16th-century Church of St. George once stood on this site, but today only the church's bell tower still stands.*

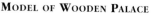

**Mead Brewery**

**Front Gate Museum**

**The Front Gate** was the ceremonial entrance to Tsar Alexis's palace. The chambers on either side of the gate now form the Front Gate Museum.

## MODEL OF WOODEN PALACE

Kolomenskoe underwent a major expansion during the reign of Tsar Alexis Mikhailovich, father of Peter the Great. He added a new centrepiece, an astonishing wooden palace with fanciful barrel-shaped roofs, onion domes and carved ornamentation, which visiting diplomats described as the "eighth wonder of the world." It was demolished in 1768 on the orders of Catherine the Great. Fortunately she had a model made, which is now displayed in the Front Gate Museum.

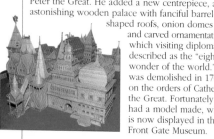

**STAR FEATURES**

★ Church of the Ascension

★ Church of Our Lady of Kazan

## Church of St. John the Baptist
*Located to the south of the main estate, this church was commissioned by Ivan the Terrible to celebrate his accession to the throne in 1547.*

**Church of St. John the Baptist**

**This wooden gate tower** was brought to Kolomenskoe from the St. Nicholas Monastery at Karelia in 1932. It was built in 1692 from interlocking sections without using a single nail.

**Front Gate Museum annexe**

**Peter the Great's Cabin**
*This simple log cabin was built for Tsar Peter the Great in 1702 when he visited Arkhangelsk (on the north coast of Russia). It was brought to Kolomenskoe in 1934 and its four low-ceilinged rooms restored.*

**Bratsk Stockade Tower**

**These ancient oaks** are said to have been planted by Peter the Great.

| 0 meters | 25 |
|---|---|
| 0 yards | 25 |

**The Boris Stone** (12th century) bears the inscription, "Strong, brave, holy Boris."

**St. Savior's Gate** is the main entrance to the complex.

**Kolomenskaya metro**

## ★ Church of Our Lady of Kazan
*Completed in 1650 for Tsar Alexis, this stunning church is an early example of Moscow Baroque (see p44). It is now open again for worship. A replica of the Icon of Our Lady of Kazan, which is believed to have helped Russia drive out Polish invaders in 1612, can be found inside the church.*

# Krutitskoe Mission ⑮

Крутицкое подворье
*Krutitskoe podvore*

Krutitskaya ulitsa 11. **Map** 8 E5.
**☎** 276 9256. **Ⓜ** *Proletarskaya.*
**Grounds** ◯ *8am–8pm daily.* 🔆

THE METROPOLITAN originally
resided in the Kremlin,
but moved to the Krutitskoe
Mission when he was super-
seded as head of the Russian
Orthodox Church by the crea-
tion of the patriarchate in the
16th century *(see p56)*. The
Mission's name derives from
the Russian *krutoy*, meaning
steep, and refers to the nearby bank of the Moskva River.

The Baroque buildings seen
today are undergoing restoration and are dominated by
the bulky Cathedral of the
Assumption, built in 1685. The
entire edifice, including the
onion domes, is built of bricks.

A covered gallery links the
cathedral to the Metropolitan's
Palace via a double-arched
gateway topped by a small
pavilion or *teremok*. The gallery and pavilion are by Osip
Startsev, who was famous in
Russia in the late 17th century
as a designer of religious
buildings. The northern facade
of the *teremok* is decorated
with intricately carved window
frames and turquoise tiles
with yellow floral motifs.

The Metropolitan's Palace
is a handsome, though plainer,
red brick building with pyra-
midal chimneys and an
impressive staircase at the rear.

Since falling into disrepair
early in the 19th century, the
Mission has served as a bar-
racks, a prison, and, after the

Revolution, a workers' hostel;
their wooden living quarters
still survive. Now, the youth
movement of the Orthodox
Church is based here.

# Kuskovo ⑯

*See pp142–3.*

# Monastery of the Savior and Andronicus ⑰

Спасо-Андрониковский
монастырь
*Spaso-Andronikovskiy
monastyr*

Andronevskaya ploshchad 10. **Map** 8
F2. **Ⓜ** *Ploshchad Ilyicha.* ◯ *11am–*
*6pm Thu–Tue.* **Museum** **☎** *278*
*1467.* 📷 ⌀ 📷 *(book in advance).*

TRAVELING BACK from the city
of Constantinople in 1360,
Metropolitan Aleksey survived
a storm at sea. To give thanks
he founded the Monastery of
the Savior on the banks of the
Yauza river. He
then appointed
the monk
Andronicus to
be the first abbot
and to oversee the
building works.

The best-known
monk to have
lived here was
Andrey Rublev,
Russia's most brill-
iant icon painter
*(see p61)*. He is
thought to have
died and been buried here in
about 1430, but the location
of his grave is unknown.
Rublev is commemorated by

**The Cathedral of the Savior, with
characteristic *kokoshniki* gables**

the monastery's Andrey Rublev
Museum of Old Russian Art.
There are no icons by Rublev
himself here, but some excellent copies of his works are
on display, along with genuine
pieces by his contemporaries.
Original Rublev icons can be
seen in the Tretyakov Gallery
*(see pp118–21)*. The museum's
collections are on
show in two of the
monastery build-
ings. The 16th-
century Abbot's
House, decorated
with tiles and just
to the right of the
main entrance, dis-
plays decorative
arts of the 11th–
20th centuries. The
Baroque Church
of the Archangel
Michael, built in
1691–94, displays Russian art
of the 13th–17th centuries.
Highlights include the 17th-
century Icon of the Tikhvin
Virgin, originally from the
Donskoy Monastery *(see p136)*,
and paintings depicting the life
of St. Nicholas of Zaraysk, one
of Russia's favorite saints. The
18th-century monks' building,
which contained monks' cells,
is being renovated and will provide additional gallery space.

The beautiful, single-domed
Cathedral of the Savior was
built in either 1390 or 1425–7.
If the former date is correct,
this would make it the oldest
church in Moscow. The interior
was painted by Rublev but
only traces of his work survive,
around the altar windows.

**Icon of St. John the
Baptist, 15th century**

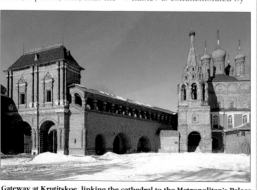

**Gateway at Krutitskoe, linking the cathedral to the Metropolitan's Palace**

# Izmaylovo Park ®
Парк Измайлово
*Park Izmaylovo*

Narodniy prospekt 17. **☎** *166 7909.*
**M** *Izmaylovskiy Park, Shosse
Entuziastov.* ◯ *24 hours daily.* &

**17th-century Cathedral of the Intercession, Izmaylovo Park**

ONE OF THE LARGEST PARKS in Europe, Izmaylovo covers nearly 12 sq km (4.7 sq miles). It features attractions such as sports facilities, children's amusements, cafés, and woods, as well as an outdoor theater, a famous flea market *(see p185)*, a cathedral, and the picturesque remains of one of the tsars' country estates.

Izmaylovo passed to the Romanov family in the 16th century and became one of their favorite hunting lodges. In 1663, Tsar Alexis *(see p19)* built an enormous wooden palace here and dedicated the land to experiments in animal and vegetable husbandry and various cottage industries.

Peter the Great later spent an idyllic childhood at Izmaylovo, secluded from palace intrigues. It was here that his lifelong fascination with the sea began, when he learned to sail an old boat on a lake. The boat was later nicknamed the "grand-father of the Russian navy."

The wooden palace has long since disappeared, demolished by Catherine the Great in 1767. However, about 500 m (550 yds) east of Izmaylovskiy Park metro, the remains of other buildings can be seen on an island near the sports stadium. The lake surrounding them was once part of a network of 37 ponds previously created by Tsar Alexis for breeding fish and irrigating experimental crops. He planted exotic species such as mulberry trees, and cotton and ordered seeds from his ambassadors in England.

The island is reached over a small bridge. The iron archway at its far end was built in 1859 and led to three buildings commissioned by Nicholas I and designed by Konstantin Ton *(see p45)* in the 1840s for retired soldiers. Rising above the trees ahead, behind the remains of the estate's walls, are the five formidable black domes of the Cathedral of the Intercession, built in 1671–9. The domes are tiled with metallic "scales." The *zakomary* gables *(see p44)* beneath them are beautifully decorated with "peacock's eye" tiles, by Stepan Polubes, a late-17th-century Belorussian ceramicist working in Moscow.

On the cathedral's right is a tiered red-brick arch with a tent roof. Built in 1671, this is the Bridge Tower, all that remains of a 14-span bridge that once crossed the estate's extensive waterways. Its tower was used for meetings of the boyars' council under Tsar Alexis. The top tier of the bridge has fine views of the whole estate.

On the opposite side of the cathedral from the Bridge Tower stands the white, triple-arched Ceremonial Gate. It was designed by Terentiy Makarov in 1682 and is one of two gates that originally led to the palace.

The flea market, just to the northwest of the lake, trails down the hill from the concrete tower blocks of the Izmaylovo Hotel, offering an amazingly eclectic variety of goods. Muscovites come here in large numbers to buy items such as second-hand household goods and vehicle parts. Tourists are likely to be greeted by a storm of shouts in English from people selling their wares.

**Triple-arched Ceremonial Gate, the surviving
entrance to the tsars' former estate, Izmaylovo Park**

# Kuskovo ⑯

Кусково
*Kuskovo*

**Statue of Minerva**

★ **Formal Gardens**
*The gardens were laid out in the French, geometrical style, which led to Kuskovo gaining a reputation as the Russian Versailles.*

**F**OR OVER 200 YEARS before the Revolution, Kuskovo was the country seat of one of Russia's wealthiest aristocratic families, the Sheremetevs. The present buildings were commissioned by Count Pyotr Sheremetev after his marriage to the heiress Varvara Cherkasskaya in 1743. Among their 200,000 serfs were the architects Fyodor Argunov and Aleksey Mironov, who played a major role in Kuskovo's construction, probably under the supervision of professional architect Karl Blank. Apart from the elaborate gardens, the main attraction is the two-story wooden palace, completed in 1777. A ceramics museum, with a renowned collection of porcelain, occupies the Orangery.

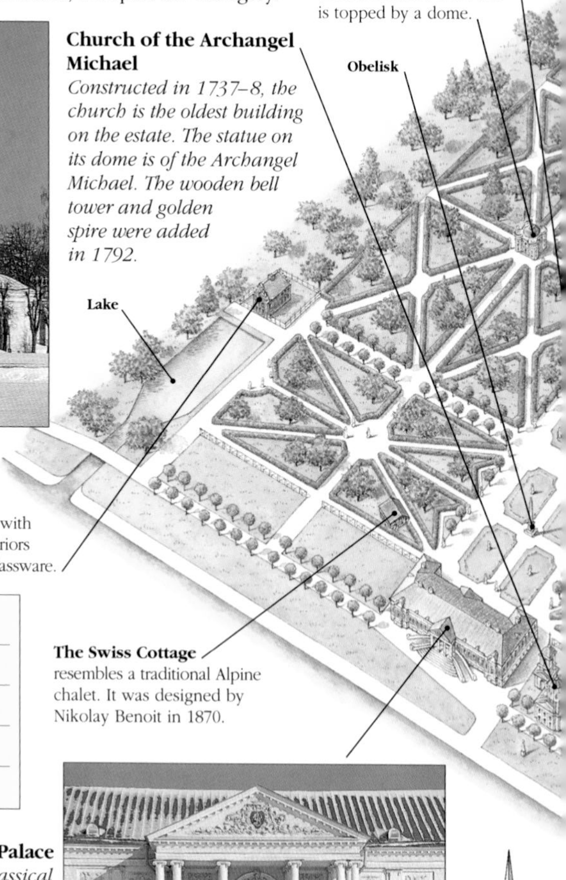

**The Hermitage** has distinctive rounded walls and is topped by a dome.

**Church of the Archangel Michael**
*Constructed in 1737–8, the church is the oldest building on the estate. The statue on its dome is of the Archangel Michael. The wooden bell tower and golden spire were added in 1792.*

**Obelisk**

**Lake**

**The Dutch Cottage** was built in 1749 in the homey style of 17th-century Dutch architecture, in red brick and with stepped gables. The tiled interiors house Russian ceramics and glassware.

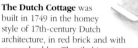

## STAR FEATURES

★ **Wooden Palace**

★ **Grotto**

★ **Orangery**

★ **Formal Gardens**

**The Swiss Cottage** resembles a traditional Alpine chalet. It was designed by Nikolay Benoit in 1870.

★ **Wooden Palace**
*Surprisingly, this Neo-Classical palace is made entirely of wood, plastered and painted to resemble stone. Carriage ramps sweep up to the main portico, which is emblazoned with the crest of the Sheremetev family.*

### ★ Orangery
*With a central hall for dining and dancing, the Orangery was built in 1761–2. It is now a ceramics museum, based on the 18th–19th-century porcelain collection of Aleksey Morozov (see p96). Pieces displayed include Wedgwood, Meissen, and items from various Russian factories.*

### VISITORS' CHECKLIST

Ulitsa Yunosti 2. ☎ 370 0160.
Ⓜ *Ryazanskiy prospekt, Vykhino.*
🚌 *133, 208 (see p219).*
🕐 *mid-April–Sep: 10am–6pm Wed–Sun; Oct–mid-Apr: 10am–4pm Wed–Sun.*
🎟 *tickets sold at main entrance for some of the individual sights within the complex.*

**The Green Theater**
was used to stage open-air plays and concerts for an audience of 50 guests.

**Allegorical statue of the Greek river god Scamander**

**Statue of Minerva, Roman goddess of wisdom**

**Aviary**    **American Conservatory**

**Italian Cottage**
*Russian architect Yuriy Konlogrivov studied in Italy prior to designing this pavilion. It was built in 1754–5 in the style of a late-Renaissance villa and now contains displays of 18th-century paintings.*

**Coach House**

**The Menagerie**, a semicircle of terra-cotta and white fenced pavilions, housed songbirds.

### ★ Grotto
*Designed by Fyodor Argunov in the mid-18th century, the Grotto is the most remarkable of Kuskovo's pavilions. The cool, spacious interior is decorated with shells and porcelain embedded in sand and stucco.*

| 0 meters | 50 |
| 0 yards | 50 |

**The kitchens** were housed in this large, imposing building, constructed in 1756–7.

**Entrance**

**Main entrance of the Style-Moderne Yaroslavskiy Station on Komsomolskaya ploshchad**

# Komsomolskaya Ploshchad ⑲

Комсомолская площадь
*Komsomolskaya ploshchad*

**Map** 4 D2. M *Komsomolskaya.*

THE THREE train stations on this large square are long-standing rivals for the affection of Muscovites. The oldest, Leningradskiy Station (formerly Nikolaevskiy Station), opened in 1851, serving as the terminus of the line from St. Petersburg to Moscow. The building was designed according to the tenets of historicism by Konstantin Ton (*see p45*), architect of the Great Kremlin Palace (*see p63*).

In complete contrast is the turreted Yaroslavskiy Station, rebuilt in 1902 by architect Fyodor Shekhtel (*see p45*). The station is a colorful Style-Moderne building with a tiled frieze and an unusual, steeply pitched roof. The Trans-Siberian Railroad starts here.

Shekhtel's radical design for his station goaded his rival, Aleksey Shchusev (*see p45*), into adopting an equally bold approach when designing the third station, Kazanskiy, on the opposite side of the square. Begun in 1912, the station has a tiered central tower modeled on the citadel in the Mongol capital Kazan. The terminal was completed in 1926 and serves the Urals.

The porticoed pavilion of Komsomolskaya metro station (*see pp39–41*) is also a striking feature of the square. It is named after the Komsomol (Communist Youth volunteers) who helped to build it. It has a luxurious interior, lit by glittering chandeliers.

Komsomolskaya ploshchad itself is a seething mass of beggars, families with apparently everything they own in tow, street hawkers, drunks, drug dealers, and, in the evenings, prostitutes. Over recent years it has assumed a disturbing atmosphere to say the least, so it is advisable not to linger here long, especially at night.

# Vasnetsov House-Museum ⑳

Дом-музей ВМ Васнецова
*Dom-muzey VM Vasnetsova*

Pereulok Vasnetsova 13. **Map** 3 A2. 281 1329. M *Sukharevskaya, Prospekt Mira.* ⏱ 10am–5pm Wed–Sun.

A GRAPHIC ARTIST, sculptor, painter, theater designer, and architect, Viktor Vasnetsov (1848–1926) was a member of the artists' colony set up by arts patron Savva Mamontov at Abramtsevo (*see p154*). He is probably best known for the highly original facade of the Tretyakov Gallery (*see pp118–21*), where many of his paintings are also housed.

**Ornate roof of the wooden house designed by Viktor Vasnetsov**

Vasnetsov designed this unusual house for himself and his family in 1893–4 and lived here until he died in 1926, at the age of 78. As an enthusiastic advocate of traditional Russian folk art and architecture, he employed peasant carpenters from Vladimir (*see pp160–61*) to build his remarkable, log cabin-like, timber house with green roofs.

The ground-floor rooms display highly individual pieces of furniture, many designed by Vasnetsov and his similarly talented younger brother, Apollinariy (1856–1933). The stoves are decorated with colourful tiles made by fellow artists from Abramtsevo.

A spiral staircase hung with 17th-century chain mail and weaponry leads up to the artist's studio, which resembles a vaulted medieval hall. This is the perfect backdrop for Vasnetsov's arresting canvases, many of which take figures from Russian legends as their subjects. For example, *Baba Yaga* portrays Russia's forest witch indulging in her favorite occupation, stealing children. The enormous painting of *The Sleeping Princess*, painted in the last year of Vasnetsov's life, shows a scene from the classic fairy story of Sleeping Beauty.

# Ostankino Palace ㉑

Московский музей-усадьба Останкино
*Moskovskiy muzey-usadba Ostankino*

1-ya Ostankinskaya ulitsa 5a. 286 6288. M *VDNKh.* ⏱ 10am–5pm Wed–Sun. ● Oct–April. gardens only. English.

LIKE THE ESTATE at Kuskovo (*see pp142–3*), Ostankino was built by the serf architects Pavel Argunov and Aleksey Mironov for the Sheremetevs, one of Russia's richest families. Count Nikolay Sheremetev was a prominent patron of the arts and built his palace around a theater, where a company of 200 serf actors and actresses performed plays of his choosing. In 1800 the Count married Praskovia Zhemchugova-Kovaleva, one of the actresses. Secluded at their palace, they

**Main facade of the imposing, Neo-Classical Ostankino Palace**

were able to shelter themselves from the disapproval of polite society, but Praskovia died three years later. The count never recovered from the loss and left the palace, which fell into disuse.

Ostankino is a handsome palace, with a shallow green dome and a restrained Neo-Classical facade. It was built of wood in 1792–8 and skillfully plastered over to look like brick and stone.

Parts of it have been restored, and the Italian Pavilion is open to the public. It demonstrates the remarkable workmanship of Sheremetev's serf craftsmen. The halls are a wonder of *trompe l'oeil* decor. Carved wooden moldings are painted to resemble bronze, gold, and marble, parquet floors are patterned in birchwood and mahogany, and a crystal chandelier hangs from the ceiling of the main hall. The pavilion also serves as a sculpture gallery, and among the sculptures is a Roman marble head of Aphrodite from the 1st century AD.

The *pièce de résistance* of the palace is the theater, a breathtaking, elliptical hall with a superb painted ceiling supported by rows of Corinthian columns. In 1796 the building was partly reconstructed to allow the installation of an ingenious mechanical device that raised the auditorium floor so that the theater could also be used

as a ballroom. In the summer, concerts of classical music are still held here.

On the road leading from the estate is the ornate Church of the Trinity, with a cluster of green domes. It was built in 1678–83 for the Cherkasskiy family, who owned Ostankino estate before the Sheremetevs.

**Theater auditorium, Ostankino Palace, once home to Count Sheremetev's serf actors**

## All-Russian Exhibition Center ㉒

Всероссийский Выставочный Центр (ВВЦ)
*Vserossiyskiy Vystavochniy Tsentr (VVTs)*

Prospekt Mira. ▮ 181 9504.
Ⓜ *VDNKh.* **Pavilions** ◯ *May–Oct: 10am–6pm Mon–Fri, 10am–7pm Sat–Sun, hols; Nov–Apr: 10am–5pm Mon–Fri, 10am–6pm Sat–Sun, hols.* ▮
**Space Museum** ◯ *10am–7pm Tue–Sun.* ▮ ▮ ▮ ▮ *English.*

O NCE ONE OF the city's main tourist attractions, the former Exhibition of Economic Achievements of the USSR (VDNKh) has now become the All-Russian Exhibition Center (VVTs). The site began life in 1939 as a major agricultural exhibition, but 20 years later

it was transformed by Soviet leader Nikita Khrushchev into a vast park extolling the nation's achievements in economics, science, and technology. After the disintegration of the Soviet Union in 1991, the pavilions were taken over by the private sector. Although more than 70 of them now function as retail showrooms for products such as electronic goods, computers and cars, the whole complex is a shadow of its former self.

A stroll around the grounds will take you past some of the sculptures for which the former VDNKh was famous. The main entrance to the park is a triumphal arch, topped by the figures of a tractor driver and a woman collective farmer, holding up a sheaf of corn.

On one side of the main gates, on prospekt Mira, is the emblematic statue *Worker and Woman Collective Farm Worker*. The two figures stride forwards together into the future, holding aloft a hammer and sickle. Sculpted by Vera Mukhina, the statues won her international recognition at the Paris Exhibition in 1937.

On the other side of the gates is the Space Obelisk by Andrey Faydysh-Krandievskiy. Over 100 m (328 ft) high, it represents a rocket lifting off on a plume of flame. The monument was erected in 1964, three years after Yuriy Gagarin became the first man in space. Nearby is the Space Museum, which houses such exhibits as *Vostok 1*, in which Gagarin orbited the Earth.

VDNKh was also intended as a recreational area, and families still flock here on weekends. The main attraction is the fairground, but there are also movies and cafés.

**Statue of tractor driver and woman atop the main entrance of the VVTs**

# BEYOND
# MOSCOW

# BEYOND MOSCOW

T HE MAGNIFICENCE OF SOME *of the palaces and churches outside Moscow and the historic interest of some of the towns make excursions there justly rewarding. Although parts of the landscape are unappealingly industrial, the large areas of true countryside are green, forested, and dotted with villages of small wooden dachas.*

Visitors may find it a good idea to take an organized tour *(see p198)* to out-of-town sights as public transit can be erratic, though perfectly feasible for those who prefer mixing with local daily life *(see p219)*. There are several places of historic and cultural importance within easy reach of the city. To the west is Borodino *(see p152)*, site of the great battle between Napoleon's army and Russian forces under the command of Field Marshal Mikhail Kutuzov. To the north is the magnificent Trinity Monastery of St. Sergius *(see pp156–9)* and to the northeast the towns of the Golden Ring *(see p155)*. The political heyday of these towns was in the 12th and 13th centuries, before the rise of Moscow, and their churches and wooden buildings make them well worth exploring.

**Field Marshal Mikhail Kutuzov**

Also outside Moscow are houses lived in by two of Russia's most famous sons, Pyotr Tchaikovsky *(see p153)* and Leo Tolstoy *(see p134)*.

On Friday nights the trains and roads into the countryside are packed with families traveling to their dacha, a migration that leaves the capital rather deserted. Each dacha has a small plot of land used for growing fruit and vegetables. For some Muscovites this was, and often still is today, an essential source of food. In the last few years, brick houses have started to spring up where farmers used to grow crops, built for New Russians who have adopted Western commuter habits. However, many have been abandoned half-built as construction companies have gone out of business in the fast-changing economic climate.

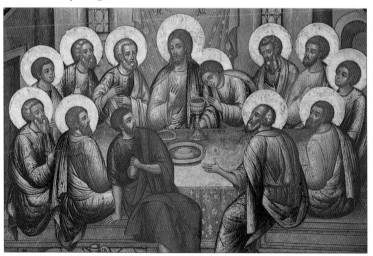

*The Sacred Supper*, painted in 1685, displayed in the Treasury at the Trinity Monastery of St. Sergius

◁ **The Church of the Prophet Elijah**, one of many picturesque churches in the Golden Ring town of Suzdal

# Exploring the Moscow Region

Despite the numerous attractions of Moscow, it is well worth spending time in the surrounding region. Several country estates lie within easy reach of the city and make for delightful one- or two-day trips. Among them are Yasnaya Polyana, where Leo Tolstoy (see p134) lived for many years, the house in Klin rented by Pyotr Tchaikovsky (see p153), and Abramtsevo Estate-Museum, a former artists' colony. However, the star attraction of the region is the Trinity Monastery of St. Sergius. Once a place of pilgrimage for the tsars, this huge complex has several superb cathedrals.

**Tiles by artist Mikhail Vrubel on a bench at Abramtsevo**

Moscow is also an ideal base for visiting the Golden Ring towns, which include Pereslavl-Zalesskiy, Suzdal, and Vladimir. Founded by Russians seeking shelter from invading tribes, these attractive settlements still have many historic buildings.

### KEY

| | |
|---|---|
| ▬▬ | Highway |
| ▬▬ | Major road |
| ▬▬ | Minor road |
| ▬▬ | Scenic route |
| ┿━┿ | Railroad |
| ≈≈ | River |
| ✦ | Viewpoint |

*Riga, Pskov*

*Minsk, Kiev*

*Kiev*

**The blue-domed Church of the Holy Spirit and the Chapel Over the Well, Trinity Monastery of St. Sergius**

## SIGHTS AT A GLANCE

Abramtsevo Estate-Museum ❹
Arkhangelskoe ❶
Borodino ❷
Pereslavl-Zalesskiy ❻
Suzdal ❼
Tchaikovsky House-Museum ❸
*Trinity Monastery of St. Sergius pp156–9* ❺
Vladimir ❽
Yasnaya Polyana ❾

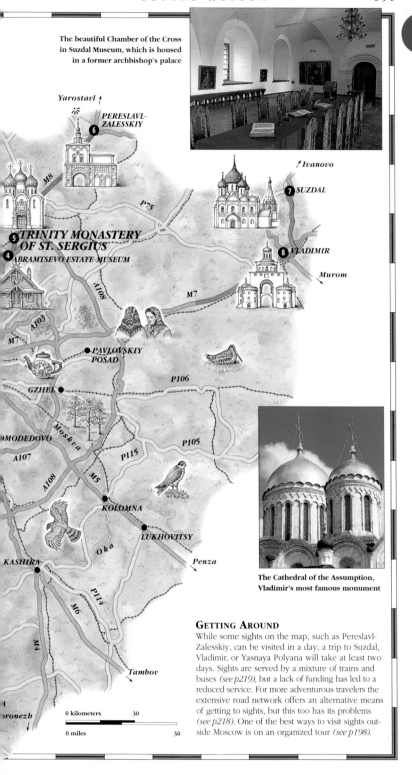

The beautiful Chamber of the Cross in Suzdal Museum, which is housed in a former archbishop's palace

*Yarostavl*

**PERESLAVL-ZALESSKIY** 6

*Ivanovo*

7 **SUZDAL**

5 **TRINITY MONASTERY OF ST. SERGIUS**

4 **ABRAMTSEVO ESTATE-MUSEUM**

8 **VLADIMIR**

*Murom*

**PAVLOVSKIY POSAD**

**GZHEL**

**MODEDOVO**

**KOLOMNA**

**LUKHOVITSY**

*Penza*

**KASHIRA**

*Tambov*

*ronezh*

0 kilometers    30

0 miles    30

The Cathedral of the Assumption, Vladimir's most famous monument

### GETTING AROUND

While some sights on the map, such as Pereslavl-Zalesskiy, can be visited in a day, a trip to Suzdal, Vladimir, or Yasnaya Polyana will take at least two days. Sights are served by a mixture of trains and buses *(see p219)*, but a lack of funding has led to a reduced service. For more adventurous travelers the extensive road network offers an alternative means of getting to sights, but this too has its problems *(see p218)*. One of the best ways to visit sights outside Moscow is on an organized tour *(see p198)*.

The southern, garden facade of the Neo-Classical, stucco-covered, wooden palace at Arkhangelskoe

# Arkhangelskoe ●

Архангельское

*Arkhangelskoe*

20 km (12 miles) W of Moscow.
🛈 560 2231. ◷ 10am–6pm
Tue–Sun. Ⓜ Tushinskaya, then bus
(see p219). 📷 ♿ grounds only.

MOST OF THE buildings on
this country estate date
from the 18th and 19th centuries. The only one to predate
them is the charming Church
of the Archangel Michael, completed in 1667, from which the
name of the estate is derived.

The Golitsyn family acquired
the estate in 1703. In the 1780s
Prince Nikolay Golitsyn began
a wholesale rebuilding, including a new palace that was
built to a design by the French
architect Charles de Guerne.
Constructed from wood, it was
covered with stucco to give the
effect of stone. When Golitsyn
died in 1809, the estate was
purchased by Prince Nikolay
Yusupov, who continued to
add Neo-Classical buildings.
Recently restored, the palace's
sumptuous rooms are filled
with fine furniture, fabrics,
and antiques. There is also
an excellent art collection.

The formal gardens were laid
out in the 18th century. Within
them stand pavilions such as
the diminutive Caprice Palace,
built in 1819 for soirees. In
1910–16 a lavish mausoleum
was erected for the Yusupov
family, but it was never used
because of the Revolution.

# Borodino ●

Бородино

*Borodino*

130 km (80 miles) SW of Moscow.
🛈 8238 51057. ◷ 9am–6pm Tue–
Sun. ◻ Mozhaisk or Borodino, then
bus (see p219). 📷 ♿ 🚫 ▢

ONE OF THE FIERCEST military
confrontations of the 19th
century took place at Borodino
on September 7, 1812. For over
15 hours Napoleon
Bonaparte's Grande
Armée and the
Russian army, led
by Field Marshal
Mikhail Kutuzov,
fought each other to
a bloody impasse.
It is estimated that
40,000 Russian and
30,000 French sol-
diers were killed.
Napoleon called it
the "most terrible"
of all his battles, but
claimed victory on
the grounds that the Russians
were forced to continue their
retreat to Moscow. Posterity,
however, awarded the laurels
to the Russians. The French
followed the Russians, but
arrived to find the city and the
Kremlin deserted. Napoleon's
army was quickly driven
out by a great fire *(see
pp24–5)* started on
Kutuzov's orders. Faced
with a Russian winter
in the open, the French
were forced to retreat.

The battlefield covers
over 100 sq km (40 sq
miles), but the main
places of interest are
reasonably accessible. A
museum 1 km (½ mile)
south of Borodino vil-
lage recounts the story
of the battle with the
aid of models and an
illuminated map. More
than 30 monuments
are strewn around
the area. Russia's
most distinguished
general to fall in
battle, Prince Pyotr
Bagration, was
buried at the base of a column
dedicated to the fallen just
east of the museum. Nearby
is the inn, now a museum,
where Leo Tolstoy stayed to
research the background for
his epic novel *War and Peace.*

The small Empire-style
Spasskiy Church of 1822 was
the first monument to be constructed on the battlefield. A
reenactment of the battle
takes place every September 7.

The gorgeously painted dome of the Yusupov
mausoleum, built in 1910–16, at Arkhangelskoe

Monument to
fallen of Borod

# Tchaikovsky House-Museum ❸

Дом-музей ПИ Чайковского
*Dom-muzey PI Chaykovskovo*

90 km (55 miles) NW of Moscow.
Ulitsa Tchaikovskaya 48, Klin.
539 8196. 9am–5pm Fri–Tue.
Klin (see p219).

The reception area in the house at Klin, containing Tchaikovsky's piano

IN A LETTER to his brother Anatoly in May 1892 Pyotr Tchaikovsky wrote, "I have rented a house in Klin. What a blessing it is to know that noone will come, either to interrupt my work, or my reading or walking." Previous stays in the village of Frolovskoe near Klin had inspired some of his best music, including the ballets *The Sleeping Beauty* and *The Nutcracker*, and the opera *The Queen of Spades*, based on Pushkin's novel *(see p73)*. Tchaikovsky enjoyed Klin for only a few months, since he died in 1893. In 1894 his younger brother, Modest, opened the estate to visitors. The ground floor of the clapboard house, once occupied

**Tchaikovsky's wooden house in Klin, in the quiet of the Russian countryside he loved so much**

by Tchaikovsky's servant, Aleksey Safronov, is closed to the public, but on entering the composer's rooms on the first floor visitors find themselves in a bright, spacious reception area. The walls are covered with photos of his family, his classmates at law school, and fellow musicians. The grand piano in the center of the room was a gift from the Russian firm Becker. Though an excellent pianist, Tchaikovsky never performed in public. The winner of the Tchaikovsky International Competition *(see p192)* gives a recital here on the composer's birthday, May 7.

Tchaikovsky was a great collector of souvenirs. On a shelf behind the piano is a Statue of Liberty inkwell, which he brought back from his triumphant conducting tour of the United States in 1891.

The bedroom is separated from the reception area by a curtain. Warm and intimate, it contains Tchaikovsky's diminutive slippers and a beautiful coverlet made by his niece. Tchaikovsky finished his *Sixth Symphony*, the *Pathétique*, at the table by the window.

Also open to visitors are the handsome wood-paneled library and the study where Modest Tchaikovsky worked as the Klin archivist until his death in 1916. A memorial room to the composer holds some of his personal possessions, including his top hat, gloves, and evening clothes.

Tchaikovsky habitually took a stroll in the garden before breakfast and after lunch. His favorite flowers, lilies of the valley, are still planted here. Concerts are held year round in a hall built on the grounds.

## PYOTR TCHAIKOVSKY

Probably Russia's most famous composer, Tchaikovsky was born in 1840. After graduating initially in law, he studied music at the St. Petersburg Conservatory. One of his teachers helped the young composer get a job teaching music at the Moscow Conservatory *(see p94)* in 1866, where he then taught for the next 12 years. It was during this period that Tchaikovsky composed his first four symphonies and the ballet *Swan Lake* (1876). In 1877 he married a student from the Conservatory in an effort to suppress his homosexuality.

**Statue of Pyotr Tchaikovsky at the Moscow Conservatory**

However, the marriage was unhappy and short-lived. Tchaikovsky composed prolifically in the 1880s, completing such works as the ballet *The Sleeping Beauty* (1889) and the overture *The Year 1812* (1880). In 1892 he moved to Klin, outside Moscow. He died of cholera in November 1893, while overseeing the premiere of his final work, the *Sixth Symphony*, in St. Petersburg. It is rumored that he knowingly drank infected water as a dignified form of suicide after the exposure of his homosexual involvement with a young aristocrat.

**Iconostasis in the Church of the Savior, Abramtsevo Estate-Museum**

## Abramtsevo Estate-Museum ❹

Музей-усадьба Абрамцево
*Muzey-usadba Abramtsevo*

60 km (35 miles) NE of Moscow.
🚊 *Khotkova or Sergiev Posad, then
bus (see p219).* 📞 *254 32470.*
🕙 *10am–5pm Wed–Sun.* 📷 📵
✔ *English (book in advance).*

Iᴎ ᴛʜᴇ sᴇᴄᴏɴᴅ half of the
19th century this delightful
rural retreat became a hive of
cultural activity. Until his death
in 1859, the house was owned
by the writer Sergey Aksakov,
whose sons were leading
Slavophile thinkers. The
estate's creative legacy was
continued in 1870 when it was
acquired by Savva Mamontov,
an industrialist and art patron.
Mamontov's generosity and
zeal led to the establishment
of an artists' colony here, and
to a reevaluation of traditional
Russian folk art and craftwork.
The work of local peasant
craftsmen, whose children
were educated in the estate's
school, was a source of inspiration for many of the artists.
Dotted around the estate
are a number of remarkable
buildings. The artists' studio,
with a spectacular carved roof,
was designed in 1872 by Viktor
Gartman. Displayed here are
ceramics by the two distinguished artists Valentin Serov
and Mikhail Vrubel. The
*teremok*, meanwhile, is a free

improvization on the typical
peasant hut *(izba)*, and was
originally built as a bathhouse
by Ivan Ropet in 1873. It was
later used as a guesthouse.
Inside are the original wooden
furnishings and ornaments,
such as carved statuettes, kitchen utensils, and a tiled stove
designed by Mikhail Vrubel.
The House on Chicken Legs
stands on stilts. Designed by
Viktor Vasnetsov, it is now a
popular children's attraction,
recalling the witch of Russian
folklore, Baba Yaga, whose
house in the forest is built
on giant chicken legs.
A woodland path leads to
the most remarkable building
on the estate. The Church of
the Savior Not Made by
Human Hand is modeled
on the medieval churches of
Novgorod, but was brought
up to date by the addition
of bands of painted majolica
tiles to its walls of whitewashed brick. The church
was built in 1881–2, to a
design by Viktor Vasnetsov;
the mosaic floor is also his
work, while the icons were
painted by Vasnetsov, Ilya
Repin and his wife Vera,
Vasiliy Polenov, and Nikolay
Nevrev. A small oratory holds
Savva Mamontov's remains
and those of his son Andrey,
who died, aged 19, in 1891.
The manor house still
contains Aksakov's original
Empire-style furnishings, left

by Mamontov out of respect
for his predecessor. Aksakov
knew the novelists Nikolai
Gogol and Ivan Turgenev, and,
here, in the red sitting-room,
Gogol would read aloud from
his masterpiece, *Dead Souls.*
The dining room features a
beautiful, tiled corner fireplace
and a profusion of paintings.
The gaze, however, is drawn
to a copy of Valentin Serov's
arresting portrait of Vera, Savva
Mamontov's daughter, seated
at the dining table. Entitled
*Girl with Peaches* (1887), the
original can be found in the
Tretyakov Gallery *(see p121).*

## Trinity Monastery of St. Sergius ❺

*See pp156–9.*

## Pereslavl-Zalesskiy ❻

Переславль-Залесский
*Pereslavl-Zalesskiy*

135 km (85 miles) NE of Moscow.
🚶 *43,400.* 🚊 *Sergiev Posad, then
bus (see p219).*

Fᴏᴜɴᴅᴇᴅ as a fortress in 1152
by Yuriy Dolgorukiy, and
overlooking Lake Pleshcheevo,
Pereslavl Zalesskiy was an
independent princedom until
1302, when it came under the
control of Moscow. Peter the
Great *(see p22)* developed
plans for the Russian navy
here. Sights of interest include
the 12th-century **Cathedral of
the Transfiguration** and the
**Goritskiy Monastery of the
Assumption**, founded in the
14th century but dating mainly
to the 17th–18th centuries.

**Cathedral of the Goritskiy Monastery
of the Assumption, Pereslavl-Zalesskiy**

# The History of the Golden Ring

THE FIRST IMPORTANT cities in Russia were Novgorod in the north and Kiev in the south, both situated on trade routes connecting the Baltic and the Black Sea. From the 11th century on, as hostile tribes invaded Kievan Rus *(see p17)* and many Russians were forced northward, new settlements were founded such as Rostov, Yaroslavl, Vladimir, and Suzdal. Like Novgorod and Kiev, these towns flourished on trade from

**16th-century icon from the Golden Ring**

Western Europe, Byzantium, and Central Asia, while Sergiev Posad, location of the Trinity Monastery of St. Sergius *(see pp156–9),* became an important center for the Orthodox Church. Moscow was also founded during this era *(see p17)* and, by the 16th century, became Russia's capital. The cluster of towns northeast of Moscow then paled, but in the 1960s they were titled "The Golden Ring" because of their historic splendor.

**THE GOLDEN RING**

*Prince Vladimir Monomakh (see p59) founded a small trading settlement in the late 11th century. It was named Vladimir in 1108. Monomakh's son, Yuriy Dolgorukiy (see p17), expanded the town ,and it was later the capital of Northern Rus.*

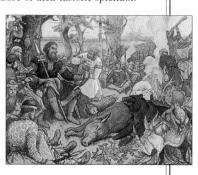

*A campaign by Suzdal against Novgorod in 1169 is the subject of this icon. Created by the 15th-century Novgorod School (see p61), it recalls Suzdal's strength before Moscow became preeminent.*

**Andrey Bogolyubskiy***, the son of Yuriy Dolgorukiy, moved his court to Vladimir in 1157, where his craftsmen were to recreate the splendor of Kiev. His boyars later murdered him for being a dictator.*

**Angels** denote that the campaign against the Mongols was blessed.

**Dmitriy Donskoy**

*The Battle of Kulikovo (see p18), in 1380, was a turning point in the history of the Golden Ring. The Mongols made many inroads into the area, sacking Suzdal in 1238 and demanding tribute from the Russians. Dmitriy Donskoy (see p18) won a decisive victory against them at Kulikovo, with a blessing, it is said, from monk Sergius of Radonezh (see p159).*

*Many churches were built in the towns of the Golden Ring, a sign of their comparative wealth. Some wooden churches are preserved in a museum at Suzdal (see p160).*

# Trinity Monastery of St. Sergius ❺

Троице-Сергиева Лавра
*Troitse-Sergieva Lavra*

FOUNDED AROUND 1345 by Sergius of Radonezh *(see p159)*, the Trinity Monastery of St. Sergius in the town of Sergiev-Possad is one of Russia's most important religious centers and places of pilgrimage. In 1608–10, during the Time of Troubles *(see p19)*, the monks survived a siege by the Polish army, and in the 1680s the young Peter the Great found refuge here during the Streltsy Rebellion *(see p22)*. The monastery was closed down by the Communists in 1919 but was allowed to open again in 1946, when it became headquarters of the Russian Orthodox Church. The headquarters transferred to new premises at the Danilovskiy Monastery *(see pp136–7)* in 1988.

**The Church of the Virgin of Smolensk** was built in 1745 to house the Icon of the Smolensk Virgin.

**The bell tower** was begun in 1741 and completed 28 years later. There are spectacular views from its gallery.

Carpenters' Tower

Hospital with Church of SS. Zosima and Savvatiy

Obelisk

Treasury

**Chapel Over the Well**
*This delightful, Moscow-Baroque* (see p44) *chapel was built in the late 17th century to mark the site of a holy spring.*

Sacristy

★ **Trinity Cathedral**
*Built in 1422–3 over the grave of St. Sergius, this splendid church contains an iconostasis painted by a team of artists led by Andrey Rublev (see p61).*

Water Tower

**Palace of the Metropolitans**
*This grand palace was completed in 1778. It was the residence of the metropolitans and patriarchs in 1946–88.*

Church of the Holy Spirit

★ **Church of St. Sergius and Refectory**
*The monks' refectory was built in 1686–92 with the Church of St. Sergius at its eastern end. The colorful facade features pillars with vine leaf decoration and checkered walls. The interior is equally lavish.*

**Tsars' Apartments**
*These apartments were built in the late 17th century for Tsar Alexis Mikhailovich. He often visited the monastery with a retinue of over 500 courtiers. The building now houses a theological college.*

**VISITORS' CHECKLIST**

75 km (47 miles) NE of Moscow.
8254 45356. from
Yaroslavskiy station (see p219).
**Trinity Cathedral** 6am–5pm
daily. **Treasury and Sacristy**
10am–5pm Tue–Sun.
**Grounds** 6am–9pm daily.
English (book in advance).

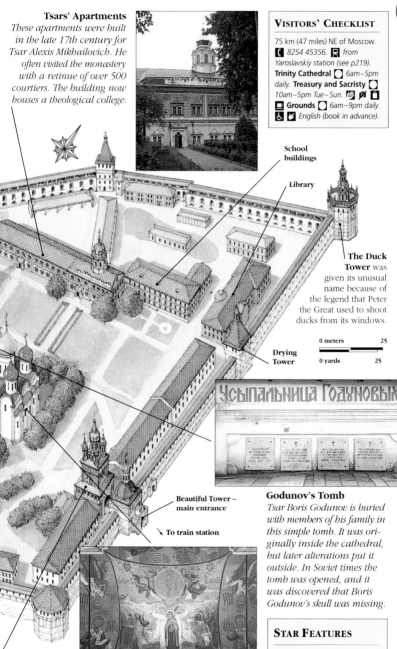

School buildings

Library

**The Duck Tower** was given its unusual name because of the legend that Peter the Great used to shoot ducks from its windows.

Drying Tower

0 meters    25
0 yards     25

Усыпальница Годуновых

**Godunov's Tomb**
*Tsar Boris Godunov is buried with members of his family in this simple tomb. It was originally inside the cathedral, but later alterations put it outside. In Soviet times the tomb was opened, and it was discovered that Boris Godunov's skull was missing.*

Beautiful Tower – main entrance

To train station

**The Gate Church of St. John the Baptist** stands over the main entrance. It was built in 1692–99 by the wealthy Stroganov family.

**★ Cathedral of the Assumption**
*Commissioned in 1559 by Ivan the Terrible to commemorate the capture of Kazan, this is the monastery's main cathedral. Its sumptuous interior was decorated by artists from Yaroslavl over a century later.*

**STAR FEATURES**

★ Cathedral of the Assumption

★ Trinity Cathedral

★ Church of St. Sergius and Refectory

# Exploring the Trinity Monastery of St. Sergius

IN THE 14TH CENTURY, Sergius of Radonezh built a small wooden church in the forests to the north of Moscow and consecrated it to the Holy Trinity. Many pilgrims were attracted to the site by reports of Sergius's piety. He organized them into a community and the Trinity Monastery was born. The monastery expanded as it gained wealth and influence, and today the huge complex is enclosed by white walls around 1.6 km (1 mile) long. Its stunning churches, grouped around the spectacular Cathedral of the Assumption, are among the most beautiful in Russia.

**The fortified Trinity Monastery of St. Sergius seen from the southeast**

**The superb 17th-century iconostasis in the Cathedral of the Assumption**

### Church of St. Sergius and Refectory

The monks' refectory was built in 1686–92 using money donated by Peter the Great and his half-brother, Ivan V, in gratitude for the refuge given them by the monastery during the Streltsy Rebellion *(see p22)*.

The exterior walls are divided into a series of panels, topped by carved scallop shells and separated by pillars decorated with sculpted vines. Each panel is painted so that it looks as though it has three-dimensional facets similar to those of the Faceted Palace *(see p62)*

**Baroque pillars on the Church of St. Sergius and the Refectory**

in the Kremlin. The refectory's main facade features a covered terrace with a wealth of ornamentation. At the eastern end of the refectory is the Church of St. Sergius. Its iconostasis was brought here from Moscow's Church of St. Nicholas on Ilinka in 1688. Delicate fretwork on the iconostasis seems to be metal, but is actually made of wood.

### Cathedral of the Assumption

This magnificent cathedral, with its central golden cupola surrounded by four blue, star-spangled domes, is located at the heart of the monastery. Ivan the Terrible commissioned the cathedral in 1559 to celebrate his defeat of the Mongols at Kazan *(see p19)*. It was completed 26 years later to a design inspired by Aristotele Fioravanti's Cathedral of the Assumption *(see pp58–9)* in the Kremlin. Painters from the acclaimed Yaroslavl school of artists, led by Dmitriy Grigorev, took just 100 days to decorate the lofty interior in 1684. Their names are inscribed beneath a fresco of the Last Judgment on the west wall. The sumptuous five-tiered iconostasis dates from the same period but incorporates a number of icons from the 16th century.

### Trinity Cathedral

This exquisite white cathedral is decorated with *kokoshniki* gables *(see p44)* above a triple-banded frieze and is the oldest stone building in the monastery. It was built over the tomb of St. Sergius in 1422, the year of his canonization. St. Sergius's remains are now

*Christ in Majesty* **(1425–7) in the Trinity Cathedral's iconostasis**

encased in a silver shrine inside the cathedral and are still a focus for visiting pilgrims.

The original decoration of the interior was the work of master artists Andrey Rublev and Daniil Chernyy. Most of their frescoes have since been painted over. Their iconostasis has survived, but Rublev's icon *The Trinity* (1420s) is a copy. The original is in the Tretyakov Gallery *(see pp118–21)*. Also in the iconostasis are two icons by renowned painter Simon Ushakov: *The Holy Face* (1674) and *Christ Enthroned* (1684).

## THE HOLIEST MONK

Sergius of Radonezh (c.1319–92) was born into a noble family but, with his brother, withdrew from the world and founded the Trinity Monastery.
Sergius was instrumental in encouraging Russia's princes to unite against the Mongol invaders and, in 1380, Prince Dmitriy Donskoy, commander of the Russian army, asked for his blessing before attacking the Mongols at Kulikovo *(see p155)*. The Russian victory, along with the discovery that Sergius' body was miraculously unharmed in a Mongol attack on the monastery in 1408, led to Sergius' canonization in 1422.

A 16th-century icon of the appearance of the Virgin and Saints Peter and Paul to Sergius of Radonezh

Open rotunda over the holy spring, next to the Chapel Over the Well

### Other Churches

There are five smaller churches within the monastery walls. The oldest is the Church of the Holy Spirit, built in 1476 by craftsmen from Pskov *(see p44)*, a town to the northwest of Moscow. The infirmary and its adjoining tent-roofed Church of SS. Zosima and Savvatiy were constructed in 1635–8.

The Chapel Over the Well was built at the end of the 17th century over a holy spring. The open rotunda next to it was added in the 19th century. Pilgrims still come to fill bottles with holy water from the spring beneath the rotunda.

Just in front of the Church of St. Sergius stands the small Church of St. Micah. This single-domed church is named after one of St. Sergius's pupils, who is buried beneath it.

The Baroque Church of the Virgin of Smolensk, a small, blue and white rotunda, was

built in 1745. The last of the monastery's churches to be constructed, it houses the Icon of the Smolensk Virgin.

### Palaces and Museums

Gifts from the tsars are among the monastic treasures in the former Sacristy and Treasury. Visitors can see jeweled icon covers, exquisite crosses, icons, gospels in gilded covers, vestments, and some wonderful tapestries, including the pall from the coffin of St. Sergius.

Built in the late 17th century for Tsar Alexis Mikhailovich, the Tsar's Apartments are now used as a theological college. Parts of the slightly shabby exterior are painted to appear

One of the frescoes depicting scenes from St. Sergius's life, on the archway of the Beautiful Tower

faceted. In the southwest corner of the monastery is the 18th-century Palace of the Metropolitans. It was the first of the buildings to come back into religious use when the Soviets allowed the patriarchs and metropolitans to return in 1946.

### Towers and Gate Churches

The Trinity Monastery was originally fortified in the reign of Ivan the Terrible *(see p18)*. Its formidable walls are 12 m (39 ft) high and date, in their present form, from the early 17th century. The monastery's main gate is in the Beautiful Tower. The frescoes on its archway depict the life of St. Sergius. Behind the Beautiful Tower is the red-brick Gate Church of St. John the Baptist.

At the north end of the walls is the Duck Tower, so called because Peter the Great shot ducks from its windows. The spire with its carved duck and the upper tiers were added in 1672–86.

The soaring, five-tiered, blue and white bell tower was built between 1741 and 1769.

## Suzdal ❼
Суздаль
*Suzdal*

200 km (124 miles) NE of Moscow.
🚶 *12,100.* 🚆 *Vladimir, then bus.*
🚌 *(see p219).* 🚍 *Sun*

NESTLING ON the banks of the Kamenka river, Suzdal is the best preserved of the Golden Ring *(see p155)* towns. Its clusters of 17th- and 18th-century whitewashed churches, built by local merchants, and its streets of low, wooden houses with traditional carved eaves and windows mean that it is also one of the most attractive towns in the area.

The first records of Suzdal date from 1024. Shortly afterward the founder of Moscow, Prince Yuriy Dolgorukiy *(see p17)*, built the town's kremlin on a grassy rampart above the river. Its dominant building is the **Cathedral of the Nativity** with its blue, star-spangled domes. Although it was built in the 13th century, most of the current building dates from the 16th century. The south and west doors are of gilded copper, etched with biblical scenes. Frescoes dating from the 13th to the 17th centuries cover the interior walls.

The Cathedral of the Nativity, in the grounds of Suzdal's kremlin

Next to it stands the former archbishop's palace, now the **Suzdal Museum**. Its collection of icons and ancient art is housed in the main room, the magnificent Chamber of the Cross, one of the largest unsupported vaults in Russia. To the northeast, on Suzdal's main street, a long, arcaded building dating from 1806–11 was the former merchants' quarters.

Suzdal also contains five important religious foundations, including the **Monastery of St. Euthymius**. Once the richest in the area, with more than 10,000 serfs at its disposal, the monastery has a commanding position in the north of Suzdal, overlooking the town. Its fortified walls are almost 6 m (20 ft) thick. The monks' cells now house the **Museum of Arts and Crafts**, which has an impressive collection, including religious paintings, and jewelry.

To the south of the monastery is the **Aleksandrovskiy Convent**. It was originally founded in 1240, but it burned down and was rebuilt in the 17th century. Its Cathedral of the Ascension was built at this time by Nataliya Naryshkina, mother of Peter the Great.

Rising from the meadows directly across the river here is the **Convent of the Intercession**. Founded in the 14th

Icon of St. Nicholas, dating from the 15th century, in the Suzdal Museum

century, it was completed in the reign of Basil III in 1510–14. Its retreat houses offer overnight lodging.

On the southwest edge of town is the **Suzdal Museum of Wooden Architecture** an open-air exhibition of wooden buildings brought from all over Russia. Particularly impressive is the Church of the Transfiguration, built in 1756. With domes made with overlapping shingles, it was built without using any metal nails.

🏛 **Suzdal Museum**
Ul Kremlyovskaya. 📞 *09231 20444.*
🕙 *Wed–Mon.* 🎟 📖 *English (book in advance).*

🏛 **Museum of Arts and Crafts**
Ul Lenina. 📞 *09231 20444.* 🕙 *Tue–Sun.* 🎟 📖 *English (book in advance).*

🏛 **Suzdal Museum of Wooden Architecture**
Ul Kremlyovskaya. 📞 *09231 20444.*
🕙 *Wed–Mon.* 🎟 📖 *English (book in advance).*

The Golden Gate, the entrance to Vladimir from the Moscow road

## Vladimir ❽
Владимир
*Vladimir*

170 km (106 miles) NE of Moscow.
🚶 *360,000.* 🚆 🚌 *(see p219).*
🚍 *Daily*

FOUNDED ON the Klyazma river by Prince Vladimir Monomakh *(see p155)* in the late 11th century, Vladimir really began to flourish during the rule of his son, Prince Yuriy Dolgorukiy *(see p17)*. In 1157 Dolgorukiy's heir, Prince Andrey Bogolyubskiy, brought his court here and made it the capital of the new principality of Vladimir-Suzdal. The town's heyday was in the 12th and

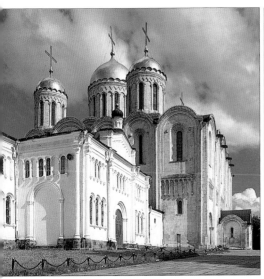

**The 12th-century Cathedral of the Assumption in Vladimir**

early 13th centuries, and most of the architectural monuments worth seeing date from this period. Like Suzdal, Vladimir was later eclipsed by Moscow in political importance, but it remained a significant trading center. Today, Vladimir looks like any industrial city of the Soviet era, although, fortunately, the chemical plants and tire factories are situated at some distance from the picturesque old part of the town, with its fine views.

When approaching Vladimir by the Moscow road, the visitor will still enter the city through the splendid **Golden Gate**. This was constructed in 1164, and combines the functions of both triumphal arch and defensive bastion. The icons above the archway were whitewashed by the Communists and have only recently been restored. The gate now contains a small exhibition on military history.

A short stroll down the main street takes the visitor past the 19th-century trading arcades and shops to the **Cathedral of the Assumption**, Vladimir's most famous monument. Built in 1158–60, high above the

**A detail of the carved bas-reliefs on the Cathedral of St. Dmitriy**

banks of the Klyazma, it was originally decorated with prodigious quantities of gold and silver, precious gems, majolica tiles, and white stone carvings. Craftsmen came from all over Russia, Poland, and the Holy Roman Empire to contribute to what was then the tallest building in Russia. The coronation of many of Russia's princes, including Dmitriy Donskoy (see p18) and Aleksandr Nevskiy (see p17), took place here.

The cathedral was damaged by fire in 1185, and when it was repaired, four domes were added. When, in the 15th century, Ivan III wanted to build the Cathedral of the Assumption in Moscow (see pp58–9), he instructed his Italian architect, Aristotele Fioravanti, to use the cathedral of the same name in Vladimir as his model.

The famous Icon of the Virgin of Vladimir (see p61) used to hang in the cathedral, but it is now in the Tretyakov Gallery (see p121). However, some superb frescoes by medieval masters Andrey Rublev and Daniil Chernyy are still visible under the choir's

gallery on the west wall.

A short distance away is the **Cathedral of St. Dmitriy**, built in 1194–7 by Prince Vsevolod III. A single-domed church of white limestone, its exterior is covered with more than a thousand bas-reliefs featuring griffins, centaurs, rampant lions, and fantastic birds and plants, as well as a portrait of Vsevolod and his family. Over the window on the south wall is a carving of Alexander the Great ascending to heaven, a symbol of princely authority.

## Yasnaya Polyana ❾
Ясная Поляна
*Yasnaya Polyana*

180 km (112 miles) S of Moscow. 📞 *0872 339118.* 🕐 *10am–5:30pm Wed–Sun.* 🚉 *Tula, then bus.* 🚍 *(see p219).* ♿

THE BELOVED country estate of Leo Tolstoy (see p134), Yasnaya Polyana is located in a peaceful valley surrounded by forests. Tolstoy was born on the estate in 1828. From the mid-1850s he spent the summers here with his wife and children, and the family moved here permanently in 1901. The house and its contents are much as they were in Tolstoy's day. The rooms on show include the study, where Tolstoy wrote *War and Peace* and *Anna Karenina*. Other buildings on the estate include the Dom Volkonskovo, where the serfs lived, and a pavilion for the guests. A small literary museum is housed in the former peasants' school that Tolstoy established.

**Leo Tolstoy's house on his beloved family estate, Yasnaya Polyana**

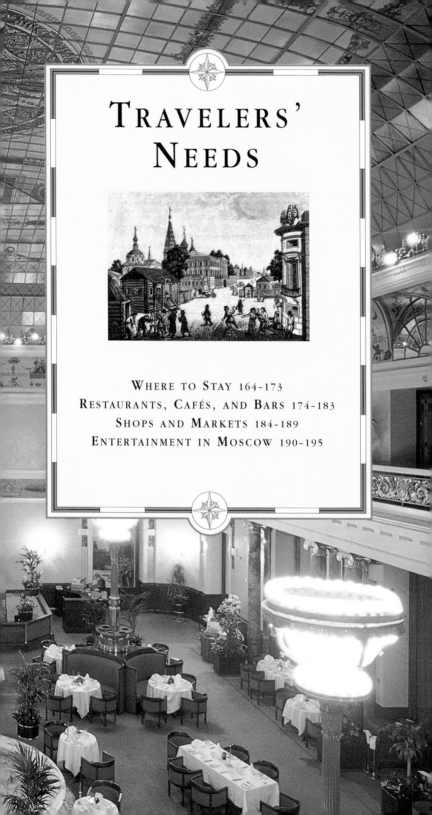

# TRAVELERS'
# NEEDS

# WHERE TO STAY

THE HOTEL SITUATION in Moscow has improved considerably since Russia became an independent state in 1992. New hotels have been built and grand old residences renovated. These works are likely to continue as Yuriy Luzhkov, the city's dynamic mayor, has made new accommodations a priority. Despite the improvements, there is still a great shortage of hotels of all types in the city. Worse still, as with much in modern Russian life, expansion tends to have

A mosaic by Aleksandr Golovin on the Metropol's facade *(see p88)*

taken place at the top end of the market and there is precious little available in the mid-price range. The selection of hotels on pages 168–71 is divided into central or farther-afield locations and arranged in price order. Prices are liable to rapid change so should always be checked. There are no accommodations agencies in Moscow, but it is possible to make a reservation at most hotels directly by phone or fax. The best alternative is to book through a travel agent in advance.

## TYPES OF HOTEL

IN THEORY there are more than 200 hotels in Moscow. Many of these, however, are little more than hostels for professional delegations, with names such as The Oncological Research Center Hotel. With occasional exceptions, therefore, the foreign visitor is in effect confined to hotels that fall into two broad categories: luxury hotels, and cheaper, plainer, "ex-Soviet" hotels.

Luxury hotels are often foreign-owned or run as joint Russian-Western ventures. Many occupy historic buildings (some pre- and some post-Revolution), and have rooms combining period furniture with modern facilities. Service is similar to that in the best hotels in the West, but a double room rarely costs less than the equivalent of $200 a night. Hotels of this type are often referred to as Western-style.

The spacious lobby at the luxurious Baltschug Kempinski *(see p169)*

The more modest, so-called "ex-Soviet" hotels that were formerly run by the state often appear tired. The service can seem to take little account of what guests actually want, but rooms are usually clean and of a good size. These hotels can offer fascinating insight into how the elite in the Soviet era used to live.

## LOCATION OF HOTELS

MOST OF THE luxury hotels are within 15 minutes' drive or metro ride of the center. Ex-Soviet hotels tend to be a little farther out, but there are some options in the center of the city, too.

For both types of hotel, the price is unlikely to be affected very much by location. However, when choosing a hotel, visitors should think about how they want to get around the city and take into consideration whether or not they will have a car, whether they want to get to the main sights on foot, or if their ability to read Cyrillic script is adequate to allow them to use buses and the metro with confidence.

## MAKING A RESERVATION

DURING THE Soviet era all accommodations had to be arranged before going to Russia. It is still impossible to obtain a tourist visa without prebooking but, once there, it is now theoretically possible to walk into any hotel and book a room on the spot. In practice, though, it is best to make arrangements before arriving, which can be done through most travel agents dealing with trips to Russia. Many of the more expensive hotels get booked up quite a while in advance, particularly for weekdays. In ex-Soviet hotels, attitudes left over from the days of restricted travel can make them wary of guests

A spacious, elegantly appointed room in the National *(see p89)*

Guest sitting room adjoining a bedroom at the Danilovskaya *(see p170)*

walking in off the street wanting a room. Almost all the hotels listed here will accept reservations by fax or phone. All the luxury hotels have staff who speak good English, but it is advisable to book rooms at ex-Soviet hotels by fax, asking for written confirmation. Luxury hotels will usually ask for a credit card number as a deposit.

## FACILITIES

ALL LUXURY HOTELS provide the facilities that would be found in an expensive hotel in the West. These include television (often satellite), business facilities, such as a message-taking service and meeting room, minibars, a laundry service, and 24-hour room service. All rooms have a bathroom

with a bath or shower, or both. Fitness facilities or a swimming pool are available in only a handful of hotels. Not even all of the top hotels have air-conditioning, which can be a drawback in the hot summers.

Rooms in an ex-Soviet hotel always contain a television, a refrigerator, and a telephone. International calls from rooms are expensive and may not be easy to make if they have to be booked through the operator. Bathrooms with a bath and shower are also standard. Ex-Soviet hotels, particularly the cheaper places, do not often have sophisticated room service, although laundry can usually be arranged.

Many ex-Soviet hotels still have a *dezhurnaya* sitting at a desk on each floor. As one of their duties, these sometimes rather fearsome ladies look after guests' keys while they are out. Visitors should make sure they do not lose the card given to them when the keys are handed in, since it sometimes has to be shown to get back in through the main entrance. Friendly relations with the *dezhurnaya* will probably increase the chances of receiving good service.

All hotels have bars and restaurants. The luxury hotels contain some of the city's finest restaurants, but

Opulent dining room at the Savoy *(see p168)*

## USING THE LISTINGS

The hotels on pages 168–71 are listed according to location and price category. The symbols summarize the facilities at each hotel.

🛁 all rooms have bath and/or shower.
1 single-rate rooms available
⊞ rooms for more than two people available, or an extra bed can be put in a double room
24 24-hour room service
TV television in all rooms
Y minibar in all rooms
▤ air conditioning in all rooms
🏋 gym/fitness facilities
🏊 swimming pool
🖥 business facilities: fax service, message-taking service, desk, and telephone in room; meeting room.
🧒 caters for children
♿ wheelchair access
🛗 lift
P hotel parking available
Y bar
🍴 restaurant
★ highly recommended
💳 credit and charge cards accepted:
*AE* American Express
*DC* Diners Club
*MC* MasterCard
*V* VISA
*JCB* Japanese Credit Bureau

**Price categories** are based on a standard double room per night in tourist season, including tax, service, and, in some cases, breakfast.
⑤ under US$100
⑤⑤ US$100–175
⑤⑤⑤ US$175–250
⑤⑤⑤⑤ US$250–325
⑤⑤⑤⑤⑤ over US$325

do not expect to find a bargain here. Ex-Soviet hotels tend to be less flexible about mealtimes, and the food is much less exciting. Continental breakfasts are the norm in luxury hotels. In ex-Soviet establishments guests usually help themselves from a large buffet that includes eggs, cold meats, and bread. Breakfast is not usually included in the room price.

The Sovietskiy's elegant Yar restaurant, where mirrored walls add to the feeling of spaciousness *(see p170)*

## PAYMENT

THE GENERAL SHORTAGE of accommodation in Moscow means that, almost without exception, hotel rooms in the city are over-priced. The rates given in this book are the standard rates quoted by the hotels. However, very few guests actually pay the full rate. Business guests usually have cheaper rates negotiated at the expensive hotels by their companies, and most tourists book through an agent, again at more favorable rates. It is worth remembering that it is rarely economical to book any hotel room personally. Travelers interested in a particular hotel should ask their travel agent to inquire about special rates, or should find a travel agent who has already dealt with the hotel. Leisure weekend discounts should be available at many luxury hotels, since most of their clients are business people staying during the week.

The luxury hotels generally quote prices in a foreign currency (usually US dollars). However, it is illegal to pay in any currency other than roubles. The easiest way to pay in these hotels is undoubtedly with a credit card (few take traveler's checks). This eliminates the necessity of carrying large amounts of cash around or changing money. Ex-Soviet hotels do not normally quote prices in dollars and mostly

Detail of an interior mosaic at the Moscow *(see p168)*

take only cash (in roubles), though some will take credit cards. They do not accept traveler's checks.

Luxury hotels frequently quote prices exclusive of VAT and city tax; this can add more than 20 percent to the bill. Visitors should also bear in mind that tax rates in Russia are liable to change at short notice.

Breakfast is rarely included in room prices and can be a significant addition to the bill. The cost of making international or even local phone calls from a hotel room can also come as a shock. The local phone network *(see p206)* is cheaper.

## TRAVELING WITH CHILDREN

RUSSIANS IDOLIZE their children, but this rarely seems to translate into hotel facilities for families. In most hotels it should be possible to have an extra bed put in a room for an additional fee, and most luxury hotels will provide babysitters. Generally, however, hotels are more interested in business guests or tour groups, so do not expect to find extensive facilities for children or favorable room rates for families.

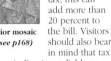

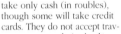

Formidable array of windows in the Moscow's expansive facade *(see p168)*

The Marco Polo Presnya, centrally located on a quiet street *(see p168)*

## DISABLED TRAVELERS

F EW HOTELS in Moscow have wheelchair access, and those that do generally have few facilities. Disabled travelers should check in advance with their travel agents or the hotels, making sure to ask about any specific needs.

## SECURITY

W HILE MANY of the dangers of life in Moscow are exaggerated, hotels (particularly those owned by foreign companies) take security very seriously. Do not be surprised to see men with walkie-talkies patrolling the entrances of even the most refined establishments. Luxury hotels all have safe-deposit boxes, and hotel

guests generally have few problems with personal safety.

Ex-Soviet hotels also have a very good record on security. Porters keep undesirables out, and the *dezhurnaya (see p165)* on each floor keeps a pretty close eye on her own domain.

However, as in other major cities, tourists are often targets for petty criminals. Take particular care when leaving the hotel, as pickpockets are known to hang around outside tourist hotels.

## STAYING WITH FAMILIES

A FEW ORGANIZATIONS now arrange stays with families in Moscow. While this can be a good option for those who want to improve their Russian or get closer to "real" Russian life, staying with a family can be difficult for visitors who speak no Russian. When booking accommodation with a family, it is important to check where their apartment is – few are centrally located, so those choosing this option will need to be confident about traveling from the suburbs into the center of Moscow. It is also important to be quite clear about whether items such as meals and laundry are included in the basic cost. Guests are normally given a separate bedroom but should expect to share the bathroom and other facilities with the host family.

## BUDGET ACCOMMODATIONS

O PTIONS FOR travelers on a tight budget are very limited. Some of the cheaper ex-Soviet hotels have rooms for the equivalent of less than $50. The service may be rather sullen and the rooms a little shabby, but they should be clean. Their restaurants may be uninspiring. **Bed and Breakfast** rents out apartments with cleaning included

The Stalinist-Gothic tower of the Ukraine *(see p169)*

The Ukraine's lobby *(see p169)*

of them close to Belorusskaya metro. Apartments for one person cost the equivalent of about $50 a night; the rate decreases for sharing.

There are very few hostels in Moscow, but the **Prakash Guest House** and the **Travelers' Guest House** specifically cater to travelers on a budget. They offer dormitory accommodation from the equivalent of $15 and $25 a night respectively. The service is friendly and the dormitories are clean.

### DIRECTORY

**STAYING WITH FAMILIES**

**Moscow Bed and Breakfast**
( 457 3508.
FAX 457 3508.

**Russian Tours and Travel**
156 Fifth Ave., New York, NY.
( (212) 741-0033.

**BUDGET ACCOMMODATIONS**

**Bed and Breakfast**
( 147 0021.

**Prakash Guest House**
Общежитие Пракаш
Profsoyuznaya ulitsa 83, korpus 1, podezd 2.
( 334 2598.
FAX 334 2598.

**Travelers' Guest House**
Bolshaya Pereyaslavskaya ulitsa 50, 10th floor.
( 971 4059.
FAX 280 7686.

## CITY CENTER

# Belgrade
Белград

Smolenskaya ploshchad 5. **Map** 5 C1.
**[** 248 1643. **FAX** 230 2129. **Rooms:**
920.  *MC, V.* **$**

The Belgrade fulfils a useful role
as a functional and economical
ex-Soviet hotel in the center of
Moscow. It formerly occupied two
imposing tower blocks built in the
later years of the Soviet era, but
now occupies just one of them.
Although the service can often
be rather perfunctory, a reminder
of pre-democracy standards, the
restaurant serves good east-
European food and the hotel as
a whole is seemingly undergoing
constant face-lifts. With the giant
Rossiya hotel scheduled for demolition, the Belgrade takes its place
as the only good hotel of its type
left in the city center.

# Budapesht
Будапешт

Petrovskie Linii ulitsa 2/18. **Map** 3 A4.
**[** 924 8820. **FAX** 921 1266. **Rooms:**
116. *AE, DC, MC, V, JCB.* **$$**

All of Moscow's central sights can
easily be reached on foot from this
hotel. The Budapesht is located on
a quiet street off ulitsa Petrovka, a
good location for music lovers as it
is close to the Bolshoy Theater.
While the Budapesht has none of
the glamor of some of the central
hotels, its prices make it a very
attractive compromise between the
expensive, centrally located, luxury
hotels and the cheaper hotels on
the outskirts of the city. The hotel
was built in 1876 and the common
areas have a slightly shabby air. The
lobby furnishings consist of a frayed
carpet and a single sofa, while the
elevators creak away in the corner.
However, the bedrooms are bright
and clean, with sparse furnishings
and a faint smell of disinfectant. The
hotel bar has been decorated as
an English pub. The restaurant,
which is being renovated, offers
traditional Russian cuisine.

# Intourist
Интурист

Tverskaya ulitsa 3/5. **Map** 2 F5. **[**
956 8426. **FAX** 956 8450. **Rooms:** 433.
*DC, MC, V, JCB.* **$**

Previously the favored destination
of foreign tour groups, these days
the Intourist is little more than a
reminder of the low standards that
Soviet hotels could get away with

before tourists were able to choose
their own accommodations.
　Despite this, the 22 stories of
identical rooms nonetheless offer
accommodation at a reasonable
price in an excellent location, with-
in five minutes' walk of Red Square.
Although rumors of a takeover or
demolition of the hotel are rife,
they seem to be unfounded and
the Intourist insists that it will be in
business well into the 21st century.
　Among the various restaurants in
the hotel the best is probably the
tiny Azteca, serving Mexican food
in two converted rooms on the 20th
floor. The bar near the lobby on the
ground floor is still the most con-
venient place in the city center to
get a cup of coffee and a slice of
cake. In the Soviet era, Moscow
gained a reputation for seedy hotel
lobbies, and the Intourist has the
dubious distinction of being where
that notoriety began. The lobby's
rather run-down aspect and the
prostitutes who sometimes frequent
it mean that is still the same today.

# Moscow
Москва

Ulitsa Okhotnyy ryad 2. **Map** 3 A5.
**[** 960 2020. **FAX** 928 5938. **Rooms:**
983. *MC, V.* **$$**

This monumental hotel is famous
for its asymmetrical facade. The
story goes that Stalin was shown
two alternative designs for a new
hotel and approved them both, so
the finished building ended up as
a combination of the two.
　The Moscow Hotel used to provide accommodations for visiting
Communist Party officials, and it
remains something of a Soviet outpost in modern, capitalist Moscow.
Today, for those who are happy to
ignore the prostitutes and dubious
characters in the lobby, the hotel
provides cheap lodgings right in
the center of the city.
　The rooms are generally clean,
of a decent size, and sound-proofed
against the passing traffic. Rooms
high up on the south side offer
views of Red Square. The hotel's
main restaurant is to be avoided,
but El Rincón Español, its Spanish
bar, is one of Moscow's oldest and
most reliable foreign restaurants.

# Arbat
Арбат

Plotnikov pereulok 12. **Map** 6 D2.
**[** 244 7635. **FAX** 244 0093. **Rooms:**
105. *AE, DC, MC, V.* **$$$**

The Arbat Hotel is on a quiet side
street leading south from ulitsa
Arbat, Moscow's most famous
souvenir-laden pedestrian street.

The hotel is a nondescript 1960s
pale brick building, nestling among
the flats that used to house the
Communist Party elite. For those
who do not want to pay the prices
of the top-class hotels in the very
center of the city, but want some-
where quiet and reasonably central,
the Arbat is a very good option.
　The rooms are quite large, and
many have a sitting area, but the
bathrooms and furnishings gen-
erally have the slightly tired look
of so many of the ex-Soviet hotels.
The bar is an exception to this. It
is an astonishing mix of shiny
black surfaces and thick purple
carpet, and there is a very nice
veranda where guests can sit and
have a drink outside in summer.

# Marco Polo Presnya
Марко Поло Пресня

Spiridonevskiy pereulok 9. **Map** 2 E4.
**[** 202 4834. **FAX** 926 5402. **Rooms:**
68. *AE, DC, MC,
V, JCB.* **$$$$**

Situated in a peaceful area near
Patriarch's Pond *(see p96)*, the
Marco Polo Presnya has one of the
best locations in Moscow. Although
it is not perfectly placed for public
transportation, visitors heading out
from the hotel on foot will pass
along some of Moscow's most
attractive residential streets. Its
smaller size compared with other
hotels in a similar category con-
tributes to its quieter atmosphere.
　The hotel itself is the poor
relation of the Palace Hotel on
Tverskaya ulitsa. Both hotels were
taken over by the Marco Polo chain,
but, unlike the Palace, the Presnya
has not yet been completely over-
hauled. The rooms are on the small
side, and the cracks in the bathroom
tiles suggest the need for renova-
tion. Despite the faint air of neglect
and the slightly sullen service, the
hotel offers a low-key alternative
to the city's grander establishments.

# Savoy
Савой

Rozhdestvenka ulitsa 3. **Map** 3 A4.
**[** 929 8500. **FAX** 230 2186. **Rooms:**
86. *AE,
DC, MC, V, JCB.* **$$$$**

Built in 1912, the Savoy was reno-
vated in 1989 and was the first of
Moscow's luxury hotels to reopen
under foreign management. It is
tucked away on a quiet side street
near Lubyanka Square *(see p112)*.
Its plain and unassuming exterior
belies its luxurious interior.
　A small lobby leads into rather
dark but luxurious surroundings,
where rich wooden fittings, red

carpets, and subdued lighting give it an atmosphere somewhat akin to a gentleman's club from a past era. The Savoy's corridors double as an art gallery, with pictures hanging along every wall.

The bedrooms are small, but they have high ceilings, reproduction furniture, and modern facilities. The Savoy has one restaurant with tables laid out around a splashing fountain, beneath ornate chandeliers and elaborate wall paintings.

## Baltschug Kempinski
### Балчуг Кемпинский

Ulitsa Balchug 1. **Map** 7 B2. 230 6500. FAX 230 6502. *Rooms:* 234. AE, DC, MC, V, JCB. $$$$$

Although it does not have the architectural grandeur of some of its rivals, the Baltschug Kempinski is still one of Moscow's finest hotels. Hidden within a handsome building dating from the late 19th century is a luxurious, modern interior which features elegant white marble and golden banisters.

The bedrooms are stylish, though rather uninspiringly decorated. Rooms on the river side offer magnificent views of the Kremlin and St. Basil's Cathedral. The hotel's restaurant is reputed to offer the best Sunday brunch in Moscow.

The Baltschug Kempinski is on the south bank of the Moskva River. Although it is centrally located, the walk across the river to the Kremlin can seem a long one, particularly if a winter wind is blowing.

## Marriott Grand Hotel
### Марриотт Гранд отель

Tverskaya ulitsa 26. **Map** 2 E3. 935 8500. FAX 937 0001. *Rooms:* 392. AE, MC, V, JCB. $$$$$

This luxury establishment, belonging to the American Marriott chain of hotels, was completed in 1997. It is another of the city's modern buildings whose architectural design has been loosely influenced by late-19th-century Style Moderne.

It offers every modern amenity, including computer ports in every room. As it has a conference hall and meeting rooms, a large number of the guests are business travelers. Its facilities also include a well-equipped fitness center with an indoor pool, a Jacuzzi, a wet and dry sauna, a solarium, and an American-style juice bar. The Marriott Grand has three restaurants: the best serves both Russian and Western cuisine; the buffet restaurant serves buffet-style breakfasts,

lunches, and dinners (often themed along national lines such as Italian, German, or Asian), and an informal Russian taverna offers a large selection of caviars and vodkas.

The hotel is conveniently and centrally situated between the Garden and Boulevard Rings.

## Metropol
### Метрополь

Teatralnyy proezd 1/4. **Map** 3 A5. 927 6000. FAX 927 6010. *Rooms:* 369. AE, DC, MC, V, JCB. $$$$$

Built between 1899 and 1905, the progress of the Metropol *(see p88)* through the 20th century mirrors that of Moscow itself. It was extremely opulent in tsarist times, but was requisitioned by the Soviets immediately after the Revolution. Following years of neglect the hotel was renovated, with foreign participation, and is now prohibitively expensive for most.

The Metropol is a wonderful example of Style Moderne *(see p45)* from the turn of the 20th century. Its spectacular interior is adorned with mosaics, golden chandeliers, and stained glass. The Metropol Restaurant is dazzling. Set beneath an impressive vaulted glass ceiling, it is lit by great rings of lamps on long gilded stalks.

Many of the bedrooms are similarly lavish, combining antique furniture with modern facilities. Of course all this luxury comes at a price, but there is a hint of complacency about the service. However, even for those not staying in the Metropol, it is worth dropping in for a cup of coffee just for the chance to see the magnificent interior.

## National
### Националь

Mokhovaya ulitsa 15/1. **Map** 2 F5. 258 7000. FAX 258 7100. *Rooms:* 231. AE, DC, MC, V, JCB. $$$$$

The charms of the Hotel National *(see p89)* are understated, and the beauty of the facade may only become apparent on close inspection. Built in 1903, the hotel was completely overhauled in the early 1990s and has now firmly reestablished itself as one of the top two or three luxury hotels in Moscow.

The bedrooms have high ceilings and wooden floors and the more expensive ones contain antique furniture and rugs. The rooms tend to get smaller and less impressive the higher up they are, and views of the Kremlin come at a premium. The hotel's cafés and restaurants

lie beyond a warrenlike lobby. The service is impeccable, but the food is astonishingly expensive. The glassed-in bar on the ground floor is thick with foliage giving it the atmosphere of a conservatory.

### FARTHER AFIELD

## Kosmos
### Космос

Prospekt Mira 150. 234 1000. FAX 215 8880. *Rooms:* 1,776. AE, DC, MC, V, JCB. $$

The Kosmos was opened in 1980, in time for the Moscow Olympics. Its huge crescent-shaped facade looks out over the All-Russian Exhibition Center *(see p145)*.

Like the exhibition, the Kosmos is not quite the flagship it once was. The cavernous lobby, decorated on the theme of space with stars and rockets suspended from the ceiling, is now a little dated, and the shops and bars that surround it are no longer Moscow's most luxurious. The swimming pool is closed for refurbishment until further notice.

The rooms, however, are a good size and get plenty of light, and those on the top floors have splendid views. The lower ground floor contains a late-night bar and a ten-pin bowling alley. The Kosmos is situated well to the north of the city center and is directly opposite the VDNKh metro station.

## Ukraine
### Украина

Kutuzovskiy prospekt 2/1. **Map** 5 B1. 243 2596. FAX 956 2078. *Rooms:* 1,600. AE, DC, MC, V. $$

The Ukraine Hotel occupies one of the seven Stalinist-Gothic *(see p45)* tower blocks that Stalin commissioned around Moscow after World War II. Located on the west bank of the Moskva River, it looks out over the White House *(see p128)* on the other side.

In some ways the Ukraine is the most magnificent of all the hotel buildings in Moscow. An interesting feature of the interior decoration is the series of mosaics of happy Soviet youth that adorns the lobby ceiling. The bedrooms have parquet floors and contain period furniture, but guests should not expect great luxury here. The whole feel of the place is now a little dated and shabby.

Nevertheless, staying at the Ukraine offers a rare chance to see the inside of a building constructed when the Soviet Union was at its most powerful.

*For key to symbols see p165*

## Danilovskaya
Даниловская

Bolshoy Starodanilovskiy pereulok 5.
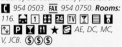 954 0503. **FAX** 954 0750. **Rooms:** 116. AE, DC, MC, V, JCB. $$$$

The Danilovskaya stands on the grounds of the fortified Danilovskiy Monastery *(see pp136–7)*, and the hotel's security guard sits in a restored 15th-century turreted watchtower. However, the hotel itself is a five-story block built in 1991.

The Danilovskaya is a remarkable place run by the Russian Orthodox Church. Portraits of Moscow's patriarchs hang in the corridors, and religious icons decorate the rooms. The intriguing blend of spiritual and secular gives the establishment a faintly otherworldly quality. This very agreeable hotel offers clean, quiet rooms, up-to-date facilities, and views of the renovated monastery and its tranquil gardens. The hotel restaurant is excellent, offering some of the best Russian food to be had in Moscow.

The Danilovskaya is located some way to the south of the city center and is not therefore within walking distance of the main sights.

## Hotel Sovetskiy
Отель Советский

Leningradskiy prospekt 32/2. **Map** 1 B1. 960 2000. **FAX** 250 8003. **Rooms:** 100. AE, DC, MC, V. $$$$

For sheer grandeur, as opposed to modern facilities, the Sovetskiy is hard to beat. In Soviet times, the hotel was the place where visiting foreign dignitaries stayed.

Built in 1957 in Stalinist style, it is wonderfully grandiose, although it does not have very many rooms. Red carpets line the marble floors and the lobby is surrounded by vast columns. The bedrooms are similarly opulent. They are large, with high, molded ceilings, wooden floors, and period furniture. However, the bathrooms are unfortunately slightly shabby.

The hotel's restaurant is named the Yar, after the famous restaurant of the same name, once owned by Frenchman Tranquille Yard in the city center. The latter was frequented by the poet Alexander Pushkin who, in one of his poems, cried "take me to the Yar." The hotel's restaurant is a spectacular mirrored hall, lit by a stunning chandelier.

The Sovetskiy is 15–20 minutes' drive from the city center by car, on the road to Sheremetevo *(see p208)*. Dinamo, the nearest metro station to the hotel, is about 1 km (1,000 yds) away along this road.

## Novotel
Новотель

Sheremetevo 2 Airport. 926 5900, 502 220 6611. **FAX** 926 5904, 502 220 6604. **Rooms:** 488. AE, DC, MC, V, JCB. $$$$

Exactly what you would expect from an airport hotel, the Novotel is clean, bright, and efficient. The rooms are a decent size and well equipped. Its restaurants and bars are good, although short on character. For visitors stuck at the airport for any length of time, the facilities at the Novotel are infinitely superior to anything in the airport itself.

## President Hotel
Президент отель

Ulitsa Bolshaya Yakimanka 24. **Map** 7 A4. 239 3800. **FAX** 230 2318. **Rooms:** 209. AE, DC, MC, V. $$$$

Opened in 1983, the President Hotel was favored by top Communist Party officials and visiting foreign dignitaries, and the official atmosphere still lingers. Staff members and the security guards sometimes seem to forget that these days it is their job to entice guests in rather than keep them out. Security at the President is extremely tight, making it a frequent choice among modern Russia's visiting foreign statesmen.

Inside, the hotel has all the hallmarks of late Soviet architecture at its most monumental. A broad marble staircase sweeps up to a lobby lit by spotlights and mirrored ceilings. The rooms are quite large and furnished functionally, if not always with good taste. The presence of several conference halls indicates that this is primarily a business hotel. It is south of the river, not far from the city center.

## Art Sport Hotel
Арт Спорт отель

3-ya Peschanaya ulitsa N2. 955 2300. **FAX** 955 2310. **Rooms:** 86. AE, DC, MC, V. $$$$

This curiously named hotel opened in November 1996. The "Art" in its name refers to the collection of sculptures in the garden, while the "Sport" comes from the fact that the hotel is located in the former Red Army Sports Compound. German-run, the hotel is clean and well maintained and somewhat resembles an upscale American motel.

The rooms are of a decent size and contain modern, functional furniture. The main attractions are

facilities (that include a sauna), an artificial waterfall, and a beer garden. The latter is a rarity in Moscow and provides a quiet, pleasant place to sit and enjoy a drink outside when the weather permits. The cuisine in the main restaurant and the bar is European, with the bar offering the specialty of hearty grilled meals.

The Art Sport Hotel is about 20 minutes by car from the center of Moscow, but not very conveniently located for public transportation. In the summer, however, it offers a rare opportunity to relax away from the heat and fumes of the city center.

## Mezhdunarodnaya
Международная

Krasnopresnenskaya nab 12. **Map** 5 A1. 258 1212. **FAX** 253 2481. **Rooms:** 547. AE, DC, MC, V, JCB. $$$$

The Mezhdunarodnaya Center (known by all as the "Mezh") is a sprawling complex of hotel rooms, offices, shops, and restaurants. It was built in 1980 on the initiative and money of the American tycoon Armand Hammer, and was to be a symbol of US-Soviet relations. Hammer was head of Occidental Petroleum as well as a promoter of US-Soviet relations. Throughout the 1980s the Mezh was almost the only place for visiting business people to stay, a Western oasis in the Communist capital. Today it is still popular with the business community, although its relatively inaccessible location makes it less attractive for visitors interested in sightseeing.

The centerpiece of the hotel's cavernous lobby is a large wooden cuckoo clock. Various bars and restaurants, including Japanese and Chinese establishments, lead off the lobby. The hotel's bedrooms are functional, if a little uninspiring.

## Palace Hotel
Палас отель

1-ya Tverskaya-Yamskaya ulitsa 19. **Map** 2 D2. 931 9700, 502 256 3000. **FAX** 931 9704, 502 256 3008. **Rooms:** 218. AE, DC, MC, V, JCB. $$$$

This hotel occupies a modern building with a simple facade of granite and mirrored glass. The interior is unremarkable, but any lack of character is made up for by the luxurious surroundings, modern facilities, and efficient and very friendly staff. Although the Palace is short on the glamour of Moscow's older hotels, for luxury and range of facilities it is unbeatable. Its entrance leads out onto an extension of Tverskaya ulitsa, one of central Moscow's busiest streets. However, the hotel itself is fully soundproofed.

## Radisson-Slavyanskaya
Рэдиссон-Славянская

Berezhkovskaya nab 2. **Map** 5 B2.
📞 *941 8020.* FAX *941 8000.*
**Rooms:** 410. 🛏 1 🏨 24 TV 🗐
🍽 🏋 ⛶ 🕭 🎅 Y 🖩 ★
🐾 *AE, DC, V.* $ $ $ $

The Radisson-Slavyanskaya is the archetypal business hotel. It has a long corridor lined with luxury shops, which leads into a large, low-ceilinged bar favored by business people. The hotel is next to Kievsky Station, out of walking range of the city center, but with good public transit connections.

Most guests stay at the Radisson-Slavyanskaya for its excellent business facilities, and visitors on vacation may find the working atmosphere and standardized rooms a little unexciting. However, it does possess one of Moscow's English-language movie houses – the American House of Cinema (*see p193*).

## Tverskaya
Тверская

1-ya Tverskaya-Yamskaya ulitsa 34.
**Map** 2 D2. 📞 *502 290 9900.* FAX
*502 290 9999.* **Rooms:** 162. 🛏 1
🏨 24 TV 🗐 🍽 🏋 ⛶ 🕭 P
Y 🖩 ★ 🐾 *AE, DC, MC, V, JCB.*
$ $ $ $

The Tverskaya Hotel was built in the 1990s and opened in 1995, but its restrained facade imitates the Style-Moderne architecture that was popular 100 years previously.

From the unremarkable lobby, glass elevators take guests up into a magnificent atrium that stretches eight floors to the hotel's glass roof. The bedrooms are very comfortably furnished and have modern facilities. Style-Moderne features, including extravagantly curved wooden handrails, colored glass windows, and brass fittings, recur throughout the Tverskaya.

The hotel is run by an American management team. Security is tight and the service is excellent.

## Aerostar
Аэростар

Leningradskiy prospekt 37, korpus 9.
📞 *213 9000.* FAX *213 9001.* **Rooms:**
413. 🛏 1 🏨 24 TV 🗐 🍽 🏋
⛶ 🕭 P Y 🖩 🐾 *AE, DC, MC,*
*V, JCB.* $ $ $ $ $

The construction of the Aerostar began before the 1980 Moscow

Olympics. However, the money ran out, and it was only when a Russian-Canadian joint venture took over that the hotel was finally finished. It opened in 1991.

From the outside the building is an uninspiring, white, concrete block, but inside, the hotel is cool and bright, with a large bar overlooking the lobby. The bedrooms are furnished in a comfortable modern style. They have windows stretching from floor to ceiling, which gives the rooms a particularly light and airy feel.

Easy access to Sheremetevo airport (*see p208*) makes the Aerostar a popular choice for short-stay guests, especially business travelers. It is situated on Leningradskiy prospekt, the main road leading from Moscow to the airport, 30 km (19 miles) away. For other visitors, the 20-minute car trip into the city center may prove a drawback.

## Renaissance Moscow
Ренессанс Москва

Olimpiyskiy prospekt 18/1. **Map** 3 A1.
📞 *931 9000.* FAX *931 9076.* **Rooms:**
475. 🛏 1 🏨 24 TV Y 🗐 🍽
🏋 ⛶ 🕭 🎅 🐾 *AE, DC, MC, V, JCB.* $ $ $ $ $

Like the sports stadium next door, the Renaissance Moscow Hotel was intended to be completed in time for the 1980 Moscow Olympics. The stadium was built on time and is now falling down. In contrast, the hotel was not completed until 1991, but it is in much better condition as a result.

The Renaissance Moscow is a luxury hotel of the modern variety. It is possibly a touch short on character, but it has excellent facilities, including the best swimming pool and fitness center in Moscow. The rooms are small and neatly fitted out with pale, functional furniture. A complex of bars, restaurants, and shops is situated on the lower ground floor. The Renaissance also offers the Dome, an English-language movie theater (*see p193*).

## Sofitel-Iris
Софитель-Ирис

Korovinskoye shosse 10. 📞 *488 8000.* FAX *488 8888.* **Rooms:** 195.
🛏 1 🏨 24 TV Y 🗐 🍽 🏋 ⛶
🕭 🎅 P Y 🖩 ★ 🐾 *AE, DC, MC, V, JCB.* $ $ $ $ $

This hotel is so named because it was built on the grounds of the eye clinic of a Professor Fyodorov. Architecturally, too, the eye motif is strong: a silver oval stares down from eight floors above the café in the lobby. The open-plan effect, with bedrooms set back on balconies running around the atrium,

gives the hotel a pleasant, airy feel. The rooms themselves are modern and well equipped. The restaurant offers excellent, if expensive, French food.

The Pullman Iris, in the north of Moscow, is a long way from the center of town. However, a free shuttle service runs from the hotel into the city and back every half an hour from 7:30am until 11:00pm.

---

## BEYOND MOSCOW

## Tour-Center
Тур-Центр

Korovnikiy ulitsa, Suzdal. 📞 *2 0908.*
FAX *2 0766.* **Rooms:** 271. 🛏 1 🏨
🖼 🕭 P Y 🖩 ★ 🐾

Visitors coming to Suzdal (*see p160*) to savor the architecture dating from as early as the 11th century may be disappointed to find themselves staying in this low building built around 1970. However, the rooms are perfectly clean and well equipped. Since it is the most convenient accommodations in the town, the best way to consider the Tour-Center is as a living slice of the conditions prevalent in recent Soviet history. Its bleak lobby, facilities that are not quite as extensive as advertised, and rather unenthusiastic staff, who have figured out that the competition in the area is limited, make it a good example of an ex-Soviet hotel.

Situated on the northwest edge of the town, the hotel is about 15 minutes' walk from the churches and other religious buildings at the center of the town.

## Moscow
Москва

Moscow Railroad Station Square, Tula.
📞 *0872 208952.* FAX *872 208952.*
**Rooms:** 357. 1 🕭 Y 🖩 $ $

Trains from Moscow arrive in Tula just across the square from the Moscow Hotel. However, the Moscow is probably not the sort of place visitors would choose for a long stay unless they are on a tight budget. For those passing through Tula on the way to Yasnaya Polyana (*see p161*), the home of Tolstoy (*see p134*), it is perfectly adequate. The rooms are clean and not very expensive, although they are rather faded and not particularly large. The level of service, though, has not caught up with the improved standards generally observed in Moscow's hotels. Staff members do not usually speak foreign languages, so guests should be prepared to fend for themselves or come prepared with advance sightseeing information. The Moscow's restaurant will satisfy only the truly hungry.

For key to symbols *see p165*

# Moscow's Best: Hotels

THE HOTELS RECOMMENDED on these pages all offer an excellent standard of modern comfort and a good range of facilities for both the leisure and the business traveler, though fitness enthusiasts will have a limited choice if they want a gym on the premises. They are all luxury hotels, known for efficient, courteous service – an attribute not always in evidence in other hotels. Their architecture ranges from early-20th-century Style Moderne to late-20th-century sleek steel and glass, plus the unique combination of a 1990s building set in the gardens of the 13th-century Danilovskiy Monastery.

*Tverskaya*

**Tverskaya**
*Both the exterior facade and the interior of this comfortable, modern hotel imitate early-20th-century Style Moderne (see p171).*

*Arbatskaya*

**Palace Hotel**
*This luxury, modern hotel is renowned for its friendly staff and excellent service. It also has simple and elegant decor, though perhaps lacks the character of some of Moscow's other fine hotels (see p170).*

**Marco Polo Presnya**
*While not as palatial as some of Moscow's hotels, the Marco Polo Presnya is attractively located in a quiet residential area. It has one restaurant serving good, standard European-style food (see p168).*

**National**
*Built and decorated in a mixtu of 19th-century styles, this famou and impressive hotel has an ai conservatory-like bar (see p169*

### Renaissance Moscow
*This large hotel, completed in 1991, offers excellent modern facilities, including Moscow's best fitness center and swimming pool – rarities in Moscow's hotels* (see p171).

### Savoy
*Although the Savoy's bedrooms are small, their luxurious fittings and soft lighting combine to give them a welcoming feel* (see p168).

| 0 meters | 600 |
| 0 yards | 600 |

Red Square and Kitay Gorod

mlin

### Metropol
*Built in 1899–1905, the Metropol is one of the best examples of Style Moderne in Moscow. Its elaborate facade features a number of mosaics and carved stone friezes* (see p169).

Zamoskvoreche

### Baltschug Kempinski
*This grand hotel was established in the 19th century, but has a luxuriously appointed modern interior* (see p169).

### Danilovskaya
*Situated in the peaceful grounds of the 13th-century Danilovskiy Monastery, this modern hotel* (see p170) *is run by the Russian Orthodox Church.*

# RESTAURANTS, CAFÉS, AND BARS

THE PASTIME of dining out is a relatively new concept in Russia, and nowhere has it been embraced more strongly than in the capital. In the restrictive Soviet era, the number of good restaurants in Moscow could be counted on one hand. Today, however, the city boasts an array of places to eat that, if not approaching the scope of New York or London, at least provides visitors with numerous desirable options, from Russian and European to Caucasian, Indian, and Chinese. Most decent restaurants are moderately expensive – Moscow is still a long way from acquiring a casual café culture – but the frequency with which new places are opening bodes well for the hungry tourist. The following pages will help you locate the best-quality food and most exciting cuisine in all price categories. A detailed review of the selected restaurants is provided on pages 180–81, and ideas for light meals on pages 182–3.

**Logo of Russkoe Bistro chain**

McDonald's, now a familiar sight all over Moscow

## WHERE TO EAT

MOST OF MOSCOW'S better known restaurants are to be found in central Moscow; almost all, therefore, are easily accessible by metro. Ulitsa Arbat (see pp70–71) has the highest concentration and variety of restaurants, from Russian and Georgian to Italian and Japanese, as well as a now ubiquitous McDonald's (see p182). There is also plenty of choice along Tverskaya ulitsa (see p89), and at Triumfalnaya ploshchad. Russkoe Bistro (see p183) is a popular new chain offering fast food Russian style.

## READING THE MENU

IN RESTAURANTS specializing in international cuisine, the menu is almost always in Russian, English, and sometimes a third language. The staff speak English in most restaurants geared toward foreigners. In smaller, local eateries, a knowledge of the Cyrillic alphabet will help with deciphering the menu.

## TYPES OF CUISINE

THERE ARE surprisingly few good, exclusively Russian restaurants in Moscow. Russians have never made a habit of dining out, nor has Russian cuisine ever enjoyed the prominence of, say, French or Italian. Georgian or Armenian cooking, both of which are delicious and relatively inexpensive, are a better option. Mediterranean and other Western European restaurants, especially Italian ones, are now increasingly popular in Moscow. Chinese and Japanese food is generally overpriced and of variable quality, but there are a few excellent Indian restaurants.

**Café sign, listing a selection of Russian dishes**

## WHAT TO DRINK

VODKA IS the alcoholic drink most often associated with Russia. However, in the years since perestroika, beer has become more widely available as an accompaniment to meals. Some restaurants now offer imported and local beer on tap, along with a variety of bottled beers. The better European restaurants have commendable wine lists, although good imported wine tends to be quite expensive. It is a shame to visit Moscow without sampling a bottle of Georgian wine (see p179). This wine tends to be sweet and is an excellent accompaniment to the food.

## PAYMENT AND TIPPING

ONE of the drawbacks of eating out in Moscow is that many restaurants, especially the less touristy ones, take only cash. This situation is gradually changing, but it is still a consideration when deciding where to eat. Generally restaurants that serve Western or Asian cuisine will accept credit cards, but it is a good idea to call ahead and check. Prices vary enormously, from the cheapest local cafeteria (stolovaya),

The Central House of Writers (see p181), one of Moscow's most exclusive restaurants

**Outdoor café in Tverskaya, a good place to watch the world go by**

where a basic Russian meal might cost the equivalent of around $5, to the exclusive Central House of Writers, where dinner will come to over $75. Most international restaurants fall in the moderate to expensive range; it can be difficult to eat cheaply in Moscow without sticking rigidly to the Russian staples of bread, cheese, and salami-style sausage (*kolbasa*).

Tipping is not as ingrained in Russia as elsewhere. A good rule of thumb is to keep to international standards – about 15 percent – in foreign or prestigious restaurants, but to leave just small change, or nothing at all, in Russian-style restaurants or cafés. Service is rarely included on the check.

## OPENING TIMES

DINNER IS THE main meal of the day, but many restaurants in Moscow have now adopted the concept of the

**Cozy interior of Cafe Margarita (see p180), a traditional café**

business lunch. These often take the form of a fixed price menu and can be good value. They are usually served from noon to 4pm. Most restaurants start serving dinner at around 6pm and stop taking orders at 10:30pm; some family-run Georgian establishments close their kitchens as early as 8:30 or 9pm. As Moscow's nightlife picks up speed, however, an increasing number of restaurants are staying open until the early hours of the morning. Several places, both Russian and foreign, also now remain open 24 hours a day.

## MAKING A RESERVATION

MOST INTERNATIONAL and tourist-oriented restaurants take reservations, and some of the most popular require them. Generally, it is best to book ahead whenever possible. However, some of the most popular Georgian and Caucasian restaurants do not take reservations, and clients may find themselves waiting for up to an hour to be seated, especially on weekends.

## ETIQUETTE

CASUAL OR semiformal dress is acceptable in almost every Moscow restaurant. It is worth bearing in mind, though, that Russians tend to overdress rather than underdress, so it is probably safer to err on the formal side. Children are a rare sight at expensive restaurants, and most menus do not have special dishes for them. However, Moscow does have a few family-style restaurants.

## VEGETARIANS

MUCH OF Russian cuisine consists of meat dishes. Even salads often contain meat, so the best option for vegetarians is often a beet or tomato platter. Georgian cuisine, featuring numerous excellent bean and eggplant dishes, is usually a much better bet. Only a few restaurants list vegetarian dishes separately on the menu – some Indian ones are the exception. European, Chinese, and Japanese restaurants usually have some items suitable for vegetarians, as well as fish dishes.

## SMOKING

THERE ARE generally no areas for nonsmokers, and smoking during meals is considered acceptable.

## DISABLED PERSONS

FEW RESTAURANTS in Moscow have facilities for disabled visitors. Some restaurants are located in basements and would therefore pose a problem. It is always best to phone in advance to check if there is full disabled access.

---

### USING THE LISTINGS

Key to symbols in the listings on pp180–81.

**V** vegetarian dishes
**X** suitable for children
**&** wheelchair access
**T** formal dress
**田** outdoor eating
**♫** live entertainment
**Y** recommended wine list
**★** highly recommended
**▣** credit cards accepted:
*AE* American Express
*DC* Diners Club
*MC* MasterCard
*V* VISA
*JCB* Japanese Credit Bureau

**Price categories** for a three-course meal with a glass of wine, but not including service or tax:
**⑤** under US$15
**⑤⑤** US$15–30
**⑤⑤⑤** US$30–50
**⑤⑤⑤⑤** US$50–75
**⑤⑤⑤⑤⑤** over US$75

# What to Eat in Moscow

RUSSIA'S VAST RANGE of climates and cultures has given rise to an incredibly diverse cuisine, which has been further influenced by European and Arabic food. Traditionally each region had its own cuisine, but today certain regional specialties, such as the Georgian dish *shashlyk*, are popular all over Russia. Staple ingredients of the Russian diet include potatoes, cabbage, beets, onions, pickles, *kasha*, sour cream *(smetana)*, curd cheese *(tvorog)*, and herbs such as dill.

A sprig of dill

### Khachapuri
*These cheese-filled breads come in various shapes and sizes. Originally from Georgia, their traditional filling is* suluguni *cheese, made from sheep's milk.*

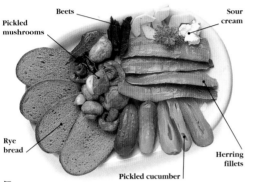

Pickled mushrooms

Beets

Sour cream

Rye bread

Pickled cucumber

Herring fillets

## ZAKUSKI
The name given for a variety of hors d'oeuvres, *zakuski* are often served as appetizers for lunch or dinner. The robust spicy and salty flavors stimulate the appetite. Caviar, smoked sausage *(kolbasa)*, and cheese are also typical.

### Rassolnik
*There are many versions of this classic soup, including recipes using chicken, fish, or kidneys. Pickled cucumbers are a vital ingredient in all of them.*

### Solyanka
*Made from either meat or fish, this soup has a distinctive rich, spicy taste. The meat version has a strong tomato flavor.*

### Borshch
*This classic soup gets its color from beets and tastes sweet and sour. It is served hot in winter and chilled in summer.*

### Shashlyk
*This version of a kebab is made from marinated mutton or lamb. The pieces of meat may be interspersed with vegetables such as onions or peppers.*

## CAVIAR & BLINI

Black caviar *(ikra)* is sturgeon roe. *Ikra* is produced by three species of sturgeon, all of which are found in the Caspian Sea. Beluga is the rarest and has a distinctive nutty taste. Osetra has a creamy flavor, while sevruga tastes of sea salt. Red caviar *(keta)* is salmon roe. Both *ikra* and *keta* are often served with blini (Russian buckwheat pancakes) and sour cream.

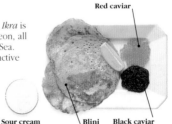

Red caviar

Red caviar jar

Black caviar jar

Sour cream        Blini   Black caviar

**Osetrina**
*The sturgeon is renowned for its roe (caviar), but the fish itself is also eaten in a variety of ways, such as salted or smoked.*

**Savory Pirozhki**
*These small parcels can be stuffed with a variety of fillings. Favorites include meat and cabbage or curd cheese.*

**Kotlety po Kievski**
*Chicken breasts are filled with garlic butter, coated in breadcrumbs, and deep fried. This is called Chicken Kiev in the West.*

**Pelmeni**
*Originally a Siberian dish, these meat or fish dumplings are typically served in soups or with sour cream, butter, or vinegar.*

**Kulebyaka**
*Puff or yeast pastry encloses a filling of salmon, rice, hard-boiled eggs, and mushrooms. This long pie is served in slices.*

**Golubtsy**
*Ground meat and rice rolled in cabbage leaves, golubtsy are boiled or baked and are often served with a tomato sauce.*

## DESSERTS

An important part of any Russian meal, most desserts are uncompromisingly rich. Russian cuisine has a wide variety of cakes, pies, tarts, pastries, and ice cream.

**Bev Stroganov and Kasha**
*Sautéed strips of beef in a sour cream, onion and mushroom sauce, this dish is often served with boiled buckwheat (kasha).*

**Vatrushki** are sweet cheese-filled tartlets.

**Vareniki** are boiled sweet dumplings with various fruit fillings.

**Khvorost** are flat, deep-fried cookies.

**Sweet Pirozhki**
*Made with yeast dough, sweet pirozhki can have a variety of fillings, including fruit or jam, and may be served with cream.*

**Sharlotka**
*This sponge cake, filled with custard and fruit purée, was devised for Tsar Alexander I by French chef Anton Carême.*

**Morozhenoe**
*Ice cream is traditionally a favorite dessert in Russia. It is often served with fresh fruit.*

# What to Drink in Moscow

**A glass of flavored vodka**

Russia is renowned for vodka, which has been manufactured there since the 14th or 15th century and was possibly originally invented by Muscovite monks. Vodka produced in Moscow has always been considered to be the finest. Peter the Great *(see p22)* was particularly fond of pepper and anise vodkas and devised modifications to the distillation process that greatly improved the quality of the finished drink.

Tea is Russia's other national drink. Traditionally made using a samovar and served black, tea has been popular in Russia since the end of the 18th century when it began to be imported from China.

**A 19th-century Russian peasant family drinking vodka and tea at their dacha**

## CLEAR VODKA

Russian vodka is produced from grain, usually wheat, although some rye is also used. Stolichnaya is made from wheat and rye and is slightly sweetened. Probably the best known of the Russian vodkas, its name means "from the capital city." Moskovskaya is a high-quality, slightly fizzy vodka, while Kubanskaya, originally produced by the Cossacks, is slightly bitter. The Cristall distillery in Moscow has been hailed as the finest in Russia and produces super-premium versions of several vodkas, including Stolichnaya and Moskovskaya, as well as its own vodka, Cristall. Vodka is almost always served with food in Russia, often with a traditional range of accompaniments called *zakuski (see p176)*. These specialties are usually spicy or salty, and their strong flavors complement vodka perfectly.

**Kubanskaya**

**Stolichnaya**      **Moskovskaya**      **Stolichnaya Cristall**

## FLAVORED VODKA

The practice of flavoring vodka has entirely practical origins. When vodka was first produced commercially in the Middle Ages, the techniques and equipment were so primitive that it was impossible to remove all the impurities. This left unpleasant aromas and flavors, which were disguised by adding honey together with aromatic oils and spices. As distillation techniques improved, flavored vodkas became a specialty in their own right. Limonnaya, its taste deriving from lemon zest, is one of the most traditional, as is Pertsovka, flavored with red chili pepper pods. Okhotnichya (hunter's vodka) has a wider range of flavorings including juniper, ginger, and cloves. Starka (old vodka) is a mixture of vodka, brandy, port, and an infusion of apple and pear leaves, aged in oak barrels.

**Pertsovka**

**Limonnaya**      **Okhotnichya**      **Starka**

## Major Wine Regions

| | |
|---|---|
| ◼ Vine-growing region | ◻ Russia |
| ◻ Moldova | ◻ Georgia |
| ◻ Ukraine | ◼ Armenia |
| | ◼ Azerbaijan |
| | — International borders |

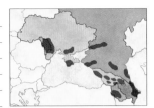

### Wine

THE FORMER SOVIET UNION was one of the world's largest wine producers *(vino)*. Many of its major wine regions, however, are now within independent republics, but their vintages are still popular in Moscow. A wide range of grape varieties is cultivated in the different regions, along with many types found in other parts of the grape-growing world. Georgia and Crimea (in southeastern Ukraine) have traditionally produced the best wines. Georgian wines include those made from the *rkatsiteli* grape,e characterized by a floral aroma and subtle, fruity flavor. Moldova produces white, sparkling wines in the south and central regions, and the south is also known for its red wines. Since 1799 Moldova has also produced vast amounts of a sweet, sparkling wine called *shampanskoe*.

**Georgian wines**    **Shampanskoe**

### Other Alcoholic Drinks

ORIGINALLY A BY-PRODUCT of wine-making, brandy *(konyak)* only began to be made commercially in Russia in the 19th century. Among the ex-Soviet republics, Georgia and Armenia both produce brandy. Armenian is considered the finer, with a vanilla fragrance resulting from ageing it in barrels made of 70–100-year-old oak. Although beer *(pivo)* is becoming more popular, it is still served in relatively few restaurants and cafés. Good Russian beers include Zhigulevskoe, Baltika, Kolos, and Moskovskoe. Various imported beers are also available.

**Baltika beer**    **Armenian brandy**

### Other Drinks

MADE FROM BARLEY AND RYE, *kvas* is a sweet, mildly alcoholic drink consumed by adults and children alike. Russia has a huge range of mineral waters *(mineralnaya voda)*, including many with unusually high mineral contents. Those from the Caucasus, Siberia, and Georgia are especially prized. Also available are fruit juices *(sok)* and sweetened drinks made by boiling fruit with sugar and water *(kompot)*. The cranberry equivalent is called *mors*.

**Mineral water**    **Kvas**    **Mors**

### Tea

RUSSIAN TEA IS SERVED BLACK with a slice of lemon and is usually drunk from a tall glass, called a *stakan*, or a cup. The tea *(chay)* is often sweetened with jam *(varenye)* instead of sugar. The boiling water for making tea traditionally comes from a samovar. The water is used to brew a pot of strong tea, from which a little is poured into the glasses. This is then diluted with more boiling water.

**A glass of tea, with jam (varenye) to sweeten it**

### The Samovar

Traditionally made from brass or copper, samovars were once used to provide boiling water for a variety of domestic purposes. Nowadays they are often made of stainless steel and are used for boiling water to make tea. Occasionally eggs are put in the top of the samovar to cook in the boiling water. The word samovar comes from *samo* meaning "itself" and *varit* meaning "to boil."

## CENTRAL MOSCOW

### Cafe Margarita
Кафе Маргарита

Malaya Bronnaya ulitsa 28.
**Map** 2 E4.  299 6534.  1pm–
midnight. V  ♬  $$

Named after the heroine of
Mikhail Bulgakov's *The Master
and Margarita*, Cafe Margarita *(see
p182)* is on the corner of the pic-
turesque Patriarch's Pond *(see p96)*,
where the classic novel begins. The
full range of Russian specialities is
served here, including cabbage
soup *(shchi)* and several types of
blini *(see p176)*. With its cozy in-
terior and dark wood furnishings,
this café is also a congenial setting
in which to enjoy tea or coffee
and a snack. Live music is some-
times performed in the evenings.

### Patio Pizza
Патио пицца

Ulitsa Volkhonka 13a. **Map** 6 F2.
 298 2520.  noon–midnight. V
♂  &  AE, DC, MC, V, JCB.  $$

An airy, spacious restaurant, Patio
Pizza is a good spot for a low-key
Italian meal. The pizzas, though
not outstanding, come with a wide
variety of toppings, and the salad
bar boasts an equally good choice
of both Russian and Western-style
salads. This is a convenient choice
for a meal before or after a visit to
the Pushkin Museum of Fine Arts
*(see pp78–81)*. Alternatively, try the
branch at No. 4 Tverskaya ulitsa.

### Starlite Diner
Свет звёзд

Bolshaya Sadovaya ul 16. **Map** 2 E3.
 290 9638.  24 hours. V  ♂
  AE, MC, V.  $$

Nestled within a courtyard off
Triumfalnaya ploshchad, this neon-
and-chrome diner is an island of
1950s' Americana, though with
considerably inflated prices. Still,
the Starlite Diner is hugely popular
with expatriate Americans and
Russians alike. Its burgers are ex-
cellent, as are the thick milkshakes.
Another draw is the jukebox
playing rock 'n' roll songs.

### Hola Mexico!
Привет Мексика!

Pushechnaya ulitsa 7/5. **Map** 3 A4.
 925 8251.  noon–5am. V  ♂
♬  AE, DC, MC, V, JCB.  $$

The historic Kuznetskiy most area
may seem an incongruous location
for tasty Tex-Mex food, but that is

exactly what this restaurant provides. All the Mexican favorites,
ranging from *quesadillas* to *fajitas*,
are offered in a spacious, brightly
colored setting below street level.
A lengthy list of fruity cocktails
includes excellent sangria and piña
coladas. The live music can get a
bit loud but, if the fun atmosphere
is to your liking, then this is a
good choice of restaurant.

### Maharaja
Махараджа

Ulitsa Pokrovka 2/1. **Map** 3 C5.
 921 9844.  noon–4pm,
5–10:30pm. V  AE, DC, MC, V,
JCB.  $$

Though pricier than its competitors,
Maharaja is a safe bet for delicious
Indian food and is conveniently
located not far from the Kremlin
*(see pp52–67)*. The decor is taste-
ful, with comfortable chairs, and
it has a quiet, low-key atmosphere
that eludes most Moscow restau-
rants. Portions are small, but the
service is attentive. The Indian
breads are excellent, as are the
spicy curry dishes.

### Samovar
Самовар

13 Myasnitskaya ulitsa. **Map** 3 B4.
 921 4688.  1–11pm. ♬
  MC, V.  $$

Samovar is a good place in which
to sample traditional Russian food,
and probably boasts the most extensive menu of its kind in town.
Satisfy your craving for *kotlety po
Kievski (see p177)*, *osetrina (see
p177)*, blini *(see p176)*, borscht
*(see p176)*, or explore all the possibilities of *pelmeni (see p177)* –
of which there are five varieties,
including steamed, grilled, and
cooked in an omelette. The food
is delicious, though expensive. As
its name suggests, Samovar also
caters to the tea connoisseur, with
two dozen blends to choose from.

### San Marco
Сан Марко

Ulitsa Arbat 25. **Map** 6 E1.
 291 7089.  noon–midnight.
V  ♂  AE, DC, MC, V.  $$

The Arbat *(see pp70–71)* abounds
with tourist traps, but San Marco
is not one of them, and is a great
place to stop when strolling along
this street. This unpretentious
Italian restaurant is one of the best
places to sample a brick-oven
pizza in Moscow. The soups tend
to be on the oily side, but the
salads and pasta dishes are com-
mendable and the prices are
reasonable for the location.

### Tandoor
Тандур

Tverskaya ulitsa 30/2. **Map** 2 E3.
 299 4593.  noon–midnight. V
♂  &  AE, DC, MC, V.  $$

Conveniently located across the
street from the Tchaikovsky Concert
Hall *(see p192)*, Tandoor is one of
Moscow's oldest Indian restaurants
and remains as popular as when it
first opened in 1994. Though some
of the curries on the main menu
are not particularly exciting, the
appetizers are strong, as are the
offerings from the *tandoor*, or
oven. Vegetarians should try the
*dhal* and the mustard leaves, and
tea lovers the sweet, milky *masala*
tea to finish off their meal.

### U Babushki
У бабушки

Bolshaya Ordynka 42. **Map** 7 B4.
 230 2797.  noon–11pm.
& limited   ♬  MC, V.  $$

The menu at U Babushki encom-
passes both French and Russian
cuisine, though it is for the latter
that the restaurant is better known.
Delicious *pelmeni (see p177)* are
served, as well as other Russian
staples including osetrina *(see
p177)* and blini *(see p176)*.

### Elegance
Элеганс

Maly Ivanovskiy pereulok 9. **Map** 7 C1.
 917 0717.  noon–midnight. V
♂  ♀  DC, MC, V.  $$

Elegance offers commendable
Caucasian cuisine prepared by an
Armenian chef, and friendly service. Try the lamb and *lobio* bean
dishes with servings of traditional,
thin *lavash* bread. Armenia is
known for its brandy *(see p179)*,
and Elegance provides its diners
with a complimentary glass. There
are two dozen varieties of brandy
to choose from here, in addition
to an excellent wine list.

### Le Gastronome
Лё гастроном

Kudrinskaya ploshchad 1. **Map** 1 C5.
 255 4433.  noon–midnight.
V  ♬  ★  AE, DC, MC, V,
JCB.  $$

Le Gastronome's most salient
characteristic is its grandeur. It is
located on the ground floor of a
1950s' Stalinist-Gothic skyscraper.
The creative menu spans sushi to
hamburgers, but concentrates on
European-style cuisine. Everything
is good, but the borscht *(see p176)*,
the eggplant salad, and the twice-
roasted duck stand out in particular.
Advance booking is advisable.

## Scandinavia
### Скандинавия

Malyy Palashevskiy per 7. **Map** 2 E4.
**(** 200 4986. **○** noon–11pm.
**AE**, DC, MC, V, JCB. **$$$$**

This Swedish-run restaurant just off Pushkin Square is especially popular in the summer, when the outdoor bar and dining area can be packed even on weekdays. The menu blends European food with American burgers and steaks, and is consistently good. Inside, the cozy bar and mellow atmosphere make Scandinavia a pleasant choice for a winter meal as well.

## U Dyadi Gillyaya
### У Дяди Гилляя

Stoleshnikov pereulok 6, str 1. **Map** 2 F4. **(** 229 2050. **○** 11am–midnight.
**AE**, MC, V. **$$$$**

The name means "At Uncle Guilly's" and the filet mignon is said to be the best in Moscow. The menu offers many more American-European options, among them a great Caesar salad and chicken parmesan sandwich. Both the bar area and the restaurant itself have a casual, intimate atmosphere, with mellow lighting.

## Artistico
### Артистико

Kamergerskiy pereulok 5/6. **Map** 2 F4. **(** 292 4042. **○** noon–midnight.
**AE**, DC, MC, V.
**$$$$$**

Artistico offers mid-range Italian cuisine in an intimate and elegant setting, just off Tverskaya ulitsa (see p89). The main courses are a bit lackluster, but the simple, freshly prepared salads and artistically presented desserts – including a delectable *tiramisu* – are enough to compensate, as is the decor, an ornate combination of wood, mirrors, and wall paintings.

## Central House of Writers
### Центральный дом литераторов

Ulitsa Povarskaya 50. **Map** 2 D5.
**(** 291 1515. **○** noon–midnight.
**AE**, MC, V.
**$$$$$**

Russian literature buffs will recall the Central House of Writers from a scene in Bulgakov's *The Master and Margarita*, and they will find that the real thing provides an equally unforgettable dining experience. The high ceilings and carved-wood decor are the utmost in tasteful elegance, the service impeccable, and the medley of Russian and European cuisine uniformly delicious. The menu includes excellent caviar (see p176) and *osetrina* (see p177), alongside more European offerings such as a delicate shrimp and artichoke salad. Reservations are required; for a table with a view, a spot on the balcony is very pleasant.

## Praga
### Прага

Ulitsa Arbat 2. **Map** 6 E1.
**(** 290 6171. **○** noon–midnight.
**$$$$$**

Until recently Praga seemed to be stuck in the days before perestroika, but it has reemerged as one of the city's best restaurants. Dating from the 1880s, its imposing rooms have been renovated to offer a varied dining experience. Customers can choose among superbly prepared national cuisines in settings ranging from the Brazilian Room, which offers a reasonable-value buffet, to the luxurious Tsar's Room.

## FARTHER AFIELD

## Guria
### Гурия

Komsomolskiy prospekt 7/3.
**Map** 6 D4. **(** 246 0378.
**○** 11am–11pm. **$**

With its hearty Georgian fare, Guria is one of Moscow's busiest restaurants. Unfortunately, it does not take reservations, so you may face a long wait, especially at weekends. The menu, although short, is more than enough to satisfy. Start with *khachapuri* (see p176). Next move on to the garlicky eggplant and *lobio* bean dishes, before sampling the *shashlyk* (see p176). Specialty drinks include sweet Georgian wine (see p179). Gypsy singers perform everything from folk songs to the Beatles. One note of caution – the service is patchy.

## Darbar
### Дарбар

Leninskiy prospekt 38, Hotel Sputnik.
**(** 930 2925. **○** noon–midnight.
**★ AE**, DC , MC, V, JCB. **$$**

It is well worth the trip out of the city center to visit Darbar. This restaurant is hailed by Muscovites as serving the best Indian food in Moscow, yet is relatively inexpensive. The menu, inscribed on a series of scrolls, includes southern Indian cuisine. With many vegetable dishes, Darbar is a great choice for vegetarians, and the lentil and tandoori dishes are recommended. Reservations are advisable.

## Brasserie du Soleil
### Брассери дю солей

Taganskaya ulitsa 23. **Map** 8 F3.
**(** 258 5900. **○** noon–midnight Mon–Fri, 6pm–midnight Sat–Sun.
**★ AE**, DC, MC, V. **$$$**

A French-managed restaurant serving modern European cuisine, Brasserie du Soleil is one of the top spots for a dependably delicious meal out. The changing menu reflects seasonal specialties, and popular appetizers include a generous green salad and a goat cheese salad. The excellent main courses are of a consistently high standard; for dessert, try the airy chocolate mousse. On weekends there is live jazz in the bar.

## TRAM
### ТРАМ

Malaya Dmitrovka ulitsa 6. **Map** 2 F3.
**(** 299 0770. **○** 24 hours.
**★ AE**, MC, V. **$$$**

Located in the basement of the Lenkom Theater (see p192), TRAM is a great spot for Russian food in a casual, enjoyable atmosphere. The drama theme extends from the decor to the menu – dishes bear the names of contemporary Russian actors. The blini (see p176) are among Moscow's best. Whether you want a simple cup of coffee or a full meal you will not go wrong here.

## U Pirosmani
### У пиросмани

Novodevichiy proezd 4. **Map** 5 A5.
**(** 247 1926. **○** 12:45–11pm.
**★ V**. **$$$**

U Pirosmani is more expensive than its Georgian competitors in Moscow but, for your money, you enjoy both a picturesque view of the Novodevichiy Convent (see pp130–33) and a stunning painted interior. The food, Georgian favorites ranging from tangy, marinated cabbage to *pelmeni* (see p177) and *shashlyk* (see p176), is excellent.

## Il Pomodoro
### Иль помодоро

Bolshoy Golovin pereulok 5. **Map** 3 B3.
**(** 924 2931. **○** noon–11pm.
**★ AE**, DC, MC, V. **$$$$**

Moscow's most genuine Italian restaurant has a homey, trattoria feel and superb cooking. The *carpaccio* (thinly sliced raw beef) and the mozzarella and tomato salad rate highly, as do the pasta dishes. Offering excellent espresso and cappuccino, which is a rare treat in Moscow, it is a very good idea to book in advance.

For key to symbols *see p175*

# Light Meals and Snacks

Moscow DOES NOT HAVE a café culture in the tradition of many Western European cities but, as the up-market restaurant boom continues, a more casual dining culture is growing steadily alongside it. Visitors to the Russian capital should be aware, however, that the word café does not necessarily promise coffee, nor tables. Many small establishments based on the traditional Soviet cafeteria (stolovaya) serve tea and sandwiches that you eat standing at a counter. But Moscow's cafés are gradually catching on to the appeal of a cozy environment in which to take a light meal, a giant step toward comfort for tourists in the city. Several American and European bars sprang up after the end of the Soviet era. They are now joined by a growing number of Russian bars, where you can sample tasty local snacks such as blini (see p176) along with your drink.

## WHERE TO EAT

THE CITY CENTER has the highest concentration of cafés and bars, although they are now springing up even in Moscow's more remote areas. Most central, top-class hotels (see pp168–173) have their own Western-style cafés and bars. For visitors who are looking for something cheaper and with more local color the best bet is probably just to wander around the city center and see what they come across.

Since new cafés and bars are opening with such regularity it is a good idea to pick up a copy of Friday's edition of The Moscow Times or The Moscow Tribune (see p207). Both of these list a selection of good venues. Another useful source of up-to-date information is The Exile, a biweekly English-language publication that focuses on eating out and nightlife. These papers are available at most hotels and at many restaurants and bars.

## CAFÉS

A CHEAP, CASUAL meal out in Moscow usually means Russian food. The menu in a Russian café tends to consist of soups – borscht (see p176) is, of course, a favorite – salads, buterbrod (an open sandwich, usually topped with salami, smoked fish, cheese, or pâté) and sweet pastries or tortes. Visitors will find excellent examples of such offerings at Cafe Margarita (see p180).

Some of Moscow's most appealing cafés are tucked away in shopping centers or arts venues. One stylish and popular option is Art Kafe Nostalgie, located inside a children's cinema complex. In a similar vein is Café Cinema, adjacent to the Cinema Center (see p193). This is a wonderful spot for a cup of coffee and a dish of ice cream after a film. Alternatively, Palm's, situated in an upscale shopping arcade, offers plenty of opportunity for people-watching.

At upscale cafés, such as those usually found in expensive hotels, the menu often has a European flavour, focusing on light sandwiches and desserts and offering different varieties of coffee and tea. Bear in mind, though, that even a cup of tea can be extortionately expensive. The Amadeus Café located in the Radisson-Slavyanskaya Hotel (see p171) and the Vienna Café in the Renaissance Moscow Hotel (see p171) are good examples of this type of establishment.

## BARS

FOR SEVERAL YEARS the most popular bars in Moscow were the foreign-run ones, such as the American Bar and Grill and the Moosehead Canadian Bar. The food at these bars strikes an appropriately American chord, with burgers, french fries, and burritos featured prominently on the menu. The Hungry Duck also serves great American

bar food, although diners are advised to arrive early, before the notoriously raucous evening party scene begins.

Somewhat surprisingly, the food at the John Bull Pub is not English but Chinese; for some reason the combination of tasty Oriental dishes and a pint of English ale has turned out to be a great success.

Taverna Miramar has an unusual gimmick. At the end of an evening of pool and great Latin American cuisine, customers can smash their empty beer bottles in the designated broken-glass area.

Moscow's Russian-managed bars cater to students at one end of the spectrum and to wealthy New Russians at the other. They usually offer food such as stolichnyy salat (meat and vegetable salad), and blini, as well as alcoholic drinks. Russian food is well suited to a bar setting due to its emphasis on zakuski (see p176). These snacks often have strong flavors and are generally chosen because they go well with a shot of vodka (see p178). The menus at Propaganda and Krizis Zhanra (see p194), though short, offer delicious salads and pastries, and the blini and borscht at Vermel are not to be missed.

## OPENING TIMES

FEW PLACES in Moscow are open 24 hours a day, but most of the more popular bars stay open until at least 2am, and some do not close until 5am. Visitors may have trouble getting food after about midnight, though.

The standby choice for after-hours dining is the Starlite Diner (see p180), which is open around the clock. The American Bar and Grill is also a popular choice for both late night dinners and early breakfasts.

## FAST FOOD

FAST-FOOD aficionados in Moscow can take refuge in the familiar at McDonald's (see p174). The branch on Bolshaya Bronnaya ulitsa, on the corner of Pushkinskaya ploshchad, is the most famous.

This was the first in the city when it opened in 1990, initially attracting huge lines of Muscovites. There are now nearly a dozen McDonald's franchises around Moscow, including one convenient for shoppers on Tverskaya ulitsa (see p89) and another on Gazetnyy pereulok, not far from the Kremlin (see pp52–67). Alternatively, visitors can grab a slice of pizza from one of the branches of **Pizza Hut**, or satisfy sweet-tooth cravings at **Dunkin' Donuts**.

Better yet, for a more authentically Russian experience, visit a branch of the **Russkoe Bistro** chain, which has been expanding rapidly thanks to support from the mayor of Moscow. Russkoe Bistro serves salads, excellent *pirozhki* – pastries filled with everything from cabbage and potatoes to liver (see p177) – and a refreshing, slightly alcoholic drink called *kvas* (see p179). Look for the green and gold Russkoe Bistro signs that are now scattered all over the city. Good central branches to try include the four that are located on Tverskaya ulitsa.

## CAFÉ ETIQUETTE

IN SMALL RUSSIAN cafés, the menu is usually a handwritten affair, in Russian only and priced in roubles. But in cafés that have a Western flavor, or that have become popular with foreigners, the menu will often be translated into English. Both Russian and expatriate bars usually have menus in Russian and English. Most Russian bars that serve food, and virtually all foreign-run bars, accept credit cards, but Russian cafés rarely do.

Tipping is, by and large, unnecessary in Russian bars and cafés, unless the service has been particularly good. However, in a Western-style venue it is usual to add a tip.

The atmosphere in Moscow's bars and cafés is notoriously smoky. Smoking is not only acceptable everywhere, but seems almost *de rigeur*. Those sensitive to smoky air may well run into difficulties.

## DIRECTORY

### CAFÉS

**Amadeus Café**
Амадэус кафе
Radisson-Slavyanskaya Hotel, Berezhkovskaya naberezhnaya 2.
**Map** 5 B2.
[ 941 8020 ext 3298.

**Art Kafe Nostalgie**
Арт кафе ностальжи
Chistoprudnyy bulvar 12a.
**Map** 3 C4.
[ 916 9478.

**Bubliki Bagels**
Бублики багелс
Ulitsa Petrovka 24/1.
**Map** 3 A4.
[ 200 0828.

**Café Cinema**
Кафе синема
Druzhinnikovskaya ulitsa 15.
**Map** 1 C5.
[ 255 9116.

**Palm's**
Пальма
*Palma*
Ulitsa Novyy Arbat 11, 2nd floor. **Map** 6 E1.
[ 291 2221.

**Vienna Café**
Венское кафе
*Venskoe Kafe*
Renaissance Moscow Hotel, Olimpiyskiy prospekt 18/1.
**Map** 3 A1.
[ 931 9000 ext 2422.

### BARS

**American Bar and Grill**
Американский бар и гриль
*Amerikanskiy bar i gril*
1-ya Tverskaya-Yamskaya ulitsa 2/1.
**Map** 2 E3.
[ 251 9671.

**Angara**
Ангара
Ulitsa Novyy Arbat 19.
**Map** 6 D1.
[ 203 6936.

**Hungry Duck**
Хангри дак
Pushechnaya ulitsa 9/6.
**Map** 3 A4.
[ 923 6158.

**John Bull Pub**
Джон булл паб
Kutuzovskiy prospekt 4/2.
**Map** 5 B1.
[ 243 5688.

**Marika**
Марика
Ulitsa Petrovka 21.
**Map** 3 A4.
[ 924 0358.

**Moosehead Canadian Bar**
Музхэд канадиэн бар
Ulitsa Bolshaya Polyanka 54.
**Map** 7 B5.
[ 230 7333.

**Planet Hollywood**
Планета голливуд
*Planeta gollivud*
Ul Krasnaya Presnya 23b.
**Map** 1 B4.
[ 255 9191.

**Propaganda**
Пропаганда
Bolshaya Zlatoustinskiy pereulok 7.
**Map** 3 B5.
[ 924 5732.

**Sally O'Brien's**
Салли о'брайнс
Ul Bolshaya Polyanka 1/3.
**Map** 7 A3.
[ 959 0175.

**Sports Bar**
Спорт бар
Ulitsa Novyy Arbat 10.
**Map** 6 E1.
[ 290 4311.

**Taverna Miramar**
Таверна мирамар
Myasnitskaya ulitsa 30.
**Map** 3 C4.
[ 924 1986.

**U Yara**
У яра
Hotel Sovetskiy (see p170), Leningradskiy prospekt 33.
**Map** 1 B1.
[ 945 3168.

**Vermel**
Вермель
Raushskaya naberezhnaya 4/5.
**Map** 7 B2.
[ 959 3303.

**The Zoo**
Зоопарк
*Zoopark*
Kudrinskaya ploshchad 1.
**Map** 2 D5.
[ 255 4144.

### FAST-FOOD RESTAURANTS

**Dunkin' Donuts**
Данкин донатс
Myasnitskaya ulitsa 24.
**Map** 3 B4.
[ 925 0289.

**McDonald's**
МакДоналдс
Bolshaya Bronnaya ulitsa 29.
**Map** 2 E4.
[ 200 5896.
Ulitsa Arbat 50/52.
**Map** 6 D2.
[ 241 3681.
Gazetnyy pereulok 17/9.
**Map** 2 F5.
[ 956 9817.

**Pizza Hut**
Пицца хат
Tverskaya ulitsa 12.
**Map** 2 F4.
[ 229 2013.
Kutuzovskiy prospekt 17.
**Map** 5 A2.
[ 243 1727.

**Russkoe Bistro**
Русское бистро
Tverskaya ulitsa 19a.
**Map** 2 E4.
[ 299 3800.

# SHOPS AND MARKETS

R USSIA'S APPETITE for Western goods means that Moscow now offers most of the shopping facilities of a large, modern Western city. There are supermarkets, department stores stocking imported goods, and exclusive boutiques with French and Italian designer clothes and shoes for the new rich.

Moscow's most interesting shopping districts are located within the Garden Ring. The main department

**Russian doll**

stores are clustered around the city center near Red Square, and the best souvenir and antique shops can be found along ulitsa Arbat *(see pp 70–71)*, a charming old pedestrian street. For the more adventurous a trip to the weekend flea market at Izmaylovo Park is a must. Here it is possible to buy everything from Russian dolls and Soviet memorabilia to handmade rugs from Central Asia and antique jewelry.

**A display counter in the sumptuously decorated Yeliseev's Food Hall *(see p186)***

## OPENING HOURS

M OSCOW'S SHOPS and businesses rarely open before 10am and often not until 11am. Most shops open until around 7pm. Many shops, especially old, state-run stores, close for an hour at lunchtime, either from 1pm to 2pm, or from 2pm to 3pm. Shops are usually open all day on Saturdays, and nowadays many are also open on Sundays, although often for shorter hours.

Markets generally operate from 10am to 4pm but it is necessary to go in the morning to get the best choice of goods.

## HOW TO PAY

M ANY FOOD SHOPS, department stores, and state-run souvenir *(berezhka)* shops use the *kassa* system of payment. This involves visiting several cashier's desks and can be confusing for the uninitiated. The first step is to select the

item to be purchased at the display counter and ask its price. It is a good idea to get the assistant at the display counter to write the item's details and price down. The next step is to go to the *kassa* to pay. Finally take the *kassa* receipt back to the display counter and collect the item. The whole process generally takes about ten minutes if the shop is not busy.

The only legal currency in Russia is the rouble, and most shops will not accept other currencies. Vendors at the tourist markets may quote prices in US dollars. However, this will not guarantee a discount and visitors should bear in mind that it is illegal. Now that the rampant inflation of the early 1990s is under control there should rarely be pressure to pay in hard currency.

Western-style supermarkets and shops, as well as some upscale Russian boutiques, accept the main credit cards.

Some shops still display prices in US dollars or, very occasionally, in units that have a fixed rate of exchange with roubles. If so the price will be converted into roubles, at a higher than average exchange rate, before payment is made. Paying by credit card avoids this as credit card slips are nearly always made out in US dollars.

Prices for most goods include 20 percent VAT. Only staples such as locally produced milk and bread are exempt.

There are a few duty-free shops in the center of Moscow and at Sheremetevo-II airport.

## DEPARTMENT STORES

T HE MOST FAMOUS department store in Russia is the State Department Store, known by its acronym, **GUM** *(see p107)*. Its beautiful edifice houses three arcades of shops under a glass roof. It was built at the beginning of the century, just before the Revolution put an end to such luxurious capitalism. During Soviet times GUM stocked the same goods as other department stores in the city and was very dingy and run-down. It has recently been renovated and now houses several top Western chains, as well as specialty shops and boutiques. Items such as cosmetics, medicines, cameras, and electronic goods are all available along with clothes and household goods.

Moscow's other large department store is **TsUM**, the Central Department Store. Formerly cheaper and a little shabbier than GUM, it has now been

**A new Western boutique in Moscow's largest department store, GUM**

Replica icons on sale at the Trinity Monastery of St. Sergius *(see pp156–9)*

thoroughly renovated and is too expensive for most ordinary Muscovites. It still uses the *kassa* system of payment.

**Detskiy Mir** (Children's World) is the largest children's store in Russia. It stocks toys made in Russia, model kits, and sports equipment, as well as imported toys. In the Soviet era the cavernous halls were often almost empty. Now the colorful displays of toys reflect the new affluence of Muscovites, and there is even a luxury car showroom for the grown-ups.

Souvenirs for sale at the flea market in Izmaylovo Park

## BAZAARS AND MARKETS

M ANY MUSCOVITES buy their cheese, meat, fruit, and vegetables at one of the big produce markets dotted around the city. One of the biggest and most picturesque food markets is the **Danilovskiy Market**, which takes its name from the nearby Danilovskiy Monastery *(see pp136–7)*.

**Izmaylovo Market** is a flea market held every weekend at Izmaylovo Park *(see p141)*. It is a treasure trove of old and new. All the usual souvenirs are on sale, including Soviet memorabilia and painted Russian *matryoshka* dolls *(see p188)*, as well as antique silver and jewelry, icons, samovars, china, and glassware, fur hats, amber, and the best Central Asian rugs in Russia. In recent years many artists and craftspeople have set up stalls, and the

range of strange and beautiful toys and decorations to browse through is enormous.

On the Moskva River embankment next to the **Central House of the Artist** there is an outdoor art market specializing in all sorts of paintings and carved ornaments.

## MUSEUM SHOPS

T HERE IS A SMALL, but excellent, souvenir shop at the **Museum of the Revolution**. Its stock includes old Soviet posters, stamps and badges, amber and lacquer boxes. Both the **Pushkin Museum of Fine Art** *(see pp78–81)* and the **Tretyakov Gallery** *(see pp118–121)* sell a good selection of art books with English commentaries.

## BARGAINING ETIQUETTE

V ISITORS WHO SPEAK a little Russian can have fun negotiating prices for their fruit and vegetables at produce markets. Many vendors come from long-established trading families and expect buyers to bargain for every purchase. However, visitors should not expect to get the better of these enthusiastic salesmen. Most vendors are from the Caucasus and southern Russia, where the best fresh produce is grown.

Many vendors at souvenir markets speak enough English to bargain, but it is not always possible to negotiate a discount as salespeople have a good idea of what they can get for an item and will not want to undercut each other.

The Central Asian salesmen at the carpet market at Izmaylovo Park are persuasive, but as a rule of thumb the first price they name

is about twice what they can afford to accept. The customer should open bargaining by halving the first price and expect to agree on a price somewhere in between. Only those who are fairly certain they want to buy should begin bargaining. Once a price is agreed it can be hard to walk away without causing offense.

A stall selling fresh vegetables and herbs at the Danilovskiy Market

## BUYING ANTIQUES

I T IS VERY DIFFICULT to take any items made before 1945 out of Russia *(see p200)*. All outgoing luggage is x-rayed by customs officials to check for precious metals, works of art, rugs, and icons, and complete documentation for all these objects is required before they can be exported. Permission to export antiques and art can only be obtained from the **Ministry of Culture**. This process takes at least two weeks and an export tax of 50 percent of the ministry's assessment of the antiques' value will have to be paid.

It is safest to restrict purchases to items less than 50 years old. However, customs inspectors at the airport may still want to see receipts and documentation that proves the age of the objects.

Samovars and other items for sale in one of the many antiques shops along ulitsa Arbat

# Where to Shop in Moscow

THE INCREASING NUMBER of Western-style stores means that buying food, toiletries, and supplies such as photographic film and batteries is much easier than it used to be. Shopping no longer involves lining up for as long as in Soviet times, or visiting hard-currency stores open only to foreigners and the privileged. However, high import duties, transportation costs, and the relative lack of competition make consumer goods considerably more expensive than in the West. Far more exciting buys are the colorful Russian arts and crafts available at many locations throughout the city. Exotic goods from the ex-Soviet Republics of Central Asia and memorabilia from the Soviet era also make interesting purchases.

## VODKA AND CAVIAR

WHEN BUYING VODKA and caviar there are a few points to remember. It is advisable to buy cans of caviar rather than jars, but even cans should be kept refrigerated at all times. It is best to avoid buying from street stalls or kiosks. Caviar is available from most supermarkets but, for a real Russian shopping experience, go to the slightly run-down **Yeliseev's Food Hall** (*see p89*). This pre-Revolutionary delicatessen, known as Gastronom No. 1 in Soviet times, boasts chandeliers and stained-glass windows.

There is a great deal of boot-leg vodka about, which can be highly poisonous. It is essential to make sure that there is a pink tax label stuck over the top of any bottle of vodka, and none should ever be bought on the street. Popular vodkas such as Stolichnaya and Moskovskaya (*see p178*) are available from most supermarkets, including **Kalinka Stockmann** and **Diplomat Supermarket**, two of the best Western-style ones. Vodka is also sold in small grocery stores. There are no restrictions on when alcohol can be sold.

Vodka and caviar are available but costly at the duty-free airport stores (*see p208*).

## ARTS AND CRAFTS

LOW LABOR COSTS mean that handmade goods are generally cheaper here than in the West, and they make exotic and interesting souvenirs to take home. The best places to buy are the markets, such as the **Izmaylovo Market** (*see p185*), and souvenir stores on ulitsa Arbat (*see pp70–71*). Lacquer trays and bowls, painted china, and *matryoshka* dolls can be bought at **Arbatskaya Lavitsa**. Handmade lace and embroidery are sold in **Russkaya Vyshivka**, while for Russian jewelry and amber visitors should try **Samotsvety**.

A wide range of arts and crafts is also available at stores elsewhere in the city, such as **Russkiy Souvenir**. The **Union of the Artists of Russia Gallery** has an exhibition of paintings for sale, as well as jewelry and lacquer boxes. For more unusual souvenirs, try **Dom Farfora**, which sells hand-painted tea sets and Russian crystal, and the **Salon of the Moscow Cultural Fund**, which has samovars, old lamps, and some whimsical sculptures and mobiles.

## ANTIQUES

THE NEW RUSSIAN rich are hungry for antiques, and dealers know the value of goods, so the bargains of a few years ago are no longer available. It is also worth noting that exporting objects made before 1945 from Russia involves a lot of expense and effort (*see p185*). However, it is still well worth exploring the many wonderful shops full of treasures.

Ulitsa Arbat has many of the best antique shops in Moscow. **Kupina Antiques** offers a good selection of icons, silver, jewelry, and china, while **Antonika** has a variety of interesting Soviet porcelain. For larger pieces and furniture visitors should go to **Tradition and Personality** and **The Commission Antique Shop**, which sells goods for people on commission. **The Foreign Book Store**, which is principally a bookshop, also sells furniture and a lot of china, lamps, and bric-a-brac.

## FASHION AND ACCESSORIES

THERE ARE MANY boutiques in the center of town around **GUM** (*see p107*) and **TsUM** (*see p184*) and along Tverskaya ulitsa (*see p89*). The center also has two arcades. **Petrovskiy Passage** has clothes and shoes as well as furniture and electrical goods. **Gallery Aktyor**, a modern, three-story arcade, contains Western and designer stores selling clothes, French perfumes, and jewelry from Tiffany and Cartier. Clothes by Russian designers are gradually appearing in Moscow's stores.

A little farther out from the center is **Sadko Arcade**, a large shopping and restaurant complex with two supermarkets as well as specialty stores and boutiques. At these more upscale arcades, most of the stores accept credit cards.

Authentic Russian fur hats are sold in Petrovskiy Passage and on the second floor of GUM, and there's a good selection in the winter at Izmaylovo Market.

## BOOKS AND MUSIC

FOR ENGLISH-LANGUAGE books, **Anglia British Bookshop**, **The American Book Store**, and **The English Book Store** are the best bets. Next door to the last is **The Foreign Book Store**, which sells Russian-language books and antiques. The enormous **Moscow House of Books** sells some English-language books and also CDs, records, old icons, and Soviet propaganda posters. The **Moskva Trade House** has Russian books, stamps, art books, small antiques, and paintings. **Melodiya** sells CDs, records, and cassettes of Russian orchestras and performers, while **Transylvania 6-5000** has the best range of non-pirated Western CDs in town.

## DIRECTORY

### DEPARTMENT STORES

**Detskiy Mir**
Детский мир
Teatralnyy proezd 5.
**Map** 3 A5.
928 2234.

**GUM**
ГУМ
Krasnaya ploshchad 3.
**Map** 3 A5.
921 5763.

**TsUM**
ЦУМ
Ulitsa Petrovka 2.
**Map** 3 A4.
292 1157.

### BAZAARS AND MARKETS

**Central House of the Artist**
Центральный Дом художника
Tsentralnyy Dom khudozhnika
Krymskiy val 10.
**Map** 6 F4.

**Danilovskiy Market**
Даниловский рынок
Danilovskiy rynok
Mytnaya ulitsa 74.

**Izmaylovo Market**
Рынок Измайлово
Rynok Izmaylovo
Izmaylovskoe shosse.

### MUSEUM SHOPS

**Museum of the Revolution**
Музей революции
Muzey revolyutsii
Tverskaya ulitsa 21.
**Map** 2 E4.
299 6724.

**Pushkin Museum of Fine Art**
Музей изобразительных искусств имени АС Пушкина
Muzey izobrazitelnykh iskusstv imeni AS Pushkina
Ulitsa Volkhonka 12.
**Map** 6 F2.
203 7998.

**Tretyakov Gallery**
Третьяковская галерея
Tretyakovskaya galereya
Lavrushinskiy pereulok 12.
**Map** 7 A3.
951 1362.

### VODKA AND CAVIAR

**Diplomat Supermarket**
Дипломат гастроном
Diplomat gastronom
Bolshaya Gruzinskaya ul 63.
**Map** 2 D2.
251 2589.

**Kalinka Stockmann**
Калинка Стокман
Ulitsa Zatsepskiy val 4/8.
**Map** 7 C5.
953 2602.

**Yeliseev's Food Hall**
Елисеевский гастроном
Yeliseevskiy gastronom
Tverskaya ulitsa 14.
**Map** 2 F4.
209 0760.

### ARTS AND CRAFTS

**Arbatskaya Lavitsa**
Арбатская Лавица
Ulitsa Arbat 27.
**Map** 6 E1.
290 4669.

**Dom Farfora**
Дом фарфора
Leninskiy prospekt 36.
137 6023.

**Russkaya Vyshivka**
Русская вышивка
Ulitsa Arbat 31.
**Map** 6 D1.
241 2841.

**Russkiy Souvenir**
Русский сувенир
Kutuzovskiy prospekt 9.
**Map** 5 A1.
243 6986.

**Salon of the Moscow Cultural Fund**
Салон Московского фонда культуры
Salon Moskovskovo fonda kultury
Pyatnitskaya ulitsa 16.
**Map** 7 B3.
951 3302.

**Samotsvety**
Самоцветы
Ulitsa Arbat 35.
**Map** 6 D1.
241 0765.

**Union of the Artists of Russia Gallery**
Галерея Союза художников России
Galereya Soyuza khudozhnikov Rossii
Tverskaya ulitsa 25/9.
**Map** 2 E3.
299 7221.

### ANTIQUES

**Antonika**
Антоника
Ulitsa Arbat 4.
**Map** 6 E1.
291 7444.

**The Commission Antique Shop**
Антиквариат комиссионный магазин
Antikvariat komissionnyy magazin
Frunzenskaya nab 54.
242 3664.

**Kupina Antiques**
Антиквариат Купина
Ulitsa Arbat 18.
**Map** 6 D1.
202 4462.

**Ministry of Culture**
Министерство культуры
Ministerstvo kultury
Kitaigorodskiy proezd 7.
**Map** 7 C1.
923 8754.

**Tradition and Personality**
Традиция и личность
Traditsiya i lichnost
Ulitsa Arbat 2, 2nd floor.
**Map** 6 E1.
290 6294.

### FASHION AND ACCESSORIES

**Gallery Aktyor**
Галерея Актера
Tverskaya ulitsa 16/2.
**Map** 2 F4.
935 8374.

**Petrovskiy Passage**
Петровский Пассаж
Ulitsa Petrovka 10.
**Map** 3 A4.
928 5047.

**Sadko Arcade**
Садко Аркада
1-yy Krasnogvardeiskiy proezd 1a .
259 5656.

### BOOKS AND MUSIC

**The American Book Store**
Американская книга
Amerikanskaya kniga
Denezhnyy pereulok 8/10.
**Map** 6 D2.
241 4224.

**Anglia British Bookshop**
Англия британские книги
Angliya britanskie knigi
Khlebnyy pereulok 2.
**Map** 2 E5.
203 5802.

**The English Book Store**
Английская книга
Angliyskaya kniga
Ulitsa Kuznetskiy most 18.
**Map** 3 A4.
928 2021.

**The Foreign Book Store**
Иностранная книга
Inostrannaya kniga
Malaya Nikitskaya ul 16/5.
**Map** 2 D5.
290 4082.

**Moskva Trade House**
Торговый дом Москва
Torgovyy dom Moskva
Tverskaya ulitsa 8.
**Map** 2 F4.
229 6483.

**Melodiya**
Мелодия
Ulitsa Novyy Arbat 22.
**Map** 6 D1.
291 1421.

**Moscow House of Books**
Московский Дом книги
Moskovskiy Dom knigi
Ulitsa Novyy Arbat 8.
**Map** 6 D1.
290 3580.

**Transylvania 6-5000**
Трансильвания 6-5000
Tverskaya ulitsa 25.
**Map** 2 E3.
200 4379.

# What to Buy in Moscow

**Intricate wooden box**

I̶T IS EASY TO FIND interesting and beautiful souvenirs in Moscow. Traditional crafts were encouraged by the State in the old Soviet Union, so many age-old skills were kept alive. Artisans today continue to produce items ranging from small, low-cost, enameled badges to more expensive hand-painted Palekh boxes, samovars, and worked semiprecious stones. Other popular items are lacquered trays and bowls, chess sets, wooden toys, and *matryoshka* dolls. Memorabilia from the Soviet era also make good souvenirs, and Russia is the best place to buy the national specialties, vodka and caviar.

### Vodka and Caviar

*An enormous variety of both clear and flavored vodkas (such as lemon and pepper) is available (see p178). They make excellent accompaniments to black caviar (ikra) and red caviar (keta), which are often served with blini (see p176).*

### Samovar

*Used to boil water to make tea, samovars (see p179) come in many sizes. A permit is needed to export a pre-1945 samovar.*

**Clear vodka**

**Flavored vodka**

**Red caviar**

**Black caviar**

**Malachite egg**          **Amber ring**

### Semiprecious Stones

*Malachite, amber, jasper, and a variety of marbles from the Ural mountains are used to make a wide range of items – everything from jewelry to chess sets and inlaid tabletops.*

### Wooden Toys

*These crudely carved wooden toys often have moving parts. They are known as* bogorodskie *toys and make charming gifts.*

### Matryoshka Dolls

*These dolls fit one inside the other and come in a huge variety of styles. The traditional dolls are the prettiest, but the models painted to represent Soviet political leaders are also very popular.*

### Chess Sets

*Chess is an extremely popular pastime in Russia. Chess sets made from all kinds of materials, including malachite, are available. This beautiful wooden set is painted in the same folkloric style as the traditional* matryoshka *dolls.*

## LACQUERED ARTIFACTS

Painted wooden or papier-mâché artifacts make popular souvenirs. The exquisite, hand-painted, lacquered Palekh boxes can be costly, but the eggs decorated with icons, and the typical red, black, and gold bowls are more affordable.

**Palekh Box**
*The art of miniature painting on papier-mâché items originated in the late 18th century. Artists in the four villages of Palekh, Fedoskino, Mstera, and Kholuy still produce these hand-painted marvels. The images are based on Russian fairytales and legends.*

**Painted wooden egg**

**Bowl with Spoon**
*The brightly painted papier-mâché bowls and spoons made in Khokhloma are coated with a hard lacquer. However, they are not resistant to boiling liquid.*

**Russian hand-painted tray**

**Tuners**          **Strings**

**Traditional Musical Instruments**
*Russian folk music uses a wide range of musical instruments. This gusli is similar to the Western zither and is played by plucking the strings with both hands. Also available are the balalaika and the garmon, which resembles a concertina.*

**Russian Shawl**
*These brilliantly colored, traditional woollen shawls are good for keeping out the cold of a Russian winter. Mass-produced polyester versions are also available, mostly in big department stores, but they will not be as warm.*

**Soviet Memorabilia**
*A wide array of memorabilia from Soviet times can be bought. Old banknotes, coins, pocket watches, and all sorts of Red Army gear, including belt buckles and badges, can be found, together with more recent watches with cartoons of KGB agents on their faces.*

**Gzhel Vase**
*Ceramics with a distinctive blue and white pattern are produced in Gzhel, a town near Moscow. Ranging from figurines to household crockery, they are popular with Russians and visitors alike.*

**Pocket watch**

**Badge with Soviet symbols**

**Red Army leather belt**

# ENTERTAINMENT IN MOSCOW

Moscow offers many forms of entertainment, from great theater productions, operas, and ballets to a wide choice of lively nightlife venues.

Attending a performance at the historic Bolshoy Theater (see pp90–91) remains a must for opera and ballet buffs. Other theaters put on an enormous range of productions, including musicals and special shows for children.

**A neon sign advertising one of Moscow's casinos (see p195)**

Moscow has several theaters screening foreign-language films. They usually show the latest Western releases only a few weeks after they are premiered in the West. The city also has around 300 nightclubs and many late-night bars and cafés, some of which have live bands. In addition, there is always plenty of free entertainment from street performers, especially on ulitsa Arbat (see pp70–71).

**A performance of the opera *Boris Godunov* at the Bolshoy Theater**

## PRACTICAL INFORMATION

Moscow does not have any conventional tourist information offices. However, listings for events such as films, plays, concerts, and exhibitions, together with extensive lists of restaurants, bars, and nightclubs can be found in the Friday editions of the English-language newspapers *The Moscow Times* and *The Moscow Tribune*. Restaurants and nightclubs are also listed in the English-language *The Exile*. These are available free at large hotels and West-ern-run restaurants and bars.

Note that the safest way to get back from late-night events is in an official taxi booked in advance (see p212).

## BOOKING TICKETS

By far the easiest way to book tickets for a concert, a ballet, an opera, or the theater is through one of the main international hotels, even for visitors not staying there. Both Western-

style and Russian-run hotels will usually offer this service. However, tickets bought in this way are often more expensive than those available elsewhere. Hotel ticket-booking desks accept payment by major credit cards, but many will charge a fee for doing so.

Visitors who speak Russian will be able to buy cheaper tickets from a theater ticket kiosk (*teatralnaya kassa*). These kiosks are scattered all round the city and in metro stations.

Another alternative is to book tickets at the venues. Although these tickets are usually the cheapest, it can require a lot of patience to obtain them since ticket offices open at unpredictable hours and do not usually sell tickets more than three days in advance.

There are scalpers outside most events,

**Posters for theater performances**

## THE MOSCOW STATE CIRCUS

Russians have always loved the circus. In the 18th and 19th centuries it was the most popular theatrical entertainment. Troupes traveled round the country performing mostly satirical shows. Today the renowned Moscow State Circus has its permanent home in Moscow. It is famous for its clowns, for the breathtaking stunts of its acrobats and trapeze artists, and for its performing animals. The latter often include tigers jumping through burning hoops and bears riding bicycles, and animal-lovers should be aware that they may find some acts distressing.

The original venue, now known as the **Old Circus**, was built in 1880 by Albert Salamonskiy for his private troupe. Salamonskiy's Circus became the Moscow State Circus in 1919. The **New Circus** was built in 1973. Both venues are now in use.

**The big top of the New Circus, second venue of the Moscow State Circus**

**The Arts Cinema** *(see p193)*, one of the oldest cinemas in Moscow

especially those at the Bolshoy Theater. However, there is a risk that their tickets are counterfeit, and they will almost certainly be overpriced.

## CHILDREN'S ENTERTAINMENT

Traditional russian entertainments for children have always included the puppet theater, the zoo, and the circus. Moscow has two puppet theaters: the **Obraztsov Puppet Theater** *(see p192)*, which puts on matinee performances for children, and the **Moscow Puppet Theater**. The **Nataliya Sats Children's Musical Theater** performs excellent shows, great for children of all ages.

The **Russian Academic Youth Theater** *(see p88)* puts

on performances suitable for children from the age of seven.

**Moscow Zoo** is a great favorite but, unfortunately, the animals often look underfed and cramped in their cages.

The **Durov Animal Theater** puts on shows that feature trained tigers, elephants, and seals, and mice operating a toy railroad. In the intervals children are allowed to play with some of the animals and have their photos taken with them. Performances at the **Kuklachev Cat Theater** include cats pushing toy prams and jumping through hoops. Visitors to both theaters may find some acts upsetting.

At **Arlecchino Children's Club** children can play with toys and computer games or be entertained by clowns.

**Miracle City** at Gorky Park is an outdoor, Western-style amusement complex

A scene from the story of Noah's Ark being performed at the Moscow Puppet Theater

**Paddle boats, one of the many attractions on offer in Gorky Park**

that opens from late spring until late October. Children under 1.2 m (4 ft) tall are given free entry to all the children's rides, which include merry-go-rounds, trains, and mini racing cars. There are also adult rides, such as a roller coaster, some of which allow children if accompanied by a grown-up.

Also in Gorky Park is the **Buran Shuttle**. This space shuttle is unusual – its single test flight was unmanned. It has now been converted into a simulator and provides a great chance to experience space flight. Visitors can also sample the tubes of foods such as soups and pâtés that Russian cosmonauts typically eat.

## DIRECTORY

**Arlecchino Children's Club**
Детский клуб Арлекино
*Detskiy klub Arlekino*
Verkhnyaya Radishchevskaya ul 19/3, stroenie 1.
**Map** 8 E3.
[ 915 1106/07.

**Buran Shuttle**
Космический корабль Буран
*Kosmicheskiy korabl Buran*
Gorky Park, ulitsa Krymskiy val 9. **Map** 6 F4.
[ 237 0832.

**Durov Animal Theater**
Театр зверей имени Дурова
*Teatr zverey imeni Durova*
Ulitsa Durova 4. **Map** 3 A1.
[ 971 3047.

**Kuklachev Cat Theater**
Театр кошек Куклачёва
*Teatr koshek Kuklacheva*
Kutuzovskiy prospekt 25.
[ 249 2907.

**Miracle City**
Чудоград
*Chudograd*
Gorky Park, ulitsa Krymskiy val 9. **Map** 6 F4.
[ 236 3112.

**Moscow Puppet Theater**
Московский кукольный театр
*Moskovskiy kukolnyy teatr*
Spartakovskaya ulitsa 26.
**Map** 4 F2.
[ 261 2197.

**Moscow Zoo**
Зоопарк
*Zoopark*
Bolshaya Gruzinskaya ul 1.

**Map** 1 C4.
[ 255 5375.

**Nataliya Sats Children's Musical Theater**
Детский музыкальный театр имени Наталии Сац
*Detskiy muzykalnyy teatr imeni Natalii Sats*
Vernadskovo prospekt 5.
Near Sparrow Hills *(see p129)*.
[ 930 7021.

**New Circus**
Новый цирк
*Novyy tsirk*
Vernadskovo prospekt 7.
Near Sparrow Hills *(see p129)*.
[ 930 2815.

**Obraztsov Puppet Theater**
Кукольный театр

имени Образцова
*Kukolnyy teatr imeni Obraztsova*
Ulitsa Sadovaya-Samotechnaya 3.
**Map** 3 A2.
[ 299 3310.

**Old Circus**
Старый цирк
*Staryy tsirk*
Tsvetnoy bulvar 13.
**Map** 3 A3.
[ 200 6889.

**Russian Academic Youth Theater**
Российский академический молодёжный театр
*Rossiyskiy akademicheskiy molodezhnyy teatr*
Teatralnaya ploshchad 2.
**Map** 3 A5.
[ 292 0069.

# The Arts in Moscow

FROM JUNE UNTIL LATE SEPTEMBER most of Moscow's concert halls and theaters close, and the city's orchestras, theater and ballet companies perform elsewhere in Russia and abroad. However, for the rest of the year the city has a rich and varied cultural scene. The Bolshoy Theater (see pp90–91), Moscow's oldest and most famous opera and ballet house, offers an impressive repertoire. Numerous drama theaters put on a variety of plays in Russian, ranging from the conventional to the avant-garde. For non-Russian speakers there is a wide choice of events, ranging from folk dance and gypsy music to classical concerts by top international musicians. Evening performances at most venues begin at 7pm or 7:30pm, while matinées generally start around midday.

Moscow's most prestigious classical music gathering is the annual Svyatoslav Richter December Nights festival (see p35). Held in the Pushkin Museum of Fine Arts (see pp78–81), the concerts attract a star-studded array of Russian and foreign musicians. In the intervals, the audience is invited to stroll around some of the museum's galleries.

In summer both indoor and outdoor concerts are held outside Moscow at Kuskovo (see pp142–3) on Tuesday and Thursday evenings.

## BALLET AND OPERA

THERE ARE NUMEROUS venues in Moscow where visitors can see high-quality ballet and opera. Undoubtedly the most famous is the **Bolshoy Theater**, originally built in 1780. Despite two major fires the theater has existed on its present site ever since. Today the Bolshoy is still the best venue in Moscow in which to see opera and ballet. Its magnificent main auditorium accommodates some 2,500 people. The world-famous ballets danced there by the company include *Giselle* by Adolphe Adam and *Swan Lake* and *The Nutcracker* by Pyotr Tchaikovsky. The theater's operatic repertoire includes a number of works by Russian composers. Among them are *Boris Godunov* by Modest Mussorgsky, *The Queen of Spades* and *Eugene Onegin* by Pyotr Tchaikovsky, and *Sadko* by Nikolai Rimsky-Korsakov.

Another much younger company, the Kremlin Ballet Company, can be seen at the **Palace of Congresses** (see p56) in the Kremlin. This gigantic steel and glass building, originally constructed in 1961 as a convention hall for the Communist Party, has a 6,000-seat auditorium. It is a prime venue for those wishing to see visiting Western opera singers, as well as for ballet.

Less grandiose, but nevertheless high-quality, operas and ballets are performed at the **Helicon Opera**, the **Novaya Opera**, and the **Stanislavskiy and Nemirovich-Danchenko**

**Musical Theater**. As its name implies, the **Operetta Theater** performs operettas, while the **Gnesin Music Academy Opera Studio** stages more experimental productions.

## CLASSICAL MUSIC

MOSCOW HAS a strong tradition of classical music and has long been home to several top international music events. One of Moscow's most famous classical music venues is the **Tchaikovsky Concert Hall**. The main feature of this large circular auditorium is a giant pipe organ, which has 7,800 pipes and weighs approximately 20 tons. It was made in Czechoslovakia and was installed in 1959.

The **Moscow Conservatory** (see p94) is both an educational establishment and a venue for concerts of classical music. It was founded in 1866 and Pyotr Tchaikovsky (see p153), then a young composer at the beginning of his brilliant career, taught here for 12 years. Nowadays the conservatory has more than 1,000 music students at any one time.

The Bolshoy Zal (Great Hall) is used for orchestral concerts, both by the resident orchestra at the conservatory and by visiting orchestras. The Malyy Zal (Small Hall) is used for recitals by smaller ensembles. Over the years many prominent musicians have performed here, and every four years the conservatory plays host to the prestigious Tchaikovsky International Competition (see p33).

## THEATER

MOSCOW HAS more than 60 theaters. Unlike those in many other countries most are repertory theaters. This means that a different production is staged every night. It is therefore crucial that those wishing to see a particular production check when it is on. Listings can be found in the Friday editions of *The Moscow Times* or *The Moscow Tribune*, or in *The Exile* (see p207).

The **Moscow Arts Theater** (see p92) stages a wide repertoire, but it is particularly famous for its productions of Anton Chekhov's plays, such as *The Seagull*. In contrast, the **Lenkom Theater** produces musicals and plays by contemporary Russian playwrights.

The **Malyy Theater**, which is situated across the street from the Bolshoy, is worth visiting since it was Russia's first drama theater and played a major role in the development of Russian theater.

The **Obraztsov Puppet Theater** (see p191) is as entertaining for adults as it is for children. It was founded in 1931 and is named after its first director, Sergey Obraztsov. The theater's repertoire is outstanding and most of the plays can be enjoyed without a knowledge of the Russian language. Evening performances may only be open to those over the age of 18.

Performances at the **Gypsy Theater** consist of traditional gypsy dancing and singing. Performances of Russian folk dancing are held at various places throughout Moscow.

## FILM

THE RUSSIAN FILM industry flourished under the Soviet regime, and Lenin (see p28) himself recognized the value of film for conveying messages. Specially commissioned films shown throughout Russia on modified trains, for example, informed much of the rural population that there had been a revolution in the capital.

Until the Soviet Union's collapse in 1991, the film industry was run by the state. Films were subsidized and their subject matter closely monitored. Russian filmmakers now have artistic freedom, but suffer from a shortage of funding. Most theaters show American blockbusters, but audiences are often small. Recent Russian releases are hard to find in theaters but can be obtained on video.

Many theaters have out-of-date equipment, muffled sound, and uncomfortable seats, but two central Russian-language theaters, the **Rossiya** and the **Udarnik**, offer digital sound and good facilities. The **Arts Cinema** is one of the oldest in Moscow. Its sound system is not as good as those at the Rossiya and the Udarnik, but it is one of the city's most popular theaters. It shows the latest Russian releases and Western films in Russian. It is also a venue for film festivals.

**Kodak Cinema World** shows the latest US releases, in both English and Russian.

Moscow also has two English-language theaters, the **Dome Cinema** at the Renaissance Moscow Hotel (see p171) and the **American House of Cinema**, in the Radisson-Slavyanskaya Hotel (see p171).

Films from Europe and India can be seen in their original languages at the **Illuzion** and the **Cinema Center**. The latter is also the spot where the Moscow International Film Festival (see p33) is held.

The listings will inform visitors what is on and in what language. Tickets for movies can be bought only at the theaters. At most payment is in cash, but the American House of Cinema, the Dome, and Kodak Cinema World accept all major credit cards.

---

## DIRECTORY

### BALLET AND OPERA

**Bolshoy Theater**
Большой театр
Teatralnaya ploshchad 1.
**Map** 3 A4.
☎ 927 6982.

**Gnesin Music Academy Opera Studio**
Оперная студия
академии музыки
имени Гнесиных
Opernaya studiya akademii muzyki imeni Gnesinykh
Povarskaya ulitsa 30/36.
**Map** 2 D5.
☎ 290 1096/290 4837.

**Helicon Opera**
Геликон опера
Gelikon opera
Bolshaya Nikitskaya
ulitsa 19. **Map** 2 E5.
☎ 290 6592.

**Novaya Opera**
Новая опера
Ulitsa Karetnyy ryad 3.
**Map** 2 F3.
☎ 200 2255.

**Operetta Theater**
Театр оперетты
Teatr operetty
Ulitsa Bolshaya
Dmitrovka 6.
**Map** 3 A4.
☎ 292 0405.

**Palace of Congresses**
Дворец съездов
Dvorets sezdov
Kremlin.
**Map** 7 A1.
☎ 928 5232.

**Stanislavskiy and Nemirovich-Danchenko Musical Theater**
Музыкальный театр
имени Станиславского
и Немировича-Данченко
Muzykalnyy teatr imeni Stanislavskovo i Nemirovicha-Danchenko
Ulitsa Bolshaya
Dmitrovka 17.
**Map** 2 F4.
☎ 229 8388.

### CLASSICAL MUSIC

**Moscow Conservatory**
Московская
консерватория
Moskovskaya konservatoriya
Bolshaya Nikitskaya
ulitsa 1.
**Map** 2 F5.
☎ 229 7412.

**Tchaikovsky Concert Hall**
Концертный зал имени
ПИ Чайковского
Kontsertnyy zal imeni PI Chaykovskovo
Triumfalnaya
ploshchad 4/31.

**Map** 2 E3.
☎ 299 0378.

### THEATER

**Gypsy Theater**
Театр ромэн
Teatr romen
Leningradskiy
prospekt 32/2.
**Map** 1 B1.
☎ 214 8070.

**Lenkom Theater**
Театр Ленком
Ulitsa Malaya Dmitrovka 6.
**Map** 2 F4.
☎ 299 9668.

**Malyy Theater**
Малый театр
Teatralnaya ploshchad 1/6.
**Map** 3 A5.
☎ 923 2621.

**Moscow Arts Theater**
МХАТ имени
АП Чехова
MKhAT imeni AP Chekhova
Kamergerskiy pereulok 3.
**Map** 2 F5.
☎ 229 8760.

### FILM

**American House of Cinema**
Berezhkovskaya
naberezhnaya 2.
**Map** 5 B2.
☎ 941 8747.

**Arts Cinema**
Художественный кино

Khudozhestvennyy kino
Arbatskaya ploshchad 14.
**Map** 6 E1.
☎ 291 5598.

**Cinema Center**
Киноцентр
Kinotsentr
Druzhninikovskaya
ulitsa 15.
**Map** 1 C5.
☎ 205 7306.

**Dome Cinema**
Olympiyskiy prospekt 18/1.
**Map** 3 A1.
☎ 931 9873.

**Illuzion**
Иллюзион
Illyuzion
Kotelnicheskaya
naberezhnaya 1/15.
**Map** 8 D2.
☎ 915 4353.

**Kodak Cinema World**
Кодак киномир
Kodak kinomir
Nastasinskiy pereulok 2.
**Map** 2 E3.
☎ 209 4359.

**Rossiya**
Россия
Pushkinskaya ploshchad 2.
**Map** 2 F4.
☎ 229 2111.

**Udarnik**
Ударник
Ulitsa Serafimovicha 2.
**Map** 7 A3.
☎ 959 0856.

# Music and Nightlife

UNDER THE COMMUNIST REGIME Moscow's nightlife was practically nonexistent. In the 1930s the bars where people used to relax with a drink and enjoy live music were establishments only for the elite. With the advent of perestroika a host of new bars and clubs began to appear, and bands, previously forced underground, were able to perform publicly. These days Moscow has a flourishing nightlife with hundreds of clubs catering to all musical tastes. Casinos are another great hit and are especially popular with the so-called New Russians, who like to let off steam by trying their luck at Moscow's numerous gambling spots. Cigarettes are still extremely popular in Russia, and many venues have rather smoky atmospheres.

## ROCK VENUES

WELL-KNOWN RUSSIAN bands tend to perform at larger nightclubs such as **Manhattan Express**, **Utopia**, or **Metelitsa**. These clubs, which often have high cover charges, are packed with young people, including a good sprinkling of New Russians and the numerous expatriates living in the city. Smaller bars, such as **Krizis Zhanra** *(see p182)*, **Bednye Lyudi**, and **Tabula Rasa**, often have bands who are just as talented, but less famous, and the drinks are much cheaper. These venues are always crowded. **Armadillo**, an American-style bar, is another alternative. It offers good live music and reasonably priced drinks and snacks, and has a young professional clientele.

The **Gorbunov House of Culture** is a popular spot for major rock concerts, which are also sometimes staged at large sports stadiums.

## JAZZ, BLUES, AND LATIN CLUBS

MOST OF THE NUMEROUS jazz clubs in Moscow also play host to blues bands. The most famous, and the oldest, are the **Jazz Art Club**, **B.B. King**, and the **Arbat Blues Club**. Concerts do not take place every night, so it is worth checking listings in the English press for details *(see p207)*. On concert nights the venues tend to be packed, and many have a cover charge. Otherwise they are often fairly empty and offer moderately priced drinks and snacks.

Another great jazz venue is **Woodstock- MKhAT**. Live jazz is performed several times a week, the entrance fee is negligible, and the decor is made up of 1960s paraphernalia. The **Brasserie du Soleil** *(see p181)* offers jazz concerts on weekends, a bar, and good French cuisine, and is often frequented by a large crowd of expatriates.

Alternatively, try **Cabana**, a Brazilian-style bar and restaurant with live music, including Latin American bands.

## NIGHTCLUBS AND DISCOS

MOSCOW'S NIGHTCLUBS have never been trend-setters, but they are gradually catching up with the clubs of the other major European capitals. There are hundreds of nightclubs in Moscow, with new ones appearing every month. Most of them are open throughout the evening, but rarely get going before 1am. Admission is usually free before 10pm and can be quite expensive after that. Some clubs offer free entry to unaccompanied women.

The city's nightclubs mostly fall into two categories: those with a floor show of some kind, often featuring strippers or erotic dancers, and those that contain various dance floors and bars. Among the latter are **Titanic**, **Utopia**, and **Soho**, which are primarily rave venues for rich kids. The Pilot disco in the Soho club has an unusual dance floor with a huge airplane in the middle.

**Mirazh**, **Hippopotamus**, and **Manhattan Express** are more straightforward rock and pop discos. Mirazh has a good-size dance floor, but the dance floors at Hippopotamus and Manhattan Express are so popular that they often fail to accommodate the crowds that pack them on weekends.

**Night Flight** is another famous nightclub, although it has a reputation as a favorite haunt of gangsters and prostitutes.

**Master** is popular with students and the younger crowd generally. Upstairs here a vast, black room is reserved for hard-core techno, while downstairs is a smaller bar, where a mixture of techno and other dance music is played. Master is a prime venue for visiting DJs and techno groups.

**Up and Down** is probably the most famous club in the city. Both Russian and foreign celebrities come here and scrawl their names on the walls. The club boasts that it has the most beautiful strippers in Moscow and it also has a gambling casino. Above the club is one of the city's most expensive seafood restaurants, Tri Peskarya, where the diners sometimes include important Russian and Western politicians.

Another nightclub with a striptease show is the popular **Karousel**. The music tends toward disco and techno.

## SPECTATOR SPORTS

Traditionally, the most popular sports in Russia are soccer and hockey. Important matches and championships are held at the **Dynamo Central House of Sports**, the **Krylatskoye Sports Complex**, the **Olympic Sports Complex** and the **Luzhniki Central Stadium**. Krylatskoye also has a racetrack and a canal where row- ing races take place.

The Olympic Sports Complex is the main venue in Moscow for tennis tournaments.

The recently renovated **Hippodrome** has a large racetrack, and a riding school where horses and riding equipment are available for a fee.

**Chance**, nominally a gay club, is favored by a heterosexual crowd. Its floor show features go-go boys and starts at about 1am, but visitors will not see much unless they arrive early. A trip requires a taxi as it is on the city outskirts.

## CASINOS

Moscow has dozens of casinos, which range from extravagant venues to tiny, seedy joints that are not worth a visit. Gambling is a favorite pastime of New Russians, and entrance fees and chip prices are quite high. Some casinos offer a free ride home to clients who either win or lose a large sum. In others, the entrance fee includes drinks and snacks. Most top hotels also have their own casinos, which are less grandiose than the purpose-built ones.

Moscow's most famous casinos are the **Aleksandr Blok**, situated on a riverboat, the **Golden Palace**, which has a Las Vegas-style interior with heavily armed guards, and fish swimming under a glass floor, and the Cherry Casino at the **Metelitsa** nightclub, favored by mafia types. The **Beverly Hills** casino waives its entrance charge for foreigners who produce their passports. The **Club Royale** is located at the Hippodrome racetrack, so visitors can follow a flutter on the horses with some serious gambling in the casino.

## DIRECTORY

### ROCK, JAZZ, BLUES, AND LATIN CLUBS

**Arbat Blues Club**
Арбат блюз клуб
Filippovskiy pereulok 11.
**Map** 6 E1.
291 1546.

**Armadillo**
Армадилло
Khrustalnyy pereulok 1.
**Map** 7 B1.
293 3553.

**B.B. King**
Ulitsa Sadovaya-Samotechnaya 4/2.
**Map** 2 F2.
299 8206.

**Bednye Lyudi**
Бедные люди
Ul Bolshaya Ordynka 11/6.
**Map** 7 B3.
951 3342.

**Cabana**
Кабана
Raushskaya nab 4.
**Map** 7 B2.
239 3046.

**Gorbunov House of Culture**
Дом культуры Горбунова
Dom kultury Gorbunova
Novozavodskaya ulitsa 27.
145 8974.

**Jazz Art Club**
Джаз арт клуб
Begovaya ulitsa 5.
**Map** 1 A2.
191 8320.

**Krizis Zhanra**
Кризис жанра
Prechistenskiy per 22/4.
**Map** 6 D2.
241 1928.

**Metelitsa**
Метелица
Ulitsa Novyy Arbat 21.
**Map** 6 D1.
291 1130.

**Tabula Rasa**
Табула раса
Berezhkovskaya naberezhnaya 28.
240 9289.

**Woodstock-MKhAT**
Вудсток-МХАТ
Kamergerskiy pereulok 3.
**Map** 2 F5.
292 0934.

### NIGHTCLUBS AND DISCOS

**Chance**
Шанс
Shans
Volocharskovo ulitsa 11/15.
956 7102.

**Hippopotamus**
Гиппопотам
Gippopotam
Mantulinskaya ulitsa 5/1, stroenie 6.
**Map** 1 A5.
256 2327.

**Karousel**
Карусель
1-ya Tverskaya-Yamskaya ulitsa 11.
**Map** 2 D3.
251 6444.

**Manhattan Express**
Ulitsa Varvarka 6.
**Map** 7 B1.
298 5355.

**Master**
Мастер
Pavlovskaya ulitsa 6.
237 1742.

**Mirazh**
Мираж
Novyy Arbat 21.
**Map** 6 D1.
291 1423.

**Night Flight**
Tverskaya ulitsa 17.
**Map** 2 F4.
229 4165.

**Soho**
Сохо
Ulitsa Trekhgorny val 6.
**Map** 1 A5.
205 6209.

**Titanic**
Титаник
Young Pioneers' Stadium, Begovaya ulitsa 21/31.
**Map** 1 B1.
213 4581.

**Up and Down**
Zubovskiy bulvar 4.
**Map** 6 D3.
201 5291.

**Utopia**
Утопия
Pushkinskaya ploshchad 2.
**Map** 2 F4.
229 0003.

### CASINOS

**Aleksandr Blok**
Александр блок
Krasnopresnenskaya naberezhnaya 12a.
**Map** 1 A5.
255 9281.

**Beverly Hills**
Kudrinskaya ploshchad 1.
**Map** 2 D5.
255 4228.

**Club Royale**
Клуб рояль
Begovaya ulitsa 22/1.
**Map** 1 A1.
945 1410.

**Golden Palace**
3-ya ulitsa Yamskovo Polya 15.
**Map** 1 C1.
212 3909.

### SPORTS VENUES

**Dynamo Central House of Sports**
Динамо – Центральный дворец спорта
Dinamo – Tsentralnyy dvorets sporta
Lavochkina ulitsa 32.
453 6501.

**Hippodrome**
Ипподром
Begovaya ulitsa 22, korpus 1.
**Map** 1 A2.
945 0437.

**Krylatskoye Sports Complex**
Спортивный комплекс Крылатское
Sportivnyy kompleks Krylatskoe
Krylatskaya ulitsa 2.
140 0347.

**Luzhniki Central Stadium**
Центральный стадион Лужники
Tsentralny stadion Luzhniki
Luzhniki ulitsa 24.
201 0955.

**Olympic Sports Complex**
Спортивный олимпийский комплекс
Sportivnyy olimpiyskiy kompleks
Olimpiyskiy prospekt 16.
**Map** 3 A1.
288 3777.

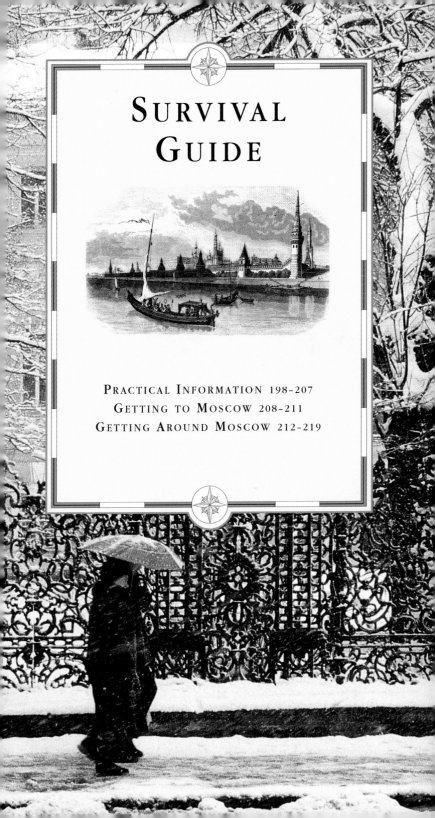

# SURVIVAL
# GUIDE

# PRACTICAL INFORMATION

Moscow is not as difficult for visitors to find their way around as it may seem at first. Certainly, the city is vast, street names and signs are in Cyrillic, and the traffic can be formidably heavy, especially in the center.

**Sign for the
Intourist agency**

On the other hand, there is an excellent metro system, and passers-by and people working in hotels, restaurants, and shops will usually help foreigners. However, it is a good idea for visitors to familiarize themselves with the Cyrillic alphabet in order to decipher signs.

With tourism still a fledgling industry in Moscow, some tourist facilities, such as information services, are fairly basic. The first port of call for visitors wanting information about events and practicalities should be their hotel. Surprisingly, Moscow can be one of the most expensive cities in the world to visit. While public transit is cheap, hotels, restaurants, and theater tickets can cost more than their Western equivalents. It is always worth inquiring about the price before booking something.

**Information desk run by concierge in the Baltschug Kempinski Hotel**

## TOURIST INFORMATION

There are no conventional tourist information offices in Moscow, so hotels are the main source of guidance for visitors. Concierges in Western-style hotels, such as the Radisson-Slavyanskaya, National, Baltschug Kempinski, and Metropol *(see pp168–71)*, will provide assistance. All the large hotels, both Western-style and Russian-run, will book theater tickets for visitors, but will add commission to the face value. Most also have a flight-booking service, accepting payment by credit card, or will put visitors in touch with a travel agency. The advice of Russian-run hotels on sights and restaurants is often indifferent, but the English-language press *(see p207)*, particularly *The Moscow Times*, *The Moscow Tribune*, and *The Exile*, has details of exhibitions, events, and opening hours.

## GUIDED TOURS AND EXCURSIONS

Hotels can book seats on group guided tours and day trips in several languages. The advice **Intourist** agency offers a wide range of tours, mainly to the most well-known sights. **Patriarshiy Dom Tours** offers a range of tours in English, including trips around the KGB Museum, the Kremlin, and State Armory, as well as hiking expeditions. The listings of forthcoming trips are published in the Friday edition of *The Moscow Tribune*. Tours should generally be booked at least 48 hours in advance.

### ADMISSION CHARGES

Many museums and theaters charge foreigners considerably higher admission fees than Russians, although still well within European and North American norms. Those that do include the Tretyakov Gallery *(see pp118–21)*, the State Armory *(see pp64–5)*, the Pushkin Museum of Fine Arts *(see pp78–81)*, and the Bolshoy Theater *(see pp90–91)*. Schoolchildren and students *(see p200)* are entitled to discounts. Credit cards are never accepted at sights.

The ticket office, recognizable by the касса *(kassa)* sign, is often some distance away from the entrance to the sight; staff at the entrance will point you in its direction.

**Tour bus operated by the Intourist agency**

**Tour operator in Red Square
signing up visitors for excursions**

**A woman leaving church after a service, appropriately dressed in a headscarf**

## OPENING HOURS

MOST MUSEUMS have standard opening hours, from 10 or 10:30am to 6pm, but ticket offices may close earlier than the museums. The majority of museums close one day a week and one day a month for cleaning. All museums open on Sundays. Some cathedrals and churches are always open, but others open only for services.

**ОТКРЫТО**

Sign for open *(otkryto)*

**ЗАКРЫТО**

Sign for closed *(zakryto)*

## VISITING CHURCHES

ATTENDING an Orthodox church service is a fascinating experience. The most important services take place on Saturday evenings and Sunday mornings, and on religious holidays. In general, services run for several hours. Russian churches do not have any chairs, and the congregation is expected to stand. It is acceptable for visitors to drop in on a service for a while, but certain dress rules must be observed. Shorts are not acceptable. Men must remove their hats, and women should cover their chest and shoulders and preferably wear a headscarf or hat. Although acceptable in town churches, women wearing pants are likely to be refused entry to monasteries.

## LANGUAGE

CYRILLIC IS the alphabet of the Russian language. It is named after Cyril *(see p17)*, the monk who in 860–70 invented the alphabet from which it developed. Various systems for transliterating Cyrillic into Roman characters *(see p252)* exist, but they do not differ enough to cause confusion. Many Russians who regularly come into contact with visitors can speak some English. However, a knowledge of even one or two words of Russian *(see pp252–6)* on the part of visitors will be taken as a sign of respect and much appreciated.

## ETIQUETTE

RUSSIAN manners and attitudes are becoming more Westernized, but the linguistic distinction between the formal "you" *(vy)* and informal "you" *(ty)* remains strictly in force. On public transport, young men are expected to give up their seats to the elderly or families with young children.

Smoking and drinking are popular pastimes. Frequent toasts are required to justify the draining of glasses. When invited to someone's home, the toast *za khozyayku* (to the hostess) or *za khozyaina* (to the host) should always be offered by the visitor.

Many Russians are superstitious. Most prefer not to shake hands across the threshold of a doorway and, if someone accidentally steps on a friend's toes, the injured party pretends to step back on the perpetrator's toes.

**Sign on apartment house with *podezd* number**

## PAYING AND TIPPING

ROUBLES ARE THE only valid currency in Russia *(see p205)*. Some large shops and hotels may display prices in US dollars or Deutschmarks, but all cash payments must be in roubles only. Credit cards are accepted in some restaurants and most hotels, but rarely in stores, except for those selling imported goods at much higher prices than abroad.

Tipping is a matter of choice, but baggage handlers at the airport and train stations may ask exorbitant sums. Visitors should simply pay what they consider to be appropriate.

## ADDRESSES

RUSSIAN ADDRESSES are given in the following order: post code, city, street name, house *(dom)* number, and, finally, apartment *(kvartira)* number. If an apartment is part of a complex, a *korpus (k)* number is also given to indicate which block it is in. When visiting an apartment, it tells which entrance *(podezd)* to use.

After the Revolution of 1917, many streets were renamed to avoid imperial connotations or to commemorate new Soviet heroes. Since perestroika most streets in the center have officially reverted to their pre-1917 names. This can cause confusion, as people often use the Soviet names, forgetting that street signs show the original ones. However, most people happily use both, and no offense is caused by using one instead of the other.

**Six-figure post (or index) code**     **Street name**

103009 Москва
Тверская улица
д. 6, кв. 25
И. А. Иванову

**House number**     **Apartment number**     **Name**

# VISAS

Visas are required for all visitors to Russia. Package tour companies will organize visas for you, but independent travelers need to arrange their own. This can be a complex, time-consuming process, and by far the easiest option is to pay a small fee for your travel agency to obtain a visa for you. The alternative is to go in person to the Russian Embassy where visas are issued. Document requirements change regularly, and it is essential to check these in advance. You will need to show proof of either pre-booked accommodations or an invitation (visa support) from a tour company, business, or private individual in Russia. **Ost-West Kontaktservice** can fax express invitations directly. Private invitations cannot be faxed, and the process of issuing them takes at least one month through **OVIR** (Visa Registration Department).

The cost of a visa ranges from around $16 for a short-term, single entry visa to about $150 for multiple entry business visas. A visa usually takes ten days to be processed, but for an extra modest fee it can be arranged in one or two days.

Inside Russia, visa extensions can be granted only by the organization that issued the initial invitation. If you overstay your allotted time, you may well expect to be stopped at the airport and turned back until you have either obtained the necessary extension visa or paid a considerable fine.

For those on package tours, tourist visas will be arranged by the travel agency or tour company. For independent travelers, the easiest way to obtain any type of visa is to pay a modest fee and allow a special travel agency, such as Panorama Travel, Ltd. in New York or Intourist Travel Ltd. in London, arrange it.

Igumnov House, built in 1893, now the home of the French Embassy

**A Russian visa**

## IMMIGRATION AND CUSTOMS

Passports and visas are thoroughly checked at immigration desks. All visitors have to fill out a customs declaration form on arrival, which is available in various languages (some airlines hand them out on the plane). This should be kept for the duration of the stay and handed back together with another declaration form at departure.

It is illegal to take roubles out of Russia (nor, by extension, are they allowed in). Essentially, there are no limits on how much foreign hard currency may be brought in, but visitors will be expected to have less when they leave (to prove that they have been buying rather than selling things). Valuables such as jewelry and computers should be declared on the customs form on entry, otherwise an import duty may be levied on them on leaving. The departure customs in Russia are generally stricter than in many other countries, particularly with regard to art and antiques *(see p185)*.

## REGISTRATION

Officially, all foreigners are supposed to register with **OVIR**, the Visa and Registration Department, within three days of their arrival. Hotels can do this for guests. Nowadays, though, about 80 percent of visitors do not bother to register. Nonregistration is rarely a problem, but sometimes people are fined or ordered to get their paperwork in order, if the authorities become suspicious of them.

## EMBASSIES AND CONSULATES

Every country that has diplomatic relations with Russia has an embassy or consulate in Moscow. Anyone intending to reside in Russia for longer than three months is advised to register with their own. Should a visitor be hospitalized, robbed, imprisoned or otherwise rendered helpless, the embassy or consular officials will then be able to help with interpretation or at least to give advice. These offices can reissue passports and, in some cases, provide emergency money.

## DISABLED TRAVELERS

Moscow has almost no facilities for the disabled. Transit is inaccessible; entrances have steps and narrow doors, and there are rarely public elevators, so it is hard for disabled travelers to get around.

## STUDENT TRAVELERS

As well as being accepted for discounts in museums, international student cards can also be used to obtain discounts on rail and air travel booked through **STAR Travel**.

# TRAVELING WITH CHILDREN

RUSSIANS ADORE children, and those accompanying visitors to Moscow are likely to attract plenty of compliments. On the other hand, it is not unknown for Russian grannies (*babushki*) to be overly inquisitive and even to offer critical, though well-meaning, remarks on the way they are dressed.

Children under six travel free on public transit, but older ones pay the full price. Museums are free for toddlers and babies, and offer concessions to schoolchildren.

**Children playing on a cannon at the Armory in the Kremlin**

## PUBLIC TOILETS

FEW CAFÉS AND BARS have facilities, and public toilets on the street are not pleasant. It is often best to find the nearest foreign hotel or a pay toilet in, say, a department store. These are usually very cheap. Though the lady who takes the money also hands out rations of toilet paper here, it is always a good idea to carry your own.

**Toilet (*tualet*) sign**

**Men's toilets**

**Women's toilets**

## ELECTRICAL APPLIANCES

THE ELECTRICAL CURRENT in Russia is 220 V. Two-pin plugs are needed, but some of the old Soviet two-pin sockets do not take modern European plugs, which have thicker pins. Hotels all have modern sockets. Adaptors are best bought before traveling, but those for old-style plugs are found only in Russia. US appliances need a 220:110 current adaptor.

## PHOTOGRAPHY

THERE ARE NO longer any serious restrictions on what visitors are allowed to photograph (unless you want to take aerial pictures). Expect to have to pay for the right to take photos or use a video camera in museums.

## TIME DIFFERENCE

MOSCOW TIME is eight hours ahead of Eastern Standard Time (EST). Russia has recently come into line with the rest of Europe, putting its clocks forward by an hour at the end of March, and back again in October.

## CONVERSION TABLE

**Imperial to Metric**
1 inch = 2.54 centimeters
1 foot = 30 centimeters
1 mile = 1.6 kilometers
1 ounce = 28 grams
1 pound = 454 grams
1 US quart = 0.946 liters
1 US gallon = 3.785 liters

**Metric to Imperial**
1 centimeter = 0.4 inches
1 meter = 3 feet, 3 inches
1 kilometer = 0.6 miles
1 gram = 0.04 ounces
1 kilogram = 2.2 pounds
1 litre = 1.1 US quarts

---

## DIRECTORY

### TOURIST INFORMATION AND GUIDED TOURS

**Intourist**
Интурист
Tverskaya ul 3/5, 1st floor.
**Map** 2 F2.
☎ 956 8402.
FAX 956 8590.

**Patriarshiy Dom Tours**
Патриарший дом турс
Vspolniy per 6. **Map** 2 D4.
☎ 795 0927.
FAX 795 0927.

### VISA FORMALITIES

**Russian Travel Bureau, Inc.**
255 E. 44th St.
New York, NY 10017

☎ (212) 986-1500.
FAX (800) 847-1800.

**Panorama Travel, Ltd.**
156 5th Avenue,
New York, NY 10010.
☎ (212) 741-003.
FAX (212) 645-6276.

**Andrew's Consulting**
Tsvetnoy bulvar 25/3.
**Map** 3 A3.
☎ 258 5198.
FAX 258 5199.

**OVIR**
ОВИР
Gorodskoye otdel viz i registratsii
Pokrovka ul 42.
**Map** 4 D4.
☎ 200 8427.
◐ Wed, Sat, Sun.

### EMBASSIES AND CONSULATES

**Australia**
Kropotkinskiy per 13.
**Map** 6 D3.
☎ 956 6070.
FAX 956 6170.

**Canada**
Starokonyushenny per 23.
**Map** 6 E2.
☎ 956 6666.
FAX 232 9948.

**Ireland**
Grokholskiy per 5.
**Map** 3 C2.
☎ 288 4101.

**New Zealand**
Ul Povarskaya 44.
**Map** 2 D5.
☎ 956 3579.
FAX 956 3583.

**South Africa**
Bolshoy Strochenovskiy per 22/25. **Map** 7 C5.
☎ 230 6869.
FAX 230 6865.

**UK**
Sofiyskaya nab 14.
**Map** 7 A2.
☎ 956 7200.
FAX 956 7420.

**US**
Novinskiy bulvar 19/23 & Bolshoi Devyatinskiy per 8.
**Map** 2 D5.
☎ 252 2451/59.
FAX 956 4261.

### STUDENT TRAVEL

**STAR Travel**
Vorontsovskaya ul 18/20, stroenie 6. **Map** 8 E4.
☎ 935 8336.

# Personal Security and Health

**D**ESPITE LURID WORLDWIDE reporting on the mafia, crime in Moscow is no worse than in any big city. Petty crime should be the visitor's only concern, but even this can usually be avoided if sensible precautions are taken. For language reasons, it is a good idea to have a card with your Russian address written on it for use in taxis and emergencies. Medical insurance is essential. Although many medicines are readily available, local healthcare compares poorly with Western care and English-speaking services and medical evacuation are very expensive.

## PROTECTING YOUR PROPERTY

**E**VERY VISITOR should take out travel insurance. Once in Moscow, visitors can avoid pickpockets by not carrying money in open pockets or displaying large sums of money in public; bags should be kept closed and roubles kept apart from foreign currency and credit cards. It is advisable to carry a small sum of money for purchases, and to keep the rest separately or at the hotel.

It is best not to stop for gypsies who sometimes frequent Tverskaya ulitsa and the central metro stations, apparently begging. Hold on tightly to valuables, walking on with determination.

Travelers' checks have the advantage that they are insured against loss or theft. However, if they are stolen, report immediately to the issuing company; they can easily be "laundered" in Russia.

It is absolutely essential to report thefts to the police in order to obtain certificates for insurance claims. It is best to report first to hotel security staff who can usually provide interpreters or deal with the whole matter. Embassies will deal with serious situations.

GAI policeman checking documents

## PERSONAL SAFETY

**T**HE GREATEST danger for visitors comes from thieves who might become violent if they encounter resistance. As in any country, it is advisable to hand over belongings immediately.

The mafia, though widespread, has scant contact with foreigners, particularly tourists, who are generally much poorer than Russian businessmen.

Women on their own may be approached by cruising men in cars, who are best ignored. Women may also be propositioned if alone in bars and restaurants. At night, it is safer to use taxis reserved in advance. The metro is also safe.

Other threats come from local drivers, who see pedestrians as a nuisance, and from manhole covers, which have a tendency to rock wildly or collapse when stepped on.

## POLICE

**S**EVERAL KINDS of police operate on Moscow's streets. They change uniforms according to the weather, wearing fur hats and big coats in winter. The *militsiya*, who always carry guns, are the most frequently seen.

The riot police or OMON *(otryad militsii osobgo naznacheniya)* are rarely seen on the streets and dress in camouflage.

Totally separate are the traffic police, or GAI *(gosudarstvennaya avto inspektsiya)*, who carry black-and-white striped truncheons and have ГАИ on their badges or uniforms. They may stop any vehicle to check the driver's documents.

Both the *militsiya* and GAI supplement their incomes by picking people up on minor offences, such as crossing Tverskaya ulitsa or Kutuzovskiy prospekt between crossings. It is best just to pay the "fine," usually the equilvalent of about five or ten dollars.

*Militsiya*

Fire engine with distinctive white stripe

Ambulance

Police car

**Pharmacy, identified by the word *apteka***

## PHARMACIES

PHARMACIES IN RUSSIA are all signed by the word Аптека (*apteka*) and usually have a green cross hanging outside. The best ones are on ulitsa Novyy Arbat, Tverskaya ulitsa, and Kutuzovskiy prospekt. These sell many imported medications, some with the instructions still in the original language. Prescriptions are not necessary for any purchase, and antibiotics and other strong medications can be purchased over the counter. All the assistants are trained pharmacists and can suggest a Russian alternative to visitors who name the drug they are seeking. However, visitors with specific requirements, particularly insulin, should bring enough with them for their whole stay. Moscow has a number of all-night pharmacies *(see directory)*.

**Sign for a pharmacy**

## MEDICAL TREATMENT

MOST HOTELS have their own doctor, and this should be the first port of call for anyone who gets sick. There are several companies, notably the **European Medical Centre** and the **American Medical Center**, that specialize in dealing with foreigners. They can provide everything that travelers are likely to need, from basic treatment where they are staying to dental care, x-rays, ultrasound scans, and medical airlifts out of Russia. Their charges are very high, but they are all used to dealing with foreign insurance policies.

Slightly cheaper is **Assist-24**, which has English-speaking Russian doctors who are well able to deal with minor medical emergencies. **US Dental Care** provides a full range of dental treatment.

For those in need of immediate attention, without the time to contact any of the above, the emergency room of the **Botkin Hospital** is the safest bet. The staff can give injections and stitches and carry out general first aid, but no English is spoken.

Anyone waking up in a local hospital should contact their embassy or one of the above medical centers. They can arrange a move or oversee care.

## HEALTH PRECAUTIONS

VISITORS SHOULD not drink the tap water in Moscow but stick to bottled water. Avoid fruit and raw vegetables that may have been washed in tap water. Food in a foreign country often unsettles the stomach, and eating the meat and sausage pies *(pirozhki)* sold on the streets is a sure way to a stomach upset.

In past years diphtheria has increased among the local population. It is advisable to be inoculated against this before going to Russia.

## MOSQUITOES

MOSQUITOES (*komari*) are the bane of everyone's life between June and late September. Plug-in chemical mosquito coils are available and are particularly good at night. Alternatives are sprays, or oil repellants used in vaporizers or burned in candle form.

In the woods or countryside, some sort of repellent is also necessary, and not all of those available locally are effective. It is best to bring repellents and antihistamine cream for treating bites from home.

## DIRECTORY

### EMERGENCY SERVICES

**Fire** *(pozhar)*
( *01.*
**Police** *(militsiya)*
( *02.*
**Ambulance** *(skoraya pomoshch)*
( *03.*

### MEDICAL SERVICES

**American Medical Center**
Американский медицинский центр
*Amerikanskiy meditsinskiy tsentr*
2-oy Tverskoy-Yamskoy per 10.
**Map** 2 D2.
( *956 3366.*

**Assist-24**
Ассист-24
Bolshaya Dmitrovka ul 7/5, stroenie 3, office 38.
**Map** 2 F4.
( *229 6536.*

**Botkin Hospital**
Боткинская больница
*Botkinskaya bolnitsa*
2-oy Botkinskiy proezd 5.
**Map** 1 A1.
( *945 0033.*

**European Medical Centre**
Европейский медицинский центр
*Yevropeyskiy meditsinskiy tsentr*
2-oy Tverskoy-Yamskoy per 10.
**Map** 2 D2.
( *251 6099.*

**US Dental Care**
Американский стоматологический центр
*Amerikanskiy stomatologicheskiy tsentr*
Shabolovka ul 8, stroenie 3.
**Map** 6 F5.
( *931 9909.*

### ALL-NIGHT PHARMACIES

Kutuzovskiy pr 14.
**Map** 5 A2.
( *243 1601.*

Ulitsa Zemlyanoy val 1/4.
**Map** 4 E4.
( *917 0434.*

Nikolskaya ul 19/21.
**Map** 3 A5.
( *921 4942.*

# Banking and Local Currency

**M**OSCOW IS SLOWLY MOVING into the credit card age, and major Western cards can now be used to pay in hotels, top restaurants, and some shops. Everywhere else, however, cash is the norm, and roubles are the only legal currency. The city is well provided with exchange points where visitors can turn their currency (US dollars still being the most popular), traveler's checks or credit cards into roubles. Rates of commission vary. Since bank exchange rates are so good, money should never be changed on the street. Apparently "better" offers from private individuals will lead to visitors being cheated.

## CHANGING MONEY

**R**OUBLES CANNOT be obtained outside Russia, but there are numerous exchange offices all over Moscow, including at the airports. Some offices are open 24 hours a day.

A passport has to be shown when changing money. Any defect on foreign bills, especially vertical tears or ink or water stains, makes them invalid in Russia, and they will be refused at the exchange. Make sure that all bills brought into Russia are in good condition and that any US dollars were issued after 1990.

On completing a currency transaction, an exchange slip is issued. All slips should be kept as they must be attached to the customs declaration filled in on arrival in Russia (*see p200*) and presented at customs on leaving the country.

**A sign for a currency exchange office (*obmen valuty*)**

**Official currency exchange slip**

## USING BANKS

**T**HERE ARE ONLY a few foreign banks in Russia, and they mostly do not offer over-the-counter services. Most Russian banks, however, do have on-the-spot exchange services. They take a variety of currencies, credit cards for cash advances, and some take traveler's checks. **Most-Bank** and **Inkombank** offer the best rates. For anyone wishing to have money sent to a bank in Russia, the most reliable are **Inkombank** and **Promstroybank**. It is always advisable to check other banks' reliability.

Western Union will transfer money to Russia for you through **Inkombank**, **Most-Bank**, **Promstroybank**, and **American Express**, but they are expensive and primarily of use to businesspeople.

Many independent exchange offices in Russia accept only US dollars and Deutschmarks.

## CREDIT CARDS

**I**T IS NOW POSSIBLE to obtain cash, both roubles and US dollars, with a credit card through the larger banks and from automatic cash dispensers at some banks and in major hotels. The local commission is between 2 and 5 percent, plus whatever the card company

**Automatic cash dispenser**

---

### DIRECTORY

#### BANKS

**American Express**
Sadovaya-Kudrinskaya ul 21a.
**Map** 2 D4.
**C** 755 9001.

**Inkombank**
Инкомбанк
Slavyanskaya pl 4, stroenie 1.
**Map** 7 C1.
**C** 956 3808.

**Most-Bank**
Мост-Банк
Vorontsovskaya ulitsa 43.
**Map** 8 F4.
**C** 785 1550.

**Promstroybank**
Промстройбанк
Tverskoi bulvar 13.
**Map** 2 E5.
**C** 200 7974.

#### CASH DISPENSERS

**American Express**
Sadovaya-Kudrinskaya ul 21a.
**Map** 2 D4.
*(Accepts American Express only)*

**Most-Bank**
Мост-Банк
Vorontsovskaya ulitsa 43.
**Map** 8 F4.
*(Accepts VISA, MasterCard, Eurocard)*

**Redisson-Slavyanskaya Hotel**
Гостиница Рэдиссон-Славянская
*Gostinitsa Redisson-Slavyanskaya*
Berezhkovskaya nab 2.
**Map** 5 B2.
*(Accepts VISA, MasterCard, American Express)*

---

charges. The most commonly accepted card is VISA, with Diners, MasterCard, and American Express much less widely recognized. The cash dispensers at **Most-Bank** take MasterCard, and VISA and charge no local commission, making them a popular option with visitors.

Lost or stolen credit cards should be reported immediately to the credit card company in the home country. No local security service is offered.

## Traveler's Checks

**B**ANKS CHARGE at least 3 per cent to cash traveler's checks. Only large banks, such as **Promstroybank**, **Most-Bank**, and **Inkombank**, offer this service. The cheapest alternative is American Express checks. The commission on these is only 2 percent if they are cashed at the **American Express** office. Traveler's checks can only be used as payment for goods or services in a few large hotels, and are acceptable only in US dollars, Deutschmarks, British pounds, and French francs. In all cases dollar checks are preferred.

## Local Currency

**T**HE RUSSIAN currency is the rouble (or ruble), written рубль or abbreviated to р or руб. The higher denominations of roubles are available in bills, which all bear images of Russian cities, the lower denominations in coins. The kopek, of which there are 100 in a rouble, is issued in coins.

The designs of the bills have changed since 1990. In 1998 the rouble was revalued owing to its stronger value and lower inflation, and new bills were issued. Values were divided by 1,000 (1,000 roubles became 1 rouble). Visitors will be given the new bills, but the old ones remain valid until the end of 1998 and prices may be shown in both.

### Bills
*There are four denominations of bills, with face values of 10, 50, 100, and 500 roubles, and they have the same designs as their pre-revaluation equivalents. After December 31, 1998, the old bills can be exchanged only at major banks.*

**10 roubles**

**50 roubles**

**100 roubles**

**500 roubles**

### Coins
*The revaluation of the Russian rouble in 1998 led to the revival of the long-redundant but much-loved kopek. Traditionally, the rouble had always consisted of 100 kopeks. In addition to coins for 1, 2 and 5 roubles, there are now coins valued at 1, 10 and 50 kopeks. Any coins issued before 1997, prior to revaluation, are essentially valueless. Visitors should therefore examine change they receive and refuse to accept old coins.*

**1 rouble**

**2 roubles**

**5 roubles**

**1 kopek**

**10 kopeks**

**50 kopeks**

# Communications

M UCH OF MOSCOW'S ANTIQUATED phone system has been brought up to date in the last few years, and there is now good, city-wide service. Many hotel and public phones have direct dialing all over the world, but phones in private homes may not have this ability. The same period has seen an explosive increase in the number of magazines, newspapers, and television channels. Sadly, Russia's postal system has not improved at the same rate.

**A sign outside a post office (*pochta*) that has public telephones (*telefon*)**

## TELEPHONE SERVICES

C OMSTAR SATELLITE phone booths, which are blue, are installed at airports, in business centers, in most hotel lobbies, and in some restaurants. They accept credit cards or phonecards on sale in major hotels, restaurants, and clubs, but calls are expensive. Moscow's local system is much cheaper. It is possible to call abroad on a direct line from one of the Moscow State Telephone Network (MГTC) blue and white cardphones, located on streets and in some metro stations. Cards for the phones come in 25, 50, 100, 120, 200, 400, and 1,000 units, and are available from kiosks, metro stations and post offices. To make an

**Token for a local phone**

**MГTC phone box**

international call, at least 100 units are needed. International and inter-city calls are cheaper between 10pm and 8am and at all hours at weekends.

Old-style, non-card MГTC phones are grey and can only be used for local calls. They take plastic *zhetony* (tokens), which can be bought in the same places as phonecards. Local calls from private phones are covered by the line rental, but call charges were to be imposed from 1998.

The **Central Telegraph Office** has rows of local and international phones, and calls are paid for at the counter.

Instructions on how to use an MГTC cardphone are given below. Comstar phones work in the same way if used with a phonecard. The instructions automatically come up first in English. If using a credit

card with a Comstar phone, insert it into the top left-hand slot and remove it again in one action. Wait 15 seconds for card verification before dialing. For non-card local phones, lift the receiver and dial the number. When someone answers, drop the token into the slot.

## USING AN MГTC PHONECARD-OPERATED PHONE

1 Lift the receiver and check that you have a dial tone.

2 MГTC phones offer instructions in Russian, English, French, and German. They always appear in Russian first. Press this button to switch between languages. Instructions are given both on the display and through the earpiece.

3 When instructed, push your phonecard into the slot in the direction of the arrow marked on the card. Wait for card verification.

**Russian phonecards**

4 Dial the number. The ringing tone consists of long tones; the busy signal of shorter tones.

5 Press this button at any time to increase the volume.

6 When they answer, press this button to speak.

7 To end a call, replace the receiver and pull out the card.

## POSTAL SERVICES

Post OFFICES such as the **Main Post Office** and those in hotels sell ordinary and commemorative Russian stamps, postcards, envelopes, and phonecards. The smaller post offices are marked почта (*pochta*), and are most plentiful in the center of the city. They generally have big glass windows and blue mail boxes outside.

**Postage stamps**

International mail is often slow and inefficient and is probably best avoided except for sending postcards. **Post International**, which also offers poste restante, provides the same service as courier companies. **American Express** runs its usual poste restante service for cardholders.

It is best to use a courier service for sending important documents. There are several in Moscow, including **DHL Worldwide Express**, **Federal Express**, and **TNT Express Worldwide**. Anything other than paper, especially computer disks, has to be checked by customs, which can delay delivery by an extra day or so.

## FAX, TELEX, TELEGRAM, AND E-MAIL SERVICES

Many HOTELS and the **Main Post Office** offer fax, telex, and telegraph services. Telegrams in foreign languages can also be sent from the **Central Telegraph Office**. In addition to postal services, **Post International** offers fax and E-mail services.

## TELEVISION AND RADIO

HOTELS HAVE long offered Eurosport, CNN, BBC World Service TV, and NBC channels. Russian-language television is dominated by imported soap operas, which are generally dubbed into Russian rather than subtitled. Channel 6 shows NBC News in

**Romanesque-inspired facade of Moscow's grand Main Post Office**

English at 8:30am every morning. The best national news in Russian is on NTV, and the best local news on TV-Tsentr. For English-language radio broadcasts the best are still the BBC World Service and the Voice of America on shortwave. Ekho Moskvy provides an excellent news service in Russian.

Good pop stations include Radio Maximum (103.7 FM) and Local Europe Plus (106.2 FM), which both play Western music, and Russkoe Radio (105.7 FM), which plays Russian music. Orfey (73.4 FM) plays classical music without commercial interruptions.

**Mailbox**

## NEWSPAPERS AND MAGAZINES

Moscow HAS two major English-language newspapers, which are published daily except Sundays and Mondays. *The Moscow Times* provides full coverage of domestic and foreign news, local events, sports and the arts. *The Moscow Tribune* is similar in quality but slightly smaller. Both papers have extensive listings of exhibitions and events in their Friday editions.

**English- and Russian-language newspapers**

The Saturday editions have television programs listed for the week, including satellite channels. *The Exile*, also in English, carries restaurant and entertainment listings. The Russian-language *Kapital* is published every Wednesday and has listings of events. All four are available free in restaurants, hotels, and in some supermarkets and fast-food chains. Current foreign newspapers can be picked up at highly inflated prices from kiosks in the biggest hotels. Other hotels and some of the kiosks on Tverskaya ulitsa may have an old edition for sale.

# GETTING TO MOSCOW

THE QUICKEST and most comfortable way to get to Moscow is by plane. Traveling overland, especially by road, can be difficult and often involves crossing numerous borders and negotiating roadwork and pot-holed roads. However, if cost is the priority, train or bus are possibilities, especially for visitors arriving from St. Petersburg or a neighboring country,

**A plane owned by the Russian airline Aeroflot**

such as Ukraine or Belarus. It is essential that visitors plan their trip before applying for a visa *(see p200)* since the Russian authorities require detailed information about travel arrangements, including which cities visitors will use to enter and leave Russia. Whichever route is chosen, it is worth shopping around to find the best deal as prices fluctuate greatly throughout the year.

**Exterior of Sheremetevo 2, Moscow's main international airport**

## ARRIVING BY AIR

THE TWO MAJOR airlines operating direct scheduled flights from the US to Moscow are **Aeroflot** and **Delta**. Connecting flights from London, Paris, Helsinki, Amsterdam, and Frankfurt to Moscow via British Airways, Northwest/KLM, TWA, Finnair, and Air France are available. However, your best bet may be to go to an authorized travel agency and let it take care of all of the arrangements, including hotel reservations, transportation to and from the airports, and visas.

There are a number of agencies in New York that arrange trips to Russia. **Russian Travel Bureau, Inc., Russian Tours and Travel** and **Panorama Travel Ltd.** cater to both individual and group tours. Many agencies will arrange special-event travel, such as art tours, history tours, and even hunting and environmental tours. Because flight arrangements are usually booked through a connecting city, a travel agency is invaluable for advance planning and getting through all the red tape.

Budget trips are often advertised in the travel sections of many newspapers and magazines.

## SHEREMETEVO 2 AIRPORT

SHEREMETEVO 2 is the main international airport serving Moscow and is the most likely point of arrival for visitors. Situated about 28 km (17 miles) northwest of the city center, it has one terminal, with flights divided between its right and left wings. Central notice boards, in both the departures and arrivals lounges indicate which wing each flight arrives and departs from.

Sheremetevo 2 is not modern, or especially convenient, but it does offer facilities such

| Зал прилёта<br>Arrivals | ⤹ ↙ |
| Розыск багажа<br>Lost and found | ↙ |
| SHERCOMSERVICE<br>Rent a phone -fax -xerox -print<br>2-nd floor, left side | |
| Хранение багажа<br>Left luggage | 🧳 ↙ |

**Airport signs, Sheremetevo 2**

as a currency exchange *(see p204)*, several shops, a restaurant, and a number of fast-food outlets. A reasonable selection of duty-free goods can be purchased at the airport, on arrival as well as departure. While some duty-free items, such as alcohol, are very cheap, others, including caviar, cost almost as much as they do abroad.

Passport control in Russia is still extremely tight, and lining up for it can take up to two hours if several flights arrive at the airport at the same time. Visitors are required to fill in one customs declaration on arrival and another one when leaving *(see p200)*.

## OTHER AIRPORTS

MOSCOW HAS four other airports. **Sheremetevo 1**, close to Sheremetevo 2, is used mainly for domestic flights, including those from St. Petersburg. It also handles all Transaero flights and some Aeroflot charters from abroad. Flights destined for the nearer parts of Russia and other CIS member states often leave from **Vnukovo** airport, which is located in the southwest of Moscow. **Domodedovo**, south of Moscow, serves more distant places in Russia and the CIS including eastern Russia, Siberia, and Central Asia. **Bykovo**, to the west, is Moscow's smallest airport and is used only by small planes because it does not have the modern runways needed by larger aircraft. Bykovo serves the less important routes within Russia and, in summer, also receives some charter flights.

Rechnoy Vokzal metro, at the end of metro line 2

## BUS AND METRO LINKS INTO THE CITY CENTER

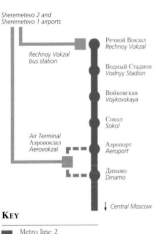

Sheremetevo 2 and
Sheremetevo 1 airports

Rechnoy Vokzal
bus station

Речной Вокзал
*Rechnoy Vokzal*

Водный Стадион
*Vodnyy Stadion*

Войковская
*Voykovskaya*

Сокол
*Sokol*

Air Terminal
Аэровокзал
*Aerovokzal*

Аэропорт
*Aeroport*

Динамо
*Dinamo*

↓ Central Moscow

### KEY

Metro line 2

Bus/minibus route

▪ ▪ Walk

**Sign at departure point of express
bus to Rechnoy Vokzal bus station**

### GETTING INTO THE CITY

ALTHOUGH THE EASIEST WAY of
getting into the city from
Sheremetevo 2 is by taxi, there
are also two bus routes. One
runs from the arrivals hall to
the air terminal *(aerovokzal)*,
around 7 km (4 miles) from the
center of Moscow, and takes
35 minutes. The air terminal
is about 15 minutes' walk
from either Aeroport or
Dinamo

metro stations. The
other bus route runs
to Rechnoy Vokzal
bus station, close
to Rechnoy Vokzal
metro. Both ser-
vices run from
6:25am to 11:30pm.
The trip into the
city center by metro
then takes about
15–20 minutes.

Sheremetevo 1 has
both bus and mini-
bus services, which
also go to Rechnoy
Vokzal bus station or the air
terminal. Again, both services
run from 6:25am until 11:30pm.
The minibuses should also run
all night, but their schedule is
erratic. The destination of each
bus is indicated by a sign displayed in its front window.

For those preferring to travel
by taxi *(see p212)* there are
several things to remember.
First, it is much easier for
travelers to book a cab
prior to arriving, either
through a travel
agency or
through their
hotel. Airport
taxis are ex-
pensive (the
equivalent of
US$50–60 to

the city center) and not all of
them are official. Anyone coming out of customs is met by a
wall of taxi drivers offering a
lift into town. These unofficial
drivers are generally safe, but
it is better to walk outside to
the stand of official taxis. These
yellow cars have black checkered designs on the roof. The
taximeters installed in most of
them are rarely used, so it is
vital to negotiate a price for the
trip beforehand. Once this has
been agreed, no tips are necessary. The trip into the city
center takes about 30–40 minutes if traffic is light, and up
to 90 minutes at busy times.

Novotel, an airport hotel *(see
p170)*, is the only hotel to operate a courtesy pick-up bus
from Sheremetevo 2. Cars can
also be rented at this airport
*(see p218)*. Should visitors
arrive at one of the smaller
airports, they will find some
public transportation and taxis.

**A minibus that takes people from Sheremetevo 1 to
Rechnoy Vokzal bus station or the air terminal**

**Passengers waiting to board a bus from
Sheremetevo 2 to Rechnoy Vokzal bus station**

**Stand of unofficial taxis outside the arrivals hall at
Sheremetevo 2, waiting for fares into the city**

## ARRIVING BY TRAIN

Moscow can be reached by train from Paris, Brussels, Berlin, and several other European capitals, but the trip will take at least a day and a night. Travelers should be prepared for a lengthy wait at the Russian border while all of the train's wheels are changed to fit the wider Russian tracks.

Three of Moscow's main train stations are situated on Komsomolskaya ploshchad (*see p144*), also known as

**Restaurant car of the Budapest train arriving at Kievskiy station**

ploshchad Trekh Vokzalov (Square of the Three Train Stations). **Yaroslavskiy** and **Kazanskiy** serve domestic routes only. **Leningradskiy** is the terminus for trains from St. Petersburg and Finland. Of the other stations, **Rizhskiy** serves the Baltic and **Kievskiy** serves Eastern Europe, while **Belorusskiy** handles trains from Western Europe and Poland. **Paveletskiy** and **Kurskiy** stations are the points of arrival for trains from southern Russia and parts of Ukraine.

**The imposing main entrance to Belorusskiy station**

Tickets for all trains have to be booked in advance. Owing to the long distances covered on many routes, the majority of trains are overnight sleepers, but there are some standard trains operating on the shorter

routes. Trains fall into four categories: express (*ekspressy*) trains, which travel the direct route between Moscow and St. Petersburg only; fast (*skorye*) trains, which operate on long journeys and stop at only a few stations; passenger (*passazhirskie*) trains, which also operate on long routes, but stop at most or all stations; and suburban (*prigorodnye*) trains (*see p219*).

## ARRIVING BY BUS

It is possible to get to Moscow by bus, but it is only usually worth it if visitors are traveling from a neighboring

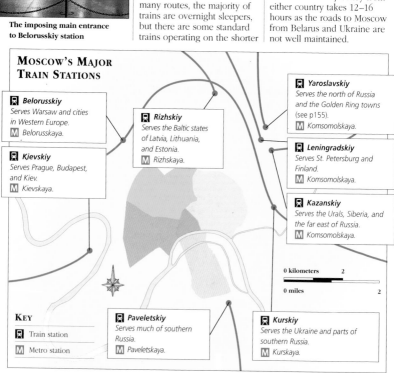

**Soviet crest on the exterior of Kievskiy train station**

country or are on a tight budget. There are bus routes to Moscow from the Czech Republic, Poland, Hungary, and Slovakia. Some run via Ukraine, while others enter Russia via Belarus. Sometimes a change of bus is necessary and the onward journey from either country takes 12–16 hours as the roads to Moscow from Belarus and Ukraine are not well maintained.

## MOSCOW'S MAJOR TRAIN STATIONS

🚉 **Belorusskiy**
*Serves Warsaw and cities in Western Europe.*
Ⓜ *Belorusskaya.*

🚉 **Rizhskiy**
*Serves the Baltic states of Latvia, Lithuania, and Estonia.*
Ⓜ *Rizhskaya.*

🚉 **Kievskiy**
*Serves Prague, Budapest, and Kiev.*
Ⓜ *Kievskaya.*

🚉 **Yaroslavskiy**
*Serves the north of Russia and the Golden Ring towns (see p155).*
Ⓜ *Komsomolskaya.*

🚉 **Leningradskiy**
*Serves St. Petersburg and Finland.*
Ⓜ *Komsomolskaya.*

🚉 **Kazanskiy**
*Serves the Urals, Siberia, and the far east of Russia.*
Ⓜ *Komsomolskaya.*

0 kilometers        2

0 miles                  2

**KEY**

🚉 Train station

Ⓜ Metro station

🚉 **Paveletskiy**
*Serves much of southern Russia.*
Ⓜ *Paveletskaya.*

🚉 **Kurskiy**
*Serves the Ukraine and parts of southern Russia.*
Ⓜ *Kurskaya.*

## TRAVELING TO MOSCOW FROM ST. PETERSBURG

THE EASIEST WAY of getting to Moscow from St. Petersburg is by train. Express trains run from Moskovskiy station in St. Petersburg to Leningradskiy station in Moscow. It is easiest to obtain a ticket through a hotel or travel agent.

**A ticket from a Moscow–St. Petersburg express**

The best nighttime trains are Nos. 1 (called the *Red Arrow*) and 3 from St. Petersburg to Moscow, and Nos. 2 and 4, from Moscow to St. Petersburg.

**Sign indicating the *Aurora* train from St. Petersburg to Moscow**

All these services leave at midnight and arrive at 8:30 the next morning and are usually on time. Other trains, including Nos. 47 and 159 (the *Aurora*) are almost as good, especially for those who prefer to make the trip in the day. On all these trains travelers should be wary of thieves. Most compartments have locks, which should be used at night.

Ticket prices start at the equivalent of US$12 for a basic seat and rise to US$80 per person for a two-person compartment. Prices are usually higher for foreigners than for Russians. There is a choice between *sidyashchyy* (sitting) tickets and a variety of more expensive sleeper options. Bedlinens cost extra. Food may be available, but visitors are advised to bring their own.

**Compartment on the *Red Arrow* St. Petersburg–Moscow express**

The alternative to taking the train is flying. The flight takes only 50 minutes, but allow plenty of time to get to and from the airports, especially in Moscow *(see p209)*. Planes depart from Pulkovo 1 airport in St. Petersburg and arrive at Sheremetevo 1 *(see p208)*. The air fare is considerably more expensive than the train.

---

### DIRECTORY

#### TRAVEL AGENCIES IN THE US

**Russian Tours and Travel by Panorama, Ltd.**
156 5th Avenue
New York, NY 10010
℡ (212) 741-0033.

**Russian Travel Bureau**
225 E. 44th St.
New York, NY 10017
℡ (212) 986-1500.

**Russian Govt. Tourist Office**
℡ (212) 758-1162.

#### AIRLINES

**Aeroflot**
Аэрофлот
Ulitsa Petrovka 20.
**Map** 3 A4.
℡ 921 8301/926 6476.
℡ (212) 265-6403 in US.

**British Airways**
Krasnopresnenskaya naberezhnaya 12, office 1905.
**Map** 5 A1.
℡ 258 2492.
℡ 1 (800) 247-9297 in US.

**Delta Air Lines**
World Trade Center, Floor 11
℡ 258 1288.
℡ 1 (800) 241-4141 in US

**KLM**
Ulitsa Usacheva 35, Floor 1.
**Map** 5 A5.
℡ 258 3600.
℡ 1 (800) 374-7747 in US

**SAS**
Ulitsa Kuznetskiy most 3.
**Map** 3 A4.
℡ 925 4747.
℡ 1 (800) 221-2350 in US

**Transaero**
Трансаэро
Ulitsa Okhotnyy ryad 2.
**Map** 3 A5.
℡ 241 7676.
℡ 1 (800) 957-2658 in US

#### MOSCOW AIRPORTS

**Sheremetevo 1 & 2**
Шереметьево 1 & 2
℡ 578 2372/ 956 4666.

**Bykovo**
Быково
℡ 558 4738.

**Domodedovo**
Домодедово
℡ 155 0922.

**Vnukovo**
Внуково
℡ 155 0922.

#### TRAIN STATIONS

**Belorusskiy**
Белорусский
Ploshchad Tverskoy Zastavy 7. **Map** 1 C2.
℡ 973 8191.

**Kazanskiy**
Казанский
Komsomolskaya ploshchad 2. **Map** 4 D2.
℡ 264 6409.

**Kievskiy**
Киевский
Ploshchad Kievskovo vokzala. **Map** 5 B2.
℡ 240 0415.

**Kurskiy**
Курский
Ulitsa Zemlyanoy val 29.
**Map** 4 E5.
℡ 917 3152.

**Leningradskiy**
Ленинградский
Komsomolskaya ploshchad 3.
**Map** 4 D2.
℡ 262 9143.

**Paveletskiy**
Павелецкий
Paveletskaya ploshchad 1.
**Map** 7 C5.
℡ 235 0522.

**Rizhskiy**
Рижский
Ploshchad Rizhskovo vokzala.
℡ 266 1364.

**Yaroslavskiy**
Ярославский
Komsomolskaya ploshchad 5.
**Map** 4 D2.
℡ 921 5914.

**General Information**
℡ 266 9333.

**Ticket Bookings**
℡ 266 8333.

#### BUS STATIONS

**Moscow Bus Station**
Московский автовокзал
*Moskovskiy avtovokzal*
Nr Shchelkovskaya metro, Uralskaya ulitsa 2.
℡ 468 0400.

# GETTING AROUND MOSCOW

**M**OSCOW'S VAST metro net work, which has stops close to all the major sights, is the most reliable way of traveling around the city. However, it can get extremely crowded. Moscow is also served by buses, trolleybuses, and trams. Services are relatively frequent, although delays are now more common than they were in the Soviet era. A knowledge of the Cyrillic alphabet will help with reading signs on these services.

**Indicates a pedestrian area**

Suburban buses are particularly useful for traveling around Moscow's outlying districts, beyond the reach of the metro network, and bus routes often start at a major metro station. Trams run as far as the outskirts of the city, but services are gradually being reduced. Trolleybuses are a good means of transport in the city center, covering the popular routes. Taxis are the most flexible, but most expensive, way of getting around.

**The Kremlin, at the heart of Moscow (see pp52–67), must be explored on foot**

## WALKING

**M**OSCOW'S CENTER is very spread out and so not easily negotiable on foot. However, the area within the Boulevard Ring, where many sights are located, offers a few good opportunities for walking. At the heart of the city are Red Square *(see p106)* and the Kremlin, which are accessible only on foot. Visitors should allow three hours to cover this area, including all the cathedrals in the Kremlin. Across the

**Pedestrian subway sign**

river from here, beautiful Zamoskvoreche *(see pp114–25)* is another district that pedestrians will enjoy.

Muscovites themselves are not great walkers but, in the evenings or on weekends, they can often be seen taking a stroll around the Old Arbat *(see pp70–71)*, a district of the city frequented by artists, musicians, and street performers. Other places to take a walk are Tverskaya ulitsa *(see p89)*, numerous parks – in

particular Gorky Park *(see p129)*, Izmaylovo Park, *(see p141)* and Sokolniki Park – and by the Moskva river.

When embarking on a walk around the city, it is a good idea to wear sturdy shoes, and preferably old ones as Moscow can be dirty. Traffic is heavy and major roads can often be crossed via subways (although, as in other cities, it is wise to be vigilant when doing so alone). Alternatively, use a zebra crossing if a green light shows: drivers in Moscow do not stop at zebra crossings without lights. It is not advisable for anyone, but especially a woman, to walk around any part of the city alone late at night. The best walking tours in English are organized by Patriarshi Dom Tours *(see p198)*.

## TAXIS

**F**OR SAFETY REASONS it is best to travel only by official taxis: yellow cabs with a black checkered design on their roofs. They can be booked through the **Moscow Taxi** company, although operators are unlikely to speak English, or alternatively through a hotel. They usually arrive within half an hour. Taxis to the airport should be booked well in advance. Some hotels have their own taxi stands, but the taxis that wait there can be very expensive. It is possible to flag down an official taxi on the street. Some switch on a green light, either on

**Official yellow Moscow taxi**

## HOT AIR BALLOONS

Taking a trip in a hot air balloon has recently become a popular pastime among well-off New Russians and visitors to the city, especially in the summer. **Avgur** launches its balloons near the Istra river in Zvenigorod outside Moscow. Rides last for about two hours, taking three passengers, who can include children, in addition to the pilot. Trips are expensive, but offer fantastic views of the city including the "Seven Sisters," Stalinist-Gothic skyscrapers *(see p45)*.

**Hailing a private car for a ride, a common practice among Russians**

their window or on their roof, to indicate they are for hire. Others do not, but if they are for hire they will stop. All official taxis have meters, but some are out-of-date and the driver may prefer to negotiate the fare. It is crucial either to agree on a fare, or to be sure that the driver turns on the meter, before setting off.

Russians themselves prefer to use private taxis (*chastniki*) to official ones. Any car can be hailed and a fee agreed for a journey. Other cars may therefore stop when an official taxi is hailed. Private taxis are cheap and generally safe. However, it is not advisable for visitors to the city who do not speak Russian to use them.

## MOSCOW RIVER CRUISES

RIVER BOATS are extremely popular in summer. They operate from May to October and cover quite a long stretch of the Moskva river. They stop at 10 or so points along the river and you can hop on and off, but must purchase a new ticket each time. All riverboats have two decks, and on sunny days the upper deck is great for combining sunbathing with sightseeing.

River cruises pass several major sites and are a good way to get a feel for the city's layout. The main pickup point for these cruises is opposite Kievskiy Station. Major stops are near Moscow State University at Sparrow Hills (*see p129*), at Gorky Park, and

near Red Square (Bolshoy Ustinskiy most). **Passengers' Port** is the main company running these cruises. It also hires boats out and organizes waterborne parties on them.

### DIRECTORY

**Moscow Taxi**
Московское такси
*Moskovskoe taksi*
( 238 1001.

**Passengers' Port**
Пассажирский порт
*Passazhirskiy port*
( 459 7476.

**Avgur**
Авгур
Ulitsa Stepana Shutova 4.
( 359 1001/1065.

**Double-decker river boat, a good way to view the sights along the river**

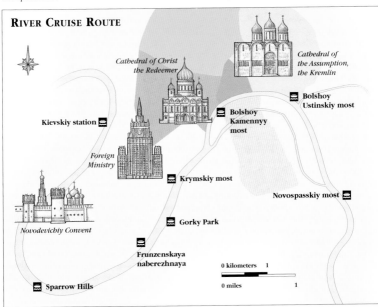

## RIVER CRUISE ROUTE

Cathedral of Christ the Redeemer

Cathedral of the Assumption, the Kremlin

Kievskiy station

Foreign Ministry

Novodevichiy Convent

Bolshoy Kamennyy most

Bolshoy Ustinskiy most

Krymskiy most

Novospasskiy most

Gorky Park

Frunzenskaya naberezhnaya

Sparrow Hills

0 kilometers    1

0 miles          1

# The Metro

M OSCOW IS A SPRAWLING, hectic city. One of its great assets, however, is its excellent metro network, which extends from the center out to many of its suburbs. During the rush hour, in particular, heavy traffic means that it is often faster to travel by metro than by car or any other form of public transportation. For years all transportation in the Soviet Union was very inexpensive; metro fares are still a very good value. These days, passengers pay the same fare regardless of the length of their trip. However, the city authorities have announced plans to introduce new variable fares at some point in the future.

**Moscow metro symbol**

The metro system is extremely reliable, with trains running frequently throughout the day. Constructed as part of Stalin's grand plan for rebuilding Moscow, it is also a tourist attraction in its own right *(see pp38–41)*.

**Main entrance to Tretyakovskaya metro, an interchange station**

**The ornate, cavernous interior of Arbatskaya metro**

## THE NETWORK

T HE MOSCOW metro network is well planned and extensive, consisting of 10 lines that cover the whole city except its outermost suburbs. One feature worth noting is the circular line connecting all the mainline train stations *(see p210)*. Changing between the metro and a mainline station is generally easy because both have the same name, but with a slightly different ending. Belorusskiy train station, for instance, links to Belorusskaya metro, and Kievskiy train station to Kievskaya metro. However, Komsomolskaya, also on the circle line, is the exception. It links to three mainline train stations – Leningradskiy, Kazanskiy, and Yaroslavskiy.

The metro lines are color-coded and numbered from 1 to 10, and all signs are in Cyrillic only. Trains arrive frequently, generally every 1–2 minutes on weekdays, while services are slightly less frequent on weekends. During the rush hour the interval between trains is less than a minute.

The Moscow metro is, on the whole, safe and reliable. All the stations are staffed, but metro attendants are likely to speak only Russian. Travelers who have a heavy bag or a suit-case will have to pay an added charge.

**Emergency intercom to driver**

## CHANGING LINES

F OR THOSE unused to the complexity of Moscow's metro system, trips can be made even more confusing by the fact that stations where it is possible to change between metro lines often have two or more separate names, one for each line involved. On the metro map *(see p216)* these interchange stations are bracketed together. For instance, near the center of the city there is an interchange between four lines – 1, 3, 4, and 9 – each of which is served by a different station. Correspondingly, four station names are given on the map: Biblioteka imeni Lenina, Arbatskaya, Aleksandrovskiy Sad, and Borovitskaya.

When changing lines at an interchange station it is therefore important to know the name of the station on the other line. It is then easy to reach the right platform by following the переход *(perekhod)* – or "interchange" – signs indicating this name.

**Metro train ready to depart from Mayakovskaya metro**

## TICKETS AND TRAVEL CARDS

THERE IS NO SUCH THING as a one-day travel card in Moscow, but monthly passes are available *(see p217)*. Apart from these there are two types of metro tickets. The first is the old-fashioned, yellow, plastic metro token *(zheton)*. These tokens can be bought at all metro stations from the ticket counter, or касса *(kassa)*. The fare for a single trip is still a flat rate, whether it is a couple of stops or the length of the network, so only one token is needed for any trip. This also means that it is possible to change as many times as necessary if exploring the metro's architectural highlights *(see pp38–41)*. Buy several tokens at a time to avoid waiting in lines, which can be long during the morning and evening rush hours.

The token is being replaced by a card with a magnetic strip on the back. This *(magnit-naya karta)* is good for either 20 or 60 rides. It works on a phonecard principle. When a card is inserted into the barrier, the passenger goes through if the card is valid. The number of trips left will be reduced by one, and this number will flash up on the display. Any number of people can travel on the same card since they all pay the same fee for their ride. Magnetic cards are sold at most stations, including all central ones.

There are no reduced-fare tickets for the Moscow metro, but children under six travel free. Metro ticket counters also sell phonecards and tickets for trolleybuses, buses, and trams *(see p217)*.

**Magnetic card being inserted into the barrier at a metro station**

## MAKING A TRIP BY METRO

**1** Study the metro map *(see p216)* and plan your trip in advance; the station names on each platform are not visible from inside the train. It is well worth learning the pronunciation of the station names as the driver will announce which station you are approaching. It is also a good idea to count the number of stops.

**2** Purchase either a token or a magnetic card from the касса *(kassa)*, the counter situated just inside the metro station. Feed the token or card into the automatic barrier to gain access to the platforms.

**Metro token**

**3** To find the right platform follow signs headed к поездам до станции *(k poezdam do stantsiy)*, which show the stops in each direction from the station you are at. These signs are sometimes color coded.

**Stops in one direction**

**4** On the platform, consult the signs showing all the stops of the line you are using. Trains always stop at each one. Look at the vertical lists beneath each interchange station. These show which subsequent stations you reach by changing at that point.

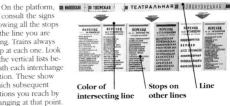

**Color of intersecting line**  **Stops on other lines**  **Line**

**5** Look at the digital board showing the time that has elapsed since a train last left the station. On weekdays another one will usually arrive within one or two minutes.

**Minutes, seconds and 100ths of a second since last train**  **Current time**

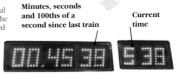

**6** If you change to a different line during your trip, follow the signs marked with either переход *(perekhod)* or на станцию *(na stantsiyu)* and the appropriate station name. Once at your destination follow signs for выход *(vykhod)* to locate the exit.

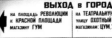

**Interchange sign**

**Exit and interchange sign**

# The Moscow Metro

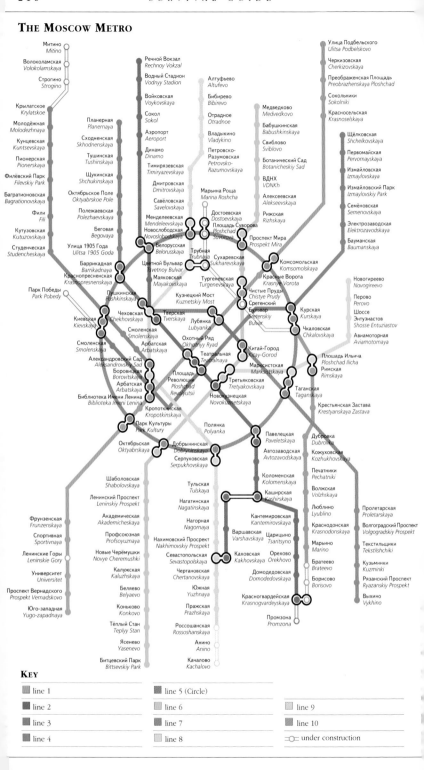

# Traveling by Tram, Trolleybus, and Bus

**M**OSCOW HAS EXTENSIVE bus, trolleybus and tram routes, and some of the most useful ones are identified on the map on the inside back cover of this book. Some routes link in with the metro network *(see pp214–16)*, often starting at one metro station and terminating at another. Main avenues are generally served by both buses and trolleybuses. Trams are less useful but, as a sedate form of transport, they are great for sightseeing. Busy routes can get extremely crowded during the morning and evening rush hours, and traffic is often slow moving at these times. Moscow's newer, more remote suburbs are well served by these forms of transportation. Stops are clearly signed and are at frequent intervals, although tram stops are occasionally farther apart.

**Line of people waiting at a bus stop in central Moscow**

## TRAMS

**A**LTHOUGH TRAMS remain Moscow's most traditional means of transportation, services are now being cut back, and some old tracks have been removed. However, they provide a bumpy, entertaining ride for children, and interest and variety for visitors.

The surviving tram services run quite frequently, especially those operating in the suburbs,

**A yellow and white Moscow tram**

**A yellow Moscow bus**

**Trolleybus, powered by an overhead cable and running on a fixed route**

linking metro stations and apartment buildings. Tram stops are marked by a transparent sign labeled Тр in Cyrillic and usually have a semicircular shelter with a bench. Trams have one or two cars, each with three doors. It was customary to get on through the rear door and leave through the front, but this practice is no longer observed.

Tram route A, which starts at Chistye Prudy metro, is useful for visitors as it travels around the Boulevard Ring, passing close to many of Moscow's central sights. A special sightseeing tram with an on-board café travels the same route. Tickets are sold as you get on.

## TROLLEYBUSES

**T**ROLLEYBUSES are very useful for traveling around the city center. Even though they are less comfortable and Muscovites prefer traveling by bus, most of the routes are still packed during rush hours. Stops are marked by a plaque with the Cyrillic letter Т.

Trolleybuses are blue, red, or yellow. Those with two cars have three working doors, and those with a single car have two working doors. As with trams, there is no established etiquette as to which door to use when getting on or off.

Trolleybus Б travels around the Garden Ring and is good for getting to know the city.

Trolleybus 15 cuts across the whole city center, starting at Suvorov ploshchad next to Novoslobodskaya metro and terminating at the Luzhniki Central Stadium *(see pp194–5)*.

## BUSES

**B**USES ARE USEFUL for traveling in Moscow's suburbs where distances between metro lines are much greater than in the center. Bus stops are marked by white and yellow plaques showing the cyrillic letter А and are the same distance apart as trolleybus stops. Public buses are yellow, red, or red and white. Bus services in the city center are limited, and there are none running along Tverskaya ulitsa. However, several bus routes run up Kutuzovskiy prospekt past the Borodino Panorama Museum, the Triumphal Arch, and Victory Park *(see pp128–9)*.

**Ticket for tram, bus and trolleybus**

**Insert ticket here**

**Push large knob to punch ticket**

**Punching machine for validating tram, trolleybus, and bus tickets**

## TICKETS AND TRAVEL CARDS

**O**NE-DAY travel cards are not available in Moscow, but monthly cards can be bought at metro stations: these cards cover the metro alone; tram, bus, and trolleybus (separately or in any combination). Individual tickets for bus, trolleybus, and tram are identical and can be bought in all metro stations, at nearby kiosks, or from drivers, but cost a little more. Insert the card into the machine on any bus, trolleybus, or tram to validate.

# Driving in Moscow

DRIVING IN MOSCOW can be quite grueling for the uninitiated. Most driving regulations, and many principles that would be considered common sense elsewhere, are ignored. For instance, although the majority of drivers will stop at red lights, some keep going, regardless. Cars travel in disorderly lanes and veer dangerously to avoid potholes. Drivers tend to be aggressive and inconsiderate about yielding to one another. Road signs mostly follow international conventions but, as all major roads are sign-posted in Russian only, it is well worth drivers familiarizing themselves with Cyrillic place names in advance.

**Gas station belonging to one of several chains operating in Moscow**

## DRIVING REGULATIONS

DRIVING REGULATIONS in Moscow are complex. GAI, Russia's traffic police *(see p202)*, have the right to stop drivers at any time and ask for documents. They can issue fines on the spot for infringements such as not having a fire extinguisher or first-aid kit and not wearing seat belts. It is compulsory for both drivers and front-seat passengers to wear seat belts, although many people do not. Drivers are not allowed to drink any alcohol at all, and fines for drunk-driving can be very high. It is illegal to make U-turns on many of Moscow's main streets.

**Priority to traffic on the right canceled**

Priority is always given to traffic coming from the right unless a yellow, diamond-shaped sign indicates otherwise.

The buying of driver's licences is common in Russia, so visitors should not assume that all road users are qualified and responsible.

## PARKING AND GASOLINE

PARKING IS EXPENSIVE in most of central Moscow. There are no meters; instead, drivers pay attendants in gray uniforms on either arriving or leaving. Parking time is by half-hour periods, with no time limit. Fines for parking in restricted areas (marked with the international signs) are high. All petrol is leaded. A98 (superplus) and A95 (super) are suitable for foreign cars; A92 is for Russian-made cars.

## CAR RENTAL

THERE ARE SEVERAL well-known companies that operate in Moscow. **Hertz** and **Europcar** have offices both at Sheremetevo 2 airport and in the city center. Other companies in Moscow include **National Car Rental** and **Rolf**. Visitors renting a car need international insurance and must show an international driver's licence and their passport and credit card when picking up. Some of the larger hotels also arrange car rental.

**Multiple lanes of traffic on Teatralniy proezd, one of Moscow's busiest roads**

## WINTER DRIVING

MOST DRIVERS use studded tires in winter as roads are often icy and covered with snow. Driving in these conditions can be dangerous and is not advisable unless visitors have had experience in other northern climates.

## DRIVING OUTSIDE MOSCOW

THE ROADS leading out of Moscow are in reasonable condition, but Kutuzovskiy prospekt is particularly well-maintained because it is used by government officials and the New Russians who own a *dacha* in this area. It is vital to have a good map because side roads to small villages can easily be missed.

---

## DIRECTORY

### CAR RENTAL

**National Car Rental**
Bolshaya Kommunisticheskaya ulitsa 1/5.
( 298 6146.

**Europcar**
Mezhdunarodnaya Hotel,
1st floor,
Krasnopresnenskaya naberezhnaya 12.
( 253 1369.
Sheremetevo 2 airport.
( 578 3878.

**Hertz**
Chernyakhovskovo ulitsa 4.
( 151 5426.
Sheremetevo 2 airport.
( 578 5646.

**Rolf**
Рольф
Shubinskiy pereulok 2/3.
**Map** 5 C2.
( 241 5393.

### EMERGENCY SERVICES

**Avto-SOS**
Авто-СОС
2-ya Magistralnaya ulitsa 10.
( 256 0636.

**Emergency Service Station (24 hours)**
Ryazanski pereulok 13.
**Map** 4 D3.
( 267 0113.

# Excursions from Moscow

ARRANGEMENTS TO VISIT SIGHTS outside Moscow *(see pp126–61)* can be made through either a hotel or a travel agency, or the trip can be made independently by train, bus, or car. Most of the places mentioned below are not far from Moscow and can be visited on a day trip. A few, such as Suzdal and Vladimir, take two days. Patriarshiy Dom Tours *(see p198)* offers a wide range of excursions to the major sights around Moscow. It is advisable to enquire in good time as reservations with them have to be made 48 hours before departure.

**Inside the carriage of one of Moscow's suburban trains**

## USING TRAINS AND BUSES

SUBURBAN TRAINS *(prigorodnye poezda)* to the nearer sights can be caught at the appropriate mainline station *(see p210)*. They usually depart from a station annex and are cheap as foreigners pay the same fare as Russians. More distant sights are served by passenger trains *(passazhirskie poezda)*.

Suburban buses *(prigorodnye marshruty)* to several closer excursion sights leave from Moscow Bus Station at Shchelkovskaya metro station in the northeast of the city. Towns farther from Moscow are served by intercity buses *(mezhdugorodnye avtobusy)*.

**An inner-city bus, which can be used to make long-distance trips**

## ONE-DAY TRIPS

BOTH NOVODEVICHIY Convent *(see pp130–1)* and Kolomenskoe *(see pp138–9)* are south of the city center, the former close to Sportivnaya metro, the latter to Kolomenskaya metro. Kuskovo *(see pp142–3)*, in eastern Moscow, is also best reached by metro, to Ryazanskiy Prospekt or Vykhino. A short bus ride will then take visitors to the estate.

Arkhangelskoe *(see p152)*, 20 km (12 miles) to the west of the city center, is served by Tushinskaya metro and then a bus. By car it is on a straight route out along Volokolamskoe shosse or Rublevskoe shosse.

It takes around two hours to travel to the village and battlefield of Borodino *(see p152)* by

train from Belorusskiy station, by bus from Moscow Bus Station or by car, leaving the city on Mozhayskoe shosse.

The Tchaikovsky House-Museum *(see p153)* is two hours northwest of the city by car on Leningradskoe shosse, by train from Leningradskiy station, or by bus from Moscow Bus Station.

Abramtsevo Estate-Museum *(see p154)* is situated to the northeast of Moscow just off Yaroslavskoe shosse. Trains leave from Yaroslavskiy station and buses from Moscow Bus Station. The trip takes an hour or so.

The Trinity Monastery of St Sergius *(see pp156–9)* is also to the northeast along Yaroslavskoe shosse and the trip also takes just over an hour. It is possible to get there by train or by bus from Yaroslavskiy station, and by bus from Moscow Bus Station.

Pereslavl-Zalesskiy *(see p154)* can be reached by car along Yaroslavskoe shosse, by train from Yaroslavskiy station, or by bus from Moscow Bus Station. The trip takes approximately two hours.

## TWO-DAY TRIPS

SUZDAL *(see p160)*, 200 km (124 miles) northeast of Moscow, is reached by leaving the city on Gorkovskoe shosse. Buses to Suzdal leave from Moscow Bus Station and take about four hours.

Vladimir *(see pp160–61)* is also situated northeast of the city along Gorkovskoe shosse. The 170-km (106-mile) trip can be made by bus from Moscow Bus Station, by train or by car in about three hours.

Yasnaya Polyana *(see p161)* is 180 km (112 miles) south of Moscow on the Simferopolskoe shosse. Trains run from Kurskiy station and buses from Moscow Bus Station. Both take almost four hours.

It is worth considering combining a trip to Vladimir and Suzdal; buses run daily between the two. Patriarshiy Dom runs tours to both towns with an overnight stopover, and day trips to Yasnaya Polyana.

**Train arriving at Sergiev Posad for the Trinity Monastery of St. Sergius**

# MOSCOW STREET FINDER

THE KEY MAP below shows the areas of Moscow covered by the *Street Finder*. The map references given throughout the guide for sights, restaurants, hotels, shops, or entertainment venues refer to the maps in this section. All the major sights have been marked so they are easy to locate. The key below shows other features marked

**A Moscow family out sightseeing**

on the maps, such as post offices, metro stations, and churches. The *Street Finder* index lists street names in transliteration, followed by Cyrillics (on maps, Cyrillics are given only for major roads). This guide uses the reinstated old Russian street names, not the Soviet versions *(see p199)*. Places of interest are listed by their English names.

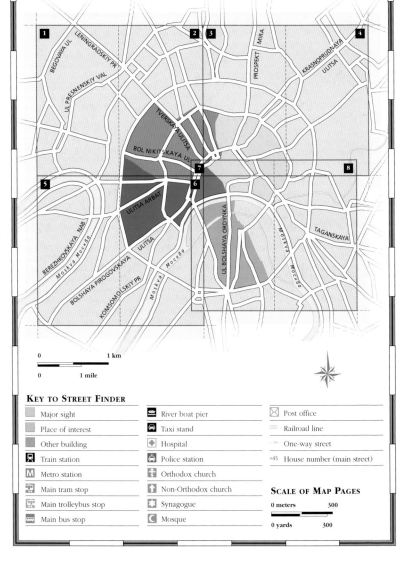

0           1 km

0           1 mile

## KEY TO STREET FINDER

| | | |
|---|---|---|
| ▢ Major sight | ▥ River boat pier | ⊠ Post office |
| ▢ Place of interest | ▤ Taxi stand | ꞊ Railroad line |
| ▢ Other building | ✚ Hospital | → One-way street |
| 🚉 Train station | ▥ Police station | *45 House number (main street) |
| Ⓜ Metro station | ✝ Orthodox church | |
| ▨ Main tram stop | ✝ Non-Orthodox church | **SCALE OF MAP PAGES** |
| ▨ Main trolleybus stop | ✡ Synagogue | 0 meters          300 |
| ▨ Main bus stop | ☪ Mosque | 0 yards          300 |

# Street Finder Index

## ABBREVIATIONS & USEFUL WORDS

| | | |
|---|---|---|
| ul | **ulitsa** | street |
| pl | **ploshchad** | square |
| pr | **prospekt** | avenue |
| per | **pereulok** | small street/ passage/lane |
| | **most** | bridge |
| | **podezd** | entrance |
| | **proezd** | small street/ passage/lane |
| | **sad** | garden |
| | **shosse** | road |
| | **stroenie** | building |
| | **tupik** | cul-de-sac |

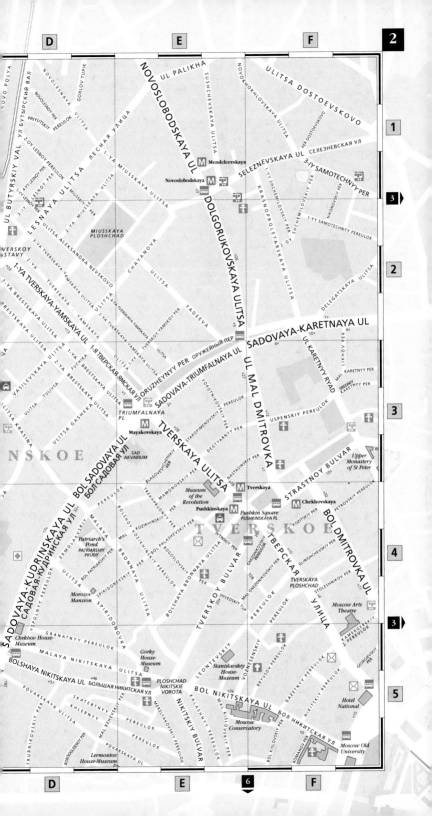

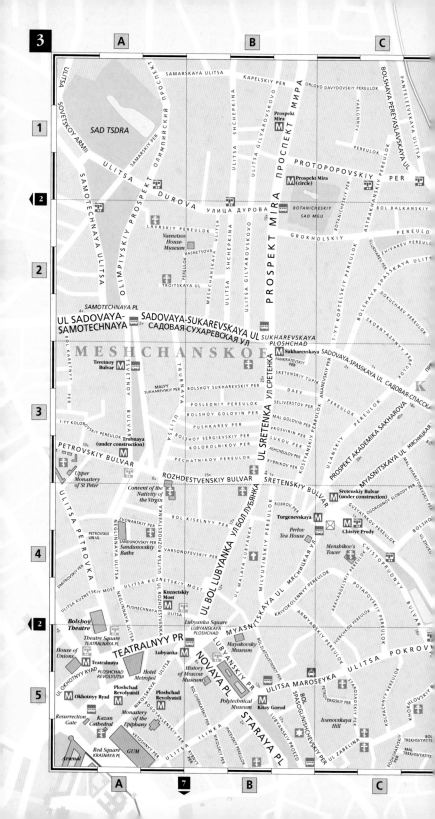

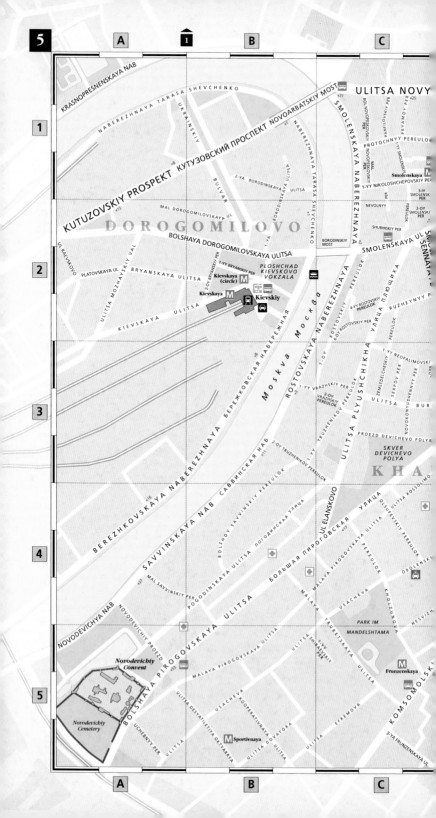

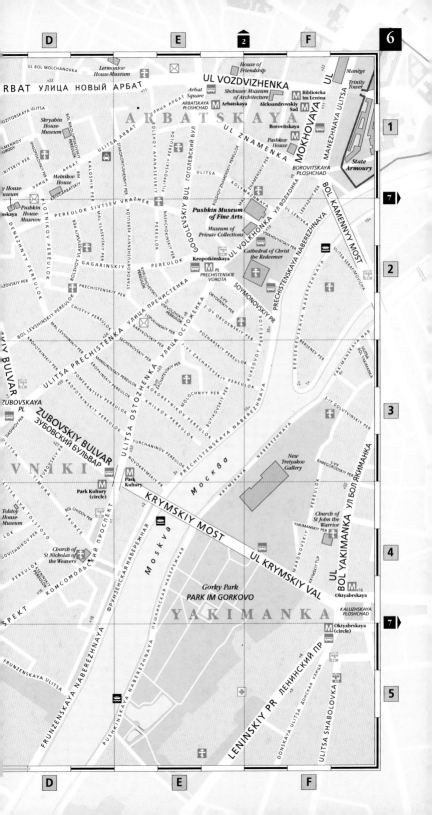

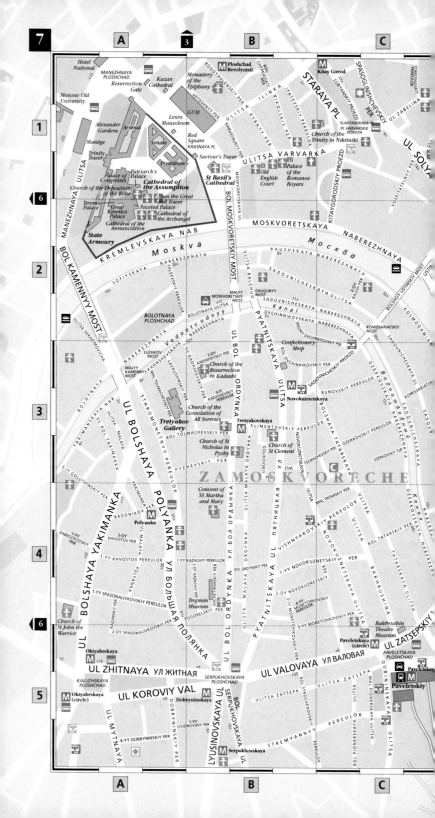

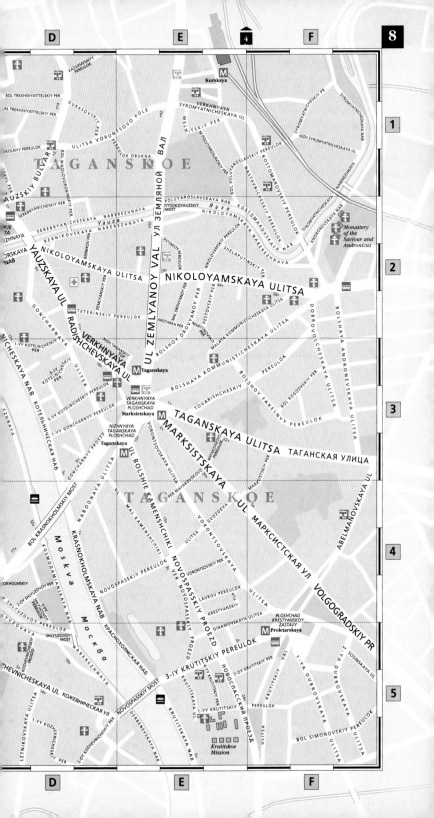

# General Index

Page numbers in **bold** type refer to main entries.

# Acknowledgments

DORLING KINDERSLEY would like to thank the following people whose contributions and assistance have made the preparation of this book possible.

## MAIN CONTRIBUTOR

CHISTOPHER RICE holds a PhD in Russian history from the University of Birmingham. He and his wife Melanie, also a writer, first visited Russia in 1978 and have been returning regularly ever since. They have written numerous travel guides to the city, and to a variety of other destinations including Prague, Berlin and Istanbul, as well as the *Eyewitness Travel Guide to St. Petersburg.*

## ADDITIONAL CONTRIBUTORS

ROSE BARING studied Russian from the age of 12. She has an MA in Modern History and divided her time between London, Moscow and St. Petersburg for much of the early 1990s. She has written guides to St. Petersburg, Moscow and other destinations, including the *Eyewitness Travel Guide to Istanbul.*

MARINA BOUGHTON has a BA in Film Studies from the University of Central London. She also studied in Russia and has worked there for a number of years. She is now a correspondent for BBC Radio in Moscow.

SERGEY KONSTANTINOVICH ROMANUIK is a graduate of the Moscow State University. Specializing in Economic Geography and the history and cultural life of Moscow, he has written around 200 articles and books about the city.

## SPECIAL ASSISTANCE

DORLING KINDERSLEY would like to thank Ian Wizniewski (food and drink author), Frank Althaus (hotels), Radhika Jones (restaurants), Natasha Linkova (researcher in Moscow), Maria Fetisova (photo permissions), Elena Mirskaya (DK Moscow), Oleksiy Nesnov (language consultant), Victoria Rachevskaya (language consultant), and Sylvain Borsi of Nikita's restaurant, London (food preparation for *What to Eat in Moscow*).

## PROOFREADER

Stewart J Wild.

## INDEXER

Hilary Bird.

## DESIGN AND EDITORIAL ASSISTANCE

Liz Atherton, Laurence Broers, Dawn Davies-Cooke, Claire Folkard, Freddy Hamilton, Leanne Hogbin, Sarah Martin, Adam Moore, Ellen Root, Luke Rozkowski, A. Sokoloff, P. Todd-Naylor, Ingrid Vienings, Veronica Wood.

## ADDITIONAL ILLUSTRATIONS

Paul Weston, Joy Fitzsimmonds.

## ADDITIONAL PHOTOGRAPHY

Andy Crawford, Erich Crichton, Neil Fletcher, Steve Gorton, Ian O'Leary, Gary Ombler, Clive Streeter.

## PHOTOGRAPHY PERMISSIONS

DORLING KINDERSLEY would like to thank all those who gave permission to photograph at the various cathedrals, churches, museums, restaurants, hotels, shops, galleries, and travel services and other sights too numerous to thank individually.

## PICTURE CREDITS

t = top; tl = top left; tlc = top left center; tc = top center; trc = top right center; tr = top right; cla = center left above; ca = center above; cra = center right above; cl = center left; c = center; cr = center right; clb = center right below; cb = center below; crb = center right below; bl = bottom left; b = bottom; bc = bottom center; bcl = bottom center left; br = bottom right; d = detail

Works of art have been reproduced with the permission of the following copyright holders:
*Goldfish*, Henri Matisse (1911–1912) @ Succession, H Matisse/DACS 1998 79cra; *Improvisations*, Wassily Kandinski @ ADAGP, Paris and DACS, London 1998 81t; *Young Acrobat on a Ball*, Pablo Picasso @ Succession Picasso/DACS 1998 46bl.

The publisher would like to thank the following individuals, companies and picture libraries for their kind permission to reproduce their photographs:

AISA, BARCELONA: 21b, 22clb, 51 (insert), 46t, 58t, 59tl, 61cr, 64b, 121t; AKG, LONDON: 17cl, 18c, 27cl, 28br, 28–29c, 29ca, 55br, 107b, 118br, 120tr, 121b, 155cra/bl; Erich Lessing 26t, 28bl, 155 clb; ARTEPHOT, PARIS: 16, 118bl; AVANT-GARDE PUBLISHING HOUSE: Victor Korniushin 4b, 196–197.

KATHLEEN BERTON MURRELL: 42cb, 62b; BOLSHOY THEATER: 90t/b, 91tl/tr; THE BRIDGEMAN ART LIBRARY, LONDON/NEW YORK: The Hermitage, St. Petersburg 25tl; Kremlin Museums 64c; Mark Gallery 159t; Novosti 21 crb, 25 crb; Private Collection 23c, 29tr; Pushkin Museum, Moscow 81b; Richardson and Kailas Icons, London 155t; Tretyakov Gallery 22t, 47bl, 118cl, 120b.

CAMERA PRESS: Richard Ellis 76–77 and 212br; JEAN-LOUP CHARMET: 18t; CATHERINE COOKE: 71bl; CORBIS UK: Dean Conger 34cr, 190cl; Library of Congress 28cl; Steve Raymer 31crb.

JAMES DAVIS TRAVEL PHOTOGRAPHY: 57t, 60t.

ET ARCHIVE: 24–25c; MARY EVANS PICTURE LIBRARY: 9 (insert), 21t, 22b, 24br, 29cb, 134t, 197 (insert).

JOHN FREEMAN: 37tl, 54cl, 55bl, 58cl, 60b, 62t, 63t/b, 96cr.

GIRAUDON: 24bl; Bridgeman 119cr; Lauros 61t; Bildarchiv Preussischer Kulturbesitz 25b.

ROBERT HARDING PICTURE LIBRARY: 63l;

MICHAEL HOLFORD: 17t, 20b, 22c; HULTON-GETTY: 163 (insert), 178t.

KEA PUBLISHING SERVICES: Francesco Venturi 47tl; DAVID KING COLLECTION: 27t, 29tl, 30t, 40c, 75t, 111br. RAYMOND MANDER & JOE MITCHENSON THEATRE COLLECTION 91b; JOHN MASSEY STEWART: 19cr, 57cl, 147 (insert).

NETWORK PHOTOGRAPHERS: H-J Burkhard/Bilderberg 32cl; A Reiser/Bilderberg 72br; Nikolai Ignatiev 31crb; NOVOSTI (LONDON): 19t, 20cla, 26cl, 27cr, 30cl, 32cr/bl, 34b, 35c, 56c/b, 61cl, 93t, 112c, 124bl.

ORONOZ, MADRID: 23t.

PLODIMEX AUSSENHANDELS GMBH, HAMBURG: 178cr/bl.

RENAISSANCE HOTEL, MOSCOW: 173tl; REX FEATURES: SIPA 2–3, 30cr; ELLEN ROONEY: 33b, 35b, 56t.

GREGOR M SCHMID: 59cr, 65c/b; SINY MOST: N Alexeiev 20clb, 37cl, 48b, 55cr, 65t; V Tetebenine 24tl, 161b; SOCIETY FOR COOPERATION IN RUSSIAN AND SOVIET STUDIES: 18b, 64t; Novosti 191c; SCIENCE PHOTO LIBRARY: SNES, 1995 Distribution Spot Image 11c; FRANK SPOONER PICTURES: Georges Merillon/Gamma 31t; STOCKMARKET: 57br.

TONY STONE IMAGES: Demetrio Carrasco 67t; TRIP: N & J Wiseman 154b; TVERSKAYA HOTEL: 172tl.

VISUAL ARTS LIBRARY: 25cra, 61c, 73t, 81c, 120tl; Over the City, Marc Chagall (1924) @ ADAGP, Paris and DACS, London 1998 119tl.

Cover: all special photography except ELLEN ROONEY: front cover left.

# Phrase Book

IN THIS GUIDE THE RUSSIAN LANGUAGE has been transliterated into Roman script following a consistent system used by the US Board on Geographic Names. All street and place names, and the names of most people, are transliterated according to this system. For some names, where a well-known English form exists, this has been used – hence, Leo (not Lev) Tolstoy.

In particular, the names of Russian rulers, such as Peter the Great, are given in their anglicized forms. Throughout the book, transliterated names can be taken as an accurate guide to pronunciation. The Phrase Book also gives a phonetic guide to the pronunciation of words and phrases used in everyday situations, such as when eating out or shopping.

## GUIDELINES FOR PRONUNCIATION

The Cyrillic alphabet has 33 letters, of which only five (a, к, м, о, т) correspond exactly to their counterparts in English. Russian has two pronunciations (hard and soft) of each of its vowels and several consonants without an equivalent.

The right-hand column of the alphabet, below, demonstrates how Cyrillic letters are pronounced by comparing them to sounds in English words. However, some letters vary in how they are pronounced according to their position in a word. Important exceptions are also noted below.

On the following pages, the English is given in the left-hand column, with the Russian and its transliteration in the middle column. The right-hand column provides a literal system of pronunciation and indicates the stressed syllable in bold. The exception is in the *Menu Decoder* section, where the Russian is given in the left-hand column and the English translation in the right-hand column, for easy use. Because of the existence of genders in Russian, in a few cases both masculine and feminine forms of a phrase are given.

## THE CYRILLIC ALPHABET

| | | |
|---|---|---|
| А а | a | **a**limony |
| Б б | b | **b**ed |
| В в | v | **v**et |
| Г г | g | **g**et (see note 1) |
| Д д | d | **d**ebt |
| Е е | e | **ye**t (see note 2) |
| Ё ё | e | **yo**nder |
| Ж ж | zh | lei**s**ure (but a little harder) |
| З з | z | **z**ither |
| И и | i | s**ee** |
| Й й | y | bo**y** (see note 3) |
| К к | k | **k**ing |
| Л л | l | **l**oot |
| М м | m | **m**atch |
| Н н | n | **n**ever |
| О о | o | r**o**b (see note 4) |
| П п | p | **p**ea |
| Р р | r | **r**at (rolling, as in Italian) |
| С с | s | **s**top |
| Т т | t | **t**offee |
| У у | u | b**oo**t |
| Ф ф | f | **f**ellow |
| Х х | kh | **kh** (like loch) |
| Ц ц | ts | le**ts** |
| Ч ч | ch | **ch**air |
| Ш ш | sh | **sh**ove |
| Щ щ | shch | fre**sh sh**eet (as above but with a slight roll) |
| ъ | | hard sign (no sound, but see note 5) |
| Ы ы | y | l**i**d |
| ь | | soft sign (no sound, but see note 5) |
| Э э | e | **e**gg |
| Ю ю | yu | **you**th |
| Я я | ya | **ya**k |

### Notes

1) Г   Pronounced as *v* in endings -oro and -ero.
2) Е   Always pronounced *ye* at the beginning of a word, but in the middle of a word sometimes less distinctly (more like *e*).
3) Й   This letter has no distinct sound of its own. It usually lengthens the preceeding vowel.
4) О   When not stressed it is pronounced like *a* in a**c**ross.
5) ъ, ь  The hard sign (ъ) is rare and indicates a very brief pause before the next letter. The soft sign (ь), marked in the pronunciation guide as ') softens the preceeding consonant and adds a slight *y* sound: for instance, *n'* would sound like *ny* in "ca**ny**on."

## IN AN EMERGENCY

| | | |
|---|---|---|
| Help! | Помогите! *Pomogite!* | pama**gee**t-ye! |
| Stop! | Стоп! *Stop!* | stop! |
| Leave me alone! | Оставьте меня в покое! *Ostavte menya v pokoe!* | as**tavt'**-ye myen**ya** pa**koy**e! |
| Call a doctor! | Позовите врача! *Pozovite vracha!* | paza**veet**-ye vra**cha!** |
| Call an ambulance! | Вызовите скорую помощь! *Vyzovite skoruyu pomoshch!* | viza**veet**-ye **skor**u-yu **po**mash'! |
| Fire! | Пожар! *Pozhar!* | pa**zhar!** |
| Call the fire department! | Вызовите пожарных! *Vyzovite pozharnykh!* | viza**veet**-ye pa**zhar**nikh! |
| Police! | Милиция! *Militsiya!* | mee**leet**see-ya! |
| Where is the nearest... | Где ближайший... *Gde blizhayshiy...* | gdye blee**zhay**shee-y... |
| ...telephone? | ...телефон? *...telefon?* | ...tyelye**fon?** |
| ...hospital? | ...больница? *...bolnitsa?* | ...bal'**neet**sa? |
| ...police station? | ...отделение милиции? *...otdelenie militsii?* | ...atdyel**yen**ye meel**eet**see-ee? |

## COMMUNICATION ESSENTIALS

| | | |
|---|---|---|
| Yes | Да *Da* | da |
| No | Нет *Net* | nyet |
| Please | Пожалуйста *Pozhaluysta* | pa**zhal**sta |
| Thank you | Спасибо *Spasibo* | spas**ee**ba |
| You are welcome | Пожалуйста *Pozhaluysta* | pa**zhal**sta |
| Excuse me | Извините *Izvinite* | eezveen**eet**-ye |
| Hello | Здравствуйте *Zdravstuyte* | zdra**stvooy**t-ye |
| Goodbye | До свидания *Do svidaniya* | da svee**dan**ya |
| Good morning | Доброе утро *Dobroe utro* | **dobra**-ye **oo**tra |
| Good afternoon/day | Добрый день *Dobryy den* | **dobree** dyen' |
| Good evening | Добрый вечер *Dobryy vecher* | **dobree vye**chyer |
| Good night | Спокойной ночи *Spokoynoy nochi* | spa**koy**nay **no**chee |
| Morning | утро *utro* | **oo**tra |
| Afternoon | день *den* | dyen' |
| Evening | вечер *vecher* | **vye**chyer |
| Yesterday | вчера *vchera* | fchyer**a** |
| Today | сегодня *sevodnya* | sye**vo**dnya |
| Tomorrow | завтра *zavtra* | **za**ftra |
| Here | здесь *zdes* | zdyes' |

| There | там | tam |
|---|---|---|
| | *tam* | |
| What? | Что? | shto? |
| | *Chto?* | |
| Where? | Где? | gdye? |
| | *Gde?* | |
| Why? | Почему? | pachyem**oo**? |
| | *Pochemu?* | |
| When? | Когда? | kagd**a**? |
| | *Kogda?* | |
| Now | сейчас | seych**a**s |
| | *seychas* | |
| Later | позже | p**o**zhe |
| | *pozzhe* | |
| Can I...? | можно? | m**o**zhna...? |
| | *mozhno?* | |
| It is | можно | m**o**zhna |
| possible/allowed | *mozhno* | |
| It is not | нельзя | nyelz**ya** |
| possible/allowed | *nelzya* | |

## USEFUL PHRASES

| How are you? | Как дела? | kak dyel**a**? |
|---|---|---|
| | *Kak dela?* | |
| Very well, thank | Хорошо, спасибо | kharash**o**, spas**ee**ba |
| you | *Khorosho, spasibo* | |
| Pleased to meet you | Очень приятно | **o**chen' pree-**ya**tna |
| | *Ochen priyatno* | |
| How do I get to...? | Как добраться | kak dabr**a**t'sya da...? |
| | до...? | |
| | *Kak dobratsya do...?* | |
| Would you tell me | Скажите, | skazh**ee**t-ye, |
| when we get | пожалуйста, | pazh**a**lsta, kagd**a** |
| to...? | когда мы | mi pree-**ye**dyem |
| | приедем в...? | v...? |
| | *Skazhite,* | |
| | *pozzhaluysta,* | |
| | *kogda my* | |
| | *priedem v...?* | |
| Is it very far? | Это далеко? | eta dalyek**o**? |
| | *Eto daleko?* | |
| Do you speak | Вы говорите | vi gavar**ee**t-ye |
| English? | по-английски? | po-angleesk**ee**? |
| | *Vy govorite* | |
| | *po-angliyski?* | |
| I don't understand | Я не понимаю | ya nye |
| | *Ya ne ponimayu* | paneem**a**-yoo |
| Could you speak | Говорите | gavar**ee**t-ye |
| more slowly? | медленнее | m**ye**dlyenye-ye |
| | *Govorite medlennee* | |
| Could you say it | Повторите, | paftar**ee**t-ye, |
| again please? | пожалуйста | pazh**a**lsta |
| | *Povtorite,* | |
| | *pozhaluysta* | |
| I am lost | Я заблудился | ya zablood**ee**lsya |
| | (заблудилась) | (zablood**ee**las') |
| | *Ya zabludilsya* | |
| | *(zabludilas)* | |
| How do you say... | Как по-русски...? | kak pa-r**oo**skee...? |
| in Russian? | *Kak po-russki...?* | |

## USEFUL WORDS

| big | большой | bal'sh**oy** |
|---|---|---|
| | *bolshoy* | |
| small | маленький | malyen'k**ee** |
| | *malenkiy* | |
| hot (water, food) | горячий | gar**ya**chee |
| | *goryachiy* | |
| hot (weather) | жарко | zh**a**rka |
| | *zharko* | |
| cold | холодный | khal**o**dnee |
| | *kholodnyy* | |
| good | хорошо | kharash**o** |
| | *khorosho* | |
| bad | плохо | pl**o**kha |
| | *plokho* | |
| okay/fine | нормально | narm**a**l'na |
| | *normalno* | |
| near | близко | bl**ee**zka |
| | *blizko* | |
| far | далеко | dalyek**o** |
| | *daleko* | |
| up | наверху | navyerkh**oo** |
| | *naverkhu* | |

| down | внизу | fneez**oo** |
|---|---|---|
| | *vnizu* | |
| early | рано | r**a**na |
| | *rano* | |
| late | поздно | p**o**zdna |
| | *pozdno* | |
| vacant (unoccupied) | свободно | svab**o**dna |
| | *svobodno* | |
| free (no charge) | бесплатно | byespl**a**tna |
| | *besplatno* | |
| cashier/ticket office | касса | k**a**sa |
| | *kassa* | |
| avenue | проспект | prasp**yekt** |
| | *prospekt* | |
| bridge | мост | most |
| | *most* | |
| embankment | набережная | nab**ye**ryezhnaya |
| | *naberezhnaya* | |
| highway | шоссе | shass**e** |
| | *shosse* | |
| lane/passage | переулок | pyerye**oo**lak |
| | *pereulok* | |
| square | площадь | pl**o**shat' |
| | *ploshchad* | |
| street | улица | **oo**leetsa |
| | *ulitsa* | |
| apartment | квартира | kvart**ee**ra |
| | *kvartira* | |
| floor | этаж | et**a**sh |
| | *etazh* | |
| house | дом | dom |
| | *dom* | |
| entrance | вход | fkhot |
| | *vkhod* | |
| exit | выход | v**i**khot |
| | *vykhod* | |
| river | река | ry**eka** |
| | *reka* | |
| summer country | дача | d**a**cha |
| house | *dacha* | |
| swimming pool | бассейн | bas**yeyn** |
| | *basseyn* | |
| town | город | g**o**rat |
| | *gorod* | |
| toilet | туалет | tooal**yet** |
| | *tualet* | |

## MAKING A TELEPHONE CALL

| Can I call abroad | Можно отсюда | m**o**zhna ats**yoo**da |
|---|---|---|
| from here? | позвонить за | pazvan**eet**' za |
| | границу ? | gran**eet**soo? |
| | *Mozhno otsyuda* | |
| | *pozvonit za* | |
| | *granitsu?* | |
| I would like to | Позовите, | pazav**ee**t-ye, |
| speak to... | пожалуйста... | pazh**a**lsta... |
| | *Pozovite,* | |
| | *pozhaluysta* | |
| Could you leave | Вы можете | vi m**o**zhet-ye |
| him/her a | передать ему/ей? | pyeryed**a**t' |
| message? | *Vy mozhete peredat* | yem**oo**/yay? |
| | *emy/ey?* | |
| My number is... | Мой номер... | moy n**o**myer... |
| | *Moy nomer...* | |
| I'll ring back later | Я позвоню позже | ya pazvan**yoo** |
| | *Ya pozvonyu pozzhe* | p**o**zhe |

## SIGHTSEEING

| castle | замок | z**a**mak |
|---|---|---|
| | *zamok* | |
| cathedral | собор | sab**o**r |
| | *sobor* | |
| church | церковь | ts**e**rkaf |
| | *tserkov* | |
| circus | цирк | tseerk |
| | *tsirk* | |
| closed for cleaning | санитарный день | saneet**a**rnee dyen' |
| "cleaning day" | *sanitarnyy den* | |
| undergoing | ремонт | rem**o**nt |
| restoration | *remont* | |
| exhibition | выставка | v**i**stafka |
| | *vystavka* | |
| fortress | крепость | kry**e**post' |
| | *krepost* | |
| gallery | галерея | galer**ye**ya |
| | *galereya* | |

| garden | сад<br>*sad* | sad |
|---|---|---|
| island | остров<br>*ostrov* | **o**straf |
| kremlin/fortified stronghold | кремль<br>*kreml* | kryeml' |
| library | библиотека<br>*biblioteka* | beeblee-at**ye**ka |
| monument | памятник<br>*pamyatnik* | p**a**myatneek |
| mosque | мечеть<br>*mechet* | myech**yet**' |
| museum | музей<br>*muzey* | moozy**ey** |
| palace | дворец<br>*dvorets* | dvar**ye**ts |
| park | парк<br>*park* | park |
| parliament | дума<br>*duma* | d**oo**ma |
| synagogue | синагога<br>*sinagoga* | seenag**o**ga |
| tourist information | пункт информации<br>для туристов<br>*punkt informatsii dlya turistov* | p**oo**nkt eenfarm**a**tsee-ee dlya toor**ee**staf |
| zoo | зоопарк<br>*zoopark* | zap**a**rk |

## SHOPPING

| open | открыто<br>*otkryto* | atkr**i**ta |
|---|---|---|
| closed | закрыто<br>*zakryto* | zakr**i**ta |
| How much does this cost? | Сколько это стоит?<br>*Skolko eto stoit?* | sk**o**l'ka **e**ta st**o**eet? |
| I would like to buy..... | Я хотел (хотела) бы купить...<br>*Ya khotel (khotela) by kupit...* | ya khat**yel** (khat**ye**la) bi koop**ee**t'... |
| Do you have.....? | У вас есть...?<br>*U vas yest...?* | oo vas yesi'...? |
| Do you take credit cards? | Кредитные карточки вы принимаете?<br>*Kreditnye kartochki vy prinimaete?* | kryed**ee**tnye k**a**rtachkee vy preeneem**a**yetye? |
| What time do you open/close? | Во сколько вы открываетесь/закрываетесь?<br>*Vo skolko vy otkryvaetes/zakryvaetes?* | Va sk**o**l'ka vy atkriv**a**yetyes'/ zakriv**a**yetyes'? |
| This one | этот<br>*etot* | **e**tat |
| expensive | дорого<br>*dorogo* | d**o**raga |
| cheap | дёшево<br>*deshevo* | dy**o**sh**ye**va |
| size | размер<br>*razmer* | razm**ye**r |
| white | белый<br>*belyy* | b**ye**lee |
| black | чёрный<br>*chernyy* | ch**yo**rnee |
| red | красный<br>*krasnyy* | kr**a**snee |
| yellow | жёлтый<br>*zheltyy* | zh**o**ltee |
| green | зелёный<br>*zelenyy* | zyel**yo**nee |
| dark blue | синий<br>*siniy* | s**ee**nee |
| light blue | голубой<br>*goluboy* | galoob**oy** |
| brown | коричневый<br>*korichnevyy* | kar**ee**chnyevee |

## TYPES OF SHOP

| bakery | булочная<br>*bulochnaya* | b**oo**lachna-ya |
|---|---|---|
| bookstore | книжный магазин<br>*knizhnyy magazin* | kn**ee**zhnee magaz**een** |
| butcher | мясной магазин<br>*myasnoy magazin* | myasn**oy** magaz**een** |

| camera shop | фото-товары<br>*foto-tovary* | foto-tav**a**ri |
|---|---|---|
| delicatessen | гастроном<br>*gastronom* | gastran**o**m |
| department store | универмаг<br>*univermag* | ooneevyerm**a**g |
| drugstore | аптека<br>*apteka* | apt**ye**ka |
| florist | цветы<br>*tsvety* | tsvyet**i** |
| grocer | бакалея<br>*bakaleya* | bakal**ye**-ya |
| hairdresser | парикмахерская<br>*parikmakherskaya* | pareekm**a**khyerskaya |
| market | рынок<br>*rynok* | r**i**nak |
| newspaper stand | газетный киоск<br>*gazetniy kiosk* | gaz**ye**tnee kee-**o**sk |
| post office | почта<br>*pochta* | p**o**chta |
| record shop | грампластинки<br>*gramplastinki* | gramplast**ee**nkee |
| shoe shop | обувь<br>*obuv* | **o**boof' |
| travel agent | бюро путешествий<br>*byuro puteshestviy* | byoor**o** pootyesh**e**stvee |
| bank | банк<br>*bank* | bank |

## STAYING IN A HOTEL

| Do you have a vacant room? | У вас есть свободный номер?<br>*U vas yest svobodnyy nomer?* | oo vas yest' svab**o**dnee n**o**myer? |
|---|---|---|
| double room with double bed | номер с двуспальной кроватью<br>*nomer s dvuspalnoy krovatyu* | n**o**myer s dvoosp**a**l'noy krav**a**t'-yoo |
| twin room | двухместный номер<br>*dvukhmestnyy nomer* | dvookhm**ye**stnee n**o**myer |
| single room | одноместный номер<br>*odnomestnyy nomer* | adnam**ye**stnee n**o**myer |
| bath | ванная<br>*vannaya* | v**a**na-ya |
| shower | душ<br>*dush* | doosh |
| porter | носильщик<br>*nosilshchik* | nas**ee**l'sheek |
| key | ключ<br>*klyuch* | kly**oo**ch |

## EATING OUT

| A table for two, please | Стол на двоих, пожалуйста | stol na dva-**ee**kh, pazh**a**lsta |
|---|---|---|
| I would like to book a table | Я хочу заказать стол<br>*Ya khochu zakazat stol* | ya khach**oo** zakaz**a**t' stol |
| The bill, please | Счёт, пожалуйста<br>*Schet, pozhaluysta* | shyot, pazh**a**lsta |
| I am a vegetarian | Я вегетерианец (вегетерианка)<br>*Ya vegeterianets (vegeterianka)* | ya vyegyetaree**a**nyets (vyegyetaree**a**nka) |
| breakfast | завтрак<br>*zavtrak* | z**a**ftrak |
| lunch | обед<br>*obed* | ab**ye**t |
| dinner | ужин<br>*uzhin* | **oo**zheen |
| waiter! | официант!<br>*ofitsiant!* | afeetsee-**a**nt! |
| waitress! | официантка!<br>*ofitsiantka!* | afeetsee-**a**ntka! |
| dish of the day | фирменное блюдо<br>*firmennoe blyudo* | f**ee**rmenoye bly**oo**da |
| appetizers/starters | закуски<br>*zakuski* | zak**oo**skee |

| | | |
|---|---|---|
| main course | второе блюдо *vtoroe blyudo* | ftaroye blyooda |
| meat and poultry dishes | мясные блюда *myasnye blyuda* | myasniye blyooda |
| fish and seafood dishes | рыбные блюда *rybnye blyuda* | ribniye blyooda |
| vegetable dishes | овощные блюда *ovoshchnye blyuda* | avashshniye blyooda |
| dessert | десерт *desert* | dyesyert |
| drinks | напитки *napitki* | napeetkee |
| vegetables | овощи *ovoshchi* | ovashshee |
| bread | хлеб *khleb* | khlyeb |
| wine list | карта вин *karta vin* | karta veen |
| rare (steak) | недожаренный *nedozharennyy* | nyedazharenee |
| well-done (steak) | прожаренный *prozharennyy* | prozharenee |
| glass | стакан *stakan* | stakan |
| bottle | бутылка *butylka* | bootilka |
| knife | нож *nozh* | nosh |
| fork | вилка *vilka* | veelka |
| spoon | ложка *lozhka* | loshka |
| plate | тарелка *tarelka* | taryelka |
| napkin | салфетка *salfetka* | salfyetka |
| salt | соль *sol* | sol' |
| pepper | перец *perets* | pyeryets |
| butter/oil | масло *maslo* | masla |
| sugar | сахар *sakhar* | sakhar |

## MENU DECODER

| | | |
|---|---|---|
| абрикос *abrikos* | abreekos | apricot |
| апельсин *apelsin* | apyel'seen | orange |
| апельсиновый сок *apelsinovyy sok* | apyel'seenavee sok | orange juice |
| арбуз *arbuz* | arbooz | watermelon |
| белое вино *beloe vino* | byelaye veeno | white wine |
| бифштекс *bifshteks* | beefshtyeks | steak |
| блины *bliny* | bleeni | pancakes |
| борщ *borshch* | borshsh | borscht (beetroot soup) |
| варенье *varene* | varyen'ye | Russian syrup-jam |
| варёный *varenyy* | varyonee | boiled |
| ветчина *vetchina* | vyetcheena | ham |
| вода *voda* | vada | water |
| говядина *govyadina* | gavyadeena | beef |
| грибы *griby* | greebi | mushrooms |
| груша *grusha* | groosha | pear |
| гусь *gus* | goos | goose |
| джем *dzhem* | dzhem | jam |
| жареный *zharenyy* | zharyenee | roasted/grilled/fried |
| икра *ikra* | eekra | black caviar |
| икра красная/кета *ikra krasnaya/keta* | eekra krasna-ya/kyeta | red caviar |

| | | |
|---|---|---|
| капуста *kapusta* | kapoosta | cabbage |
| картофель *kartofel* | kartofyel' | potato |
| квас *kvas* | kvas | kvas (sweet, mildly alcoholic drink) |
| клубника *klubnika* | kloobneeka | strawberries |
| колбаса *kolbasa* | kalbasa | salami sausage |
| кофе *kofe* | kofye | coffee |
| красное вино *krasnoe vino* | krasnoye veeno | red wine |
| креветки *krevetki* | kryevyetkee | shrimp |
| курица *kuritsa* | kooreetsa | chicken |
| лук *luk* | look | onion |
| малина *malina* | maleena | raspberries |
| минеральная вода *mineralnaya voda* | mineral'naya vada | mineral water |
| мороженое *morozhenoe* | marozhena-ye | ice cream |
| мясо *myaso* | myasa | meat |
| огурец *ogurets* | agooryets | cucumber |
| осетрина *osetrina* | asyetreena | sturgeon |
| пельмени *pelmeni* | pyel'myenee | meat or fish dumplings |
| персик *persik* | pyerseek | peach |
| печенье *pechene* | pyechyen'ye | biscuit |
| печёнка *pechenka* | pyechyonka | liver |
| печёный *pechenyy* | pyechyonee | baked |
| пиво *pivo* | peeva | beer |
| пирог *pirog* | peerok | pie |
| пирожки *pirozhki* | peerashkee | small parcels with savory fillings |
| помидор *pomidor* | pameedor | tomato |
| продукты моря *produkty morya* | pradookti marya | seafood |
| рыба *ryba* | riba | fish |
| салат *salat* | salat | salad |
| свинина *svinina* | sveeneena | pork |
| сельдь *seld* | sye'ld' | herring |
| сосиски *sosiski* | saseeskee | sausages |
| сыр *syr* | sir | cheese |
| сырой *syroy* | siroy | raw |
| утка *utka* | ootka | duck |
| фасоль *fasol* | fasol' | beans |
| форель *forel* | faryel' | trout |
| чай *chay* | chai | tea |
| чеснок *chesnok* | chyesnok | garlic |
| шашлык *shashlyk* | shashlik | kebab |
| яйцо *yaytso* | yaytso | egg |
| слива *sliva* | sleeva | plum |
| фрукты *frukty* | frookti | fruit |
| яблоко *yabloko* | yablaka | apple |

## TRANSPORTATION

| | | |
|---|---|---|
| north | север *sever* | **sy**ever |
| south | юг *yug* | yook |
| east | восток *vostok* | v**a**stok |
| west | запад *zapad* | **za**pat |
| airport | аэропорт *aeroport* | aera**po**rt |
| airplane | самолёт *samolet* | samal**yot** |
| traffic police | ГАИ *GAI* | Ga-ee |
| bus | автобус *avtobus* | aft**o**boos |
| bus station | автобусная станция *avtobusnaya stantsiya* | aft**o**boosna-ya stantsee-ya |
| bus stop | остановка автобуса *ostanovka avtobusa* | astan**o**fka aft**o**boosa |
| car | машина *mashina* | mash**ee**na |
| flight | рейс *reys* | ryeys |
| metro (station) | (станция) метро *(stantsiya) metro* | (**s**tantsee-ya) my**e**tro |
| no entry | нет входа *net vkhoda* | nyet fkh**o**da |
| no exit | нет выхода *net vykhoda* | nyet v**i**khada |
| parking | автостоянка *avtostoyanka* | aftost**o**yanka |
| gasoline | бензин *benzin* | byenz**ee**n |
| railroad | железная дорога *zhelezhnaya doroga* | zhel**ye**zna-ya dar**o**ga |
| train station | вокзал *vokzal* | vagz**a**l |
| round-trip ticket | обратный билет *obratniy bilet* | obr**a**tnee beel**yet** |
| seat | место *mesto* | m**ye**sta |
| suburban train | пригородный поезд *prigorodniy poezd* | pr**ee**garadnee **po**-yezd |
| straight on | прямо *pryamo* | pr**ya**ma |
| taxi | такси *taksi* | taks**ee** |
| ticket | билет *bilet* | beel**yet** |
| token (for a single metro journey) | жетон *zheton* | zhet**o**n |
| to the left | налево *nalevo* | nal**ye**va |
| to the right | направо *napravo* | napr**a**va |
| train | поезд *poezd* | **po**-yezd |
| tram | трамвай *tramvay* | tramv**ay** |
| trolleybus | троллейбус *trolleybus* | tral**ye**yboos |

## NUMBERS

| | | |
|---|---|---|
| 1 | один/одна/одно *odin/odna/odno* | ad**ee**n/adn**a**/adn**o** |
| 2 | два/две *dva/dve* | dva/dvye |
| 3 | три *tri* | tree |
| 4 | четыре *chetyre* | chyet**i**r-ye |
| 5 | пять *pyat* | pyat' |
| 6 | шесть *shest* | shest' |
| 7 | семь *sem* | syem' |
| 8 | восемь *vosem* | v**o**syem' |
| 9 | девять *devyat* | d**ye**vyat' |
| 10 | десять *desyat* | d**ye**syat' |
| 11 | одиннадцать *odinnadtsat* | ad**ee**natsat' |
| 12 | двенадцать *dvenadtsat* | dv**ye**natsat' |
| 13 | тринадцать *trinadtsat* | tre**e**natsat' |
| 14 | четырнадцать *chetyrnadtsat* | chyet**i**rnatsat' |
| 15 | пятнадцать *pyatnadtsat* | pyatn**a**tsat' |
| 16 | шестнадцать *shestnadtsat* | shestn**a**tsat' |
| 17 | семнадцать *semnadtsat* | syemn**a**tsat' |
| 18 | восемнадцать *vosemnadtsat* | vasyemn**a**tsat' |
| 19 | девятнадцать *devyatnadtsat* | dyevyatn**a**tsat' |
| 20 | двадцать *dvadtsat* | dv**a**tsat' |
| 21 | двадцать один *dvadtsat odin* | dv**a**tsat' ad**ee**n |
| 22 | двадцать два *dvadtsat dva* | dv**a**tsat' dva |
| 23 | двадцать три *dvadtsat tri* | dv**a**tsat' tree |
| 24 | двадцать четыре *dvadtsat chetyre* | dv**a**tsat' chyet**i**r-ye |
| 25 | двадцать пять *dvadtsat pyat* | dv**a**tsat' pyat' |
| 30 | тридцать *tridtsat* | tr**ee**tsat' |
| 40 | сорок *sorok* | s**o**rak |
| 50 | пятьдесят *pyatdesyat* | pyadyes**ya**t' |
| 60 | шестьдесят *shestdesyat* | shes'dyes**ya**t |
| 70 | семьдесят *semdesyat* | **sy**em'dyesyat |
| 80 | восемьдесят *vosemdesyat* | v**o**syem'dyesyat |
| 90 | девяносто *devyanosto* | dyevyan**o**sta |
| 100 | сто *sto* | sto |
| 200 | двести *dvesti* | dv**ye**stee |
| 300 | триста *trista* | treest**a** |
| 400 | четыреста *chetyresta* | chyet**i**ryesta |
| 500 | пятьсот *pyatsot* | pyat's**o**t |
| 1,000 | тысяча *tysyacha* | t**i**syacha |
| 2,000 | две тысяч *dve tysyach* | dvye t**i**syach |
| 5,000 | пять тысяч *pyat tysyach* | pyat' t**i**syach |
| 1,000,000 | миллион *million* | meelee-**o**n |

## TIME, DAYS, AND DATES

| | | |
|---|---|---|
| one minute | одна минута *odna minuta* | adn**a** meen**oo**ta |
| one hour | час *chas* | chas |
| half an hour | полчаса *polchasa* | polchas**a** |
| day | день *den* | dyen' |
| week | неделя *nedelya* | nyedy**el**-ya |
| Monday | понедельник *ponedelnik* | panyedy**el**'neek |
| Tuesday | вторник *vtornik* | ft**o**rneek |
| Wednesday | среда *sreda* | sry**e**da |
| Thursday | четверг *chetverg* | chyetv**ye**rk |
| Friday | пятница *pyatnitsa* | p**ya**tneetsa |
| Saturday | суббота *subbota* | soob**o**ta |
| Sunday | воскресенье *voskresene* | vaskryes**ye**n'ye |

# TITLES PUBLISHED TO DATE

## THE GUIDES THAT SHOW YOU WHAT OTHERS ONLY TELL YOU

### COUNTRY GUIDES

AUSTRALIA • FRANCE • GREAT BRITAIN • GREECE:
ATHENS & THE MAINLAND • THE GREEK ISLANDS
IRELAND • ITALY • PORTUGAL
SPAIN • THAILAND

### REGIONAL GUIDES

CALIFORNIA • FLORENCE & TUSCANY
FLORIDA • HAWAII • LOIRE VALLEY
NAPLES WITH POMPEII & THE AMALFI COAST
PROVENCE & THE COTE D'AZUR • SARDINIA
SEVILLE & ANDALUSIA • VENICE & THE VENETO

### CITY GUIDES

AMSTERDAM • ISTANBUL • LISBON • LONDON
MOSCOW • NEW YORK • PARIS • PRAGUE
ROME • SAN FRANCISCO • ST PETERSBURG
SYDNEY • VIENNA • WARSAW

*TO BE PUBLISHED IN SPRING 1999*
MADRID • BUDAPEST • DUBLIN

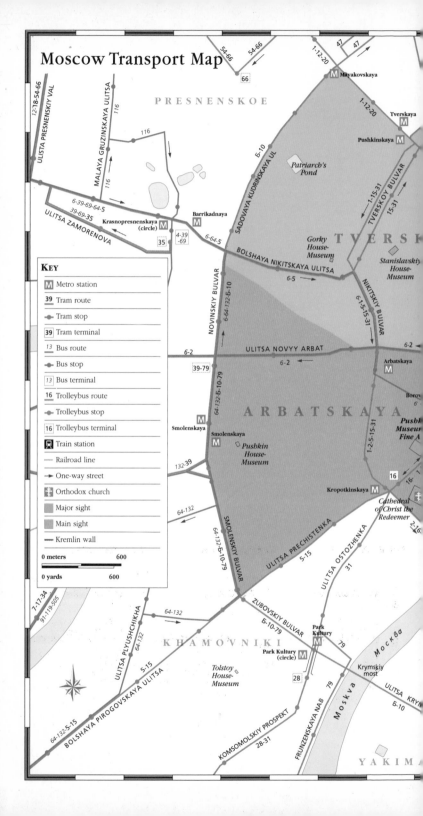